The War Diaries of Oliver Harvey
1941–1945

Also edited by John Harvey

The Diplomatic Diaries of Oliver Harvey
1937–1940

THE WAR DIARIES
OF OLIVER HARVEY

Edited by

JOHN HARVEY

COLLINS
St James's Place, London
1978

William Collins Sons & Co Ltd
London · Glasgow · Sydney · Auckland
Toronto · Johannesburg

First published 1978
© John Harvey 1978
ISBN 0 00 216148 6
Set in "Monotype" Imprint
Made and Printed in Great Britain by
W & J Mackay Limited, Chatham

Editor's Note

This second and last volume of my father's diaries leaves out the year from June 1940 during which he was at the Ministry of Information after his return from France. It starts when he went back to work again at the Foreign Office as Private Secretary to Anthony Eden in June of 1941. Similarly, although there are several pages dealing with the period after the Conservative defeat in 1945 up to April 1946, when he discontinued his diary, it seemed right to bring this volume to an end in August 1945, when Eden took farewell, for the time being, of his war-time colleagues in the Foreign Office, and Ernest Bevin moved in.

Even so, there have had to be considerable cuts to bring the book down to an economic size. But they are cuts only, and there has been no alteration of the original words. For those interested, the complete diaries, with supporting letters, etc. can be read in the British Library, to whose authorities I would like to express my thanks.

J.H.

Contents

Introduction

Oliver Harvey got back from Bordeaux by destroyer on 24th June 1940 with his Ambassador, Sir Ronald Campbell, and the rest of the Paris Embassy staff, reaching London on the morning of the 25th. The Britain which he had left at the end of 1939 had been still wrapped in the languors of the phoney war. In France he had witnessed the impact of real war upon a divided and irresolute democracy. He returned now to the euphoria of post-Dunkirk Britain, its spirits uplifted by the loss of its Allies, preparing to die upon the beaches, in defiance of the underlying realities of the situation.

In fact, Harvey was out of a job, but after leave was attached to the Ministry of Information where he was put in charge of Allied information to the exiled Governments of the Nazi-occupied countries, then re-grouping in London.

His diary begins again on July 16 1940 and soon records renewed contacts with political friends, including Anthony Eden, now Minister for War, and immersed in the task of re-organising the British Army after Dunkirk. The new War Cabinet had Churchill as Prime Minister and Minister of Defence; Halifax as Foreign Secretary; Attlee, Lord Privy Seal; and Greenwood, Minister without Portfolio. Neville Chamberlain was Lord President of the Council, but in failing health.

Though a great improvement on the last Government, Harvey felt that the new brooms had not swept clean enough, and his diary is full of complaints at the continued presence of the appeasers. He was especially critical of the Foreign Office – "Halifax a disaster at the F.O." he notes in October, ". . . he has sought to appease both Franco and Petain . . . we should now take a firmer line, with America at our back and start a definite democratic crusade. . . ."

His chief anxiety was that Roosevelt might be defeated in the Presidential election in November, and when he was returned Harvey hailed his success as ". . . perhaps the most important in the war".

"Our enemies will know [he wrote] that henceforward even if they could succeed in wearing us down in a long war there is a man across the Atlantic who would certainly bring America to our rescue, and would carry on the fight if we failed. A whole new continent ready to fight Hitler. . . ."

9

On November 15th he notes, ". . . worried about F.O. policy. It seems altogether on wrong lines. After being ahead of public opinion before the war, it is now behind it and wrong . . . it is like a piece of the Chamberlain Government still going on . . ."

By the end of November the possibility of Eden returning to the Foreign Office was in the air. Harvey was all in favour. Just before Christmas Halifax was made Ambassador to the U.S. and Eden replaced him at the F.O. "What a signal justification of his previous period there," Harvey commented, "He now succeeds his own successor who leaves with a very dusty reputation."

In January Eden told him he would like him back as Private Secretary. "I said I would be only too pleased to come back if he thought I could be helpful. He asked whether I would be too senior to be P.S. again. I said of course not. . . ."

The victories in Libya and the Greek resistance to the Italians cheered the country, but were quickly followed by the German recovery of Benghazi, and the invasions of Yugoslavia, Greece and Crete, the last a severe defeat which was not easy to explain to the British public. These depressing events made Harvey feel he was stuck in a backwater at the M. of I.

On May 12th he heard from Eden that all was fixed for his transfer to the F.O., but another month passed before Duff Cooper told him he had been asked for, and he finally started work again as Principal Private Secretary on 27th June 1941.

A few days earlier the Germans had invaded Russia and the war had taken on a fresh dimension. But Russian resistance was still an unknown quantity, and Harvey's sanguine hopes of American aid were largely unfulfilled.

It was therefore at a time of crisis for the Government that he began work with Eden, when the halcyon period of the "finest hour" had given place to more sober assessment of the future and a grim awareness of the need for greater professionalism and expertise if the country were to survive.

Biography

Oliver Harvey was born in 1893, at Tasburgh, near Norwich, the son of Sir Charles Harvey, Bt., and educated at Malvern and Trinity College, Cambridge. In the first World War, he served with the Norfolk Regiment in France, and later in Egypt and Palestine. He entered the Foreign Service in 1920, serving in Rome, Athens, and Paris. He became Principal Private Secretary to Anthony Eden in 1936, and later, to Lord Halifax. He was made Minister in Paris in 1939, returned to be Private Secretary in 1941, was Assistant Under-Secretary in 1943, Deputy Under-Secretary in 1946, and Ambassador in Paris 1948. He was made Lord Harvey of Tasburgh on his retirement in 1954. He died in 1968.

Diarist's Note

... Its [the diary's] whole value, if it has a value, lies in its "hotness", in the immediate impression and atmosphere. I am the first to recognise how many of the first reactions and impressions and judgements were proved wrong and would be admitted wrong by myself now, but that is not the point. This is how we saw things at the time.

... The more light that can be shed on the circumstances in which impressions were formed, decisions and actions taken, the better ...

Harvey of Tasburgh May, 1958

1941

June 25

To-day we came down to A.E. and B.[eatrice] for the week-end. I start work with him on Monday.

We had some long talks. He told me how difficult the P.M. was; in spite of splendid qualities as popular leader, he had a devastating effect on planning. A.E. thinks great need of a Minister of Defence independent of P.M. He sees Trenchard in this post.[1]

He also spoke of difficulty of getting a move on with service departments – Air Force were proposing to have a holiday from bombing tomorrow because it was a Sunday, in spite of the urgent need of bombing Germany continuously just now while she was occupied with Russia. In my presence he rang up Archie Sinclair[2] to urge the need of this. Always excuses.

We talked about Egypt. Wavell is to leave and Auchinleck to take his place.[3] Wavell very upset over W. Desert reverse though A.E. said it was not his fault. Both Dill[4] and Wilson[5] had thought there were sufficient tanks in Egypt to hold up Germans (they were not a surprise) but new general from England was outmanoeuvred. Wilson now in Palestine, was very good. Difficult to get younger men into higher commands.

A.E. had some doubts about F.D.R[oosevelt]. He hears his health is not too good, and he and P.M. fear he may be slackening up – great difficulty in getting him to come on. A disturbing prospect.

July 6

End of my first week's work as P.S. again. Very exhausting after the comparable leisure of M. of I.!

1. 1st Viscount Trenchard.
2. Sir Archibald Sinclair, M.P., (later Lord Thurso) Minister for Air, and Leader of the Liberal Party 1935–1945.
3. General Sir Archibald Wavell had been Commander-in-Chief, Middle East since 1939. General Sir Claude Auchinleck had been Commander-in-Chief, India.
4. General Sir John Dill, Chief of the Imperial General Staff, 1940–41.
5. General Sir Henry Maitland Wilson had been 2nd in Command to Wavell in Egypt, before being sent to Palestine.

Nothing very much to note. A.E. is continually pressing for speeding up of the Syrian operations[1] – but without much success. Our slowness is having a devastating effect on Turkey, on U.S.A., on all our friends.

Russia is doing better than was expected and the Germans' advance has slowed up.

A most important development is the beginning under adversity of Soviet–Polish rapprochement. Maisky[2] called on Saturday with a message to say Stalin was ready to recognise Polish national committees, to release Polish prisoners of war and to sign a treaty recognising an ethnographical "Poland". A.E. at once informed Sikorski[3] and finally the two – Sikorski and Maisky – met in Alec [Cadogan]'s room at the F.O.[4] last evening. S. asked to appoint a Polish Ambassador to Moscow, for formation of Polish army in Russia – discussion of frontiers to be left for the present. Maisky is to put these proposals to Moscow. Point of greatest difficulty is Polish political prisoners.

I met Winant[5] last week-end at the Edens'. He is a constant and very privileged visitor to the F.O. – a most impressive man – earnestness personified – a contrast to the flippant Kennedy.[6] Yet F.D.R. is moving very slowly – too slowly for us.

July 8

A.E. again pressed P.M. for more support to be given to Russia, Maisky having again appealed for naval or military operations in addition to the air activity over the West. This is important too as apart from harassing Germany and heartening Russia, it would have the best effect on neutral and American opinion.

A.E.'s speech at Leeds on Saturday great success. He got over 10,000 on a football ground. Alas! he is no orator. We worked hard on it all Friday, had a good dinner at Boodles and then on again till 2 a.m.

1. An Anglo-French force had invaded Syria on June 8, meeting heavy resistance from the Vichy French forces.
2. Ivan Maisky, Soviet Ambassador to Great Britain, 1932–1943.
3. General Sikorski, Polish Premier and Commander-in-Chief Polish Forces in England, 1939–1943.
4. Sir Alexander Cadogan, 1884–1968, Permanent Under-Secretary of State at the Foreign Office 1938–1946.
5. John G. Winant, U.S. Ambassador since February 1941.
6. Joseph P. Kennedy, U.S. Ambassador 1937–1941.

– Jim [Thomas],[1] C. Ponsonby,[2] A.E. and me – pruning and dictating – but it wasn't bad and went extremely well, especially his firm declaration that H.M.G. would never on any subject at any time treat with Hitler. This was to forestall Hitler's peace offensive if and when he has finished with the Soviets. (A.E. didn't even ask the Cabinet before saying it – it was an after-thought added after dinner – but they docilely approved it on Monday.) A.E.'s speeches are a case of personality triumphing over wordiness.

July 9
Cripps[3] telegraphed last night to say he had seen Stalin (to whom he had delivered a personal message from P.M.), who had offered that we should conclude an agreement pledging ourselves (a) to mutual aid and (b) to no separate peace. Winston saw it last night and rang up A.E. *at 2 a.m.* to suggest that he came across and talk about it. A.E. was already in bed and the talk took place to-day. W. already had an enthusiastic reply prepared expressing his personal approval and saying he had summoned the Cabinet to-night to consider it. A.E. insisted that P.M. shouldn't reply directly again, and himself produced a draft of acceptance. W. is so impetuous though his instinct here was absolutely sound. There must be no hanging back with Russia, but it is after all for the Foreign Secretary to do these things. (A. is having some difficulty with the P.M. who likes to take all the decisions and get all the credit!)

But what is important is not so much these paper undertakings but the action here which we can take to help the Russians. Here the P.M. is less helpful. The Navy are non-cooperative about operations in the North. The Air Force are doing a lot in the West. The Navy suffer from excessive caution as A.E. said to-day – they always want to be safe two moves ahead.

On returning to A.E., I find he is still driving and urging and pushing H.M.G. to get on with it.

July 10
Very tiresome Cabinet last night over Russian proposal, A.E. says. P.M. most arbitrary and insisted on replying personally to Stalin (It is

1. J. P. L. Thomas, M.P., (later Lord Cilcennin) Assistant Commissioner of the Treasury 1940–43, had been Eden's P.P.S. during his first spell at the F.O. (see Diplomatic Diaries Vol 1).
2. General Sir Charles Ponsonby, Parliamentary Private Secretary to Eden.
3. Sir Stafford Cripps, Ambassador to Russia 1940–42.

just like Neville and Musso!, A.E. said) Anyway the telegram has gone off proposing a formal declaration. A.E. very fed up with P.M.'s monopolistic tendencies. I told him we can't have him resigning from Winston's Government.

July 11

A hustle to-day to get Soviet Agreement signed. Cabinet have agreed to text and telegram is to go to Cripps to-day.[1] A.E. is to tell Maisky and Poles – the latter are having a relapse of punctilio over their relations with the Soviets. We hope to stage a three-cornered meeting this afternoon.

July 12

I drove down to Frensham this morning with A.E.'s box. He greeted me with the news that Winston had been on the telephone five times over a government reconstruction. He wished to send Duff[2] to Far East as coordinator à la Lyttelton,[3] Brendan Bracken[4] to M. of I., R.A.B.[5] to Ministry of Education and Dick Law[6] to be Under-Secretary at F.O. A. was against Duff going to Far East and thought it preferable to make no change at M. of I. but to see how new arrangement worked there. He said he would miss R.A.B. who was good with the House of Commons and took a lot of work off his shoulders, but he had always wanted Dick – though latter suffered from diffidence and lack of authority. I said I was sure this would be a good change and it was important to bring Dick on. Anyway we get rid of Chips [Channon][7]! I think A.E. feels R.A.B. was useful in keeping Munichers in Parliament in order. He also wondered whether he should have had a Labour Under-Secretary – but who? I think this is the best arrangement and Dick deserves the opportunity.

Instructions were sent to Cripps last night to sign Anglo–Soviet Declaration – we expect news of it at any minute.

1. For text see Churchill Vol. III p. 341–2.
2. Alfred Duff Cooper (later Lord Norwich) 1890–1954, was Minister of Information at this time.
3. Oliver Lyttelton (later Lord Chandos) President of Board of Trade 1940–41 had been sent as Minister of State to Cairo earlier in the year.
4. Brendan Bracken was M.P. for Bournemouth.
5. R. A. Butler (later Lord Butler) was Under-Secretary for Foreign Affairs.
6. Richard Law (later Lord Coleraine), was Financial Secretary to the War Office.
7. Sir Henry Channon, M.P., socialite and diarist.

The Polish–Soviet conversation on Friday went fairly well. Maisky agreed to most of the Polish points. The trouble is that half the Polish Government here is violently anti-Russian. There is also an ugly snag in the Polish political prisoners whom the Poles want released and who are believed to have been "liquidated". A.E. is using all pressure to bring them together.

There was a last-minute hitch last night over Syrian armistice, Dentz[1] refusing to treat with us if Free French were also included. But this seems to have been got over and we hear French plenipotentiaries crossed our lines early this morning.

Meanwhile things don't look too bad. Russians are doing far better than was expected and must have badly delayed German programme. The Russian Mission here are getting on very well with our staffs. But I still wish it were possible to do more to help them than bombing in the West.

A most important thing is how well A.E. and the P.M. get on. Latter, I think, really trusts him and listens to him, headstrong though he is. He apologised to A.E. for being so tiresome over his personal telegrams to Stalin. He is an eternal schoolboy.

July 14
Anglo-Soviet Agreement duly signed on Saturday and announced on Sunday.

Lunch with old Namier[2] to-day – very worried at ominous lack of references to Jews in connection with the announcement of independence for Syrians[3] and other Arabs. I fear he is right and the Government intends to do them down if it can. The war hasn't made people more pro-Jew.

Russo–Polish negotiations sticking badly because of Poles.

July 15
Long talk with Victor Cazalet[4] and Ronnie Campbell[5] about our

1. General Dentz, Vichy commander in Syria.
2. Sir Lewis Namier, the historian.
3. The Armistice Convention set up the Free French as responsible for internal affairs and the British for defence. Both pledged themselves to independence for Syria and the Lebanon, and after independence the British would recognise the predominant position of France in the area.
4. Victor Cazalet, M.P.
5. Sir R. I. Campbell, British Minister in Washington 1941–45.

Embassy in Washington and Halifax.[1] Latter is evidently being pretty hopeless – the old trouble of being unable to make real personal contacts apart from just charm. He knocked over the President with his charm on first meeting and then has made no progress since. Again, all business in the U.S.A. is now transacted by telephoning and "popping-in", both of which H. can't abide. He only goes to see the President on business – and naturally usually to ask for things – he has never got on to a more intimate chat basis with him.

Nobody really knows what is in the President's mind. He works through different people for different things. He has moreover a tremendous down on "governing classes", whether in America or elsewhere, (not a bad "down" either) – it is said because he wasn't a success at Harvard or in business as a lawyer. Anyway now he loathes everything that stands for that. But poor Halifax is the embodiment of it.

July 16
A.E. said he was worried about Persia and German infiltration there.[2] The Chiefs of Staff have been asked to report on possibilities and they must be stirred up. He also wondered if something can't now be done to bring about a Soviet–Turkish rapprochement. I talked to Moley[3] about this and we are going to tackle Maisky about the possibility of the Soviets giving the Turks assurances.

Continual appeals from Maisky and Cripps for more action to help the Russians. They want some land operations. A.E. is worried at the lack of support of the Chiefs of Staff and even of the P.M. who, for all his brave words, is reluctant to agree to raids. He wants either enormous raids with armoured divisions or nothing at all. A.E. thinks, and so do I, that we ought to stage small smash-and-grab raids up and down the coasts. We know the Germans have no armoured divisions in France now. Yet nothing can be got to move and all we do is to bomb Germany and Northern France, though that is important too. A.E. says he finds Winston "dated" in military matters – he doesn't understand the tank and aircraft technique.

July 17
Sikorski went off deep end last night. Made a speech in the country

1. Lord Halifax, Ambassador to the U.S. 1941–45.
2. There were about two thousand German engineers, technicians etc in Persia at the time.
3. Sir Orme Sargent, Assistant Under-Secretary at the F.O.

saying he had said his last word to Maisky. We have retorted by putting a censorship ban on his utterances pending Maisky getting a reply from Moscow.[1]

July 18

A.E. told me it is agreed that Dick Law should come here. He told Dick yesterday. He thinks Brendan Bracken is to be the M. of I. and Duff to go "on a visit of coordination" to the Far East – accompanied by Lady Diana! That is bad. It will create the worst impression among the poor soldiers and sailors who cannot have their wives. Hankey is to go and be replaced as Chancellor of the Duchy by Duff.

A.E. had another very negative Defence Committee last night. He says we have enormous armies in U.K. and Egypt and neither of them can do anything. Chiefs of Staff are too old, he says.

Polish–Soviet negotiations are proceeding not very well – Poles most to blame.

A.E. anxious to stiffen up to Franco who is behaving badly again, making pro-Axis speeches and sending troops against Soviet Russia. A.E. feels that the argument that we can do nothing to annoy Franco or upset him because if we do the Germans will march in, applies no longer as the Germans are fully occupied in the East. He has always hated this appeasement policy which incidentally has been contrary to American wishes.

July 19

Meeting in A.E.'s room about Spain. It was recognised that the Germans can come in whenever they are ready and Franco will welcome them. At present the Germans aren't ready. What was the good of our present policy? We get certain fruits and iron ore from Spain – so long as Spain is at peace we have unmolested use of Gibraltar as harbour and staging airplane base – these could be interrupted if we upset Franco. A.E. wondered if we could incite the Spanish Reds to revolution. Dept. thought they were broken reeds – Negrin[2] discredited. Question of "PUMA"[3] not possible after September. If it is important if not vital, to have done this, if Germans

1. The Soviet Government's Policy towards Poland after the Russo–German partition in 1939 had been ferociously repressive, with large areas being annexed to Russia. This was the background to the new situation created by the German invasion of Russia.
2. Dr Juan Negrin, Spanish Republican Prime Minister.
3. The occupation of the Canary Islands.

came into Spain – then decision should clearly be taken now. A.E. is going to raise it at Defence Committee next week.

Polish–Soviet Agreement very near settlement. A.E. hopes for a signature on Monday.

Persia – Wavell (now in India) favours strongly a forward policy there, joining hands with Russia. This works in very usefully with A.E.'s ideas.

July 20

Maisky brought P.M. a personal message from Stalin on Saturday asking for establishment of a front in N. France and another in the Arctic to relieve pressure on Russian armies. P.M. has replied regretting N. France impossible but speaking of impending naval and air operations in Arctic.

The miserable Dawson[1] has resigned from the Times under the age limit. His place is taken by Barrington Ward[2] – a nicer man but still a wet one.

July 22

A.E. says War Cabinet and after that Defence Committee spent 7 hours yesterday in so-called discussions – all of which could have been boiled down to one hour, the rest being interminable speeches by P.M. It is really a very serious situation. No decisions are taken nor proper plans thought out.

He is also worried because Roosevelt, according to Hopkins, sees himself as the man of the Peace Settlement and fears we may have great difficulty there – another Wilson over again. A.E. is very anxious to develop the work of the Allied Governments here and has planned a meeting to deal with surplus foodstuffs etc. for feeding Europe after the war. He had referred to Winant to make sure United States would not object and now a long and negative reply is coming back. I agree that these tendencies of Roosevelt who wants all the limelight (so like the P.M.) want watching. But at all costs these two (A.E. and R) must be made to work together.

July 23

Defence Committee discussed Spain last night and decided on PUMA for August. I don't feel quite happy about PUMA as it can't be done after August or September and once it is done it must inevitably

1. Geoffrey Dawson, Editor of *The Times* 1923–1941.
2. R. Barrington Ward, Editor of *The Times* 1941–1952.

precipitate Spain into war against us. Yet by August or September it is almost certain the Germans won't have invaded Spain. But if they do so in October, say, then it is too late for PUMA and we are done. Clifford [Norton][1] is rather uncertain if PUMA would be successful – and failure would be awful – also he sees the danger of precipitating events in Spain unless absolutely necessary.

A.E. has a speech to the Foreign Press Association on Tuesday. He wishes to return to the No Peace with Hitler theme and show why. I think he might also say something of the necessity of making war impossible in future but also of leaving Germany economically prosperous.

July 24
An encouraging telegram from Angora. According to Turkish Chief of Air Staff, Turks are now most anxious to have further staff talks with us and to build up an anti-German front. A.E. is very pleased at this as he has always backed the Turks though most of us have become sceptical.

July 25
It has been decided to let the Russians have some of our aeroplanes.

Meanwhile Russo–Polish negotiations are on verge of success or failure, Soviets refusing to advance any more and Sikorski's opposition refusing to allow *him* to advance any more. Maisky says that so reactionary is the country that the Generals are the most enlightened element there!

July 28
Some agitation over weekend over Soviet–Polish negotiations. Just when agreement had been more or less achieved on a text in London, Cripps weighed in from Moscow with a new text which he had agreed with Stalin himself. As this was in some ways better than the text Maisky had agreed here, we wish to get this substituted for ours. The Poles aren't aware of this yet and are in a state of ferment, Zalewski[2] and other Ministers having resigned over it. We had hoped to get signature this afternoon, and Sikorski we understand is ready to sign anyway.

Our anti-Jap measures, freezing Jap assets and denouncing commercial Treaties, are well on the way. Japs now landing troops in Indo-China. America taking same steps as ourselves. Maybe their

1. Sir Clifford Norton, later Minister in Berne and Ambassador to Greece.
2. Foreign Minister in Polish Provisional Government.

primary objective is to consolidate themselves in Indo-China with a view to operations against the Burma road and China from that side rather than an advance into the Dutch East Indies or Singapore at present.

Henry Hopkins[1] is now off to Moscow to clear up supply questions. P.M. is developing a regular correspondence with Stalin by private telegraph – much to A.E.'s concern. P.M.'s style is becoming so sentimental and florid that Cripps has telegraphed privately to A.E. to try and restrain him. We fear that it will have the worst effect on Stalin who will think guff no substitute for guns. It is worrying how little we apparently can do by way of military operations to help Russia – though we are sending her aircraft. The slowness and lack of imagination of our Chiefs of Staff are enough to frighten one.

July 29
A.E. made a speech to-day to Foreign Press Association. Principal points. 1. Germany must be prevented from ever making fresh wars, but 2. she must not be allowed to collapse economically or she would poison the rest of us. Point 1. went with a swing. Point 2. in dead silence. It is essential, however, to rub in these simple lessons.

Sikorski also spoke and declared he was going to make a treaty with Russia "on honourable conditions".

July 30
A last harum-scarum as to whether the Poles will sign. Sikorski is determined to sign but Raczkiewicz, the Polish President, has been got at by Zalewski and the anti-Russians, and may refuse to endorse it. Dormer[2] is being sent round to see the President – signatures arranged for 4.30.

Treaty finally signed at 4.30.[3] All very friendly – photographers and films. P.M. pulled out of his afternoon sleep to come and sign – looked very bleary – eyes very watery in the spotlight. Dormer reported just before signature that he had seen President who was highly nervous and undecided, but promised to do his best to get all parties to agree. It appeared from the conversation however that he

1. Henry Hopkins, Head of Lend Lease Programme 1941. Adviser and assistant to President Roosevelt 1941–45.
2. Sir Cecil Dormer, Ambassador to Polish Government in London.
3. The Treaty annulled the Russo–German agreement with regard to Poland, and the two countries promised to support each other in the war against Germany.

was completely ignorant of fact that Sikorski was at that moment off to F.O. to sign. Latter had evidently refrained from telling him. Dormer felt unable to tell him either. What happens next? We don't believe Sikorski can be thrown out. But Sosnkowski,[1] who is very popular with the Army, is dead against him. Anyway, there can be no doubt of the vision and courage of Sikorski in signing.

July 31
Explosions still going on in Polish camp. Final results not yet known. President said he wouldn't authorise Sikorski to sign. S. said it wouldn't make any difference.

Discussion in A.E.'s room about Far East. He wishes to propose to U.S.A. that we should all undertake to help each other if any one of us is attacked, and secondly, that we should issue a general warning to Japan against any further step. Thailand has now asked us definitely whether or not we will help them if they are attacked. Finally, the U.S., after their Freezing announcement,[2] show signs of intending to allow oil and cotton to go through to Japan all the same in normal amounts. A.E. is to discuss the whole problem with Winant to-day. Whatever the U.S.A. do, he feels that H.M.G. must go steadily and apply *their* freezing to the full extent.

August 1
P.M. has finally agreed to our giving the Dutch an assurance in general terms to help them in Dutch East Indies if attacked. Meanwhile the other problems of U.S. cooperation are being referred to Roosevelt.

A.E. very cross to-day after again spending 5 hours in Defence Committee – completely wasting time while P.M. discoursed on strategy to Auchinleck. A.E. finds P.M.'s views on strategy disastrous: he pressed Auchinleck to undertake an immediate offensive in Western Desert which Auchinleck refused to do as he hadn't got enough tanks. P.M. very rude but General very calm and answered well. If Wavell hadn't been made to undertake the offensive at Sollum 2 months ago with inadequate forces which lost us 200 tanks, Auchlinleck could have undertaken a proper offensive now with adequate forces. Now however it is necessary to wait till forces are reasonably adequate. The meeting broke up in some confusion, P.M.

1. General Sosnkowski became Polish C-in-C 1943–44.
2. The U.S. and British Governments had announced an order freezing all Japanese assets which took effect from July 26 1941.

grumbling and growling – purple in the face and with streaming eyes. A.E. is really worried at the P.M.'s management or lack of management – feels he is wearing out the Chiefs of Staff to no purpose.

A.E. was to see him again at Chequers tomorrow but wonders now whether he had better go. I said I thought P.M. would probably ring him up himself tomorrow and say he was sorry, but in any case he had much better go.

August 3

It looks to me problematical whether P.M. will survive the course. His health may fail – his headstrong qualities may outweigh his great abilities and he may have to go if we are to win the war. A.E.'s accounts of his conduct of the Defence Committee are disturbing – a monologue – any opposition treated as factious – policy and operations decided by impulse – no proper planning. His handling of the H. of C. especially over the supply debate has caused misgiving there: his treatment of the subject has been arbitrary to a degree and embittered by personal feelings. The recent Government changes including the promotion of his son-in-law have gone badly. If this is so, A.E. seems the only possible successor. He alone has a grasp of the strategic situation as well as drive and imagination. Above all, he has youth and is modern. P.M. is still obsessed with the methods of the past and does not yet grasp the need for speed. I should much regret an early change for A.E.'s sake as I'm sure it would be better that P.M. should finish the war. But if it must come, then A.E. has the combination of qualities necessary which no one else possesses. Fortunately his conduct of foreign affairs recently has been bringing him laurels. Polish–Soviet Pact, Anglo–Soviet agreement, Czech recognition, his two last speeches. He will have to speak in the H. of C. this week before the recess and he is to make another public speech at the end of August. Each speech must be marked by a further clarification of our war–peace aims so that he thus builds up his doctrine for the peace settlement and identifies himself with those who are thinking of the future. He must come to be regarded as their spokesman and leader.

August 4

A.E. told me today that he had been over to Chequers on Saturday and – as I had expected – P.M. was most penitent, apologising for having kept him so long and even saying "Yes, I'm afraid sometimes I do talk rather a lot. I'm quite ashamed of myself!" A.E. said at

Chequers it was like a Russian play. He arrived at 6 p.m. having motored at speed from Frensham to get there in time for the Defence Committee, to find P.M. and Auchinleck sitting in two chairs in the garden. P.M. said "I'm afraid you will be very cross with me but I've put off the Defence Committee till after dinner, as I think I'll now go off and have a sleep!!" When dinner came, P.M. suddenly said "I don't want to do any more tonight. I want to see that film again of Nelson and Lady Hamilton!" It was then found that the film unit had already set off back to London. P.M. said it must be got back and so telephoning went on at intervals through dinner which was very prolonged. "Put people across the road to stop them!" However the film unit slipped through the net, and there being no cinema the P.M. finally and reluctantly settled down to work at midnight and they then worked solidly up till 2 a.m.; A.E. getting back to Frensham at 4 a.m.! P.M. in the highest spirits at the idea of his jaunt.

Things however seem to be clearing up. The Far Eastern problem is being put squarely to Roosevelt and meanwhile it looks as if there had been misunderstanding and the Americans have no intention as we feared of going slow with their economic sanctions.

A.E. in very good spirits. Government has been left in more or less joint charge of Attlee and himself. A.E. to do all defence questions.

We hear P.M. has made Randolph liaison officer between War Cabinet and Lyttelton in Cairo – another bad appointment.

A.E. told me today he thought he would go to Moscow after P.M. comes back – probably early in September. I said I hoped he'd take me too. He said yes.

August 5
The carefully guarded secret of P.M.'s visit to President Roosevelt (he left on Sunday)[1] has leaked out from German sources at Lisbon. We are having to announce it.

August 6
Roosevelt strongly opposed to announcement of his meeting with P.M. being made until it is over. Meanwhile it is leaking heavily all round.

August 7
Visit from Weizmann[2] back again from U.S.A. full of grievances

1. The Atlantic Conference.
2. Dr. Chaim Weizmann, President World Zionist Organisation and Jewish Agency for Palestine 1935–1946. He became the first President of Israel.

against H.M.G. and A.E. in particular for their pro-Arab policy and omission of any references to Jews' part in the war. He said both Frankfurter[1] and Roosevelt expressed great concern over Palestine and need for making it a Jewish state. I entirely agree with W. about the worthlessness of the Arabs as Allies – but at the moment, with the precarious balance of forces in the Middle East, we mustn't give them excuses for making further trouble. Nor is opinion in this country so pro-Jewish as it was. The Jews are their own worst enemy by their conduct in cornering foodstuffs and evacuating themselves to the best billets. However, that I know is no excuse for us not to do our duty by them. I am still firmly convinced that Palestine should be a Jewish State as part of an Arab Federation of States if necessary and the Palestine Arabs should be paid to go away.

Sam Hoare[2] is full of rosy reports of Spanish generals being about to overturn Suner and Franco – all being reasons why we should go slow and easy with Spain. I wonder! We've so often heard of these Generals – like the German Generals who were always going to bump off Hitler. But it always ends in talk.

We also hear that Weygand[3] is causing the Americans (who have always had excessive faith in him) fresh grounds for optimism in N. Africa by alleged anti-German and anti-Darlan sentiments. I doubt his doing anything too.

I hear 1922 Committee waited on A.E. yesterday to urge respectfully that he should not make important utterances on British policy except in the H. of C. (e.g. Leeds and Press Association speeches). That is nonsense. What we have to do is to educate British and world opinion and that can only be done by public speeches in the country. This H. of C. is completely discredited and nobody reads its debates. The poor old 1922 Committee are out of date.

August 8

Great progress in Russo–Turkish rapprochement. We had already suggested in Moscow that Soviet should give assurances to Turks regarding their loyalty to Turkey who was increasingly mistrustful at progress of Anglo–Soviet friendship and success of Soviet armies. All

1. Felix Frankfurter – Judge of U.S. Supreme Court.
2. Sir Samual Hoare (later Lord Templewood), Ambassador to Spain 1940–44.
3. General Weygand was Vichy Governor-General in Algeria, and Delegate General in North Africa.

the old latent hostility has been aroused and the spectre of Russia coming down on the Straits or the Black Sea revived. Yesterday Maisky came to say Stalin agreed to A.E.'s proposal of a joint statement of a reassuring character and produced a text disclaiming any Soviet intentions in regard to the Straits. This was agreed with the inclusion of a clause to say that if Turkey were attacked both Soviet and G.B. would be ready to provide help.

At the same time it was agreed to inform the Turks of action proposed as regards Persia, viz insistence on expulsion of Germans there. Finally, A.E. and Maisky discussed text of our joint note to Tehran – whole question is whether it should be an ultimatum or not. This is to be further considered. Meanwhile our troops are collecting at Basra for occupation of oil areas if necessary.

The Chiefs of Staff are disquieting. A week ago Maisky came and proposed a joint Anglo–Russian descent on Spitzbergen where there are Russian miners who could be armed and act as garrison. We told the Norwegians who agreed, and we explained to both that we didn't want to land troops because of difficulty of maintaining them but we would do naval and air protection. Good. Preparations go ahead. A few days later Chiefs of Staff say, no. They wish to make it a purely British operation. We could land British troops and maintain them there. Good. A.E. tells Maisky, who agreed, and also Norwegians who were sending some men too. Two days later they get a report from the Admiral who says it cannot be done and anyway it would be useless – so the whole operation is to be abandoned! This again had to be put to Maisky who was most disappointed. A.E. is furious at this blowing hot and cold. But it is typical. One day they would have us rush forward. The next day they wish to rush back.

August 10
Cripps has written to suggest that his task is now done with Soviet Russia in the war and he should come back to England and be used as a link for co-ordinating post-war relations between the two countries. Poor man – he flatters himself that it was he who brought Russia into the war. But he is so quarrelsome with the Russians and has such acrimonious exchanges with them, and lectures them so much that he has really become more of an obstacle than a help, and so perhaps should come home. But the Government don't want him back here to be a thorn in their side. They realise Stalin won't pay attention to any ambassadorial blandishments and the work in Moscow can be done perfectly well by a professional. Cripps is an extraordinary man –

jumping here and there one never knows in which direction – a nice man, it seems, but odd and awkward, if brilliant.

August 11
The British–Soviet assurances to Turkey were made yesterday. This is another good development but the Turks are mistrustful as ever of the Russians and some of them at least are corrupt. I have little faith in anything they say. They will only be persuaded to stand firm, still more to help us, if they see we are winning. What they would admittedly like to see is Germany crushing Russia and herself being exhausted and crushed in turn by us after.

Lunch with A.E. at the Perroquet. We discussed the future of the party and of the party system. I said it was vital that both parties should rejuvenate very quickly or the young, who were most critical, and rightly, of existing leaders and parties, would go elsewhere. He entirely agreed and said he would feel quite differently himself about going on with politics after the war if this were done. He hates the old Tories and would rather join the Labour Party if they remained dominant. "You and I must work together", Bevin had said to him. He told me about the visit of the 1922 Committee to him at the H. of C. the other day. They had complained about his not making enough speeches in the H. of C. and also about only promoting Left-wing people in the F.O.! I said I thought that must be me, but when he asked them for names, they could only think of poor Collier,[1] who was made Minister to Norway.

He cannot see how politics will be after the war. He feels it would be fatal to have an election immediately after the war, and the peace must be put through first; then he said he thought they should go to the country as a coalition. I said I disliked that because the party system alone really made Parliament work properly. Anyway, it was essential to get as many young people as possible into the seats now as they fell vacant.

He would like to see military service kept on for the good it does to the young people, mixing them up, feeding them well and keeping them in the country. I said I thought it would be impossible: the country would hate it but much of what he had in mind could be done by schools holding summer courses in country camps.

August 11 [later]
Further telegram from P.M. at sea. Joint Declaration is to be issued

1. Sir Laurence Collier, Ambassador to the Norwegian Government.

on Thursday. Also a joint telegram to Stalin containing congratulations and promise of further material support. Finally P.M. proposes that Beaver should go to Moscow later to discuss supply.

A.E. not too favourable to idea of U.S. occupying Azores and doubts Salazar welcoming it to extent F.D.R. suggested to P.M. A.E. rather isolationist where Americans coming into Europe is concerned. He wants us, not them to be the predominant partner. But I think it is vitally important, both for war and for peace, to get America into Europe – even at the cost of bases.

August 12

I found A.E. very indignant this morning at having been aroused at 2 a.m. by a telegram from P.M. marked "Attend to at once!" containing text of a joint declaration[1] which F.D.R. had proposed that they should both issue as a result of their meeting. A terribly woolly document full of all the old clichés of the League of Nations period. The Cabinet hastily got together and met to consider it. There is obviously no alternative but to accept it, woolly though it is. The Cabinet is considering it again to-day in the cold light of morning. A.E. feels that F.D.R. has bowled the P.M. a very quick one – such a document might well have been communicated in advance. However, I think it will go well in America where they like resounding phrases and also in Liberal and Labour circles here – though A.E. said Bevin[2] was very critical.

I had a letter from Charles Peake[3] and A.E. saw Eager (of *Louisville Star*) yesterday, and both confirm that F.D.R. means to keep out of the war and dictate the peace if he can, a consummate politician much quicker than Winston. Eager said the worst thing we had ever done was Winston's speech "Give us the tools and we'll finish the job" – it gave F.D.R. exactly what he wanted. C.P. says he is out to put the U.S.A. on top and he doubts if F.D.R. believes much or at all in his democratic slogans. I wonder if F.D.R. is as bad as that. But what is certain is that we are dealing with a headstrong man who means to monopolise the limelight at the Peace but whose political ideas are still those of 20 years' ago. We must begin building fast ourselves with our Allies here, and get peoples' minds working and firm foundations laid.

1. The Atlantic Charter.
2. Ernest Bevin, Minister of Labour 1940–1945.
3. Sir Charles Peake, later Ambassador to Yugoslavia and to Greece, was Counsellor at the British Embassy in Washington.

August 15
Keynes[1] just back from America. He gave most amusing description of chaotic conditions of work of U.S. Government departments – each department letting down the other – no coordination and no over-riding authority – no records or written decisions are kept of anything – all oral and all that can be repudiated – not because of trickery but simply because in view of above conditions no Government depart-ment felt able honestly to bind itself to deliver the goods. President R. did not intend to have any war debts arising from Lease Lend Act but felt it wrong that we should go scot free; he would like to feel we were making some political concessions in return. Keynes very anxious to tie up this matter – the so-called "consideration" – soon, before the American appetite grows. President was thinking of an international police force for after war in which however we should be the leading partner. "New-Dealers" were like the Jesuits or the German General Staff and had their representatives in any Government department who were more loyal to each other than to their departments.

A.E. somewhat concerned at idea of Menzies[2] returning to London. He is in league with the Beaver[3] (who is boosting him) and would like to get into English politics via the War Cabinet.

August 15 [later]
The much-awaited Roosevelt–Churchill Declaration came out yester-day – broadcast by Attlee at 3 p.m. – P.M. still being at sea – which seems dangerous to me, though Admiralty say they are quite confident. I hope they are right.

Declaration has gone well in the press, though in fact there is nothing new in it.

August 17
Week-end with A.E. at Frensham. Talk about Persia. Notes requiring liquidation of Germans delivered in Tehran by Bullard[4] and Soviet

1. J. M. Keynes (later Lord Keynes), at this time member of Chancellor of Exchequer's Consultative Council.
2. Mr. R. G. Menzies had just ceased to be Prime Minister of Australia after the loss of the election.
3. Lord Beaverbrook was Minister of Supply and Member of the War Cabinet.
4. Sir Reader Bullard was Minister and later Ambassador to Persia 1939–1946.

Minister.[1] What is the next step? Should we and Russians go in after a few days without further warning, or should we give now an ultimatum? I think if, as is probable, Persians don't eject all the Germans, former is the best, accompanying our action with a reassuring note to Shah about respect for territorial integrity and independence etc. We don't want to upset the Shah, and would like him to bow to *force majeure* about occupation of oil fields, and then to cooperate. Our troops are all ready and it is important to occupy the oil fields before serious risk of Russian defeat in the South arises.

We talked about P.M. and A.E.'s fear that he is deteriorating. It is for instance entirely due to him that we cannot now do more for Soviet Russia. If it hadn't been for the last ill-starred and costly campaign at Sollum,[2] Auchinleck would now have been able to overwhelm Germans and Italians in North Africa and recover all the lost ground. He feels too that P.M. and Chiefs of Staff are entirely negative – no effort is being made to help Russia elsewhere. There is crying need of P.M. having someone like P. J. Grigg[3] (his former private secretary) to take charge of No. 10 instead of his present collection of amateur toughs. A.E. had suggested it to P.M. but latter said he and Grigg would quarrel too much – a bad sign. He wants only "yes-men".

August 18
Discussions about next step in Persia. General view is that with weakening of Russian position in Black Sea area, sooner we get into Persia the better. The best solution will be if after display of *force majeure* Shah will fall in with Russo-British plans and cooperate. But it is anticipated that all this will send cold shivers down the Turks' backs.[4]

August 19
P.M. and party returned to London this morning.

At Cabinet later P.M. approved A.E.'s Persian policy and was anxious to move in as soon as possible. I'm glad of this – yesterday's

1. The Persian Government in fact replied that, though they were reducing the number of Germans, to expel them would be incompatible with their neutrality.
2. "Battleaxe" which had been the last operation undertaken under Wavell's command.
3. Later Sir James Grigg who became Minister for War 1942–45.
4. On account of their traditional fear of the Russians.

Cabinet was wobbly and time is not on our side in this. I only hope the military are capable of doing their part quickly and efficiently – but of that I feel no certainty, nor does A.E.

Turks very mistrustful still not only of Russians but of us. A.E. is sending for Aras[1] to-day to impress on him our *bona fides* in Persia, our record in Iraq. He has also asked Maisky to get Molotov to see Turkish Ambassador in Moscow who is very bad. Cripps unfortunately has had the worst effect by getting into bad relations with the Turkish Ambassador and by his clumsy and indiscreet handling has confirmed the latter's suspicions that we mean to collar Southern Persia for keeps whilst the Soviets seize the North.

Cripps is so clumsy and impetuous in his work. He is quarrelsome with the Russians in matters where quarrels aren't wanted, and it is certainly time he was changed. He himself wants to come home, but he must be put at once into the Government or he'll be an infernal nuisance. But it will need careful handling, or else the F.O. will be accused by the press of having jockeyed out Cripps which won't be true.

A.E. told me to-day they were looking for a new Viceroy as Linlithgow[2] wouldn't stay on. Had I any ideas? I said I knew of one who could do it, that was Halifax. But A.E. didn't altogether agree that he had been such a great Viceroy – as I'm sure he was. I said he was a man for the East, not for the West – all his qualities of masterly detachment very valuable there, though worse than useless for the dynamic West. It wasn't a bad thing to have an "appeaser" in India where I feared there was trouble ahead unless great care was taken. However A.E. said he didn't think it would be possible to send him from Washington where it would seem to imply failure. I then suggested Sam H[oare]. He laughed and said he always wanted it: Kingsley Wood[3] had also favoured Sam, on the ground apparently that he would be such a nuisance at home – which is true. But he wouldn't be bad probably – he knows his stuff, would do it well and would work hard.

P.M. told A.E. he thought it might be well that he, A.E., should go to Moscow with the Beaver. A.E. isn't particularly keen to go now – a long journey and much to do here. He said he thought it would depend on who the Americans send. I agreed, and he has telephoned to Winant to ask him to find out.

1. Turkish Ambassador in London.
2. Lord Linlithgow had been Viceroy of India since 1936.
3. Sir Kingsley Wood, Chancellor of the Exchequer 1940–1943.

August 20

P.M. now says he won't agree to Cripps coming home – he doesn't want to turn anyone out of the Government to make room for him, and so he must stay put.

Roosevelt has given his warning to the Japs.[1] Battle of Atlantic now going much better. Roosevelt has agreed to take over escort for convoying as far as Iceland: thereby releasing fifty destroyers. Henceforward the Germans must either sink U.S. destroyers (and bring America into the War) or let the convoys pass (and enable us to get in all we want).

Anglo-Soviet advance into Persia now fixed for August 23. Russians to Tabriz, we to oil fields. An Anglo–Russian Military Mission is to meet and co-ordinate at Mosul. I only hope the soldiers don't make a mess of it. We shan't get in any too soon.

P.M. is not at all anxious for Menzies to come back here. He has sent him a stiff telegram accordingly. The truth seems to be that Menzies would like to get out of Australian politics and many in Australia would like him to go. But we can only have a Dominion representative in the War Cabinet if he is P.M. and a P.M. clearly cannot stay in London indefinitely. A Dominion Minister who wasn't P.M. would soon be out of touch with his own Government, would be less useful than the High Commissioner and would only serve to swell the Cabinet. Short ad hoc visit by the Dominion P.Ms. seems the best way. Fraser from New Zealand has just been here. Mackenzie King is just arriving from Canada. We had a good dose of Menzies early in the summer.

August 22

Date for beginning of Persian operation now fixed for Monday August 25. Persian reply received – a prevaricating document evidently put up after consultation with German Minister with a view to gaining time till Germans are nearer and can help. Halifax arrived to-day. Weizmann gave A.E. such a depressing account of him in America yesterday that A.E. actually said perhaps I was right, and he should go to India after all.

1. ". . . The U.S. Government now finds it necessary to say to the Government of Japan that if she takes further steps in pursuance of a policy of force towards neighbouring countries, the U.S. Government will be compelled to take all necessary steps towards safeguarding rights and interests of U.S. nationals and U.S. security."

August 25

Great broadcast by P.M. last night[1] – "Words, words, words, –" very little about what we are actually going to *do* to help Russia which is what the people want to know. The Persian operation began at dawn. The Shah has announced his intention of resisting – we know he thinks the Russians will shortly collapse and the Germans will be able to help him. We are accompanying our action with assurances of respect for integrity and independence of Persia.

Our first act of "naked agression". A.E. rather ashamed of himself, so too is P.M. But I tell him it is essential for us to get our base and the oilfields secure while the going is good. Late tonight we had a further telegram from Bullard describing his interview with the Shah in which there looks a hope that the Shah will only put up a token resistance.

August 26

Meeting with Halifax to discuss the Azores question.[2] H. said that Roosevelt didn't wish to go into Azores without an invitation or if fighting was involved. We think it most unlikely that Salazar would ever invite Americans rather than us, but that it might be possible for us to go in first and then hand over to Americans as in Iceland. The next question was that of the Canaries. The Chiefs of Staff – who are always changing their opinions – now say that it would be possible to attack these islands later than mid-September and in October even. There is increasing reluctance to attack them unprovoked, and in anticipation of Spain being violated by Germany. P.M. is most reluctant and A.E. not at all keen. Chiefs of Staff, however, are definite that Azores are not a substitute for Canaries and latter with better harbour facilities are necessary bases for control of Straits if we lose Gibraltar.

Maisky insistant today on the need to do more for Russia. A.E. has spoken to P.M. who has promised to send 200 fighters – to the horror of the Air Ministry, who have piled up an immense reserve.

As regards Persia, we have drafted a reply to the Shah which we have asked Moscow to concur in, providing for occupation of oil area in south, an area round Tabriz in the north, with guarantees for through communications. Meanwhile the press, and especially the American press, highly approve our action. If this goes according to

1. This broadcast also warned Japan against further expansion, and stated that Great Britain would be on the side of the U.S. if the latter became involved in war with Japan.
2. The Azores were of strategic importance in the Battle of the Atlantic.

plan and we get the Shah to acquiesce, it will be a minor triumph and much strengthen our position in the Middle East.

P.M. was furious to learn yesterday that just as these operations were to start which are under his directive, Wavell, now C. in C. in India, was proposing to come home on leave! This has been quickly stopped – but how could the man have thought of it even? Really these soldiers. We aren't very good at making war, as A.E. is always saying.

Great uncertainty about the Russian visit. A.E. in two minds about his going himself. And so am I. The Americans (and the Beaver) are now talking about delaying it till October and the Russians not unnaturally, want it as soon as possible. It certainly oughtn't to be later than mid-September. Neither the British public nor the Russians would understand a longer delay. But it really rests with the Americans, who alone can provide the armaments which the Russians need. It might perhaps be wise for A.E. to go. I hate to think of the Beaver going anywhere as a sole representative of G.B. Yet it is hard to see what they would have to discuss in Moscow except supply matters at this stage.

August 28
Lunch yesterday with Weizmann who poured out his fears of failure of American production. He is very worried. Roosevelt himself tired and necessity for short absences from work increasing. He complains too of lack of drive here and of complacency – especially at Ministry of Supply. He is convinced that there is not enough oil in America to provide us all if real fighting begins in the West. He has prepared a substitute and proved its efficacity, but no interest whatever has been taken in it – presumably because of opposition of oil companies.

W. had been very gratified at his recent talks with A.E. (He suspects him of anti-Zionism.) W. also very worried over his Jews – no mention of them in P.M.'s broadcast – "Even the Luxembourgers were mentioned!" Jews in America are most influential ethnic front – discouraged by what is felt to be reluctance over here to have Jewish cooperation, and concern to conceal it for fear of Goebbels. Morgenthau[1] very keen on settlement of Palestine with more Jews. President's entourage very Jewish. Anyway W. advised all there that nothing could be done now in the middle of the war with the Arab situation as it is. The Americans must make their views felt at the Peace Conference.

1. Henry Morgenthau, U.S. Sec. of Treasury 1934–1945.

I am convinced that our whittling down of Zionist pledge – White Paper[1] – is wrong. We must try a new approach – and deal with Middle East as a whole and Palestine as a part. What about an international Police Force and control for the whole area? – no independent warring, shifting states, but a federation under international control? I have written A.E. a paper. The problem so-far has been vitiated by the narrow pro-Arab views of our Eastern Department and of Colonial Office.

Discussion with Dick Law about Moscow meeting. We are both worried at proposed delay till October due to reluctance of Beaver and Americans to face Stalin and say they can give him so little help. I discussed this with A.E. this morning. He is worried at delay and yet does not see any useful purpose in his going there alone in advance. I said I couldn't see point of delaying until October. Our supply position won't be any better by then – yet psychological effect of speedy meeting after announcement at Atlantic meeting[2] will be lost. He agreed. Dick and I talked again with him this afternoon. And he then dictated a minute to P.M. urging earlier meeting for these reasons. He is not anxious to go himself, especially if he has nothing to offer. We must concentrate on getting the supply mission off urgently in September. *6 p.m.* We hear that Shah has ordered resistance to cease. A.E. telephoned at once for Maisky to urge need for speedy dispatch of telegram containing our conditions which Moscow has not yet concurred in. We should act quickly and clinch the Shah.

August 29
Persians have asked for Armistice, a new Government having been formed. We are stirring up Russians and Maisky is coming at mid-day with proposed joint reply. Meanwhile we favour pushing our forces on till they join hands with Russians coming from the North and so secure north–south communications – no occupation of Tehran if possible.

Further discussion yesterday by Chiefs of Staff of the Portuguese and Spanish islands. Chiefs of Staff now say Canaries should be tackled after October if necessary, so we are let out of painful decision of either violating Spanish neutrality now, before Germans go in, or having no base at all if Gib goes. Meanwhile we are to press on with negotiations with Salazar about Azores. Americans are being informed

1. Of 1939.
2. At the Atlantic meeting, a message had been sent to Stalin promising help in supplies, and suggesting a conference in Moscow to discuss this.

of this latest development. I think this is now fairly straight. Our Anglo–American Western base is taking shape.

Maisky has got his instructions and we are now both agreed to terms to be given to Persians. Telegram has now gone off. P.M. has sent a personal telegram to Stalin offering him another 200 fighters, making 440 in all.

August 31

Long talk on Saturday morning with Charles Peake. Gloomy about prospects of F.D.R. bringing America in soon – He even doubts his being very keen to bring her in at all. F.D.R. not a leader. Hitler, on the other hand, will never help us by provoking America or sinking a U.S. warship. A sort of impasse. Meanwhile war production sagging in America. More motor cars and refrigerators than ever. C.P. thought nothing less than brutal warning of the facts from the P.M. would rouse America or frighten F.D.R. into activity. He says P.M. has probably more hold over U.S. opinion than F.D.R. himself and latter knows and fears this.

Persia seemed neatly tied up before we left. Armistice and our Anglo–Russian terms put forward. Reasonable terms to assure us our oil and communications to Russia. A thoroughly sound and well-executed operation – it has gone excellently with opinion here and in the U.S.A. A credit to A.E. without whom the P.M. and the Chiefs of Staff would never have moved.

September 8

Back from leave – the usual rush of work. Persia not cleared up yet. Office meeting this morning to discuss next step in view of Persian prevarication over acceptance of our demand for expulsion of Germans. General view was that Russians and ourselves should advance into Tehran and see to seizure of Germans ourselves. Also felt that Shah was a liability owing to his extortionate policies and should be turned out. As a successor there is a young Kajar in England, who might serve.[1] We can't falter, and occupation of Tehran will give us best position to control railway. Cabinet and Defence Committee are to consider it to-night.

Last week Stalin sent a reply to P.M. appealing urgently for further assistance, notably an offensive in West or in Balkans. To this a further reply was sent showing that this was impossible for lack of equipment.

1. The Kajar Dynasty had ruled Persia all through the 19th century till deposed in 1925 when Shah Reza Pahlavi had taken over.

I fear the Russian situation is bad indeed and public opinion can't understand – neither in Russia nor here – why we can't do more about it. Nobody realises the truth which is the failure of production in America.[1]

September 9
Cabinet and Defence Committee last night agreed a somewhat modified procedure about Persia. We are to go into Tehran but to precede this with a 48 hour ultimatum demanding internment of Germans and certain Government reforms. The latter will put us on the right wicket with the Persian people who loathe the Shah. This has been put to Maisky to-day for Moscow concurrence.

Great excitement about 5 p.m. when telegram from Tehran announced that Persian Government had accepted all our conditions including handing over the Germans and expulsion of Axis diplomats. This necessitated reconsideration of this morning's decision to enter Tehran. It was decided (a) to publish acceptance and (b) to instruct our Minister to take note and to require fulfilment in 48 hours. A.E. is now anxious to work for alliance with Persia coupled with internal reforms. Shah to be eliminated sooner or later. Persians are already suggesting to us that we should turn Shah out.

September 11
Situation in Far East examined yesterday. Freezing and blockade measures of U.S.A. and ourselves are slowly strangling Japs. Sooner or later they must decide, I think, whether to go to war or to climb down. Whether or not Japs decide to attack depends on solidity of democratic front. But the Americans persist in having talks with Japs with a view to gaining time, yet though this may be desirable, we feel here that fact of talks only serves to convince Japs that democratic front is not solid and so to encourage them to attack. Department feel now is the time to increase pressure on the Japs, and any attempt at appeasement such as Americans are trying is doomed to failure. The Japs are bent on expansion and will push on fast or slow as circumstances permit, while offering every assurance of pacific intention.

September 13
Persia going all right. I cannot see how the present Shah can remain.

1. See Churchill III page 403–412 for this exchange of messages. It was this crisis which had led the F.O. to urge an earlier date for the supply conference.

He has lost "face" with the Persians. He is very unpopular anyway, and we are bound to insist on internal reforms which will strike at the roots of his position. There is no outstanding General or politician to supplant him, so we come back to the old dynasty – which is also discredited.

Roosevelt broadcast yesterday marks a good step forward. A direct warning to Axis shipping to keep out of neutrality zone. I have the impression there is a slight improvement in American situation. Anyway Hitler is sinking some American ships at last.

September 14
Talk with Weizmann about Palestine. His chief trouble now is Jewish Army. This was approved by P.M. a year ago and all organised; then held up for lack of equipment, and now again held up because of cold feet in Cairo and Jerusalem. The Jewish Army was to have been recruited in America where it would have aroused great enthusiasm among powerful pro-Ally Jewish elements. On other hand, no doubt such an army would have scared the Arabs, though they could hardly have been more unhelpful to us than they have been. Apart from Jewish Army, now thus held up, there are certain Palestinian units (Jew *and* Arab) who do exist and have seen service in Middle East. These come entirely from Palestine and trouble here is that Jewish volunteers far outnumber Arabs, who in spite of all nonsense talked about pro-British feeling, show greatest reluctance to fight for us. These units have now also stopped recruiting for fear of upsetting the Arabs. Trouble is – however we put it – Arabs dislike us, and we are afraid of them. Jews must be on our side anyway and we aren't afraid of them – we are ashamed of them. All this largely due to pro-Arab mentality of Cairo Embassy and of its influence over F.O. through Eastern Department. C.O. are also badly pro-Arab for reasons of appeasement.

I told Weizmann that much as I symphathised personally on both these questions, I felt nothing must be expected until war was over. Then, in my opinion, whole of our Middle Eastern policy would have to be revised. It must be dealt with on larger lines embracing whole of M.E. in one policy. Failure in past was due to dealing with each M.E. place separately; independence for Irak, independence for Syria etc. None of these states fit to govern themselves – yet creation of an independent Jewish Palestine in midst of three or four independent Arab States would certainly lead to trouble which H.M.G. are anxious to avoid. But if whole area were dealt with as one – individual States "federated" under a larger authority – then to my mind it would be easier to fit in a purely Jewish Palestine. Police, finance, hygiene, trade etc. would have to be common and controlled. Also international police bases would be needed in Mediterranean, in furture, e.g. Haifa, Tripoli, Crete. These might be leased like West Indian bases on 99 years' lease. Their existence would facilitate international control of Middle East. But control must be international, not purely British because British taxpayer would not stand for it alone. Here was the chance for Jewish Americans. At the Peace Conference they must press for some such generalised solution with American participation – as moreover in Europe also. We must have America "mixed" up in Europe after war – even if only by a token. Equally they should be "mixed up" with us in Middle East – through strong bases and sharing controls.

Such was my discourse. W. took it and approved of it.

September 15

Over week-end it was decided in view of obstruction at German Legation and ineffectiveness of Persians that we should advance, with Russians, into Tehran in order to supervise delivery of German colony and Legation. Advance on Tehran has begun. Shah has now abdicated in favour of his son.[1] The latter is a bad lot hand in glove with the German Legation. We are consulting Moscow and Bullard as to alternative successors.

Halifax is anxious to persuade A.E. not to publish the collection of British Diplomatic Documents covering the last fifteen years. H. himself while Foreign Secretary had agreed to their being put together with a view to possible publication. Then A.E. came along and was very reluctant to publish for fear of stirring up old controversies about Munich. Department here, however, (including Van) were very anxious to publish in order to forestall a German version of events, which might otherwise get in first (as after 1919) and "sell" the German case to all the innocent pedagogues and publicists here and in America. I finally persuaded him to agree to publish on this ground and also, still more justifiably, on the moral ground that the British public is entitled to see these documents as a result of which the war is being fought. The documents are not discreditable to the British case. They only prove, as Van says, that our Ministers were fools, but not knaves. But this prospect is no doubt distasteful to Halifax – and

1. The present Shah of Persia.

42

still more to Horace Wilson[1], who is kicking wildly at his part in the Munich proceedings.

September 17
Persia again. Shah abdicated yesterday in favour of eldest son, but it now appears that latter, if made a constitutional King and required to accept reforms, might prove satisfactory. Soviet Ambassador in Tehran takes this view and it is proposed to try him out.

Cripps is showing fresh restiveness in Moscow and wants to leave for home. Neither P.M. nor Cabinet want him back to play politics as leader of Opposition – which is of course his intention. A flattering reply is being sent about his services in Moscow and importance of his remaining there – though in point of fact he has become more of a liability than an asset owing to his quarrelsomeness with Soviet departments and the uncertainty as to which way he is going to jump. He is a hopeless Ambassador. What an odd man he is! Very brilliant, and well-meaning, very unstable, no judgment whatever, as much a menace to his friends (as Labour knows) as to his enemies – but *au fond* obviously a very nice, kind man. A.E. told me that if Cripps insisted on going, P.M. thinks of appointing Hore-Belisha there. I am horrified.

Moscow meanwhile is menaced with a visit from that bogus booster, Citrine[2] and a T.U.C. party. How Cripps will hate it! Citrine comports himself as a little Fuhrer, ordering Cabinet Ministers (or their Secretaries) about. He is puffed up with conceit, very energetic and *remuant*, but a better friend to the House of Lords than to the workers. He will probably end there. He hates Soviet Russia and is one of those Labour leaders who are throwing dust in the eyes of Labour. He could easily become an appeaser for fear of Communism.

Bevin a much better man, I should say, more downright even in his weaknesses, less bogus, definitely not an appeaser.

September 18
A.E. and I are much perplexed at the curiously persistent press campaign which has been going on against the Foreign Office over Persia. It began with *The Times* (Dawson personally as we know) on the ground that the F.O. were being dilatory and feeble in their handling of Persian procrastination over the Germans etc. in Tehran. This has been taken up by other papers and persistently pursued. *Daily*

1. Sir Horace Wilson, Permanent Secretary to the Treasury.
2. Sir Walter Citrine, General Secretary T.U.C. 1926–1946.

Mail, Daily Herald, Evening Standard. It infuriates A.E. as he has taken special trouble to keep the diplomatic correspondents informed. The Persian operation, moreover, has worked out perfectly as everybody wanted – no major operations, no tying-up of troops, no bloodshed. Shah gone, control of through communications, Persian people on our side. So persistent has been the denigration that A.E. thinks it may be a deliberate campaign with Rothermere[1] and Southborough[2] hunting in couples, as they always do, and with the Beaver possibly in the background. Is it possibly the beginning of a gambit to discredit A.E. by discrediting his Department? Perhaps a connection with the peace offensive from appeasing quarters this winter? Not impossible.

Stalin and P.M. have exchanged further messages.[3] Stalin asking for the establishment of a second front, either in the north or in the south via Persia, to join on to the Russian wings. P.M. undertaking to look into all the possibilities.

September 19

Long talk last night at dinner with Henry Hopkinson[4] (back from Lyttelton in Cairo). Mainly about Syria, Middle East and Egypt. Henry gave poor account of British Staff in Middle East. All rather indifferent. We all found ourselves in agreement over need for a purely Jewish Palestine (or possible quarter of Palestine) where Jews could immigrate as much as they wanted. We thought somehow Syria, Palestine and Transjordan might be linked up. P.M. is believed to favour an Arab Fed. underwritten by Ibn Saud, including a Jewish Palestine. Cyprus and the Dodecanese, we all thought, must go to Greece.

NOTE TO S. OF S. DATED 21 SEPTEMBER

"You are discussing the publication of the British Diplomatic Documents with Lord Halifax on Tuesday. Before then I think you should read this correspondence with Sir Horace Wilson. I hope you will agree that his attempts to stifle and bowdlerise the Documents, for which he is responsible, must be resisted. The British Public is entitled to know the lengths (however mis-

1. 1st Viscount Rothermere, proprietor of the *Daily Mail.*
2. Lord Southborough, representative of the Petroleum Board and Director of Shell Petroleum Company.
3. Stalin was asking for 25–30 divisions.
4. In the F.O. attached to Minister of State, Middle East. He later entered politics and became Minister for the Colonies 1952–1955. He was made Lord Colyton in 1957.

guided) to which H.M.G. went to prevent War. These particular conversations are the most convincing and graphic of the Munich period. Why should Wilson's papers receive a different treatment from those of our Ambassadors and Ministers?

O.C.H.

September 22
Lunch with A.E. who had spent the weekend with the Polish forces in Scotland. He asked what I thought of the idea of giving Poland East Prussia after evacuating the German population. He thought that this might be one of the best ways of providing for Polish security and access to the sea. I was rather sceptical. It would mean, I said, a mass movement of population which had been there since the 13th century. It would make it impossible to resist similar demands from the Czechs. The latter had much stronger grounds, I thought, for such a method. But as for Poland and Germany, it was a very big surgical operation. We agreed that minority treaties had been a curse – causing minorities to be often impossibly obstructive and obliging us to intervene perpetually in internal affairs. We thought next time there should be no minorities. They must opt between exchange and absorption, having no special national privileges. I said the Poles must not seek to have the old Eastern frontiers at Russian expense or there would be trouble with public opinion here.

September 23
Lyttelton arrived back from Cairo yesterday on short visit. He dined with P.M. and A.E. last night. P.M. in a mood of deep depression, A.E. said, very bitter about the constant nagging of the Press against the Government. "As if they were doing nothing."

September 24
De Gaulle crisis has suddenly blown up. De Gaulle, after being pressed to broaden his movement by appointing a national Committee, has suddenly done so, but omitting Admiral Muselier[1] and others of weight in the Movement, who had been urging the change. The immediate background to this was Admiral M., who, stung by de G.'s delays, put in an ultimatum demanding these changes, with himself as President of the Council, under threat of handing the Free French Fleet over to the Admiralty. De G. replied by threatening M. with imprisonment. Chief trouble is de G.'s insistence on retaining a

1. Head of the Free French Navy 1940–1942.

certain Passy as head of his secret service who is suspected of Fascist inclinations, and if he is kept on, others will leave. P.M. sent for A.E. for a midnight confabulation about it all with First Lord.[1] It was agreed A.E. should send for de G. and get him to agree to hold up publication of his list of the Committees and to include names we approved of including Admiral Muselier's, whilst First L. was to get M. to withdraw his offensive ultimatum to de G. De G. is as obstinate as a mule and wants only yes-men with him.

A.E. saw de G. at 5. Meanwhile Alexander had persuaded M. to withdraw his ultimatum and both M. and de G. had met. When de G. came, he said he was ready to give M. post of Marine in Executive Committee, but he would not have Labarthe[2] who was impossible (knowing L. I can only agree with de G.), and finally that Passy would go "shortly" as he was to have a command. De G. is full of sweet reasonableness when A.E. sees him. The question now is, will M. accept this? And will de G. let the Committee really work and not make it a farce? Alexander is to urge M. to give it a try.

September 25
A.E. had to have a further encounter with General de G. last night after I had gone. He had de Gaulle in one room and Admiral Muselier in the other. Latter wouldn't meet former who he said had insulted him after he had withdrawn his offending letter. Anyway de G. was ready to give him a place in his Government and every pressure was brought on M. to accept. Finally latter agreed to sleep on it. This morning we think agreement has at last been reached.

September 26
Free France. General de Gaulle finally issued his list of members of the Executive Committee last night, while Admiral M. agreed, somewhat reluctantly, to give it a trial. We are going to define our position in a letter to General de Gaulle, saying we note these changes but must make clear we do not regard it as setting up a Government and we will deal with Committee as representing all those who have joined Free French Movement. Our attitude is this:– we welcome the creation of this body as broadening the basis of the movement and we are anxious to spread our recognition of de Gaulle over the Committee as a whole,

1. A. V. Alexander (later Lord Alexander of Hillsborough), 1st Lord of the Admiralty 1940–1945. Minister of Defence 1947–1950.
2. André Labarthe, previously editor of *La France Libre*.

while keeping de G. as the figurehead. At the same time we do not wish to give de G. jurisdiction over those Frenchmen outside France who do not wish to be Gaullists. We therefore only recognise the Committee as affecting the Gaullists and the Gaullist colonies. We hope however that the still wider body – the National Assembly or whatever it is called – which de G. now proposes to set up in addition to the Committee – will embrace all the best names – Cambon,[1] Comert, Maritain, Barrès, Jules-Romains, etc. who so far have held off. Like this, we may be able to build up gradually a broader and more impressive movement which in its turn will exercise more attraction on France itself and bring more of those there over to its side.

September 29
Press campaign against F.O. has resumed again with attack in *Evening Standard* on Saturday. A.E. has drawn P.M.'s attention to it, adding that the paper is owned by a colleague. To-day we see in the *Daily Express* an encomium by Margesson of what the W.O. is doing Evidently this all fits in with what we suspected – a campaign against A.E. under cover of attack on his department as a preliminary to getting the appeasers back again.

A.E. and I at lunch together discussed the Beaver's campaign and agreed what a scamp he is. A.E. said again how well he got on with Bevin and Attlee both of whom were very decent people and wondered whether he couldn't work with them after the war. This Beaver attack has nettled him and made him more conscious of his incompatibility with the Right. I urged, as I always do, that he should keep very close touch with the Labour people in the Cabinet but that we should also keep together his own band in the Conservative Party. He couldn't go over to the Labour Party without arousing their jealousy and hostility but he could work with them if he had a group of his own.

September 30
General complaints in Cabinet last night, I hear at attitude of press to Government. A.E. quoted *Evening Standard* and *Daily Express* on F.O. Morrison complained about *Daily Express* and the blackout, while Bevin complained of *Daily Herald* (backed by Citrine) which is attacking him on man-power. I'm glad that Bevin is standing up to Citrine. The latter's overbearing behaviour is quite intolerable. A.E. very much on the side of Bevin.

1. Roger Cambon, Minister at the French Embassy in London 1924–1940.

October 1

P.M. had great success in H. of C. yesterday when he made statement on war situation. He made vigorous defence of F.O. over Persia – as a result of A.E.'s expostulation at attacks in *Evening Standard* etc., declaring that it was one of the most successful operations of the F.O. – and yet it didn't satisfy "the crabs". Dawson was sitting in the Gallery. P.M. told A.E. yesterday that the British public were magnificent in times of crisis, but in the hour of triumph they would be intolerable.

Bevin complained to A.E. to-day of the intolerable way in which the Beaver was behaving over man-power, never giving him any idea of what he wanted and moving people off one job to another. He said the B. was concentrating on producing numbers of tanks and neglecting the manufacture of spares. The tanks would be useless without the spares. It was exactly what he had done over aircraft, all window-dressing designed to show large totals – what a menace!

October 3

A.E. told me Winston has a plan he is now absorbed by, for a landing in Norway. He is desperately keen on it and wishes A.E. to work it out with him. He has a pathetic confidence in A.E. – his instinct tells him that he is the only "live" one of his colleagues to whom he can turn for confidence and understanding. But it is a big query and it would be an alternative to the M.E., and is that wise? A.E. is much perplexed – he feels as I do so many of W.'s gorgeous schemes have ended in failure. The war is now going fairly well for us – but a false step – a faulty short-cut – would set us back years.

October 6

A.E. and I had our usual Monday lunch together. He had been staying with Moyne[1] and had been much amused by Simon,[2] who was staying there, immediately tackling him about the proposed publication of the British Diplomatic Documents. S. said Halifax had spoken to him about it and he, S., thought that, in the interests of Neille's reputation, delay was desirable. A.E. told him – which Halifax had omitted to tell S. – that it was Halifax himself who had originally authorised the selection of the Documents.

1. Lord Moyne, Sec. of State for Colonies 1942–1944. Minister of State, Middle East, where he was assassinated in 1944.
2. Sir John Simon, Chancellor of the Exchequer 1937–1940, became Lord Simon and was Lord Chancellor from 1940–1945.

I told A.E. that I thought the time had come when the F.O. should begin preparing their plan for the Peace Treaty – we had a staff of professors at Balliol working on our behalf in close touch with the departments of the F.O., but they required a directive. If we hadn't our plan all ready, Roosevelt would produce one of his own out of his pocket like the Atlantic Charter. A.E. was interested and agreed. He said he would have a meeting in the Foreign Office to discuss it. He was prepared to authorise plans being worked out for an international police force based on a large measure of Anglo–American participation.

October 7
A general complaint from the Office of the failure of Cripps to provide us with any information of what is going on in Russia – no background, no account of his interviews with Stalin or his colleagues, no impressions. At the present moment we have absolutely no account of the Moscow Mission's doings, the effect it produced, whether the Russians were pleased or not – except Beaverbrook's own account which obviously cannot be trusted. A very dangerous position which no professional Ambassador would ever have allowed to arise. Cripps is quite hopeless and unteachable in this respect, but a politician can get away with anything. He nearly involved us in a first-class row with Stalin the other day over the withdrawal of three Naval officers whom Stalin had complained of.

We are slowly edging the British Documents along towards publication. Bobbety[1] has now written to A.E. strongly in favour of publication – all except one document, the worst of all, that of Chamberlain's interview with Hitler over the Czechs which he thinks will harm us in America and with the Czechs themselves, so shameful is it. A.E. is to discuss this with Bobbety.

Further discussion to-day in F.O. about an Allied declaration of abhorrence in regard to German atrocities in occupied countries. A.E. felt that these should not go unnoticed and that some minatory message should be issued. A draft declaration was prepared for Cabinet accordingly. A.E. was anxious to avoid saying we were actually making lists of war criminals for future execution in view of the sorry story of the Hang the Kaiser movement in the last war. But he wished to put in the maximum of threat about our taking records of the crimes without committing himself to exactly what the Governments would do about it. Either you must hang Hitler and, say, half-a-dozen of his

1. Lord Cranborne, Sec. of State for Dominions 1940–1942.

gang or else you must hang them as well as thousands of subordinates who were carrying out orders. Public opinion, especially in America, and probably here, would be unlikely to endorse the latter in the atmosphere of peace – even if they approve the former. At the Cabinet however there was a general demand for lists to be drawn up – this was supported especially by Dalton[1] and the Labour Ministers. To-day we had a redraft of the Declaration which is to go before the Cabinet again, stiffening it but still without the lists which A.E. proposes to oppose. I think this is right. I am in no wise averse to hanging Hitler & Co. – if we can do it. The fact that we didn't hang the Kaiser, Hindenberg and Ludendorff in the last war brought us no benefit and is if anything an argument in favour of this deterrent action in the case of these fresh war criminals. But I don't like the idea of lists of subordinates.

October 8

P.M. again grumbling at Dill, A.E. says. O. Lyttelton, as an ex-Guardsman, had been pressing on him the virtues of the brave but brainless Gort[2] as an alternative C.I.G.S. on the ground that with a strategist such as Winston a more intelligent C.I.G.S. was not required! Ye Gods. What foolish advice some people can give – P.M. rather in favour of Brooke.[3]

A.E. groans to me at the inactivity, the lack of results of work at the F.O. and longs again for the Army or the W.O. "I like excitement." He loved the Army and is as much of an amateur strategist (a better one, I think) as the P.M. himself. He might have gone on in the Army after the last war if there had been any prospects for him in the Sixtieth.

October 9

A.E. dined with P.M. last night. They had a long and intimate evening. "I regard you as my son" Winston said – "I do not get in your way nor you in mine". He said he wished A.E. were back again at W.O. where Margesson,[4] though good in H. of C., was making no

1. Hugh Dalton, Minister of Economic Warfare 1940–1942. President of Board of Trade 1942–1945.
2. Field Marshal Lord Gort, Commander-in-Chief of the B.E.F. in 1939.
3. General Sir Alan Brooke, C.I.G.S. 1941–1946.
4. Captain David Margesson (later Lord Margesson), Minister for War after Eden had switched to the F.O. He had been Chief Whip under Chamberlain.

headway. Both P.M. and A.E. very anxious and eager about forth-coming desert campaign. The soldiers are very confident.

October 10
A.E. had his talk with the Chief Whip[1] yesterday. He told him that he thought more prominence should be given to the younger men and that Dugdale might be made Chairman of the Party in place of Hacking.[2] The C.W. agreed and said he was thinking of doing this but not till February or so as he didn't wish to appear to yield to pressure by the Twenty Two Committee – but he thought it a good idea itself. The C.W. is an intelligent reactionary – a sort of Buccleuch – and was very pro-Munich. I doubt if he is very anxious to promote A.E.'s policies. I rubbed into A.E. the great importance of getting his own people into these posts in the H. of C., but he never takes it seriously enough. He feels so happy now with Winston that he refuses to look ahead.

Baddish news from Russia. Hitler's offensive against Moscow making steady progress. Beaver back to-day and saw P.M. and A.E. They are both going to Chequers for the night. But the Beaver was fairly confident that the Germans would not get Moscow and that Stalin would fight on. We have no reliable accounts from Cripps at all.

A.E. much worried to-night at outcrop of press attacks on the Government for doing so little for Russia. He much fears the effect on the Government if things in Russia do go badly wrong. He wonders, as I do, if there may be a plot of the Beaver's to weaken the P.M. by striking down his lieutenants – much as the Fifth Column in France, Flandin & Co.[3] attacked Daladier[4] and Reynaud[5] for negligence and lack of energy in order to get in themselves and make peace on the ground that further warfare was impossible. I wonder – it is not impossible.

October 13
Fresh attempt by Cripps to come home. He now proposes to come home and "discuss" whether or not he returns. P.M. is determined to keep him at his post.

1. James Stuart (later Lord Stuart of Findhorn), Government Chief Whip 1941–1945.
2. Sir Douglas Hacking, Chairman of Conservative Party.
3. See note on p. 223.
4. Edouard Daladier, Prime Minister of France 1938–1940.
5. Paul Reynaud, Prime Minister of France 1940.

I saw a letter to-day from one of our people in the Embassy at Moscow. He described how the Beaver had behaved – rude to everybody, overriding everybody, letting no-one know what he was doing, making every sort of promise regardless of how it was to be fulfilled, leaving all the ends untied and unsettled. The Beaver then goes off and leaves to others the responsibility for being unable to carry out his impossible promises. Cripps had been completely ignored. Our man also said with regard to Cripps and our constant complaint that he sends no reports, that the truth was he didn't want to send any reports which weren't of the most rosy description – he couldn't understand that an Embassy should report dispassionately what was going on but wanted to colour everything according to his political ideas. As a matter of fact there was already a good deal of pessimism and grumbling in Moscow as well as much evidence of Fifth Column work in Ukraine, failure to "scorch earth" etc.

Our first meeting to-day in F.O. to discuss the future of the world. This was really the first fruits of my own efforts to get the F.O. to start planning the peace settlement.

October 14
Staff examination of P.M.'s scheme for Norway has resulted in very cassant criticism. I'm rather relieved. On technical grounds it sounds quite hopeless, but P.M. far from satisfied.

October 15
When Beaverbrook was in Moscow, Stalin expressed the wish to him that Anglo–Soviet relations after the war should be put on a more permanent basis and suggested an alliance – this raises a big question. On one hand, obviously desirable to keep Russia tied to us and Western Europe – on the other, not really desirable to envisage a postwar world with old-fashioned bilateral alliances. We mustn't snub them, but we mustn't compromise the future settlement. We are trying through Maisky to get more particulars of Stalin's ideas.

Defence Committee to consider Norway operation again this evening, in connection with the devastating report of the Staff thereon. I discussed this with A.E. this morning, and said I couldn't help feeling relieved. It seemed more in the nature of a desperate sally than a seriously reasoned plan. A.E. was inclined to agree and said he thought too we weren't particularly good at combined operations or at operations in cold countries – we were better in the heat. I said it would surely be much better to tackle Germany from the South and through Italy. Italy was near to cracking, and once the W. Desert had been recovered, it would be far easier to mount an offensive from there against Sicily – bases would be easier, we could use both ends of the Mediterranean. He agreed and said he had already put this to P.M.

October 16
Defence Committee last night. A.E. spoke out strongly against Norway proposition and urged consideration of action against Sicily in continuation of action in Western Desert. This latter idea was much more acceptable to Chiefs of Staff who are being instructed to report on it in detail. P.M. still very grumbly – not convinced Norway impossible and quite sure that Chiefs of Staff report on Sicily operation when it comes will be equally negative. He thinks they are always negative.

Bad news again this evening. Resignation of moderate Konoye[1] Cabinet in Tokio, following on Russian difficulties, seems to portend a forward movement by Japanese extremists, who were never enamoured of K.'s United States conversations and may now take control in belief that time has come to strike. But where? North against Vladivostok or South against Siam? We are considering despatch of a capital ship to Far East. That would make a difference. Japs so hysterical a people, one can never be certain they may not rush themselves off their feet.

October 17
I hear that Beaver's broadcast last Sunday has not gone well. People were shocked that he should have been allowed to broadcast at 9 which is reserved for the King and P.M. and his ranting was thought to be that of a dictator.

Maisky yesterday very anxious about events in Russia, pleaded for despatch of troops to Murmansk and to Caucasus. We have proposed to release Soviet troops in Persia by taking it over entirely (but Soviets are suspicious of that!) and possibly to send a token force to Caucasus. Cripps strongly urges latter too because of effect on Soviet morale. Maisky also worried at Japs and anxious to know what we think.

October 18
A.E. told me yesterday in high glee that Defence Committee had decided on Sicily – very much to be forgotten about!

1. Prince Konoye, Japanese Prime Minister 1940–1941.

General Tojo, an extremist soldier and M. of War, has taken Konoye's place as new Jap P.M. We must look out for squalls.

October 20

A.E. much cast down this morning by learning at Defence Committee that Western Desert Operation must be postponed three weeks owing to delay in unloading tanks and to necessity for altering axles. Really, really, it is almost incredible that it should be so slow and that news of delay should not come till now. Whose fault is the muddle? Whilst on military grounds delay is bad, on the home front where the clamour for action to help Russia is increasing it is the very devil.

Meanwhile the Beaver is agitating in the Cabinet for more and quicker action against Germany – formation of a second front. Short term measures instead of long term measures etc.

New Jap Government under Tojo so far blowing hot in public and cold in private. They are anxious to continue talks with U.S. We are asking U.S. their views as to future. We don't want to appease them.

October 21

P.V.E.[1] told me more to-day to confirm my hunch of the Beaver's intrigues. He had heard from Harold Macmillan[2] that B. was saying he was fed up with the methods of this Government – too many committees and no decisions. All of which has a certain amount of truth in it. B. was also busily entertaining Conservative Members of Parliament of the 22 Committee. He has installed himself in No. 12 Downing St. and gives dinner parties there to Conservative M.P.s, whilst his newspapers are backing the shop stewards' movement (which is pseudo-Communist) against the Trade Unions. The *Sunday Express* excelled itself on Sunday by describing Soviet Russia as a workers' paradise! He is obviously playing up to the stupider and more venal Conservatives, and at the same time trying to wean the masses away from confidence in the Labour Party.

But I gather from A.E. that the P.M. has his eyes open. Beaverbrook put in a paper to the Defence Committee which was considered last night in which he attacked the Government for failure to help Russia. The P.M. at once tackled him about it and asked what more he thought the Government could do – the Norway operation regarded as technically impossible had been superseded in favour of Sicily operation which would take effect only four days later than the

1. Paul Emrys-Evans, M.P. Under-Secretary for Dominions 1942–1945.
2. Harold Macmillan, at this time Under-Secretary for the Colonies.

former. B. blustered and growled and finally acquiesced. P.M. told
A.E. he didn't think he meant to go out – but if he did, it would mean
war to the knife against him.

October 23
All day in H. of C. – most depressing. The sight of this H. of C. on
such a day is not inspiring. Quite gone is my pristine enthusiasm for
Parliament or any wish to belong to it. I so well understand A.E.'s
distaste for the place and its inhabitants, though I urge the young to
go into it.

October 25
Decision of U.S. Government to give up use of Vladivostok for
supplies for Soviet has had an unfortunately heartening effect on
Tokio extremists who ascribe it to new Government's firmness.
Whether this is the real reason or whether it is because Archangel
route is better, it was singularly bad moment to make the change.

De Gaulle broadcast on Thursday advising French not to assas-
sinate German soldiers and so expose themselves to reprisals. This
sent P.M. off the deep end who wanted to send for de Gaulle on the
spot. He has been calmed down, however, because all here feel that
de Gaulle was right and it was making it too easy for Vichy and
Germans to "liquidate" Gaullists by making them hostages.

I hear that it was Sikorski who hotted up P.M. over this by calling
de Gaulle a Pétainist! We must be careful of the Poles. They are most
insinuating. We must guard against the mistake of the French in the
last war who by their infatuation for the Poles and support of their
wildest claims, sapped the foundation of the Peace Settlement.
Sikorski is very busy courting A.E. as well as the P.M. S. is a good
Pole and courageous over his Russian settlement. Nonetheless he
wants watching. He is trying to "sell" the idea of deporting the
Germans from E. Prussia and giving it to Poland.

Anyway we have Hitler's authority for mass deportation and it may
be a solution. If for Poland, it must also be for Czechs too (Sudeten).
One thing I'm sure of, there must be no minorities treaties this time –
minorities must either emigrate or else remain without any special
privileges.

October 26
I fear position in Russia is increasingly grave, not perhaps so much
from military point of view which is bad enough but because of

Russian suspicion that we are sitting back and doing little or nothing to help. Cripps inists that Soviet morale will suffer seriously if we do not participate in active operations with them – *viz* send troops either to Murmansk or to South. He fears morale may collapse during winter in spite of efforts of Soviet Government, unless this is not done.

All this is being considered here including despatch of two divisions to Tiflis area in New Year, but it is a long way off.[1] What we want to do is to get Soviets to withdraw their divisions from Persia (which we will then replace) to strengthen Caucasus garrisons, also to bring Polish divisions down from Central Russia to the South area (where we can the more easily equip them as we have undertaken to do). Added to this, we are considering the despatch of the British division to Caucasus, although it raises complications of supplies and maintenance which are very difficult. A further complication is that Soviets don't want our troops merely in Caucasus – they wish them to be in the fighting line itself. They evidently mistrust our presence in the Caucasus.

Against this background, we have the Beaver manoeuvring for his get-away as the only man who wanted to help Stalin but who was obstructed by the blimps of the Government. This is the beginning of a peace offensive gambit. Beaverbrook–Laval! He has written A.E. a very stiff official letter asking to be shown copies of a letter which Cripps sent A.E. – marked personal – about the Beaverbrook mission, and of a telegram from Cripps about B.'s ramp to get Quentin Reynolds to Moscow as *Daily Express* correspondent. I've advised A.E. to discuss it with P.M. before replying. It is a very slippery wicket!

NOTE TO S. OF S. DATED 26 OCTOBER

"I have shown Sir O. Sargent Ld Beaverbrook's letter and the papers referred to.

As regards Cripps' letter, we both think, in view of its references to Ld Beaverbrook and of the marking 'Secret and Personal', that it would be a breach of confidence to the Ambassador to send Ld B. a copy. You could of course ask Cripps if he agreed to your doing so, but that places a rather awkward baby on Cripps' shoulders. If he declined, then Lord Beaverbrook would have a grievance against Cripps. I think it would be rather unfair to put Cripps in this position. Ambassadors have an undoubted right to send private and secret letters intended for the eye of the Secretary of State alone. The fact that they use this

1. The Russians were still requesting 25–30 divisions.

method is proof that they *don't* want the contents circulated as a
telegram or a despatch. But Lord Beaverbrook's request contains
a trap either way. If *you* refuse he will assume that Cripps *does*
make damaging criticism of him!

As regards the Quentin Reynolds' telegram, the P.M. himself
decided that it would be better *not* to let Ld. B. see Cripps' telegram because it might create 'bad blood' – In Ld. B.'s letter to
you of October 6th he says however 'I have seen the exchange of
telegrams between Sir S.C. and yourself about Q.R.' and 'I have
already examined the file in Moscow'. Can we assume from this
that he has seen this particular telegram? It is not safe to assume
it without Cripps' confirmation.

As it looks very much as if Ld. B. were collecting *pièces à
conviction* and wants copies of these two papers for future use to
prove (a) his personal success in Moscow, (b) the efforts of his
colleagues to sabotage him, all this wants very careful handling,
and Sargent and I can only suggest your discussing it with the
Prime Minister himself before any reply is sent. The peculiar
position of Cripps himself who is anxious to return into politics
here makes it doubly complicated!

O.C.H."

October 27
A very long day. A.E. and I dined together at Ritz after he had had a
prolonged Cabinet mainly taken up with Beaver's antics. Latter in his
most film-star mood. P.M. told A.E. afterwards that B. had written to
resign over the weekend, saying "he wouldn't be here much longer"
etc. P.M. however had reasoned with him as result of which he had
written saying "he would serve under P.M. in any capacity", which
had of course immediately melted P.M.'s soft heart. It was quite
evident tho' from what A.E. said that B. was being as bloody as
possible – in his true colours in fact. A.E. has no delusions about him
now, I'm thankful to say. He is a scamp but he is a big scamp and such
is level of Cabinet that he is a giant among them. A.E. says he misses
Attlee (off to New York for ILO conference) badly.

P.M. is disquieting A.E. by giving very evident signs of anti-
Bolshevik sentiment. After his first enthusiasm, he is now getting
bitter as the Russians become a liability and he says we can't afford the
luxury of helping them with men, only with material. No one stands
up to him but A.E. – not even the Labour Ministers who are as
prejudiced as the P.M. against the Soviets because of their hatred and
fear of the Communists at home.

October 28

A.E. had another Defence Committee late last night. He told me this morning that it was a depressing meeting as the Chiefs of Staff had recommended against adoption of Sicilian operation – just as Winston had predicted they would! Now it was the Admiralty who objected because of the locking-up of ships and escorts involved by the operation. Anything is better than a premature offensive and a flop which might put us back years. Whatever public clamour we must wait and wait until we can strike with reasonable certainty.

October 29

Press this morning full of reports that Beaverbrook may have to resign owing to his asthma and the hard strain he has had etc – obviously all put out by himself.

This led to a crop of rumours in London that a number of Government changes were impending – all diplomats agog. All this having reached A.E.'s ears, he went over to P.M. late to point out undesirable effects abroad such rumours as indicating Government instability. P.M. then sent for B. who came along at once and had a long palaver with P.M. and A.E. together. B. did a lot of shouting, said everyone was against him, Bevin was thwarting him – he wanted to go – a conspiracy against him and so on. P.M., according to A.E.'s account to me, stood up firmly and dealt fairly faithfully with him – all nonsense that anyone was against him and after a time B. calmed down. B. at one point said "Why don't you send me as Ambassador to Moscow? I'll keep them in the war!" A.E. doesn't know whether B. is still resigning or not. I rather wish he would. B. made a great fuss again about the Cripps letter which A.E., after consulting P.M., refused to let him take a copy of tho' he let him read it. P.M. quite firm over this.

November 1

Saw Weizmann. He told me that before he went to America last time, he had seen Winston who had sketched out his idea of an Arab Federation including a Jewish Palestine under the suzerainty of Ibn Saud. Shortly after this Weizmann had seen Philby,[1] Ibn Saud's man and a converted Moslem, who had said that he believed Ibn Saud would be willing to give Palestine to the Jews as part of a general federation of Arab States provided that the Jews financed it and that

1. St. John Philby, our representative at Jedda.

H.M.G. backed him. Weizmann said he would be willing to guarantee that the finance would be forthcoming and asked Philby to put it to Ibn Saud. Philby is now in London again and he is to see Martin, the P.M.'s Private Secretary and a friend of Weizmann, and tell him the reply.

I know Winston is much attracted by such a plan. But although it has been referred to Cairo, Jerusalem, Bagdad etc for a report, our representatives have said they didn't think it was feasible because of the jealousies and mutual mistrust of the Arabs. Even granted that Ibn Saud is the best, or the only big Arab, he is an oldish man who holds together a kingdom of sand by personality alone.

Anyway Weizmann is much interested and sees possibilities in it. He would prefer to confine Ibn Saud to a federation of Palestine, Transjordan and Arabia alone to start with. W. much discouraged tho' at the way H.M.G. have wriggled out of their promise of a Jewish force, and very anxious lest they should enter into any commitments now with Arabs which would compromise the future. I told him I thought this most improbable – our whole policy being to avoid any commitments to anybody before the peace settlement. I encouraged W. to try to come to terms with Ibn Saud. W. said there was no half-way house now possible with Palestine, either the Jews must all be driven out or they must become the dominant race there. The present arrangement was the worst of both worlds, too many ever to be acceptable to the Arabs, too few to be a strong stabilising element.

I didn't tell W. that Jews are ratting on him. Rabbi Lazarus of America and Anthony de Rothschild here both representing that Zionist claims are excessive.

Strong telegram in to-day from Cripps arguing against P.M.'s reluctance to send British troops to Russia – very closely reasoned with some bitterness. A.E. was away and won't get it till the afternoon. P.M. wishes to discuss it with him and the Beaver. I read it over to the Beaver down the telephone to his country house where he is having asthma.

November 3
A.E. got back late owing to weekend at Ditchley with P.M. He said Sam Hoare had been there and had got on the blind side of P.M. by abusing Baldwin, so much so that the P.M. had agreed to his suggestion that he should seek an interview with Weygand in N. Africa. I was horrified as was A.E. but the latter says he will stop it. It would be an absolutely fatal move. The whole world would think we were

going to sell out – a new Hoare–Laval – What an industrious little schemer Sam is! I thought he must be up to something. He has been sitting in my room as quietly as a little cat.

November 4

A.E. told me this morning of an idea he had of going to Moscow. What had started it was this. Twice recently the Beaver had suggested to the P.M. that he, the B., should go on a mission there to keep them in heart and to discuss war-plans with Stalin. A.E. and I agreed that it would be the greatest mistake for B. to go again now, and not on Ministry of Supply business. It has already been decided that Wavell and Paget[1] should go – and A.E. was rather attracted, as he always is by the idea of a trip, to join them – He could visit Cairo and Tehran on the way and stir up the Abyssinian question and the Persian Treaty negotiations as well as see Hugessen[2] whom he could summon to Bagdad. But it would mean a longish absence from London which I don't like. A.E. would like to be in Russia just after the W. Desert business is done, as then we might have more stuff available to offer the Russians.

I'm in two minds – certainly B. mustn't go and maybe A.E. must go to prevent B. going – but on its merits I am doubtful. It would certainly be valuable in stimulating and gratifying the Russians. But if A.E. is away, who knows what the P.M. may rush into? A.E. is the only real sane influence over him – and I mistrust a long absence – at least a month or six weeks.

Long discussions about the Far East – Chiang-Kai-Shek has sent an impassioned appeal to Roosevelt and Winston for help, especially aircraft, against the imminent offensive he believes the Japs are about to launch against Burma Road. A telegram from P.M. to Roosevelt is being prepared to ask what U.S.A. can do. We can't send aircraft from Singapore unless America can make it good. Our blockade is forcing Japan to a decision. She believes she can get away with an attack on the Road without necessarily bringing us and America in, tho' once she had knocked out China, which might well follow the cutting of the Road, she would be free to attack us or the Dutch or Siam. One by one in fact.

November 6

Telegram has gone to Stalin from P.M. offering Wavell and Paget to

1. General Sir Bernard Paget, Commander-in-Chief Home Forces.
2. Sir Hugh Knatchbull-Hugessen, Ambassador to Turkey 1939–1944.

go and talk over military possibilities. The idea of the Beaver going, A.E. assures me, has been definitely squashed. A.E. now favours going later himself after Xmas to discuss Spring plans with Stalin, in any case not till the results of the W. Desert operation are clearly established. We must now await Stalin's reaction to Wavell idea.

November 8
A.E. has suddenly developed a fresh qualm about the publication of the British Diplomatic Document. We've got Halifax and Hoare to agree, and now are only waiting for Simon. A.E. is anxious about the effect on his own reputation and fears he may look like an appeaser too. I've to-day read all the documents through which concern him and he really has nothing to fear. The truth is everybody was an "appeaser" of Germany at one time or another – "appeasement" began at Locarno under Austen and went on till Munich under Neville. But it was carried on too long, there was a point where it ceased to be wise or defensible and became stupid and criminal. The exact point when it became clear that it had failed may be disputed. I feel satisfied myself that Locarno was right and that it would have been wrong to go to war over the Anschluss or the Rhineland occupation. British people, rightly, I think, would not have tolerated war over these two latter, even tho' we admit, what is very arguable, that if we had gone to war over the Rhineland, Hitler would have collapsed and the world war would have been avoided. But certain it is to me that once Hitler had completed the absorption of German country and began tampering with Czech and Polish country, the time had come for a complete change. It was Halifax and Neville who went on tinkering with appeasement at others' expense and without massive rearmament long after it was clear that they were being hoodwinked. They were not knaves and Halifax was not a fool. But his mind is woolly and refuses to accept inconvenient facts. A.E. resigned over Italy. He might equally well have resigned over rearmament, or over the rejection of the Roosevelt initiative. In some ways these might have been not more justifiable, but from a political point of view, more profitable grounds. He certainly would have resigned over Munich. In any case he went because the policy of appeasement had become unreal and disgraceful.

November 10
Long telegram from Cripps over weekend exclaiming against the way Beaverbrook had kept him out of the Moscow discussions. This had

been aroused by his receipt of an account of the Beaver–Harriman talks which include references to Stalin's suggestion of a postwar alliance between us. B. certainly behaved like a cad in Moscow by cold-shouldering the Ambassador. On the other hand, B. claims that Stalin's references to political matters during the Moscow conference were very perfunctory and casual.

A mollifying reply is being sent to Cripps. A.E. proposes to add that he hopes to pay him a visit "in the not too distant future" to discuss political collaboration now and after the war.

November 11

Maisky brought the P.M. and A.E. this morning Stalin's reply to the message about Wavell. It was pretty stiff and Stalin is evidently feeling out in the cold. He complained that there was no real confidence or cooperation between the two countries because there had been no discussion about future military strategy or post-war cooperation. If the British generals could discuss both these problems, they would be welcome, if not, Stalin wouldn't have time for them. Finally, Stalin said our attitude in refusing to declare war on Finland etc. after his repeated requests was "intolerable".

P.M. bit Maisky and said that it was not our fault that there had been no planning before Russia came into the war when coordination of plans would have made the whole difference.

Nevertheless this isn't helpful. I have always felt Russia attached real importance to declaring war on Finland etc. and we were wrong not to. Russia is terribly suspicious. She knows we and America don't really like her. She feels she can't stand alone – she must either work with the West or with a Communist Germany. We must keep her in our counsels.

A.E.'s first reaction is that it is no use the Generals going alone: either he should go with the Generals or no one, and if the party goes, it should be after the battle is over. And he must be able to discuss long-term policies. We had already discussed the visit on our morning walk before hearing the reply, and he had made up his mind to go about December. Who would he take? Me, I said. And also a soldier, such as D.M.O.

Later

A.E. back from Cabinet very late – about 8.30. He had had terrible trouble over Russia and declaring war on Finland etc. Only the Beaver supported him strongly, but the opposition came from the

Labour leaders, Bevin and Greenwood – shocking! They could only see Communists in the Russians and their hatred of Communism blinded them to any other consideration. A.E. had to say he had been dealing with Soviet Government for years, and knew them better than they did. The Beaver played up well and supported A.E. "Things are in a terrible mess. We must send Anthony there and he'll put it all right". P.M. also very sore about Russia.

November 12
Beaver, who after his nerve-storm, is now behaving in exemplary fashion, went off to see Maisky and told him how difficult his task and that of Foreign Secretary was made by such messages as that from Stalin. He says he said to Maisky, "You ought to work to get Eden to Moscow".

A.E. dined with P.M. last night and much to his embarrassment Winston said three times that if anything happened to him, A.E. would have to take on. As the Chief Whip was there, this will have done no harm.

November 14
A.E. and Maisky have had a heart-to-heart with a view to getting things on a better footing. It now looks as if A.E. would go fairly soon and would have to be ready to talk of the future both military and political. Moley says we should have a Volga Charter as a counterpart to the Atlantic Charter. And I'm sure he is right, an Anglo–Russian charter to make Stalin feel good. I'm most anxious to get our brains thinking about the future. Lie,[1] the Norwegian M.F.A., has now written to *The Times* urging need for a practical plan of Allied postwar cooperation. He also wants to see an Anglo–American base in Norway. The Greeks too want an alliance with us for after the war. All these threads want taking up and knitting together. But the Russian visit has brought matters to a head and we must now get on with a plan to discuss with Stalin. America is a complication. Roosevelt has made us pledge ourselves not to get tied up with a postwar settlement before the peace. We obviously can't make definite pledges about frontiers – but we cannot remain with vacant minds till the moment of the peace conference. We can and must at least settle certain general principles like the Atlantic Charter. And Russia is fighting the war and America is not. We shall have to bear the brunt of the peace, even if we can get a measure of American cooperation.

1. Trygve Lie, later Secretary-General of United Nations.

We must have our plans thought out, and it is high time we began because there are plenty of others already thinking for us.

November 17
At Cabinet this morning approval given to telegram to Cripps explaining our readiness to cooperate to the full with Soviet during and after the war, our inability to produce a cut and dried scheme of war aims for Stalin as yet because we haven't got one and A.E.'s readiness to go to Moscow to discuss this as well as military help and future strategy in a few weeks' time.

On the other hand, no progress made over declaring war on Finland. P.M. most obstinate. At the same time Maisky continues to insist on profound misgiving which this policy is causing in Russia. A.E. doesn't see how to advance matters now. He has next to no support except from the Beaver.

Dawn tomorrow is zero hour for our Western desert offensive.

Dill is being retired on his sixtieth birthday tomorrow and is to go to Bombay. A.E. very sorry but P.M. who dislikes him has decided it. He will be succeeded by Brooke, the C. in C., who in turn is to be succeeded by Paget.

November 18
First discussion in the office today of what could be said to Stalin if A. goes to Kyuibeshev.[1] We felt the important thing is to convince Stalin that we mean to work with him during and after the peace. If we can convince him of this, then the fact that our ideas for postwar are still nebulous needn't matter – all that should be studied properly later. But the Americans may prove difficult, they like Russia less than we do, being more old-fashioned, and they dislike our having any postwar plans which they haven't shared in from the start – or rather they want an American plan, not a British, still less a Russo–British plan. It was also thought we must bring Russia into all the economic discussions (commodities, wheat etc.) on which we have embarked with the Americans. We must make clear that the Big Three will be Gt. B., America and Russia in all these questions.

November 19
Far East – talks between Japs and Americans still proceeding while Tojo makes blustering speeches.

1. The Soviet Government was preparing to move to this town.

64

No news at all of our offensive in Libya. The weather has been frightful and there is some reason to think the German's don't even know yet we've started!

November 21

Maisky yesterday produced an olive branch in the shape of an explanation of Stalin's rude message to the P.M. (This was plotted by A.E. with Maisky to mollify Winston and get things started again.) Now to-day comes another long, querulous and argumentative telegram from Cripps. We discussed it all this morning and it is now proposed to reply quickly to the olive branch by sending as soon as possible to Moscow a full military and a political appreciation of our position, our plans and ideas, and say S. of S. is prepared to come to Russia to develop and discuss the contents of the appreciation in the spirit of the fullest collaboration. As to Cripps, we all think now the sooner he is home the better as he will make any negotiation in Moscow impossible. A.E. would like to get him away now before he goes himself. This must now be discussed with the P.M. and the Cabinet on Monday. Cripps will be a nuisance wherever he is but more so in Moscow as Ambassador now than here as M.P. where he will soon discredit himself.

Later in the day this procedure was changed because of the P.M.'s determination to send a personal telegram to Stalin – which we all think a pity. Anyway a personal message has gone referring again to Finland and saying if she doesn't stop fighting in a fortnight we will declare war, reiterating our wish for collaboration now and after and suggesting if Libyan battle goes well that A.E. should go with military experts to discuss all these matters. P.M.'s wording is not altogether happy and rather argumentative.[1] However there it is. A.E. will see Maisky on Monday and try to fill in the gaps and make clear we mean a full, serious and honest discussion on all problems military and political.

As for Cripps, P.M. won't have him back yet and he is to remain in Russia over the visit. A.E. very fed up as he thinks he will be a nuisance to him.

November 24

Hull has told us of the results of his talks with the Japs. The latter have put forward a series of specious proposals in return for which

1. See Churchill III pages 471–472.

they require relaxation of freezing. Hull is considering a slight lifting of freezing in return for reduction of Jap forces from Indo-China as a temporary measure. P.M. is rather in favour as he wants present situation in Far East to endure and not get worse. F.O. feel that this is a thin edge of wedge, that Japs have no intention of letting up themselves but are seriously pinched by blockade. If U.S. is firm, our experts believe Japs will give way further rather than fight. Meanwhile our heavy ships are on the way to reinforce Singapore.

Russia – a draft Volga charter is now being prepared for Cabinet to see showing what we could sign and what discuss. Latest idea is to start next week by sea. But I'd prefer a little later when Libyan battle clearer, also France and Far East.

Battle not going too well. German tanks are resisting encirclement and fight still continues.

November 25
Stalin agrees to visit to Russia. Time and route still to be settled. In S.'s message he repeats his request for declaration of war on Finland etc.

November 26
I was woken up in the night by the arrival of a telegram from Auchinleck and Lyttelton saying that they had decided to remove Cunningham[1] from command of the battle because he was badly shaken. He had been replaced by a General Ritchie.

What a business! We really don't run to good Generals. But the battle is reported to be going fairly well in spite of the General, and A. and L. are confident that it may yet be won.

We also had another shock in the night in the shape of a message from Roosevelt to the P.M. and another from Hull[2] thro' Halifax showing that they proposed to appease Japan by falling in with the last Jap offer subject to very insufficient safeguards. I have never seen anything like it since Munich. But the Americans want to gain more time in the Far East and believe this is the way to do it. I'm afraid it is not and it will only serve to get the Japs round a difficult corner at the expense of the Chinese. It will also convince them that we won't fight if pressed. We have sent an urgent message to say we hope they'll give further consideration to our views.

1. Sir John Cunningham had commanded during the Abyssinian Campaign.
2. Cordell Hull, U.S. Secretary of State 1933–1944.

November 27
Hull seems to have stayed his hand for the moment and has only
handed to the Japs some general declaration and not the proposed
modus vivendi[1] which we feared so much. The Chinese have remon-
strated vigorously against the proposed sell-out.

November 29
P.V.E. in a great flap about the visit because of the danger and because
of the effect on the Tory Party. Bobbety he says holds the same views.
Certainly A.E. is now in position we want him as recognised No. 2.
If P.M. had a fit, he could take over at once. If A.E. perished, it
would be a national disaster. It is equally certain that he mustn't be
away for a day longer than is necessary because he is the only one who
can keep the P.M. right.
    Hull has finally decided not to put in his *modus vivendi* to the Japs
owing to Chinese remonstration. He recoiled before his own intention
but he is very cross about it and thinks we and the Chinese have spoilt
his peace effort. But now we are told the Japs are about to advance on
Thailand and our C. in C. then wishes to resist if they try to land in
Kra Peninsula. Chiefs of Staff, as usual, don't like it unless U.S.A.
promise in advance to back us, which of course they can't and won't.
A.E. discussed it with P.M. tonight and decided to telegraph to
Washington explaining that if Japs look like doing this, we may have
to occupy Kra to deny it them and what would U.S. views be. P.M.
has also sent a personal message to Roosevelt urging that it is time for
a warning.
    Cabinet tonight turned down proposal to publish our Diplomatic
Documents. It is really disheartening and makes one despair of our
Government, such lack of confidence in the people, such signal failure
to realise the right of the people to see these official documents.

December 2
Tête à tête lunch with A.E. He began at once that he was very perturbed over Far East and at P.M.'s reaction to it. It looks pretty
certain now that Japs mean war. But we've had a much better telegram
from Halifax saying that he had seen Roosevelt on his return and that
he was in fact ready to support us in whatever action we thought
necessary if Japs attacked. This is the contrary of the line P.M. has

1. The terms of this were to last for three months, and involved economic
   concessions and an end to the embargo in force.

assumed and is pressing, viz. that we must wait for the Americans to act. A.E. wants to send a good forthcoming telegram in reply, saying we mean to occupy Kra and help Dutch, and presume U.S.A. will support us. But P.M. is defeatist and appeasing where Far East is concerned and so, as usual, are the Chiefs of Staff.

A.E. is even more perturbed at P.M. himself who is again showing increasing signs of weary and dictatorial behaviour. His eye is getting watery again as before the Atlantic Meeting. He says he won't go to Cabinet any more! How is this going to be if A.E. is away for a month? He feels himself now he oughtn't to be away at such a juncture.

On the other hand, our instructions for Moscow are in a mess. The Chiefs of Staff are anxious to do nothing. I told A.E. whatever he did, he should not go unless and until he has "a full basket". Beaverbrook has told him the same and he realises it.

For all these varied but weighty reasons, a postponement seems likely. Our own Libyan battle is still in a mess too and what we can do for Russia must depend a little on that. But it will be important to convince Stalin our postponement is genuine (which it would be) and that could best be provided by the Japs.

We repaired this evening to the W.O. to be fitted with Arctic clothes. We found an indignant Maisky there saying "I'm not satisfied. It is not fur! I must have fur!" What the W.O. were offering were some garments in a white flimsy material which they assured us the best Arctic explorers wore and were scientifically windproof. But Maisky was not to be convinced and we all shook our heads and said we must have fur.

December 3
Yesterday and to-day interminable discussions about Far East and Russia. About the latter A.E. protested at refusal of Chiefs of Staff to produce troops for S. Russia and P.M. ordered them to look again. He was most anxious that A.E. shouldn't postpone the visit and said he would go himself if he did. A.E. said we must get clear what we could supply, Wavell must be consulted and if we could only offer very little, then Stalin should be told in advance of our departure.

On Far East P.M. wishes to wait for Americans and see a Jap–American war start (which we would immediately enter) rather than a Jap–British war which the Americans might or might not enter. He fears that anti-British and isolationist opinion in America would react unfavourably to a Jap war if we were first in it. We here feel that this

68

is the wrong way round and that Roosevelt has given us a straight undertaking to support us and he can't and won't do more, and American opinion is more likely to be impressed unfavourably if, when we or our Allies are attacked or threatened, we then wait for the Americans.

A.E. came back late from Defence Committee where the question of our Russian problem had been finally thrashed out. He had become convinced by the arguments of the Chiefs of Staff that it was not best from the war point of view to send a small packet of troops into S. Russia, it was better for us to concentrate on Africa and drive the Germans out. That was the ground for us to fight them on, it was a second front, it involved sea transport for them, and we could sink them and wear them. For Russia it was best that we should kill Germans like this and instead of men, to give Stalin machines. Beaverbrook said he was convinced Stalin wanted machines, not men, and he had never asked for men while he was in Moscow: it was only Maisky who pressed for men. At the same time it was agreed that A.E. in breaking this to Stalin, should be empowered to offer a big packet of machines – 500 aircraft and 200 tanks instead. As part of this, it was agreed that we should undertake to continue the war ruthlessly against the Germans in North Africa, on and on without letting up, pushing in troops and tanks there continuously.

A.E. was well satisfied with this and convinced in his own mind that this was sound military strategy. But before we go, the departments must look round and see that the stuff is really there to give.

December 6
At last we[1] are all set to start to-morrow.

Far East was very satisfactory yesterday when Roosevelt agreed to a general warning by us individually to Japan that if she went on and went further, we would fight her together. Today news not so good – Roosevelt is considering giving his warning to the Emperor and until he has done so, he doesn't want us to act. Also Kuruso, the special Jap negotiator in Washington hints at an arrangement and has sketched in vague language what it might be. Roosevelt is nibbling at this piece of time-wasting designed by the Japs to enable them to complete their preparations and to break the united front.

1. On this visit to Moscow, Mr. Eden was accompanied by Sir Alexander Cadogan, Oliver Harvey, and Frank Roberts from the Foreign Office; and General Sir Archibald Nye, Vice Chief of the Imperial General Staff with a military delegation.

December 7
Started off from Euston in special train at 1.15 p.m. In the evening
we heard that according to the wireless Japan had declared war on us
and America – but could scarcely credit it. But I was woken up at
2 a.m. by a message from the P.M. that it was in fact true and that
Roosevelt had summoned Congress for the next day. P.M. wished to
telephone at 9.30.

December 8
Arrived at Invergordon about 8 a.m. and drove to Naval Commander's
office where we proceeded to get through to No. 10. A.E. has developed a chill during the night and is already rather under the
weather. A.E. spoke to P.M. who was in highest spirits at America and
Japan and blandly announced that he was going off to America himself! A.E. who thus first heard of it, asked when and was told "next
Thursday". Wouldn't it be a bad thing for both to be away at once?
Oh no! Alec and I who were with A.E. were horrified. We both felt
he would not be wanted in America at such a moment and there was
nothing for him to do there if he went. But I am aghast at the consequence of both being away at once. The British public will think
quite rightly that they are mad. A.E. saw this too and telephoned to
Winant who had only understood the P.M.'s visit was for later on, he
didn't favour it now. We felt it most important to try and stop P.M.
especially as it would be fatal to put off A.E.'s visit to Stalin to enable
P.M. to visit Roosevelt. It would confirm all Stalin's worst suspicions.
A.E. decided to speak to Attlee too. The latter knew nothing of the
project but entirely agreed with A.E. that it ought at least to be postponed. He promised to urge this in Cabinet to-day. Finally, A.E.
spoke again to P.M. to communicate his fears, but P.M. would have
none of them.

Really the P.M. is a lunatic: he gets in such a state of excitement
that the wildest schemes seem reasonable. I hope to goodness we can
defeat this one. A.E. believes the Cabinet and finally the King will
restrain him, but the Cabinet are a poor lot for stopping anything.

We embarked on destroyer at 11.30 for Scapa to join our ship. We
are to telephone P.M.

We got to Scapa by 4 p.m. after a very fair journey. We went
alongside the *Kent* which is to be our ship; Admiral Tovey[1] met us.

1. Admiral Sir John Tovey (later Lord Tovey), Commander-in-Chief of the
   Home Fleet 1940–1943.

Alec and I went off at once in the Admiral's barge to the flagship (*George V.*) to telephone the P.M. as A.E. was too chilly to go. Alec talked to the P.M. who said at once that the Cabinet had agreed to his going in a day or two! Alec spoke of A.E.'s anxieties at both being away at once but P.M. said "Anthony will be just where I want him and I can communicate with him in Moscow." We felt there was nothing more to be done and so came back to report to A.E. who had gone to bed.

We're all astounded over Japan. We never thought she would attack us and America at once. She must have gone mad.

December 10

Very rough indeed. Personal telegram came in early from P.M. to say America had had a major disaster at Hawaii and was recalling her battleships from Atlantic and had for the moment suspended all export of munitions. Germany and Italy were expected to declare war on her any day and launch a ruthless campaign. We ourselves were likely to have very heavy fighting in Malaya against Japan and A.E. musn't offer Soviets the 20 squadrons. Russia was doing magnificently[1] and war effort in Tobruk was going on well. He hoped to start on his trip on Thursday "if invited". A perturbing telegram. We only hope Roosevelt will refuse to have him now. But it is a poor look-out if the Americans are going to get into a flat spin and concentrate entirely on Japan. Welles has even suggested that Russia should join in war against Japan – a bit stiff when America isn't yet fighting Germany.

Very cold in the ship today and almost perpetual night outside – dawn about mid-day. Just heard that the *Prince of Wales* and *Repulse* have been sunk by Japs. Almost incredible to us. *Prince of Wales* supposed to be proof against anything. Very grave because it alters the whole balance in Far East and will put us definitely on defensive there. Surely P.M. can't leave now.

December 11

A.E. much better. We are to have a conference this afternoon. A cheerful day. Long conference this evening as to how the conversations are to be handled – also on publicity. Maisky and Captain of ship would prefer that there should be no publicity until after our return

1. The German offensive against Moscow had collapsed, and the Russians were counter-attacking.

because of enemy submarines and destroyers en route, but it is almost certain that leakage will occur thro' Angora or Tehran when our representatives there come to Moscow.

December 12

Maisky tells us there are 3 aeroplanes and 2 armoured trains waiting to meet us. A British Naval Officer has also come off: he says it takes 6 days to get by train to Moscow – Maisky says 60 hours! I wonder which is right. Aeroplane takes 6 hours if it can fly at all. Here we are only 25 miles from the enemy. 20 degrees of frost. Maisky breathing deep breaths, says "Ah, now I can breathe"!

Flying seems hopeless. It means flying to Archangel first and you have to allow time to go there and get back in daylight in case you can't land there. Only about 4 hours' daylight. Maisky went ashore with the Russians to discuss our future movements and finally returned about 6 and it has been decided that we start tomorrow at 4 by train. He still maintains that it is only 60 hours, and if that is so we ought to be in Moscow by Tuesday evening. This is far best for A.E. as he should be warm and comfortable and well fed in the train as against the cold and hazards of the air.

A.E. very anxious to know whether P.M. has gone or not, fears if he does it will take all the limelight off the Moscow visit.

December 13

Telegram received early from P.M. said "just off" – A.E. very anxious to let Stalin know in advance of publication of news, has sent tel. to F.O. asking for necessary authority to do so at first meeting next Tuesday. We must work with Stalin on basis of absolute confidence.

We reached the quay in about 20 minutes and found a battalion of Soviet troops drawn up on the quay and a band and our two flags – the Soviets all in grey fur caps and fawn sheep skin coats turned inside out and long padded trousers. We then got into waiting motor cars and drove some 12 miles to Murmansk town over roads invisible in the snow, a rolling sort of country with stumpy trees. M. is quite a big town – over 100,000 inhabitants, having been developed from a fishing village by the Bolsheviks.

We climbed into a very warm and comfortable looking old-fashioned sleeping car train with saloon, which was waiting for us. All plush and silk curtains and tassels, just like a nineteenth century drawing room. We started about 4.30 and almost immediately an enormous and delicious tea was served. Russian tea, caviar (our first sight of caviar), smoked salmon, ham, sausages and black and brown bread and butter, and cheese. Wines galore as well. Maisky's eyes glistened at the good Russian food.

The train is full of troops; 200 of them drawn from the battalion that received us, as protection against the Finns. We have also our own anti-aircraft guns. The soldiers jump out at each stop and form a guard. They are also posted night and day as sentries in the spaces between the coaches. We went to bed about 10 after another enormous meal. I began my vodka course and managed a glass and a half. I feel I must be in good training by the time we reach Moscow.

December 14
Slept like logs till 8 – dressed and came into the saloon. It was already light by 10. Talked to A.E. Thinks it best to have first talk with Stalin entirely alone, without Cripps as Stalin has evinced a strong preference for this. It is difficult to leave Cripps out but the important thing is to get S. to talk freely.

Intermittent discussions about the forthcoming talks. A.E. very keen that our arrival in Moscow should be published before the P.M.'s in America. He now favoured a short announcement on Tuesday or Wednesday just to say we are there, to be followed by the longer one recording our joint declaration which can be released after we have left. For our security it is important to keep dark any dates and our routes of coming and going.

December 15
We hear we are to arrive tonight at about 10 p.m. A.E. worried lest, as we all think, P.M. now loses interest in Libya and wishes to starve our operations there for the Far East. The Americans being in a panic, will do their utmost to persuade him of the need for this. But Africa is the one place where we can at present embarrass the Germans – the more success we have there, the more they must reinforce from overseas. Cripps joined our train this evening about 5 p.m. He confirms the great defeat the Russians are inflicting on the Germans in front of Moscow. He says however food is short and will get shorter before winter is over.

We arrived at Moscow at 11.30 p.m. We then all got into cars and drove through the blackout to our hotel. Here we've been allotted magnificent rooms – like an old-fashioned French hotel – very nineteenth century. All dead tired and so to bed about 1.30 a.m.

December 16

When I looked out of my window this morning, I saw the Kremlin! A grey snowy morning and the Kremlin looking grey rather than pink. This hotel is on the Revolution Square which is vast. Cripps has already weighed in with a memorandum on our proposals. He is going to be an infernal nuisance butting in everywhere. We found telegrams on arrival which were decyphered this morning saying that President Roosevelt had invited Stalin and Chiang-kai-Shek to hold Allied military conferences in Moscow and Chungking to recommend combined action against the common foes. Recommendations should be sent to Washington by December 20th when they would be examined there – presumably by President and Winston (who, we hear, expects to arrive on December 21st). We think this a rather woolly eyewashy proposition. Stalin is not yet at war with Japan: America has no properly qualified military representatives in Moscow. Roosevelt and Chiang are now most anxious to get Russia into war with Japan. We are doubtful of wisdom of this and certainly will not press Stalin against his will. We felt Russia can do most by concentrating on Germany.

A.E. is to see Stalin at 7. Maisky is coming at 5. We spent the morning preparing A.E.'s brief. We hear Murmansk was raided the day after we left. The talk here is that we came by the Middle East.

A.E. got back about 11 after 4 hours with Stalin including a champagne supper at the end. I think he has made a most successful start. Stalin was quite realist and did not press at all for our airforce or men to be sent to Russia but he would like still more tanks. His armies are doing extremely well and while they were talking, news came of recapture of Kalinin. But he thought Germans might be able to reorganise and make a fresh offensive in two months. On political side he was responsive also, and he is in favour of our signing 2 treaties political and military, which however would contain much the same as our own draft declaration we brought with us. He is ruthless in his views of Europe. Germany to be treated drastically and cut up. He would cut off Rhineland into separate state: make Austria and possibly Bavaria independent: and give large pieces to Poland in East. Czechoslovakia to be completely restored. He would like us to have bases in France, Belgium, Holland, Norway – he showed no wish to share them and in fact said the West and North West was our responsibility. He would like bases for himself in Finland and in Rumania. He wants Bessarabia and Bukovina. He would give East Prussia to the Poles and return to Curzon Line for Polish–Russian frontier. He would like to give large pieces of Bulgaria to Turkey, Greece and Yugoslavia "to punish her". He also wants to "punish" Hungary by giving bits to Czechs and Rumanians. Oddly enough he wants to appease Turkey by giving her the Dodecanese. A.E. made clear we wouldn't agree to a secret protocol (which he would like) defining these peace plans and that in fact we couldn't commit ourselves to any territorial changes at present. As regards the Far East, Stalin said he couldn't help there yet, but he might be able to in the Spring. He thought the Germans were running the Japs' airforce and campaign for them. He didn't express surprise at P.M.'s jaunt, but gave impression of being critical of Roosevelt. He laughed at the President's idea of 3 military conferences in Moscow, Chungking and Singapore.

December 17

A.E.'s interview with Stalin fixed for 7 p.m. has been postponed till midnight. He is taking with him the drafts for our political and military agreements which Alec and Maisky have worked on all day.

December 18

A.E., Alec and Nye returned about 3 a.m. I had gone to bed. They had had, however, a sticky time. Stalin, before looking at the 2 draft agreements, opened up with a request for recognition of the Soviet Western frontiers, notably the Baltic States, but also in Finland and Rumania. A.E. said at once he couldn't agree to any territorial changes without reference to Cabinet and Dominions and without consultation with Roosevelt, to whom we had given a definite promise. Stalin was most reluctant to accept this and said that in that case it was better to postpone the agreements which without it would be valueless. A.E. insisted again and again on his point of view but undertook to take up the question with the Cabinet and Roosevelt as soon as he got back. Stalin was not comforted and the conversation ended inconclusively. On the military side S. expressed considerable confidence and satisfaction. He evidently is convinced he has got the Germans almost on the run. Hence no doubt the stiffness on the political side. Another meeting is arranged for tonight at 7, and Maisky is coming round beforehand, but A.E. does not propose to budge. We are inclined to think it is a try-on by Stalin and that in the end he will see our position and agree to sign the agreements.

But it is an unrealistic controversy. We cannot commit ourselves now, without much further thought and consultation, to definite frontiers for E. Europe, but if at the end of the war Russia is in occupation of the Baltic States no one is going to turn her out. The Baltic States clearly must go back to Russia but their fate cannot be signed away by us without any further thought.

Maisky came round and told us that Stalin was insisting on something being said about the Russian frontiers. A.E. can go no further and is not anxious to telegraph the P.M. or the Cabinet for instructions (as Russians urge) as from neither is he likely to get a good reply – I suggested that what we might do is to offer to Stalin that there should be a tripartite conference (Russo–American–British) as soon as possible after our return to examine the political and territorial problems of the peace settlement. A.E. likes this which is the logical course. First, the Anglo–American Atlantic Charter, then an Anglo–Russian Charter, both laying down general principles, after that a tripartite discussion to deal with practical application. It is quite evident that we must soon begin to clear our own minds about political and territorial questions (not only Russian frontiers, but all frontiers); these cannot be left vague till the peace conference or else the peace conference will resolve itself into an unseemly wrangle between the Allies from which Germany alone can profit.

A.E. intends to put this idea to Stalin and show him a draft letter which he would send him undertaking to propose such a tripartite meeting at the earliest possible date. The Americans may be shy but they are in the war now and may be more realistic. In any case if they want Russia to fight for them against Japan, they will have to pay a price.

A.E. and Alec went off at 7 to the Kremlin, and the rest of us went off to a cocktail party. Roberts and I were called out at about 9.30 by a telephone message to say A.E. had returned, and so we hurtled back. I found A.E. and Cripps and Alec; they had had a complete lemon from Stalin. The latter had rejected our offer of a tripartite meeting with U.S.A. on the political frontiers as insufficient and wanted our recognition of the 1941 frontiers of Russia *now* or nothing. The atmosphere had been unpleasant and A.E. had left saying that he must return to London on Saturday. We had a long talk. Stalin wishes to bind us to this recognition. He feels he is strong now and can do what he likes. We can't give any such recognition without the U.S.A. The P.M. is on the high-seas, the Cabinet without the P.M. consists of washouts. I am worried because (a) we cannot win the war without Russia, (b) we cannot make peace without Russia (c) the 1941 frontiers of Russia (in Finland, Baltic States, Rumania) are not too bad in themselves. On the other hand Stalin is rejecting a golden opportunity. A.E. is the one man in England who is ready to put their case (P.M. anti-Russian, Cabinet contemptible, Labour leaders, Bevin, Attlee, Morrison violently anti-Soviet). If Stalin could sign our proposed agreements, it would be fairly easy for A.E. to move Winston to next stage of getting the Cabinet to agree to get Roosevelt to tackle the whole question.

The Russians have admittedly a strong inferiority complex and they feel now they are playing the major and most successful part in beating the Germans. Frankly I don't see how we can meet them, as one ought always to go forward to meet those with inferiority complexes, without breaking our pledge to America. "Anyway, I'm not worrying", is what A.E. said to me as he went to bed. He is going to the front tomorrow which means a day off for me. Cripps is going to tackle Molotov[1] and put to him what fools the Russians are being.

Meanwhile our Chiefs of Staff, who only 2 days ago advised that it would not be to our interest to press Russia to go to war with Japan, have now completely reversed this opinion and sent us a telegram to say they hope we will urge the Russians to go to war with Japan! But there is not a hope in hell of this and A.E. won't even put it to Stalin. We are evidently in a bad way in Malaya and in almost as much of a flap as the Americans. But the Germans are our principal enemy and whatever it means losing elsewhere, we should concentrate on them.

December 19
A.E. got back about 7 p.m. from his day at the front and Maisky came round. The latter held out hope that the Soviet Government might agree after all to sign the military agreement and a revised political agreement, leaving the frontier questions for a later agreement. Cripps has meanwhile seen Molotov (who is a dreadful obstructionist in our affairs) and put strongly to him the advantage of such a course. Well, we shall see.

December 20
The river is camouflaged here to look like streets and houses by putting wooden roofs on to the ice.

We have had a reply from F.O. to say that Cabinet agree that we couldn't sign now, in view of our pledges to Roosevelt, a document recognising the 1941 frontiers, although this doesn't mean that we

1. V. Molotov, Soviet Foreign Minister 1939–1949.

might not eventually recognise them. P.M. isn't due in Washington till December 22nd or get-at-able. Maisky has telephoned to say that he had seen Stalin again last night but that he had nothing to report. A.E. will see Stalin again tonight at 7 p.m. to say good-bye and then leave tomorrow about 4 p.m. He must anyway discuss publicity for our visit and agree on a communiqué for issue after we have left. It is always possible the Russians will agree to sign something in the end.

December 21

We were just having dinner last night about 9 p.m. when A.E. and Alec suddenly came back from their interview and told us we were all expected to dine at the Kremlin at 10! The conversation had gone most amiably – Stalin had produced a communiqué which in fact contained all about war and post-war collaboration which had been contained in the two agreements whilst all reference to Russian frontiers was dropped. This communiqué is to be issued on December 25th by when we should be well away.

Having had one dinner in the hotel we all set out for our second dinner at the Kremlin. The party was carefully checked in at the Kremlin gate. The sentry asked all our names and compared them with a list. It was pitch dark and so we could see nothing of the buildings inside the Kremlin. At the palace itself we went up a long straight staircase and found ourselves in a suite of very large rooms, white and gold. The dining room which somebody said had been Catherine the Great's throne room, was of magnificent malachite with white marble pillars, a vaulted ceiling white and gold, and cream damask walls. We were received in another room with heavy gilt tables and chairs and dark green damask walls and painted ceiling. Molotov received us, dressed in a little buff uniform coat and Russian boots. Timoshenko, the victor of Rostov, an enormous man with shaven head and red face, and Voroshilov[1] were both there. Our party was about 20 and when we had all arrived, Stalin came padding in, very like a kindly bear. He is not very tall, hair slightly grey; he wore a grey uniform suit and walked quietly round among us all shaking hands without any sort of ceremony. There is nothing striking about him except his extreme simplicity and quietness.

Hardly had we started dinner than the drinking of toasts began. Stalin got up and drank to A.E., then A.E. drank to Stalin, and so on until almost everybody had proposed toasts – Molotov, Maisky, the

1. Marshal Voroshilov was Commander-in-Chief on the North Western Front.

Marshals, the Military Mission, the Royal Navy, the Soviet Transport Workers were all toasted and replied to. To-day was Stalin's birthday so just after midnight A.E. proposed his health again. The old boy was most genial. A.E. on one side and Alec on the other. He told A.E. he always went to bed at 5 a.m. and got up at 11.30 a.m. We drank and drank – pepper Vodka – which is like fire – wines red and white – champagne and brandy. All Russian wine from the Crimea or Caucasus and we had 36 toasts in all.

The two Soviet Marshals were obsequious to a shaming degree to Stalin. Timoshenko soon got very drunk and kept getting up and making speeches out of turn and going round to clink glasses with Stalin. Stalin said to A.E. "The better my generals are the more drunk they get!"

Eventually we moved into another room where we sat and talked round tables, still having our glasses filled up. Then we made a further move to a cinema room where we saw two of the longest battle films I've ever seen. At last at 5 a.m. the films stopped and we were able to say good-bye to Stalin and get away – what a party! We were all dead this morning. I slept till 12, A.E. till 3. No work done.

December 22

We are very anxious lest Chiefs of Staff should lay off the Libyan battle as soon as the present phase[1] is over and not press on to Tripoli. This would be a fatal mistake as if the job is not completed this time the Germans will reinforce and get back again, and we shall either have to retreat or else keep large forces locked up there. But it depends on Singapore and how much of a fright they are in about that. The P.M., who only thinks of one thing at a time, would readily throw up Libya in which he has lost interest, for the Far East. The Americans would also urge this. A.E. must take this up as soon as he gets back. But to clear N. Africa should be our first and major objective. We are all much struck by the confidence of Stalin and the Soviet generals in their power over the German armies, and the demoralisation which they said has set in. We hear today Hitler has sacked Brauchitsch[2] and taken over the command himself. This points to the need in Germany for reassuring public opinion. The miserable clothes of the German prisoners A.E. saw when at the front were also significant. Stalin said he believed the war would be over by next autumn.

1. The Afrika Korps was withdrawing to Agheila.
2. General Von Brauchitsch, German Commander-in-Chief.

We left for the station at 6 after A.E. had had a final goodbye meeting with Stalin. Molotov saw us off and we got back into the same train which had brought us. Bands and guards of honour as before. Our meals on the train got rather mixed up. We had what we thought was a cold Sunday supper about 7 – and then it turned out only to be tea and we were threatened with a large dinner at 8.30. This we refused, and went early to bed.

December 23
Much colder again today as we go North. Meals still muddled – we had 2 breakfasts in succession at 9.30 and 1.30 but no lunch. However we hope to get dinner straight.

December 25
Yesterday – a long day in the train. When it got light to-day we were getting near Murmansk. We reached Murmansk 3 hours later at 12. We then did our sixteen miles drive to the place where the ship was anchored. We did not sail till about 4.30 p.m. owing to some confusion over our luggage which was sent off to another ship by mistake. I thought we would never get off.

It took about an hour to get down out of the estuary into the open sea, and then we were for it! Very rough, ship pitching in all directions – no Xmas dinner for me! I rushed to my cabin, piled all my coats on, went to bed practically in my clothes it was so bitter – far the coldest spot in all our journey.

December 28
Better weather – somewhere off Faroes – went on deck at 12 – fairly nice day and a little sun – stayed on the bridge for a bit.

After lunch talked with A.E. about what he should say to press on arrival and also in his broadcast. He is a little jealous of Winston with all his limelight in Washington but feels, as I do, that he talks too much. An officer of the ship spoke to me today of his speech "as so much soap". No harm therefore in A.E. sitting pretty and getting on with the job.

December 29
A.E. very annoyed at inadequate publicity given to our visit on B.B.C. midnight news. I assured him that morning papers will give it the fullest treatment but he won't be comforted. He has written a telegram he wants to have sent off as soon as possible this morning. (We can't

break wireless silence till midday.) He thinks we should have had both a photographer and a press officer with us. All this largely because at our cinema show we saw the film of the Beaver's arrival in Archangel and Murmansk.

What a curse publicity is. I can't really feel it matters very much, though it is important that the Russians should not think we don't attach enormous importance to the visit and to their hospitality and that the British should also understand this. If publicity is needed for this, then it can't be overdone. Alec Cadogan no help on such occasions – he just grunts and goes away to bed. "All prima donna", he says.

1942

January 2
Simultaneous absences of P.M. and A.E. don't seem to have aroused criticism I had expected. I learn Roosevelt did his best to put Winston off but latter persisted – criticism fastens rather on the defeats and losses in the Far East, i.e. Service departments and also P.M. who is suspected of undue interference in operations and preparations. Parliament is to meet on Thursday and there may be a rumpus. No news yet of P.M.'s return.

January 6
Telegram has been sent to P.M. to tell him of our view of necessity for recognizing Soviet 1941 frontiers if we are to have any useful collaboration in future and suggesting that he should take it up with Roosevelt.

P.M. won't like this, nor will Roosevelt, but we are convinced it is necessary. A.E.'s idea is, if P.M. agrees, to sign the proposed treaty with Soviets including required reference to 1941 frontiers, and then to proceed to tripartite discussion with U.S.A. on general frontier question for Europe. But we are a long way off that!

Meanwhile Far East is pretty bad for us. Japs making fast progress towards Singapore: our own reinforcements (very modest even so) are still en route. American Pacific Fleet (including submarines) showing no activity whatever.

January 7
A great speech from Roosevelt today to Congress announcing enormous increases in arms production. I only hope they will impress the enemy and the goods will be delivered.

As between Russia on one side, who thinks she is doing all the fighting against the Germans, and America, who thinks she can dictate the peace on the other, poor H.M.G. are going to have a difficult time. We shall be in trouble with both. We must take a realistic view of Russia's claims, but we must somehow avoid a collision with U.S.A. who mean so much in supplies now and postwar reconstruction after. America far more old-fashioned and anti-Russian than Gt. Britain – a hundred years behind us in social evolution.

January 8

P.M. replied today to A.E.'s telegram advocating a realistic acceptance of 1941 Soviet frontiers. A flat and shocked refusal! All the arguments about the Atlantic Charter, our promise to Roosevelt to make no promises before the Peace Conference, these poor little peoples brutally invaded, dressed up afresh. I'm afraid we're going to have great difficult over this. A.E. will have a lone fight as no one else in the Cabinet will speak up to the P.M. – least of all Bevin & Co.

A.E. thinks P.M. staying away too long and getting out of touch with opinion here which thinks much more of Russia than of America at present. Winston is *au fond* a diehard imperialist – bad about India (much trouble coming to us here over his refusal to countenance Dominion status) and bad about Russia. He not only hates the Bolsheviks but is jealous of them because of their bigger and more successful armies.

January 11

Long talk with Charles Peake today – just back from U.S.A. He told me American Navy had had 6 out of 8 battleships knocked out in Pearl Harbour. No one believed air attack by Japan was possible. About 300 aeroplanes took part and the Americans shot down 2! America had been stunned by the disaster, tho' they didn't yet know the full truth. Two days before the Jap negotiator Kurasu had come to see Roosevelt secretly to tell him that Japan was prepared to clear out of China provided her face was saved. This was evidently to lull the Americans to sleep while the Jap expedition was on its way.

C.P. confirmed that F.D.R. is determined to run the peace but that he is much more advanced and realistic than Sumner Welles[1] or the State Department.

January 19

P.M. (who returned by air on Saturday night) is in the highest spirits and the most truculent mood. A.E. is appalled. There is great political discontent against the Government and a general feeling that all is far from well. Yet P.M. says "there never was a better Government" and the war is going marvellously!

News from Singapore very bad – even if it holds out, as we hope it may, it is useless as a base.

I told A.E. he must somehow get together with P.M. after he has

1. Sumner Welles, U.S. Under-Secretary of State 1937–1943.

86

calmed down a bit, and get him to see realities. He takes more from
A.E. than from anyone, but as A.E. is the only one who fights him,
it is a bit invidious.

January 20

P.M. has asked A.E. to lunch today and I urged him to go for the
opportunity of a heart-to-heart talk. We discussed Government
changes and the need for rejuvenating the Cabinet. He would like to
see Kingsley Wood [Exchequer], Margesson [War], Greenwood
[Min. without Portfolio] and Amery [India] go. They are the light-
weights and contribute nothing. He favours Cripps being given a post
which I said would certainly be popular.

After his lunch today A.E. told me he had had a long talk to P.M.
on best of terms. P.M. prepared to give Cripps a post in M. of Supply
– but not prepared to get rid of Kingsley "who had been very helpful
to him". "I'd rather have a Cabinet of obedient mugwumps than of
awkward freaks!" A.E. mentioned Crookshank[1] and Llewellyn[2] as
having deserved promotion but P.M. said there were no places for
them if Cabinet Ministers didn't die.

P.M. most anxious to have record made for broadcasting after of
his speech in H. of C. next week. A.E. much opposed to it because it
will mean practice couldn't be restricted to P.M. but would have to be
extended to all, and it would end by speakers talking to microphone
instead of to House. But P.M. mad to do it and it is to be tried as
experiment.

January 22

P.M. finally prevailed upon to drop broadcasting of his speech in
H. of C. because of chilly reception of the idea.

January 24

Saw Cripps today. He is to lunch with P.M. at Chequers on Sunday
(? and be offered post of Minister of Supply). Government apart from
P.M. is being attacked more and more and the big debate is this week.
P.M. is disposed, tho' without enthusiasm, to make Cripps M. of
Supply, while making the Beaver a sort of super Cabinet Minister
overseeing the whole field of production.

1. Captain H. Crookshank (later Lord Crookshank), had been Secretary of
   State for Mines, 1935–1939, and was then Financial Secretary to the
   Treasury.
2. P.P.S. at Ministry of Aircraft Production.

THE WAR DIARIES OF OLIVER HARVEY

Cripps said things were getting bad again in Russia. Stalin hadn't even seen him to say good-bye.[1] All the suspicions reviving.

January 25
Australia in greatest possible flap. Their clamour[2] compares unfavourably with the relative calm of New Zealand. Curtin[3] seems a second-rate man. I'm afraid Australians don't like good or big men – they've flung out Bruce, Casey, Menzies, all far bigger than Curtin.

January 27
Bad news from Libya. Rommel has again broken loose and over-run our people – he is back past Benghazi.[4] What a General! I wish some of ours were half as good. There can be no defence for our failure to hold him. He can't have the resources which we have.

P.M.'s speech today. I haven't heard how it went. Meanwhile Wavell and Chiefs of Staff want us to urge Russia to help against Japan. How are the mighty fallen! The despised Russians are now the only successful ones.

I hear Cripps has been offered the post of Minister of Supply and is thinking it over. He is reluctant to serve under the Beaver's supervision.

He says he thinks we must offer the Russians "all or nothing" as regards their frontier demands. A.E. now favours putting the dilemma to Roosevelt. I see great difficulties in the path of Anglo–Russo–American harmony. But we can't possibly beg them to help against Japan if we don't pay a price.

January 29
Bad news again from Libya. Benghazi evacuated. A plain case of out-generalling by Rommel.

P.M. seems to have got well out of his debate.[5] A minority of one voted against him. Cripps, I hear, has not accepted, or rather insists on conditions *vis à vis* Beaver. But we need more than that to win the war and to satisfy the country. I'm sure Beaverbrook is one of our liabilities – he is turning out quantities at the expense of qualities. Not

1. Sir Stafford Cripps had been relieved as Ambassador in Moscow by Sir Archibald Clark-Kerr.
2. At the approach of the Japanese.
3. John Curtin, Prime Minister of Australia 1941–1945.
4. From El Agheila.
5. He had asked for a vote of confidence.

the right guns or the right tanks. Our tank, the Churchill, has been a scandal.

Had Weizmann to lunch to meet Harold Caccia[1] and put him wise to Palestine. W. said he expected from his talks with Benes and Sikorski that there would be from two to three million Jews from Central and Eastern Europe who could never again be reabsorbed there after the war. For these the only hope was Palestine, but even there only 100,000 or so could be placed each year. He is off to America to see Roosevelt. We explained the importance of an American share in Middle Eastern responsibilities. If America would back and help maintain by a police force a Jewish state in Palestine after the war, there would be no difficulty. What H.M.G. feared was to establish a Jewish State and so to antagonise the Arabs, if Britain alone was to carry the baby. He fully saw this and means to work for it in America. I think that is the only solution, an Anglo–American solution. But the Jewish problem must be settled – the emigration from Eastern Europe is there and cannot be prevented. As W. said, the Jews will swim to Palestine whatever we do.

January 31
I hear that Auchinleck has got himself into a complete mess in Western Desert, all his reserves back in the Delta refitting, exactly as happened before. There will soon be a pogrom of the British General Staff by the British public if this sort of thing goes on. Incidentally it completely disposes of the myth circulated hitherto that our previous disaster in Cyrenaica was due to having sent troops to Greece.

February 1
Singapore now besieged. We've evacuated the mainland and blown up the bridge. I can't see how it can hold, and it is now in any case useless as a naval base. At best it may prove a Tobruk. But the Japs are also making progress towards Rangoon which seems to me even more serious.

Curtin has calmed down a bit after screaming for help both to Roosevelt and to Chiang kai Shek. After living for a century in a fool's paradise, after refusing British emigrants since the last war lest they depressed the local standard of living, Australia has suddenly woken up to the cold and hard fact that her very existence as a white country depends not on herself but on protection from Gt. Britain. Like so

1. Later Lord Caccia, Ambassador in Washington 1956–1960.

many fine states in Europe she has flourished under a British umbrella.

But I hate to think of the harm Japan may do and the business it may prove to get her out of all these places. I am nervous of India and of the effects of our pawky approaches to Dominion status in the face of flamboyant offer of independence from Japan. Here Chiang kai Shek is helping us – he wants to pay a brief visit to India and see Gandhi and Nehru (who is his great friend). We must do better for India.

The theory is that we recover command of the sea in the summer and then begin to starve out these Japanese outposts and even bomb Japan itself. Wavell is Supreme Commander – there is to be an American air C. in C. and a Dutchman naval C. in C. The international Police Force at work!

Now Roosevelt has weighed in over "consideration" – which is the undertaking we are to give under the Lease-Lend Act (in return for its benefits) for elimination of Ottawa[1] in return for reduction of American tariffs. We here all feel it must be done. The P.M., as head of the Tory Party, is reluctant and told us – quite wrongly as it appears – that when he was in Washington, Roosevelt was clearly not interested and it could be left to slumber till the end of the war. Kingsley Wood and Amery,[2] the Tory diehards, are outraged at any sapping of Ottawa and wish to resist.

February 3
The Lease–Lend business – "consideration" went wrong in the Cabinet last night. A.E. the only Minister to urge acceptance of the clause – the main obstructionists being Kingsley Wood and Amery, Labour leaders saying nothing – shocking. The article in question is entirely hypothetical and contingent in its wording but the President is pressing for it. We feel we could agree with the President *now* but if we don't, it will mean agreeing with Congress later – and a very different thing. Keynes some time ago feared America might well insist on a cash payment, or else payment in raw materials (rubber or tin), or even surrender of S. American securities. To be asked to agree only to a clause of so pious and self-evident a character is more than luck. The Cabinet will be great fools if they miss it. Even the Dominion Governments favour it. It has been decided to postpone decision on the point, to say we are ready to hold economic discussions with the U.S.A. at an early date on our post-war economic policy

1. Ottawa agreement on Imperial Preference.
2. L. S. Amery, Secretary for India 1940–1945.

including Ottawa but that it would be inappropriate meanwhile to agree to Article. This draft reply is to be considered at another meeting.

February 4
Winant offers some hope that Roosevelt would not be averse from our meeting the Russians over the Baltic States question. The P.M. is being very sticky and it is to come before the Cabinet again on Thursday. Winant suggests going over to the States himself and exploring the ground. He is strongly in favour of some such policy as ours.

Cripps has finally refused to join the Government and to work under Beaverbrook. I don't blame him. A large part of our misfortunes are due to B. and having upset the Ministry of Supply as previously he had upset the Ministry of Aircraft Production, he is now seeking (and getting) another job – that of Minister of Production.

A.E. had Bevin to lunch today – a long heart-to-heart talk. B. very anxious to work with A. A. likes B. But Bevin very worried about Beaverbrook and his swelling functions. Bevin worried also about India and thinks something must be done now without waiting till the end of the war.

February 5
Roosevelt has now sent a personal telegram to Winston telling him of the importance he attaches to getting the "consideration" question settled now on the lines of Article VII of the Agreement. It is to be considered on Friday. This much strengthens our hands against Kingsley and Co. We suspect that it is Winant who has elicited this utterance from the All-Highest.

Russia is to be discussed tonight. P.M. very grunty about it. (At the back of his mind and unconsciously, I believe, the P.M. is jealous of Stalin and the successes of his armies.)

February 6
At Cabinet last night A.E. shook them, he thinks, over "consideration" and is now hopeful that he will get them to agree to Article VII plus an explanatory exchange of notes. On Russia he has greater difficulty. Beaver, Bevin, Morrison on our side, P.M., Attlee against. Sinclair floating "on his Liberal principles" between. General opinion favoured throwing the whole problem at America *without* expressing any view of our own at all. This is clearly impossible. Discussion is to be resumed today.

February 7

A.E. at Cabinet on Friday only managed to get through a grudging and peevish acceptance of Article VII (Lease-Lend "consideration") subject to conditions, viz. – an explanatory exchange of notes at the same time saying exactly what we mean by it – i.e. exactly nothing at all. We had prepared a much more satisfactory and forthcoming draft exchange but the wiseacres of the Conservative and Labour Parties in the Cabinet would have none of it. Zero hour is Monday when the bill has to be considered by the Congress Committee. There is thus just time for Roosevelt to fling it back in our faces and insist on something better. Talk of looking the gift horse in the mouth!

Russia is to come up again on Monday.

How does the British Government think it's going to win the war without meeting the requirements of either Russia or America? Are our armies so victorious in all theatres?

Weizmann very pleased with his interview with A.E. yesterday. I always have a job to get A.E. to see him, and when he sees him, he is always impressed. What is to be done with the three or four million Jews of Central Europe who can never be reabsorbed? That is now the problem or rather the right approach to the problem. Palestine then falls into its proper perspective as the only possible outlet for a large part of these Jews. Palestine is not a sort of Zionist luxury to be set up at the expense of the Arabs – as it has been regarded wrongly hitherto. A Jewish Palestine is a necessary part of European settlement.

February 9

A.E. told me today in the greatest secrecy that P.M. is considering going to India next week (by air) to meet Chiang-kai-Chek and also to consult with Indian leaders as to formation of an Assembly to work out a constitution for after the war. On his return he would stop in Cairo and clear up the mess there (as to which he is very worried). The complication is that the doctors have told him that his heart is not too good and he needs rest.

A.E. asked him what he felt himself and he said he would go if the Cabinet wanted him to go. He confessed that he did feel his heart a bit – he had tried to dance a little the other night but found that he very quickly lost his breath!

A.E. asked my view. I said I thought no one else could do such a job successfully unless it were A.E. himself but he hadn't got the Cabinet status to reform India or deal with the military in Cairo. Halifax could deal with India if he were sent on a special mission and this had occurred to me as a way of handling that particular impasse. He is held in high regard both in India and at home on India. But we agreed he would be useless with Chiang or with the generals. P.M. was the only person who could do it all. But for his heart there could be no question he was the right one to go. But the heart? A.E. and I finally thought that if he won't rest here (and he told A.E. he meant to go on "till he dropped"), then perhaps the journey would be a sort of rest and it would be best that he should go. There should, however, be a secret War Cabinet of members only to decide.

What a decision to take, and how gallant of the old boy himself! But his age and more especially his way of life must begin to tell on him. He had beer, 3 ports and 3 brandies for lunch today, and has done it for years.

P.M. said he was very worried over Libya and thought Lyttelton had failed badly in not looking after the tanks and the Generals more. L. was taking too much interest in local politics and foreign affairs, and not enough in what he was intended to do. Auchinleck had been bad over his choice of generals in spite of advice from home to use Wilson and Gott.[1] Now at last, after these defeats, he had appointed Gott to take charge of the battle – but why this delay and obstinacy?

February 10

At Cabinet in morning it was agreed to send off the telegram to Halifax about Russia, explaining Stalin's demands and our strong feeling that they should be met either in full or by means of an immediate agreement on bases in Baltic States. Halifax is to discuss the whole thing with the President. Beaver very helpful over this.

But our grudging offer on Lease-Lend has brought forth raspberries both from Winant (who says he can help no more) and from Halifax after he had seen the State Department who say we must either agree to Article VII or not: it would only store up future trouble to say we agree and exchange letters at the same time saying in fact we don't agree – which is sound sense. We are waiting to see if Roosevelt himself is now going to weigh in again. A.E. feels he can do no more with the P.M. for the moment and it would be tactless anyway. Much evidence in the press of growth of isolationist and anti-British feeling in America.

With the arrival of U.S. troops in Australia all criticism of Britain

1. Lt. General W. H. E. Gott was commander of 7th Armoured Division in the desert.

has died down as if by magic. We hear that the Americans are finding the Australians with their peace-time exigencies rather trying.

Long talk with A.E. today about the future. I tell him he must be prepared to take over. I think he is. He is remarkably calm about it. He said he would make Bobbety Foreign Secretary and have a separate Minister of Defence. He wouldn't combine it with being P.M. He would get rid of the Beaver if he could (I hope he will but it will be difficult). He feels he is on good terms with Bevin who would work readily with him. Bevin is certainly the biggest and the best of the Labour people.

February 11

P.M. is not going on his trip because of Singapore. He feels he must be here when it falls.

The naval situation in the Far East should be better by the summer. We may even have command of the sea again if the air strength is also great enough. That should make the Jap hold precarious. But before that we may lose much. We've bogged our chances in N. Africa where now we should be in command from Tunis to Egypt. We must expect a terrific German offensive towards the Caucasus in the late spring. On the other hand, the Germans are not doing too well at present, and Italy has ceased for practical purposes to be more than a liability to them.

Winant is going to America next week. A.E. talked to him about Russia today. We've already told Halifax to discuss it with the President.

February 12

Further talk today with A.E. about P.M. He says Bracken now knows state of his health and doctor's report, so it will soon be known all over Fleet St. A.E. and I both very worried at turn of events, P.M.'s obstinate refusal to make serious changes in Cabinet after his return from America or immediately after the debate and before Singapore falls means that he will have to sustain whole weight of criticism with this discredited team. A.E. feels he is more and more obstinate and at the same time losing grip. I spoke of the rising of public opinion at successive disasters and failures which we both agreed was entirely justifiable. There might be an explosion which would sweep the whole Government out. The War Cabinet is now quite ineffective and so is the Defence Committee. A most disturbing situation which can't last. A.E. hesitates to say more to the P.M. who knows his views well enough. A.E. repeated them to Bracken who will certainly pass them on – viz. move Morrison[1] to Greenwood's place (G. to go), Cripps to Home Office, and appoint a Vice-Minister of Defence. Bracken said he thought A.E. should become Minister of Defence but he doesn't want to do that with Winston as P.M. – it would mean a continual tussle with him.

Roosevelt has sent a further personal message to P.M. about Lease–Lend consideration, as a result of which P.M. has capitulated. He has agreed to sign agreement as it stands without any exchange of notes to explain it away.

February 14 and 15

Very gloomy days. Government's position rapidly deteriorating. I think a crisis likely this coming week. I've written to A.E. giving my views of absolute necessity of P.M. reforming Cabinet or of going, of shortness of time available and of hopeless negativism of present lay-out. He thinks events have made P.M. more stubborn rather than less. It is essential to get a separate Minister of Defence, but I think in my heart of hearts nothing less than the departure of Winston and Beaverbrook will now avail. Poor Winston! A bitter position to find himself in, after all that he has done for the country.

Talked to A.E. on the telephone. He said he had got my letter and agreed with it. I said I thought all was very serious. He said he thought so too, but he'd just been for a walk on the Downs and felt grand!

P.M. broadcast tonight. In his usual style he painted a magnificent backcloth for the fall of Singapore – but it didn't meet the point which is that nobody believes the Government machine is working efficiently. He never mentioned the Channel episode.[2]

February 16

A.E. got back about 11 a.m. Meanwhile P.M. has asked him to lunch today and Erskine Hill (22 Committee) has asked urgently to see him. A.E. had discussed with Ned Grigg[3] over weekend how things were worked in Lloyd George's time. Then there was an inner War

1. Herbert Morrison (later Lord Morrison of Lambeth), was Home Secretary, 1940–1945.
2. The escape of the *Scharnhorst* and the *Gneisenau* up the Channel from Brest on 12 February.
3. Sir Edward Grigg (later Lord Altrincham).

Cabinet of 5 or 6 who had no administrative functions but each of whom dealt with a group of departments or questions. The press is strongly urging a separate Ministry of Defence. I thought the crisis might come in 2 stages if P.M. yielded now – a stage with Winston and a separate M. of D., and then a later stage when Winston faded out. Dick said country had lost all confidence in Government, and A.E. should tell P.M. so and that if he didn't make change, then it would lose confidence in him (the P.M.) – Jim Thomas who joined us, confirmed this – A.E. agreed and said he would say this and urge appointment of a separate M. of D. What if Winston offered M. of D. to A.E.? A.E. was pretty sure he wouldn't. As regards Erskine Hill, A.E. was most anxious not to lend himself to any intrigue. He proposed to say we must all rally round P.M. and try to strengthen the Government.

A.E. said if it were his choice as P.M. he would favour putting a professional in as M. of D., e.g. Dill. I suggested Trenchard but A.E. said too old and too identified with separate air force controversy.

Bobbety has written to A.E. from the country, advocating A.E. as M. of Defence if P.M. permitted as best solution and urging that all Ministers should place resignations in P.M.'s hand to facilitate reconstruction.

When Erskine Hill came, it was to ask A.E. for advice as to the line to be taken in the debate on Tuesday. A.E. said he didn't know there was to be a debate but anyway he felt they should say what they could to carry the P.M. through in so far as their consciences allowed them. E.-H. had been to see Beaverbrook who advised that they should say everything in the garden was lovely.

An unpleasant feature is that the American press is now demanding changes in the Government here.

Later
When A.E. returned from his lunch, he told Dick, Jim and me under seal of absolute secrecy that he found P.M. truculent but yet prepared for changes. These were Greenwood to go and Cripps to come in as M. without Portfolio and Leader of House (but Greenwood's reconstruction work to be taken over by R. A. Butler), Attlee to become Deputy P.M. and Assistant Minister of Defence, Margesson to go and possibly Sinclair, Lyttelton to come back from Cairo and go to W.O. He was wondering if Duff would do for Cairo. P.M. said the Attlee move to be Deputy P.M. was compensation for Greenwood going but it would in fact make no difference as he was already deputy chairman

of Defence Committee. No one else could be Minister of Defence except P.M. himself as he was "soaked" in it.

A.E. strongly approved Cripps idea; but he feared Duff would be no good in Cairo. P.M. wondered if Dick Law could do Cairo.

On talking it over with us A.E. expressed doubt about Attlee becoming Deputy P.M. as giving some blessing to idea of him as successor – also, as P.M. confesses, the whole thing is eyewash leaving M. of Defence as before. The ideal would be A.E. as Minister of Defence and Bobbety at F.O.

February 17
On our usual morning walk round the lake in St. James' Park, A.E. told me that last evening the P.M. had talked to both him and Attlee, quoting A.E. as the authority for the need for drastic changes. Attlee had disagreed and didn't think any changes necessary. What irresponsible and foolish advice! I'm afraid it shows Attlee to be what I've always thought him, a little man. He dislikes Cripps being brought in. A.E., however, is now satisfied that P.M. has got it firmly in his head that he, A.E., does regard changes as necessary and that this is weighing with him. "Anthony thinks changes are necessary", he keeps saying. A.E. feels he cannot and won't do any more to press the P.M. as that would mean risking all the influence over him he has.

I told A.E. I thought this was right. Their relations of friendship do not allow of more pressure, especially as A.E. would appear as the chief beneficiary: it must now rest with the H. of C., the 22 Committee and the Watching Committee to do more if they think fit.

A.E. back from H. of C. where P.M. had made his statement on Singapore and ships, said he really thought he was riding for a fall, so *cassant* and ill-tempered he seemed. H. of C. not unfavourably disposed, surprisingly so, but P.M. petulantly defiant.

Demand in the press (which is almost unanimous) now concentrated on appointment of a War Cabinet free from department duties and appointment of a separate Minister of Defence.

February 18
General agreement on all sides at lamentable effect on H. of C. of P.M.'s manner and temper yesterday. Watching Committee (with Lord Salisbury) getting fussed, I hear. Yet later in the evening, A.E. says, P.M. presided with admirable calm and tact at Pacific Council Meeting. What everybody wants is for P.M. to remain and to have a real War Cabinet.

Events are moving today. A.E. was sent for by P.M. at 11.30 and he is to see him again at 5.30. Meanwhile No. 10 are frantically trying to find Cripps.

I saw A.E. at 3. The P.M.'s plan was to make Attlee, deputy M. of Defence, Cripps deputy leader of H. of C., Lyttelton Chancellor of Exchequer but no smaller Cabinet. Beaver thought Cripps would upset H. of C. and then P.M. suggested A.E. should lead H. of C. but keep F.O. Beaver also thought there should be a small Cabinet of P.M., Attlee, Cripps, A.E. – with Beaver himself, Bevin etc. outside.

A.E. discussed all this with Dick, Jim and me. He wants to keep F.O. and doesn't much like taking on H. of C. We also advised that he couldn't do both F.O. and leadership of H. of C. We also said we didn't think the big Cabinet would be a success at all with the public, tho' the smaller Beaver plan would go well. Finally, A.E. thought he would urge a small Cabinet of 4 (Attlee, Cripps, A.E. and P.M.) in which he would be willing to lead H. of C. and give up F.O. if necessary – but he would decline to lead H. of C. in big outfit and suggest his remaining at F.O.

Cripps asked to see A.E. at 5 (A.E. then with Beaver but when A.E. came back, Cripps told him P.M. had offered him leadership of H. of C. "unless A.E. wanted it". A.E. rather annoyed at P.M. offering it to Cripps before he had had A.E.'s views and rather bitten now with leading H. of C. as a stepping stone to being P.M. later. He doesn't want Cripps to groom himself for P.M. Beaver was dead against Cripps as leader and against large Cabinet. Bobbety came in just before A.E. went back to No. 10 at 5.30 and was also anti-large Cabinet or A.E. as leader in it.[1]

A.E. returned from No. 10 about 6.30. He said P.M. had offered Cripps leadership of H. of C. and he had accepted – he was rather annoyed at this and felt P.M. had bowled him a quick one. On the other hand, P.M. was more disposed towards a small war cabinet. P.M. said, altho' he would make Attlee Deputy P.M., this didn't mean he had any claim on succession as P.M. must be a Tory and because if the P.M. fell down dead, he had told King that he should choose either A.E. or Anderson and he should wait 4–5 hours to see which way opinion went. He wanted to keep Anderson in War Cabinet and not send him to Cairo as M. of State because he was so useful for home affairs. Attlee was also at this discussion.

A.E. rather disturbed at this and felt he should insist on having Leadership of H. of C. Both Dick and Jim and Bobbety pressed

1. See Eden, *The Reckoning* p. 321–322.

importance of H. of C. Leadership if A.E. was to inherit from P.M.
We think Whips' Office are up to usual game of trying to side-track
A.E. by keeping him out of leadership. Much discussion between us
all. A.E. and Attlee seeing P.M. again at 10 and 15 tonight "to fix it
all up between them". Apparently P.M. favoured idea of Bobbety
coming to F.O. if A.E. goes: Lyttelton hovers between Chancellor of
Exchequer and W.O.: Greenwood goes anyway.

We all strongly urged on A.E. need of a small cabinet of relatively
unattached Ministers. The real lightweight of course is Attlee himself
in the smaller set-up but he must be included as head of Labour Party.
It looks however as if some combination of P.M., Attlee, A.E., Cripps,
with or without Anderson[1] and Bevin would emerge now. What a
disillusioning business Cabinet making is!

Bobbety, who has been in all our discussions and may or may not
become Foreign Secretary, quite detached and unmoved.

February 19
This morning A.E. went off to No. 10 at 10. Before he went he told
me it now lay between his staying at F.O. or being Leader, in either
case in a Cabinet of 7 or 8. He came back after half an hour to say it
had been more or less decided now that there should be a War Cabinet
of 7 and that he A.E. should remain at F.O. and Cripps lead. A.E. had
pressed his preference for Leadership but Attlee didn't back it and
Chief Whip was clearly opposed to it. P.M. said to A.E. "You are a
man of action and not of talk and I can't think why you want it".
Lyttelton now to be Production, Beaver to go out and do travelling,
K-Wood to remain C. of Exchequer but outside War Cabinet, P. J.
Grigg to W.O.

Dick and Jim very shattered at this, Dick furious indeed and said
"This shows Winston is not fit to be P.M. and that A.E. is not fit to
be P.M.!" Jim more philosophic, doubts if new Cabinet will last
anyway.

A.E. rather sore and feeling, I think, he hadn't pressed himself
enough. We urged that anyway the opportunity must be taken to
clear out the Whips' Office – that nest of Munichism and Chamber-
lainism. He is speaking to P.M. of this.

Alec Hardinge came later to see A.E. and I had a word with A.H.
after. He takes a much more detached and long-term view naturally
and is positively glad Cripps is to lead H. of C. which he thinks will be

1. Sir John Anderson (later Lord Waverley) was Lord President of the
Council.

popular with country, while he does not think A.E.'s long term chances will be prejudiced in the least by his remaining at F.O. He thinks new Government will go well, especially the departure of Beaverbrook and the arrival of Cripps and Lyttelton. A.E. much relieved and reassured by this. He doesn't want to lead H. of C. now, but he doesn't want either to prejudice his chances of being P.M. later. So A.H.'s views cheered him.

Personally, I would like to see A.E. as M. of Defence but that is impossible with Winston – and I should regard his leading H. of C. as a waste in war time as he does himself, but how far it is necessary for him to undergo this trial if he is to be P.M. eventually I can't say. In the country A.E.'s stocks are very high. I tell him that, whatever he does, he should get the P.M. to cleanse the Augean stables of the Whips. With a new and younger lot there his enemies in the Tory party will be discomfited.

February 20
A.E. saw P.M. again this morning when latter promised not to bring out the new list till Monday and not without consulting him about it. A.E. has also seen Bracken who is being helpful in urging P.M. to make drastic changes. A.E. has given Bracken his own list of changes and B. is going to take this to P.M. on Monday. I haven't seen the list myself. I gather P.M. is being firm about Margesson going, tho' he still stands out for Duff in Cairo. It is proposed to move Dalton from M.E.W. possibly to Health.

February 22
No more names out yet. I hope this business is soon over now and the Government will get down to the war.

For the first time the possibility that we may be defeated has come to many people – to me among them. The extent of the Jap successes is bad enough; our failures against Rommel, and the escape of the Channel ships are worse because, whatever the W.O. or Admiralty or A.M. excuses, there should not have been failure. What is worse is disquieting reports that British troops are not fighting well – this comes from both Libya and the Far East. Are we too soft, are we too civilised, are we touched with the French infection?

There seem to me certain faults – a lack of grip and coordination between the higher strategy of the War Cabinet and the execution of its decisions, bad General Staff work and again lack of coordination (indeed jealousy) among Army, Navy and Air, the P.M. himself making too many decisions impulsively without proper study and discussion (he is so much bigger than the rest of his colleagues), bad and old generals and admirals steeped in the last war, afraid of the implications of new warfare (younger men, faster machines). Then there is the great difficulty of coordinating America, G.B., Russia, China. We are all fighting separate wars. G.B. and U.S.A. are beginning to get together, Russia is entirely independent. We have size, numbers, resources – look at a map and it is almost indecent how much bigger we are than our enemies.

At a certain point in time (? next year) our side should have overwhelming resources of machines and men – can we reach that point before being defeated in detail by the lightning moves and blows of the Japs and Germans who have immediate strength and decision? It is painfully like David and Goliath.

Winston has so much to give and yet he has such disadvantages. His enormous courage and confidence, his hold over the country as a rallying force, his imagination and refusal to be bound by old ways – against that, his impulsiveness, his obstinacy in counsel, his refusal to give up full control of Defence. But the new Cabinet should be some improvement. The fresh mind of Cripps should wake it up – he is no "yes" man and will get what he wants or leave. It is smaller and has shed the Beaver.

February 23
Situation in Burma very bad. We've tried to get Curtin to agree to Australian Division on way home being diverted there as it is essential to hold this flank. But he has refused point blank in spite of personal approach from both P.M. and Roosevelt (latter is sending heavy U.S. reinforcements to Australia).

February 25
Cripps and A.E. are getting together. I'm glad. C. had an hour and a half with P.M. Cripps told A.E. that he and himself (C) were the only people who had any hold over the country and they must see to it that the P.M. agreed to what they said. They must pull the machine together and drive it along. A.E. very pleased at this and realises obvious importance of these two pulling together. I'm thankful. I was afraid he might resent the assumption of equality.

Cabinet already much more business-like, A.E. says: P.M. no longer getting away with it undisputed, indeed was in a minority of one. And P.M. does not like it.

Russia on the agenda today. Halifax has had his talk with Roosevelt who reacted not unfavourably but then saw Sumner Welles who was full of difficulties and objection.[1] Latter then went to see President and converted him to a less helpful frame of mind. President wants to take it up direct with Stalin (cutting us out). We don't feel that Stalin would welcome this as he wants a treaty with us. Our ideal would be a tripartite arrangement.

February 26

Cabinet last night approved idea of giving Winant a memorandum setting forth our views about Stalin's demands which he should take back with him in Washington. The memo was handed to Winant late last night and he has gone to America today. Our line roughly is to suggest a tripartite agreement between Russia, America and us, as a result of which Stalin should receive recognition of his pre-war frontiers. We deprecate Roosevelt charging in alone and advocate a tripartite body here – Winant, Maisky, A.E. – to deal with such questions which concern us all equally.

February 27

We hear that the view of the wiseacres in the lobbies is that the new Cabinet stocks are going up and those of the P.M. going down, and that before long the younger men, Cripps, A.E. and Lyttelton, will take over. Not unlikely I should say. P.M. does seem to be losing both grip and ground; he is exhausted by his superhuman efforts.

A.E. told me he would be quite happy to see Cripps at No. 10, if he himself could be Minister of Defence and run the war side. This surprised me. A.E. oscillates between wanting to be P.M. and wanting to stay where he is. I said whatever happened it was most important that he and Cripps should work together. But would the H. of C. agree to Cripps as P.M. and not a Tory? Of course if Cripps were P.M. now, A.E. could become the Tory P.M. later when parties divide again. But Cripps is still untried. I'm still afraid of the crank in him.

3.30 p.m. – A.E. had a long talk with Bracken early this afternoon: the P.M.'s health was getting worse, the state of his heart was affecting his circulation and this in turn might affect his powers of coordination of thought and speech. It was essential, if he was to go on, that he should do less. He was already most depressed and said he could only

1. Regarding Anglo–Russian Agreement.

go on for another month and then he would be finished. B. said the only way of sparing the P.M. was for A.E. to become deputy Minister of Defence. A.E. was the only person in whom P.M. had confidence and to whom he might be persuaded to yield – he wouldn't let anyone else touch it. Would A.E. take it on if it were offered him and could he combine it with F.O.? A.E. said he would certainly be willing to do it and keep F.O. as well, but he didn't wish to press for it. He would do whatever the P.M. wished but he must leave it to B. to put it to P.M. and for P.M. to make the first move. Apparently the Chiefs of Staff Committee is at sixes and sevens, the soldiers and sailors quarrelling and the P.M. no longer able to grip the thing. A.E. also said if he were to take it on, it must be made clear to Attlee that A.E. would work direct to P.M. and that Attlee would have no status as Deputy P.M. to intervene. (Attlee is being very petty over Cripps.) B. is going to see P.M. at Ditchley over the weekend and try if he can put it to him.

A.E. really delighted at the prospect tho' doubtful whether P.M. will ever agree. He would love the Defence work (far more than the leadership of H. of C.) and has the mind to grapple with it. He gets on with the soldiers and could pull the army together. The F.O. work can be severely rationed and Dick and Alec [Cadogan] take over more. A.E. far more interested in this even than in No. 10. He said again he would work under Cripps if he could keep Defence.

We are all convinced that the P.M. cannot last much longer and the present is only a temporary arrangement which can at most go on for two or three months. But it will be far better than an abrupt change-over.

March 2

I lunched with A.E. He had heard no more from Bracken and we wondered what if anything had happened. He feels more and more that the present set-up by which the P.M. keeps all control over operations severely in his own hands can't last, altho' he sees himself saddled with a difficult if not impossible task if P.M. agrees to his being Assistant Minister of Defence. I tell him that this would only be a transitional stage which would prepare the country for the larger change if the P.M. drops out. In any case, I said, the present situation in which the management of the war is not being controlled or co-ordinated at all owing to the P.M.'s spasmodic and hand-to-mouth methods cannot last. These are the vital months when the war may be won or lost and when we must play the few cards we have with the greatest skill and foresight if we are to reach the point in time when

Allied production will enable us to overwhelm our enemies. He is going to talk it over with Cripps tonight and meanwhile find out from Bracken what happened over the week-end. It is fantastic that there should be no War Cabinet meeting daily to deal with the war, but only an occasional defence committee meeting at 10 o'clock at night once or twice a week at the whim of Winston. A.E. doesn't believe P.M. will ever agree to give up anything.

Later. Bracken reports that the P.M. didn't take too badly to the proposal that A.E. should become Assistant M. of Defence but that their talk was interrupted. I am heartened at this. A.E. saw Cripps this evening and told him of Bracken's idea. C. said he had already himself put it to P.M. Cripps still doesn't see the Defence Committee papers – he only sees F.O. tels. He says he knows no more about the actual conduct of the war than the man in the street.

March 3

A.E. most depressed again this morning. A very long and unsatisfactory Defence Committee (old style) last night. 10 p.m. till 2 a.m. P.M. at his worst, discoursing, complaining, groaning. Lyttelton there, not Cripps. P.M. wished to send a snorter to Auchinleck. Lyttelton said generals were not to blame but the badness of our tanks (i.e. Beaverbrook's responsibility) which were definitely inferior to German tanks. This is what I always suspected. P.M.'s remedy is to suggest going out to Cairo with Beaverbrook and leave him there as M. of State! A.E. in despair. I said I thought the only thing to do was to try and merge the Defence Committee in the new War Cabinet. When the W.C. met on political questions, e.g. Russia and India, it was already working well and a great improvement on the old body, the P.M. no longer able to dominate it. It was important to get Cripps into the war discussions, and if he wasn't allowed in, he might very well present the P.M. with an ultimatum. I thought the new War Cabinet should insist on merging with the Defence Committee. A.E. thinks P.M. is determined to give up nothing, as he had always feared. A tragic situation. The P.M. has still such vitality and drive and yet it all spends itself in futile action.

But yet on India the Cabinet are about to take an immense step, an offer of complete independence like a Dominion after the war. This idea originated with the P.M. himself who cut across the obstructionism of the Viceroy and the India Office and it has been pushed on by the new War Cabinet – an excellent example of what this Cabinet can do if it is allowed. But even this won't win us the war. We must have day-to-day attention and regular hours by the best brains in the War Cabinet working on a plan and planning.

Later
A.E. had rather a touching interview with P.M. this evening when he showed him the list of Under-Secretaries. "Anyone can have my job. Anything may happen to me at any time now. But remember if it does, you are the one who must succeed." A.E. urged that Cripps should become a member of Defence Committee but P.M. did not respond.

March 4
P.M. has deputed A.E., Lyttelton and Attlee to enquire into Army Reform in view of recent failures.

March 5
P.M. is now having a revulsion about India and doesn't wish to broadcast personally the new Declaration or to let it be announced at all until next week. A.E. reasoned with him last night and got him a little better but before going any further he wishes to submit the whole thing to the junior Ministers of the Government as well.

This happened to-day with disastrous results! P.M. put the plan to the assembled ministers with such an ill grace that beginning with Kingsley Wood the reactionary Tories all piped up strongly against it in spite of the fact that it had been approved by the War Cabinet. P.M. then said he must consider it again.

A.E. says the War Cabinet has been made to look ridiculous – which it has – and Cripps says he won't go on unless it is accepted. They are going to tackle the P.M. again to-day.

Here is a further example of the P.M.'s lack of grip. We are now getting the worst of both worlds by drifting between two policies.

March 6
P.M. dined with A.E. last night. Now at last P.M. has come round about Russia. He says he agrees that we should accept Stalin's demand for recognition of 1941 frontiers and that Roosevelt must be pressed to agree or let us agree; he promises to send a personal message to Roosevelt to back up Winant's representations there. (Winant is just about arriving at Washington.) Meanwhile he will send a personal message to Stalin saying that Lyttelton has now taken over Beaver's

work[1] and he has instructed him to continue supplies to Russia on same scale as before. So bitten is he now with need for making progress with Stalin that he is actually thinking of setting off to meet Stalin himself, say in Tehran or Astrachan, accompanied by Beaverbrook, clearing up Cairo on the way. This from a man afflicted with heart who may collapse at any minute. What courage and what gallantry, but is it the way to do things? The statesman or even the opportunist would have realised the necessity for meeting Stalin like this months ago or at least when A.E. was sent to Moscow. But now as in so many other cases we are late, too late if we are to extract any benefit. We've roused Stalin's suspicions by delay and only come forward when it is obvious our Far Eastern situation forces us to be compliant.

But on India the P.M. has swung in the opposite direction. He says he won't announce the plan now, he will merely tell India he has a plan which he'll produce after the war. This is hopeless. Yet, as A.E. reminded him, it was Winston who originated the idea of an imaginative appeal to India on the broadcast. A.E. said Cripps would resign and the P.M. gave the impression that he would welcome it! Cripps is going anyway to Chequers for the weekend and may make him see sense. But talking last night, and perhaps in his cups, Winston said if the Labour leaders did not resign too, the Government could go on without Cripps, but if they resigned, then P.M. would resign too and advise King to send for A.E.! Lyttelton who was there, said he didn't think anyone would resign, not even Cripps.

I told A.E. it seemed absolute madness. Of course Cripps would have to resign and the Government would fall within 48 hours. He could knock them to pieces with what he knows now of how the war is being conducted – or *not* being conducted. In any case the Labour leaders could hardly not resign too without looking supremely ridiculous. A.E. said in such a case it would really be for the King to call Cripps – he, A.E., could never form a Government with the Tory Party divided as it would be. But he would be quite ready to serve under Cripps. I said, whatever happened, he and Cripps must work together – they alone, I thought, could pull the country through the war.

March 7
War Cabinet met this morning at short notice to discuss India. A fresh development is the receipt of telegrams from Viceroy and Wavell both

1. See Churchill IV 293–294.

saying they think the plan inopportune, Wavell in particular adding that it would have disastrous effect on Indian Army. This latter has rather shaken A.E. as Wavell is no blimp. At Cabinet proposal emerged that Cripps should go to India with the plan, on behalf of the War Cabinet, and see if he could put it across. This is being slept on over the weekend. A.E. rather likes it. P.M. thinks Cripps very gallant to offer to take on such a difficult and, as P.M. thinks, suicidal task. It certainly has merit. A plan backed by Cripps should have great appeal (not only in India) and if Indians reject it (as seems to be anticipated) H.M.G. will be on stronger ground.

P.M. has despatched his promised message to Roosevelt strongly pressing acceptance of Stalin's views about the 1941 frontiers.

Burma news rather better. We've got reinforcements in there. Alexander, who is a "tiger", has just arrived to take command.

March 8
We are having one of our periodical bust-ups with de Gaulle. He has sacked Admiral Muselier and refuses to take him back. The trouble is M. is a good sailor and has made a success of the Free French Navy so the Admiralty – who used to hate him – now adore him. But as between the General and the Admiral there can be no possible doubt that the former is the better man and also the only leader of the Free French. Admiral M. means nothing to France but General de G. is a living symbol of resistance. The General is a most difficult man and almost intolerable to work with. Every Frenchman, as usual, is against every other Frenchman. The French at H.Q. here do not present a pretty picture. They fill the restaurants of London with their gossip and intrigue. So bad is their propensity to chatter that we cannot confide to them any of our secrets. Worst almost of all are the Free Free Frenchmen – i.e. Roger Cambon, Comert and Co. who won't join de Gaulle and crab his movements from outside. Among all these minnows de Gaulle is a giant, awkward, obstinate, suspicious as he is. We cannot afford to get rid of him.

March 9
Halifax has had a preliminary encounter with Roosevelt and Hopkins about Russia and the P.M.'s message. R. is still hostile. He thinks it would be a mistake to begin setting commitments down on paper and is opposed equally to our acting alone. He favours himself telling Stalin that he is opposed to this procedure, that he fully appreciates Russia's need for security, but that the future of the Baltic States

depends on the Russian war effort – if Russia gets there, nobody is going to turn her out.

Agreement has been reached in the Cabinet over the offer to India and Cripps is to take it out at once. Meanwhile A.E. is to take on leadership of H. of C. until Cripps returns. P.M. insists on this and won't hear of Attlee doing it. A.E. most reluctant because of pressure of F.O. work. We are all rather pleased.

March 10

Secretary of State

I am a little worried by the de Gaulle trouble.

I am *quite certain* that however tiresome he is (and he is intolerable) he is the only leader of the Free French and far more important to the war effort than Muselier.

The Admiralty work up M. to intrigue against G. and that must be stopped. But if G. insists on sidetracking M., I'm sure we should acquiesce.

But de Gaulle is a real symbolic force in France and if we liquidated him, we should hand Vichy a first-class triumph.

O.C.H.

March 11

I'm feeling slightly less depressed – is it the spring or is it more knowledge of American potential?

March 12

The de Gaulle–Muselier row rages still. The Admiralty are behaving most improperly in backing Muselier against de Gaulle – how sailors intrigue! But it is more and more clear that de Gaulle is the Free French Movement and M. has got himself quite in the wrong. But the P.M., who used to be violently pro-de Gaulle, is now as violently anti. Only the F.O. preserve their senses in the confusion and see the wood for the trees.

March 14

The latest is that Beaverbrook wishes to go to America on a special mission. He has invited himself or got himself invited to stay at the White House. After that he wishes to go to Florida for his asthma. And after that to Moscow! All that we can say of it is that it is a good thing to get him out of this country.

We wonder what he is up to. Ever since he left the Government he has been writing and telephoning to A.E. about supplies for Russia – is he preparing a case against the Government for not helping Russia? No one wants to help Russia more than A.E. (who has taken B.'s place as Chairman of the Allied Supplies Executive which organises those supplies) and Cripps who is a far better friend to Russia than B. will ever be. I very much doubt whether B. cuts much ice with either Roosevelt or Stalin who know their gangsters. B. is in any case incapable of discussing either strategy or postwar problems.

Anyway Roosevelt is being difficult about Russia. He has dug his toes in about giving or our giving recognition to Stalin's prewar frontiers and is taking it up with Litvinov[1] himself. Maisky is worried at this and so are we because Stalin will suppose we've passed the buck to Roosevelt and are hedging. I fear this is the hand of Sumner Welles who is another Wilson only 20 years out of date. Meanwhile our relations with Russia are deteriorating.

March 15
A most tiresome situation is developing over the Russian frontier question. Roosevelt has seen Litvinov and told him squarely U.S. opinion would disapprove of anything affecting the Baltic States and he can't agree to any treaty in respect of definite frontiers until the war is won, tho' U.S. would support "legitimate measures of security" for Russia; he also made it quite clear he resented Stalin talking to H.M.G. and not to Roosevelt direct. This as a result of our suggestion of tripartite discussions on the subject!

Whilst F.D.R. can legitimately claim that we should decide nothing without consultation with him, he cannot properly claim that he can over-rule our foreign policy or deny us a foreign policy at all. Russia and we were allies before U.S.A. came in. We are both Europeans and nearer the German menace. We must wait and see what Stalin replies.

Meanwhile Maisky has received a message from Stalin for delivery to P.M. and A.E. together. P.M. is staying at Chequers over Monday. (He has had some mysterious minor operation.) A.E. and Maisky are to go there to lunch tomorrow.

March 17
Maisky gave his message to P.M. and A.E. yesterday. It turned out to be both agreeable and anodyne, a friendly acknowledgement of our present difficulties and confidence in the future, pleasure at our

1. Russian Ambassador in U.S.

continuing supplies and reference to need of further exchanges of views before treaty is signed. Maisky did not in any way confirm the pessimistic view which we took of the Litvinoff–Roosevelt talk. We must now await Stalin's own reaction to Roosevelt. On the whole A.E. favours our going on with the Anglo–Russian Treaty on our own. It is noticeable that opinion seems to be veering more and more in favour of meeting the Russians (e.g. Bruce says the Australian Government is strongly in favour, R. A. Butler is in favour).

P.M. is amazing. He is still proposing to go off to Cairo at the end of the month and clear up the military situation there, then to go on and meet Stalin at somewhere like Baku. He told Maisky this yesterday and asked him if he thought Stalin would come to meet him. M. said he was sure he would. But what courage!

March 18

MacArthur[1] has been got out of Philippines and is to command Australian Pacific sphere. That is to the good. He and our Alexander in Burma should be a vast improvement on the old duds there before.

Meanwhile the dispute between Auchinleck and the P.M. as to whether the former should attack or wait still rages. Cripps and Nye are looking into it on the spot and the P.M. threatens to go himself at the end of the month. A. says his tanks are less numerous and inferior to the enemy's.

March 19

Cabinet has decided that de Gaulle must be allowed to sack Muselier who has quite put himself out of court by his foolish intrigues. This is the only possible course. The Admiralty who have been backing Muselier *à outrance* have to climb down. They are already hedging on their statement that the French Navy will split over it.

Cabinet met last night at 6.30 and left off at 8.30. Defence Committee met at 10 p.m. and went on till 2 a.m. P.M. not appearing till 11.30! This shows how hopeless the present methods are. I said to A.E. that when Cripps returns from India, they really must make a frontal attack on the old gentleman and insist on regular meetings at proper hours. Even when the Defence Committee does meet, it is nothing but endless talk from the P.M. A.E. wishes Cripps wasn't away at this juncture. It will be the end of April before he returns.

1. General Douglas Macarthur, U.S. Supreme Commander in the Pacific 1942–1945.

Meanwhile A.E. is making a great success of his leadership of the House and is no longer afraid of it.

March 21
The appointment of Casey[1] as Minister of State in Cairo has infuriated Curtin, who, although the P.M. had consulted him in advance and secured his approval, has now come out in a childish fit of temper, saying "it was against his wish!" He has published a string of telegrams to which Winston is retorting by a string of our telegrams.

Curtin is behaving deplorably but I'm afraid even he is better than most of them. We hear the Americans, who are sending troops there, are having great trouble with Australian red tape. Australian party politicians pursue their strife with the enemy at the gate and Australian morale is low. The Curtin Government have screamed for help from the Americans, making it quite clear that they think us broken reeds. I'm afraid it is the "good life" in Australia which has made them soft and narrow. But they will learn like all democracies, if they are to survive. Not so the New Zealanders, however, who have been models of restraint, dignity and helpfulness.

At last we've got the King of Greece and the Diadoch[2] off to Egypt. But he was most reluctant to go and visit his troops and wanted to go to America instead. Harold [Caccia] tells me that even during the fighting in Greece he could never be got to go near the front. A.E. tried to take him up with him when he was in Greece but the King refused to go. The fuss the King has made about his journey and his party, in spite of the known restrictions on air space, has sickened us all. The Greek Royalties are quite the stupidest of their kind and their misfortune is to have to try and govern the most quick-witted of subjects. The F.O. has done its best to convince him of the absolute need to show himself and to come out as a constitutional leader but he hedges and havers. I've always said these small countries are better as republics.

At last too the Beaver has been got off. Fifteen film-stars couldn't have been more temperamental, changing his mind and saying he didn't want to go (which he did) and saying he wouldn't go unless the P.M. *asked* him to go. What the effect of him on Roosevelt and America will be I really don't know. He will advocate our Russian

1. R. G. Casey (later Lord Casey), Australian Minister to U.S. 1940–1942. Minister of State Cairo 1942–1944.
2. Head of the Greek Church.

policy at any rate. Russia has become his obsession and for that we must be thankful.

March 22

Long letter from Cripps in Cairo to P.M. reporting on his military discussions there with Auchinleck. He had been convinced that Auchinleck can do nothing till May but then he should be able to mount an offensive. A.E. doesn't think this date too bad as it would coincide probably with German offensive against Russia. A.E. had previously dictated a minute to P.M. urging vital importance of action against Germany *this year* when she is committed to fight Russia. Germany must beat Russia this summer or else she is sunk. If she does beat her, the war may be prolonged indefinitely. We should therefore do everything by resuming the offensive in Middle East and by landing operations on Western European coastline to harass and disperse Germany's effort, whilst remaining on defensive in Far East. I am sure this is sense. Germany is the principal enemy. Japan cannot stand up without her. Russia is stronger this year than last year, and Germany weaker.

Meanwhile there is appearing a dangerous rift in Anglo–American relations over Russia. Stalin has sent a snubbing reply to Roosevelt's message – as indeed he was entitled to do. At the same time our new Ambassador Clark-Kerr[1] has had a cordial reception from the usually frozen Molotov.

March 24

Meeting in Office about Stalin's demands. A.E. favours telling Roosevelt we now propose to go ahead and hope that he will acquiesce. It is felt that this may go badly in America but that the issue is unreal and we should never be forgiven if the spring offensive went badly for Russia and we hadn't faced it.

March 26

A.E. brought before Cabinet his proposals for going ahead with Treaty negotiations with Stalin. A telegram has been approved to Halifax instructing him to see Roosevelt at once (the Beaver is already there) and to explain that we feel obliged to go ahead because of the necessity for us of closest collaboration with Russia and of evident

1. Sir A. Clark-Kerr (later Lord Inverchapel), Ambassador to Russia 1942–1946. He succeeded Cripps on the latter's entry into the Cabinet.

refusal of Stalin to deal frankly with us until the frontier question is out of the way. We therefore ask Roosevelt to agree that we've done our best to consult him before taking action and we hope if he cannot approve, he will not openly disapprove. Reference is made to our own public opinion which is demanding utmost helpfulness towards Russia.

Meanwhile Sikorski who has also just arrived in Washington, is running about with typical Polish folly stirring up opposition to our Russian policy. The Poles are very brave but almost incurably foolish and short-sighted. They are outraged now because they hope to secure Lithuania for themselves. We must be very firm with the Poles, not forgetting that it was they who just after the last war drove the first breach in the new treaty and League of Nations system by attacking and annexing Vilna. That was the first step on our downward path.

March 30

We've just had the account of Clark Kerr's first talk with Stalin in Moscow. Very friendly and so most encouraging. S. spoke of dangers of mutual misunderstandings but wasn't at all grumpy – much gratified at regularity of our supplies as compared with Americans who are far below schedule. Unfortunately our telegram to Halifax was so delayed in despatch by last-minute dallying by the P.M. that Roosevelt is away and won't be visible before Tuesday when he is to see Litvinov again. The Beaver has done his stuff at the White House and left again for Florida. I'm afraid this negotiation won't be easy at all. Roosevelt will not like being left out but yet won't come in – he will probably try again some middle course proposal which will please nobody.

The India Plan was revealed today. Cripps seems fairly hopeful.

April 1

I'm afraid we are in for trouble with Roosevelt and Sumner Welles over Russia. Halifax was to have seen Roosevelt today, but has been put off, although the Beaver was to have had a crack at him yesterday. I'm afraid our plan of going ahead won't go with a swing.

April 2

A.E. came up from the country today unexpectedly for a special Cabinet on India. Cripps has sent back a gloomy picture of the Indian scene, Gandhi opposed to the plan, Nehru doubtful, Moslems in favour. Congress are expected to turn it down. Great agitation over question of immediate control of Defence which all seem united in demanding quite apart from our long-term offer. Indian and local European morale very low indeed. Agitation also over the local option clause which raises the ugly spectre of partition. It is proposed that Nehru should discuss defence problems with Viceroy and Wavell and see if any plan can be devised.

Cabinet agreed to consider any proposals thus put forward. Trouble is that C. in C. India is under War Cabinet and must remain so at present,[1] just as MacArthur in Australia is under Roosevelt. Meanwhile Jap advance in Burma is progressing and an ugly moment may come when the enemy reaches the borders of Bengal. Jap ships are already in the Bay.

A.E. worried as usual over P.M.'s methods of running the war. He is convinced it cannot go on and says that when Cripps returns a frontal attack must be made.

In spite of our fears, Roosevelt hasn't reacted too severely over our Russian plan. Welles told Halifax more in sorrow than in anger that President couldn't himself take part in negotiations regarding Baltic States for internal reasons and he would do his best to avoid hostile comment; it would much help him if Stalin could agree to a provision in his treaty with us giving right of option for local inhabitants to leave with their possessions if they so wished. This is really satisfactory. H. says the Beaver was a great help. We are now going ahead with an easy conscience. Draft treaty is to go before Cabinet on Wednesday.

April 6
Late Cabinet about India. Cripps reports that all parties have fixed on question of control of Defence now as vital, and efforts are being made to meet this as far as possible without endangering Wavell's control as C. in C. But it is difficult. I fear it looks tho' that the Indians don't mean to accept the Plan anyhow and are manoeuvring for a specious ground to break on. A pity! It was a generous offer.

April 7
Bevin came to see A.E. about getting Jouhaux[2] out of France. A certain Pineau[3] (whom I knew of while last in Paris) has come over to urge the importance of this with a view to strengthening the Left side of the Gaulle movement. Pineau said that the General enjoyed

1. In view of Indian demand for control of defence.
2. Léon Jouhaux (1879–1954) French Trade Union leader.
3. Christian Pineau, afterwards Socialist Deputy and Minister.

great symbolic prestige in France where little was known of him, and it was important to link up with the movement of resistance inside France. I'm all in favour of this – indeed, (with Jack Sandford (formerly of *Daily Herald*)) I struggled in M. of I. to increase contact with Left Wing and C.G.T. opinion in France – always to be obstructed there by the F.O. and Political Warfare people. It is amusing to see it happening at last.

April 8
Cabinet today approved A.E. proceeding with negotiations with Maisky for Soviet political and military treaty including recognition of 1941 frontiers. At long last. Maisky is to be told today; Molotov is to be invited to come for the signature. Meanwhile, Hopkins is due today too with the famous Roosevelt plan whatever it may be – Molotoff is also invited to Washington.

April 9
Indian negotiations at critical stage – issue now is the formula describing functions of Indian Minister of War and his relation to Wavell as C. in C. Roosevelt's representative Louis Johnson[1] has become an active intervener with Cripps and Nehru to the dismay of the Viceroy. What we don't seem to know is whether *if* we can reach agreement over the Defence question in the intermediate period, Congress etc. will accept our plan for the future. Cabinet today on all this.

April 11
India negotiations finally broken down and Cripps leaving on Monday. Congress turned the Plan down on all counts, not merely on that of the interim period in Ministry of Defence etc. There was some friction between Cripps and London at the last stages owing to C. apparently (tho' this is not clear to me) having gone beyond Cabinet instructions to meet Indians over interim period. The American Johnson turned out to be taking too much on himself in giving out that he was the President's personal representative. Hopkins told the P.M. that this was not the case, he was only in India to deal with supply questions and the last thing Roosevelt wished was to be drawn into these Indian discussions. Anyway I think Mr. J. proved helpful because the fact that he and Cripps did work together

1. Later U.S. Secretary of Defense 1949–1950.

strengthens our case over the breakdown. But what a pity! It is beginning to be clear to me that Nehru was afraid of the Plan because of the difficulty it involved for Indian leaders in squaring the Moslems with the Hindus – they used the Ministry of Defence question as a pretext merely. Obviously if they had given us a firm offer to accept the future arrangement if we could meet them over the interim period, we might have been justified in going even further to meet them. But without some such clear understanding it would have been folly to discuss the present in terms which jeopardised defence. The truth is we have wet-nursed India so long in our grandmotherly way that Indians perforce have lost all sense of political realism.

April 13
Poles in a great flap about our Anglo-Soviet treaty negotiations. Sikorski and Raczinski just back from America most anxious to get us to delay. They object particularly to Lithuania and Bukovina being included because of designs of their own. But they are getting little sympathy. In fact they are doing themselves much harm by these efforts to mobilise American opinion against us. They have drawn heavily on their credit with A.E.

April 14
A.E. dined with P.M. and Casey. Apparently Roosevelt has sent P.M. a critical telegram about our handling of India, to which P.M. had returned a polite raspberry. And not only that but he had sent for Hopkins at Chequers over the week-end, making it quite plain that we were bearing the whole burden of the war and America was giving no adequate help at all.

A.E. is urging that we should press America to send us an aircraft carrier or two to India to help there. American fleet are still doing nothing. Hopkins himself has said that there was complete lack of liaison or cooperation between the two Navies which were operating as completely separate units. This is very bad. Is it due to Pound again, and his American equivalent? A.E. would like to go over himself to America about it but can't get away now until the Russian negotiations are terminated. But it is most urgent. Jap fleet is slowly mopping us up.

April 15
A.E. said to me today that with Cripps away he is the only man in the Cabinet anxious to help Russia. Lyttelton and Attlee both very bad.

Do they not see that Russia is bearing the whole burden of the war on land – neither ourselves nor Americans yet seriously fighting? I told him of the growing demand to hear more in the country of the future England. That is why enthusiasm is flagging at present – he must give more attention to it. It should be the chief feature of his Edinburgh speech.

The return of Laval is ominous,[1] but yet he represents to France German collaboration in its most odious and Quisling form. Why has Germany imposed him unless she is afraid of early invasion?

April 16
More and more evidence comes in of the deplorable behaviour of all responsible in Singapore. No preparations, troops (British and Australian) refusing to fight, looting by troops, petty squabbling between officials, officials leaving their posts – 60,000 British troops beaten by 5,000 Japs! It must be hard to beat as a national disgrace. Many disturbing resemblances with the fall of France.

April 17
A.E. had a long and useful talk with Harry Hopkins last night. He told him he would much like to come over to Washington himself to discuss future plans. Hopkins was strongly in favour and said he should stay in the White House and perhaps make one speech. A.E. also said Dick Law wanted to go over too to talk about post-war economic cooperation and to demonstrate our interest in all this in which we feared the U.S. thought we were not sufficientlyinterested. Hopkins said exactly the same view was held there about us! They thought we were taking a great interest in it, more than they were as President R. was not really interested at all at present and was shelving it all by giving different people and bodies different problems to work out in corners.

This is rather comic and makes me think that there may be more resemblance between President R. and Mr. C. than we suspect.

Hopkins said the Beaver had been magnificent in handling the President over Russia. The latter was extremely difficult and cross. He wouldn't listen to Harry Hopkins or to Winant, but the Beaver had held his ground and gone on and on at him. "Isn't he grand at selling his stuff?"

1. He became Head of the Vichy Government, and Minister of the Interior, and the Foreign Office, in succession to Flandin.

April 21
The horrid Laval is now master of France. There could be no more
ironic comment on the claim of Pétain to be "regenerating" the
country after the excesses of the Third Republic – *"ce glorieux
vieillard"*. But it is proof of the concern of the Germans that there
should be no risk of fifth-column work in France against German
interests during the coming months when they are fighting in the
East and fear raids in the West.

April 22
Victor Cazalet is flapping about the H. of C., stirring up opposition
to our Soviet Treaty because of the Baltic States. This is part of the
Polish offensive but it threatens to assume serious proportions. There
is only too much anti-Soviet feeling about in influential quarters on
both sides of the House to make trouble easy. The Chief Whip is by
nature on that side, the Cabinet itself is lukewarm, even or especially
the Labour members. But Cripps is now back, thank goodness, and I
hope Stalin doesn't make matters difficult by haggling. If he does
he won't get his treaty. A special aeroplane is flying from Moscow
today presumably with the reply.

The Americans are being maddening about their ships. Pound,
who went over specially with Harry Hopkins, reports that they decline
to move in the Pacific or to send us aircraft carriers to help in the
Indian Ocean. They will send a battleship as far as Newfoundland
but no further.

Cordell Hull has returned to life and a recrudescence of pro-Vichy
sentiments in Washington is to be feared. Sumner Welles has got
quite tough with Laval, withdrawing Leahy,[1] but Hull refused to
comment on Laval's speech with its shameless attacks on us and
flatteries to America. How odd the Americans are. Winant has been
away now for weeks, leaving only a very nice but quite junior Chargé
d'Affaires.

April 23
A big and pleasant surprise to-day. Stalin, in a personal and most
secret telegram to P.M., says he is sending Molotov over at once to
discuss the Treaty with us and plans for a second front. He has also
telegraphed to Roosevelt to say he is sending Molotov there too. The
Roosevelt plan of operations which Hopkins and Marshall came to

1. Admiral Leahy, U.S. Ambassador to Vichy.

discuss here, has stirred Stalin and we hope we may now get something like a real exchange of views and a combined plan on strategy.
Into all this our proposed treaty will fit very suitably.

M. is to arrive in a non-stop aeroplane direct.

Cripps is staking out his claim to be a member of Defence Committee. I'm glad, it will greatly strengthen that body vis-à-vis the
P.M.

April 25
The P.M. for the moment is in a chastened and more cooperative
mood. He told A.E. yesterday that he thought the combination of
A.E., Cripps and Lyttelton with himself, made a pretty strong team"
and said he intended to merge the Defence Committee more into the
War Cabinet; but Attlee was the great weakness there, both he and
Bevin being quite useless on strategic questions. This is a most
welcome sign if the mood endures. A.E. and I both doubtful of this.
Meanwhile the Beaver from New York has come full out for a second
front in the West this year – which he declares the United Nations
have now the means of achieving. Having come straight from the War
Cabinet himself he should know, so people will think, tho' they won't
know how far the material available is either unsuitable or faulty
because of the Beaver himself. However I'm inclined to think it is
healthy for this clarion to be sounded. The Chiefs of Staff won't
attack for 10 years if it is left to them. They will never think they are
sufficiently prepared. And, as the Beaver says, if we miss the opportunity this year and the Russians are knocked out, we shall never
have such a chance again. Roosevelt also is rather "next-year minded",
having little wish to play second fiddle to Russia or to us as would be
the case if he came into action this summer. So I think the Beaver is
doing good.

We are waiting impatiently to hear when Molotov is to arrive.
He may drop from the sky at any moment.

April 29
The first party of Russians arrived this morning – six hours' flight
from Moscow.

Dined last night with Dick Law – Harold Butler there. He told
us many stories of the turpitude of Horace Wilson. The chief obstructionist now to any forward planning is Kingsley Wood. He is
like a Bourbon and believes we need do nothing for anybody. What a

disaster that the P.M. didn't drop him at the last reconstruction as he was minded to do.

May 2

Maisky came yesterday bringing alternative drafts for Anglo-Soviet Treaties. These were not so good. All reference to any facilities for those in Baltic States, such as local autonomy or option to leave, which we had pressed for to help us with American and our own public opinion, left out. Stalin repeats his request for a secret protocol in addition by which each side should recognise the other's needs as to security, notably by a Soviet guarantee treaty with Finland and Roumania permitting stationing of troops at bases to be balanced by a similar British treaty with Holland and Belgium providing for bases. This makes me laugh. It was the Bolsheviks who in 1917 published all the secret treaties of the last war and put the democracies to shame. So much so that H.M.G. at least learnt their lesson and will never have another secret treaty, not even to please Stalin. As A.E. said, it is going to be a very difficult negotiation.

Still no news of date of arrival of Molotov.

Winant has returned at last and has gone to A.E. for weekend. He says A.E. is regarded as a Bolshevik in America!

May 3

Cripps' mission to India has properly put the cat among the pigeons. The Congress Party are now split between the younger and more statesmanlike ones who see the necessity of coming to terms with the Moslems, and the old stiffs of the Congress machine.

May 4

Cripps broadcast last night about the future England. Lyttelton did the same ten days' ago. I cannot get A.E. to take the lead in this. He is hanging back. For months I've urged him. The country is really anxious about the future and will follow the first statesman who responds, whatever his party. Perhaps A.E. will do so now that these other two have. He is to speak at Edinburgh on Friday.

Winant reports that Roosevelt is adamant about Russia. He thinks no treaty necessary and it is only a question of supplies being kept up. Hence no doubt his pressure on us to send bigger convoys than we can safely escort. Hull and Sumner Welles are equally bad, and neither the Beaver, nor Hopkins nor Winant himself made any impression. Russia remains unpopular in the U.S.A. in spite of all.

May 5
Our long prepared attack on Madagascar[1] was launched this morning.
Complete secrecy! Poor General de Gaulle is outraged at hearing it
first on the news. A.E. had asked him to come at 12 noon to tell him
and to say that we would discuss with him the conditions of handing
it over later. But he refuses to come. Charles Peake has been sent to
try and mollify him. There couldn't have been any question of consulting him beforehand because no Frenchman can keep a secret but
we want to hand over the island to him as soon as possible.

A.E. saw Maisky – a very difficult interview. M. offered no promise
that Soviet Government would alter their attitude appreciably.
Molotov was waiting to hear how the discussion went before starting.

May 6
We discussed Russia again late last night. It was decided to draft a
final version of our treaty, shorn of all frills and containing only the
hard core on which we must insist. At same time a fresh draft altogether should be prepared of a treaty for 20 years mutual assistance,
much on the lines of our treaty with Turkey. This would have no
mention of frontiers, would avoid that issue and it could be offered
as an alternative to the other treaty if the Russians won't have it. It
would merely serve to mark our intention of close post-war cooperation and no more.

A.E. afterwards went across to see P.M. with whom Beaver, just
back, was dining. B. was apparently in favour of our now being firm
with Russians in view of their complete dependence on us for supplies.

Negotiating with Russia is a wearisome and exasperating business.
But I think we should justifiably agree to recognise 1941 frontiers
provided Polish position is safeguarded. We cannot look at a secret
protocol nor can we approve the idea of Soviet-Finnish and Soviet-
Roumanian guarantee pacts.[2] The latter would have a bad smell and
any way deal with post-war problems of European security etc.
which should not be prejudged at this stage when the rest of the
European security lay-out is not clear. But we should go as far as
indicated above and put it to the Soviets "take it or leave it". If they
won't take it, tant pis – we should have done all we could be expected
by public opinion to do to meet them.

1. It was important to deny this island to the Japanese, and Vichy were
   suspected of allowing Japanese submarines to refuel there.
2. These were to be in the secret protocol.

All the same I much doubt now whether there will be any treaty or any visit by Molotov.

Beaverbrook last night with P.M. was saying how great had been our failure to put our case across in U.S.A. There was no conception there that we were doing anything. Halifax hopeless for all his tours and speeches, his one asset that he got on well with Sumner Welles. B. much in favour of A.E. going over there "at once" on a visit to retrieve the situation. (A.E. rather bitten with this, tho' he has now Russia on his hands and couldn't go quite yet. Also Winston has ideas of his own of going again in June).

I asked A.E. what he thought B. himself was after. Was it the Embassy for himself? A.E. said he couldn't make out, tho' he feared that this might be the idea of the P.M. from something he had said of the possibility of Halifax going to India again. I said that it would be dreadful to think of Beaverbrook as Ambassador. The country would be profoundly shocked. He agreed. But equally the Beaver, if he held any other post there (as co-ordinator of supplies for instance), would make the life of any Ambassador impossible and Halifax has quite rightly let it be known that it would be impossible for him to carry on.

Beaverbrook was most fulsome to A.E. whom he was continually buttering up to the disparagement of Cripps and Lyttelton.

May 7
Cabinet today very stiff over Russia. Bevin insistent on the clause regarding option of Baltic citizens to leave. Attlee ditto about blessing of federation in E. Europe. Maisky, on the other hand, equally firm and says he doesn't think there can be agreement now.

A very serious situation in Middle East. Auck. doesn't now wish to attack till July which spells the loss of Malta because it can no longer be supplied without the use of the Cyrenaica aerodromes. P.M. very upset and told A.E. that he thought of replacing Auchinleck by Alexander – a good fighter if there was one. A.E. was told a disconcerting story of his friend General Gott being in favour of hanging on at Benghazi before, and General Auchinleck having wished to go right back to Matruh. We shan't win wars with such generalship as that.

I can't make out these Generals. Are they any good or not? They are never successful but that is not necessarily their fault.

May 9
We heard during the night that Molotov would be leaving "in the

very near future!" An agreeable surprise as we all thought he had put it off for good and because it looks as if he really wanted his treaty with us.

May 11
Molotov still not here. We had a great hurroosh on Saturday night when Maisky told us he'd be arriving on Monday. He wished to go up to meet him in a train and bring him back in a train – no flying in British aeroplanes in fact! So a special train was laid on and left with Nicholas L. on Sunday morning early. Finally, late last night we heard from Moscow that weather conditions prevented his departure, but he hopes to get off tonight or tomorrow night.

May 12
After further Cabinet consideration Auchinleck has been told he must start his offensive in June to forestall the fall of Malta, in spite of his misgivings. I think this is right. I cannot see any argument for delay when according to every calculation the Germans must get stronger as time goes on and they can reinforce more with Malta knocked out. But I have grave doubts about A. as the right general. A.E. thinks it is only Scotch caution.

P.M. has opened out to A.E. about his idea of sending the Beaver to Washington in place of Halifax. He wants to recall H. because he is a flop and make him leader of H. of L. (Bobbety's health won't permit of his going on with this as well as C.O.) and to make the Beaver Ambassador where he says he will put our case across, get the aeroplanes we want out of America and have daily touch with Roosevelt. A.E. not at all keen, he told P.M. he thought it would be unpopular here, and he was not at all sure that Roosevelt would welcome it. As Ambassador B. would be very difficult to control and to work with. He finally got P.M. to agree to send a personal wire to Harry Hopkins to ask him, as a friend and "off the record", what he feels about it.

I said I was sure it would be most unpopular here, and it was dreadful to think of such a man in the Embassy. A.E. said he thought P.M. was determined to keep him out of the country because he feared the attacks of his papers. Both A.E. and I agreed that he need have no fear whatever. B.'s influence – as of all newspaper proprietors – was grossly exaggerated. But there it is, and I think it would be a calamitous appointment.

May 15
Still no Molotov. This delay is tiresome because uninformed and obstructive opinion against the negotiations is taking shape. The Foreign Affairs Committee of House of Commons is working itself up. The egregious Simon has written to the P.M. about it on the high moral tone: Duff too is anti. So the sooner we get it over the better. I don't myself believe the opposition will come to anything, and I think the country will be wholeheartedly on our side in this.

The Beaver problem is still unsettled. No reply has yet come from Harry Hopkins. A.E. spoke to Winant (who had seen the P.M.'s message to Hopkins which went through his Embassy). Latter very guarded, said he could only suppose we wanted to get rid of B. He mentioned that Roosevelt had recently asked that Halifax should remain because he felt he was absolutely honest and he knew where he was with him, therefore he wondered whether the President would like any change. A.E. begged the Ambassador to ensure that an absolutely frank and honest reply was sent to the P.M.'s enquiry.

May 16
Rumours percolating about that Germany may make a separate peace with Soviet Russia. Coming from different sources they all look mischievous. It is just possible that the Russians are helping them in order to frighten us into a second front. Indeed Moley has a theory that Molotov is only coming here to threaten us with this. Not that the Russians mightn't make a separate peace if it suited them but unless they are at the last gasp or unless Hitler offers them their 1941 frontiers, I cannot see that it would suit them. But they are obviously not at the last gasp but much stronger than last year, and how could Hitler offer such humiliating terms unless he was at the last gasp? We must expect the strongest pressure for a second front, and indeed why not?

May 18
Still no Molotov.

Meanwhile Harry Hopkins has replied about the Beaver. It amounts to a very cold and perfunctory acquiescence, quite clearly a hint that the President would prefer no change. The P.M. interprets it as an enthusiastic acceptance! A.E. much concerned, discussed over weekend with Bracken and Jim T., both equally opposed to the changes. The Chief Whip, who is working hard to get H. back for his own purpose, says the changes would be most popular in the H.

of C. If he really thinks that then he is indeed a fool. A.E. lunching with P.M. today. I am sure A.E. should resist the proposal by all means. From every point of view it will be bad. H. bad here. B. bad there. Bad for the Government.

More defeatism from the Chiefs of Staff. They wish to terminate the Madagascar operation (which they were kicked into) with the occupation of the North bit only, whilst concluding a *modus vivendi* with the Vichy governor as regards the rest. A.E. up in arms against this, is pointing out to P.M. that Vichy can never be trusted. Their first reaction was to appeal to Japs against us and they will now provide nests for German and Italian agents. A.E. wishes to clear the rot out and put in a good Free French Governor (General Legentilhomme). The trouble is the P.M. now so loathes de Gaulle, he almost prefers Vichy itself – as the Americans do.

May 19
A recrudescence of hope of Molotov tomorrow. Maisky in great to-do about secrecy and security having heard from Molotov that he wishes absolute secrecy preserved. We say that is impossible in London because the Soviet Embassy will be closely watched. He now says, "Well then, could he not live in the country, merely come up in a car each day to the F.O.?" A.E. thinks Chequers the only possibility and has consulted the P.M. who is delighted to put it at M's disposal.

May 21
Molotov arrived yesterday. He came down from Scotland by special train and was then sent off to Chequers from a wayside station. A.E. said he was in cracking form, all smiles and in a smart brown suit – very different to the usual Molotov.

Talks begin this morning at No. 10.

I met A.E. at lunchtime. He told me the conversations were perfectly amiable but the Russians were opening their mouths very wide. They were asking not only for the 1941 frontiers but also for the secret protocol covering Russian guarantee pacts to Finland and Roumania. Molotov had said he would much like to have a Treaty but if he couldn't get what he wanted he would perfer to have none at all. He is proposing to go on to America to discuss the second front.

We agreed that we couldn't accept either a secret protocol or guarantee pacts, and that the 1940 frontiers were as much as we could properly give. I think we should agree to them without the frills which the Americans want and which would be pure eye-wash;

but we cannot possibly give way over Finland and Roumania. To acquiesce in these guarantee pacts would be tantamount to handing them over body and soul to Russia. The absorption of the Baltic States began with guarantee pacts. It would also hopelessly compromise future discussion of the future reorganisation of Europe.

May 22

Further Russian talks yesterday afternoon. Main obstacle now the Polish frontiers. Molotov wants to leave these to be settled between Russia and Poland: we say we cannot disinterest ourselves as an ally; we would welcome Russo-Polish agreement but we must define our position. Molotov would agree to Curzon Line plus some modifications in Russia's favour. (The Curzon Line is fair in itself but it represents considerably less than Poland had before the war). In any case we would favour the Curzon Line but for the Poles it would be difficult to expect them to acquiesce in giving up territory to Russia till they know what they will get from Germany in compensation. Molotov confirmed that Russia favoured Poland getting East Prussia. Molotov still very amiable and didn't seem to mind if he didn't get a treaty at all. Yet he takes our swallowing of the Baltic States demand as nothing and says we owe him a concession for the sacrifices *he* is being asked to make over Poland.

This morning the second front is to be discussed. Chiefs of Staff are as usual most unhelpful in their attitude. I fear that M. will find the Americans much more forthcoming on this question and we shall be in the position of appearing the obstructive ones both on the political and on the military questions.

May 23

Further political talks yesterday afternoon after which both P.M. and A.E. went down to Chequers for the night with the Russians. We are pretty well stuck over the political treaty. Apart from the Polish front, the Russians are asking us to endorse now the Finnish–Soviet and Roumanian Soviet non-aggression guarantee pacts which they wish to conclude after the war, this point to be covered in a secret protocol attached to the Treaty. They say they would be prepared similarly to endorse similar pacts between H.M.G. and Holland and Belgium. Our point of view is that we aren't as yet contemplating such agreement with Holland and Belgium, and we cannot see why we should be brought into it at all at this stage. There can of course be no question for us of a secret protocol.

Further talks for today. A.E. will probably propose a new treaty altogether, agreeing to 20 years' alliance and cooperation, in place of the texts over which we are stuck. The new treaty would not touch frontier questions at all, but would nonetheless mark our willingness to cooperate with Russia postwar. It would be something *faute de mieux*.

May 24

At yesterday's talks the Russians agreed to drop the secret protocol, provided something was embodied in the text of the treaty expressing the interest of the Soviets in the Gulf of Finland and the "North West area" of the Black Sea. A.E. produced his new treaty for a 20 years' alliance but it was received with marked lack of enthusiasm, not to say suspicion. Molotov said he would study it and report on it when he got back to Moscow but he couldn't do so before. Meanwhile, P.M. has sent a message to Stalin strongly urging that Molotov should be allowed to return here again, after his visit to America, on his way home.

The meeting broke up on the understanding that it should be resumed on Sunday or Monday as soon as Molotov was ready. (He is evidently expecting instructions from Moscow). The Polish difficulty remains, so does that of Finland and Roumania, even tho' we have got them to drop a secret protocol. A.E. inclines now to the idea of the new treaty without its embarrassing references to frontiers, but it is clear the Russians don't like it and would much prefer the other. Indeed, our interest in the new treaty is acting as something of a spur on them to meet us over the old treaty. The fact remains we must safeguard our treaty position to Poland – we cannot sign away all interest in her and endorse a Russian claim to settle with her without interference. We have conceded the Russian point about the 1941 frontiers in Baltic States and Finland and Roumania, which I'm convinced is right and defensible and which is what they asked of us in Moscow. But again we cannot, I think, endorse the proposed Russian interest in Finland and Roumania over and above the frontier concessions, at any rate at this stage in advance of a Peace Conference. That would look like handing them over bound hand and foot. There is a great difference between recognising Russia's pre-war frontiers and prejudicing the peace lay-out of the states beyond those frontiers. Why cannot the Russians be satisfied with this and leave the self-evident fact of Russia's interest in these states to take effect at the Peace Conference when her position will be unassailable?

Meeting this evening again. Russians unexpectedly forthcoming, have met us over Poland to an extent which even Alec Cadogan says would be difficult for us to refuse. But they still cling to a reference to Finland and Roumania, and still refuse to agree to any emigration from the Baltic States which is what Roosevelt would like, tho' they offer to agree to emigration for national minorities, e.g. Poles from Lithuania but not Lithuanians from Lithuania. They clearly do not want our new treaty of alliance only.

Meanwhile Winant is expressing despair at the prospect of our agreement with the Russians over the frontiers and says he can't exaggerate the bad effect it will have in America. He begs that at least we shall not sign until Molotov has been there.

A.E. getting hesitant about the treaty because of this American opposition coupled with that of elements in the H. of C. Even Cardinal Hinsley[1] has written to express abhorrence of it. A.E. now obviously eager to get away from the old treaty and on to the new. I tell him it is no use listening to the Catholics, they are on the side of darkness anyway. As for the H. of C. opposition it is of the worst and wettest elements. And in assessing American criticism we must bear in mind the unlikelihood of America cooperating in policing Europe after the war. Russia and ourselves are part of Europe and we must contrive to work together or be prepared to fight each other. We should be very careful, after the Russians have come so far, not to break with them lightheartedly. They will snap back into a dangerous isolationism. A.E. says he doesn't think that this would necessarily happen from what he judges Molotov's attitude. The latter very amiable and apparently learning much from his visit here. A.E. feels he should hold out for emigration facilities from border states, for dropping of references to Finland and Roumania and for initialling now but signature after Washington visit.

Worrying –

Just at this point – midnight – A.E. rang up to say he had received a message from Molotov that he wished to come and see him tomorrow afternoon at 3 to discuss the *new* treaty. Winant had previously rung up to say that he had seen the Russians and put to them the American attitude about the old treaty, and that they were very friendly and didn't seem to have realised it before. A.E. much intrigued and encouraged by this.

All very mysterious. We shall see better to-morrow. But it is pretty clear the Russians want to sign something with us and are not being

1. Archbishop of Westminster.

put off by our conditions. Our objective remains the same – to go as far as we can to dispel Russian suspicion of us without sacrificing our own principles.

May 25

Meeting this afternoon went most smoothly and rapidly. Russians cheerfully adopted new treaty and dropped the old. The new treaty is a straight alliance for 20 years unless superseded by a new order for Europe. It should gratify the Poles and please those who are pro-Baltic States. Winant says the Americans will be delighted. Anyway there seems no doubt of the willingness of the Russians to accept it instead of the original treaty.

There are one or two points to clear up. One point is whether we *both* have to agree on the acceptability of a new order in Europe before we are released from our obligations and, supposing the Russians don't agree with us about the new order, whether thereby they can hamstring our participation in the new order, e.g. in taking part in collective security. But by and large, no new order will be worth much if it doesn't include Russia. If Russia stays out then it is essential for us to have some sort of string on her.

I'm not sure whether I like this treaty as much as the old because of this extension into the post-war period. The old treaty would have fixed the frontiers of Russia and nothing much more. As to the future our hands were not tied. If I were America, I would be more shocked by this new treaty than by the other. However we have Winant's word for it.

May 26

Molotov accepted all outstanding amendments to draft of new treaty last night and signature is today. P.M. and Cabinet delighted, especially P.M. who is beside himself with pleasure at A.E.'s new treaty which saves him from the old. Bouquets, bouquets all round!
Later –

All went with a swing. The treaty was signed at 6.30 in S. of S.'s room at F.O. – originally it was to have been 5 but translating and typing and a last minute difficulty over one word held us up. The P.M., Attlee and Sinclair there as well as A.E. Immediately after, the Russians left for their train which is to take them North whence they start for Iceland, Greenland and Washington. Stalin has agreed to their returning this way, so we shall see them again in about a fortnight. Meanwhile nothing is to be said of the new-born treaty till Molotov gets back to the Kremlin.

Our intelligence reports seem to show that the Germans are about to attack in Libya and go for Tobruk. They will thus anticipate our own offensive. But our stay-at-home generals seem readier to be attacked than to attack and believe it an advantage.

May 27

A.E. and I dined together last night at the Ritz to "celebrate". A.E. pretty tired, it's an exhausting business negotiating, every wit all the time extended. He feels immensely relieved and satisfied, feels a good job of work done, his biggest day yet. He feels his position will be much strengthened and he is more than ever convinced that he was right to stay at F.O. and not to have taken on the leadership of the H. of C. This treaty would never have come off without him. His Russian record, his visits in 1935 and last December, alone made it possible. Nor could any Labour Foreign Secretary have done it. The Tory Party would have made too much racket. In any case none of the present Labour leaders would have had the courage or the vision to try – except perhaps Cripps but here again the Russians themselves didn't want to play with him. Nothing is more revealing than C's failure in Moscow, in spite of every sympathy, the rudeness of Stalin towards him, the studied neglect etc. Stalin wished to take Russia out of party politics here and for that purpose a treaty with Cripps or Labour would have been valueless. He wanted to negotiate with a Government which politically speaking, could deliver the goods.

But why the sudden agreement to the new treaty when they had got us to swallow the principles of the old? As P.M. said to A.E., we would never have got the new treaty at all if we hadn't given over the 1941 frontiers. Was it really in the end due to realisation of the American point of view and to Winant's eleventh-hour intervention? The turning point came on Sunday afternoon after we had stood out over Roumania and Finland and over permission for emigration from the Baltic States and when Winant had visited them and put the U.S. point of view personally. Then came A.E.'s midnight call to me from the country to say they wished to come the next afternoon to discuss the new treaty. One lesson at least sticks out, the importance of having an alternative ready against such a moment.

I told A.E. that all this reinforces the need for him to go to U.S. in the autumn, as he is thinking of doing. He must not get into the position of being the Red Eden – to work the future he must stand equally well with Russia and with America.

May 28
Rommel's offensive against Tobruk in full swing.

June 3
Western Desert battle going quite well. Rommel undoubtedly getting a bad shaking, if not worse. And we may still have a rod in pickle for him.

Molotov and Co. in Washington. President R. has sent a message to P.M. to say he is keeping him a few days longer. He says they are getting on famously but M. has spoken with real anxiety of next 3 or 4 months. R. feels Russian position may be precarious and we should do all possible to take action on continent this year.

June 9
Molotoff arrived back today.

Western Desert battle not too good. American tanks moreover proving better and more resistant than our own.

Luncheon with A.E. for Molotov. Beaver, Leathers,[1] Cadogan, Maisky. Beaver outshone all. He told Molotov whom he was sitting next, he had made three cardinal mistakes in the war – that the French would fight well, that the Russians would fight badly and that the Japs couldn't drive us and Americans out of Pacific Asia. In England public opinion is ahead of the Government, in America the Government is ahead of public opinion. When Molotov told him what the Americans were doing for us in the way of supplies of tanks and aircraft (as a reason why they couldn't do more for Russia) the Beaver said "Balls! They are doing nothing like that. Their promises are always greater than their performance." Speaking of the German offensive in Libya, Beaver said it was directed against the Second Front.

June 10
Molotov has pressed very hard for a Second Front in 1942.[2] Roosevelt encouraged him to do so, although the whole burden this year must fall on us. P.M. very firm on the limitations of what was possible

1. F. J. Leathers, M.P. (later Lord Leathers), Minister of War Transport 1941–1945.
2. On his return from Washington.

for us this year: he would not authorise any large-scale operation which didn't offer fair prospect of success, since a failure would not help Russia either. Roosevelt had calmly told Molotov he would be prepared to contemplate a sacrifice of 120,000 men if necessary – *our* men. P.M. said he would not hear of it.

June 11
Statement in H. of C. this evening on Russia.[1]

June 12
Press today most full and satisfactory. Many telegrams for A.E. from workmen's clubs and groups of workers in factories.

Desert battle bad, Rommel too much for our Generals again, pushing us about as he likes.

June 15
P.M. going to Washington this week for two days! All about second front plans. He suggested to A.E. on Thursday in the enthusiasm of the Russian Treaty that he should come too. "Would you like a little trip?" A.E. rather embarrassed as to reply, didn't want to go just now, thought it wrong to go and wanted to go later alone when he could discuss post-war questions with Roosevelt. However P.M. has said no more about it and is starting off now on Thursday.

June 17
Roosevelt is seriously turning over the idea of an American expedition against Dakar this summer. The P.M. (who starts off to-day) is also taken with it. A.E. asked me what I thought of it. I said I thought anything which committed the Americans to operations over here was to be encouraged. Vichy were less likely to fight the Americans than if it were us. It might have the effect of bringing the Germans into Spain but I couldn't see that would matter now – more commitments for Germans and a further thinning out of her military resources.

But things are going badly at the moment. Libya very nasty – we seem to be back again on the Egyptian frontiers tho' Auchinleck

1. There was also a communiqué issued stating that "in the course of conversations full understanding was reached with regard to the urgent tasks of creating a Second Front in Europe in 1942". This was accompanied by an aide-memoire to Molotov making it clear that we made no promise over this.

thinks he is exhausting the Germans by our still fighting. On the other hand, the Americans are hitting the Jap fleets in the Pacific by aircraft attack,[1] and the Russians are holding fast at Sevastopol and Kharkov.

June 18
P.M. is suffering from a fresh access of anti-de Gaulle feelings, so much so that he is becoming almost pro-Vichy. He wants to keep the Free French out of Madagascar, so do the soldiers who cannot get out of their stupid heads that de Gaulle is a "rebel" whereas Vichyites are "loyalists".

Another striking and significant feature which Libya has revealed is the badness of our tanks as compared with the excellence of our aircraft. We never seem to have the tank with the right armour and the right gun. In aircraft design we lead the world. The case for "leaving it to the airmen" grows with every operation. In the last two big American engagements with the Japs in the Pacific the ships never fired at each other at all – all fighting was done by aircraft, either from carriers or from land.

June 21
4 p.m. I've just heard Tobruk has fallen. I'm telephoning to A.E. in the country to tell him. How right Beaverbrook was when he said the Germans were fighting here against the Second Front! I fear this must put us back a lot and even Egypt itself be endangered.

A.E. much worried, fears there wan't sufficient garrison left there. He had had doubts about it. There is to be a Defence Committee tonight.

June 22
This morning he told me that the Defence Committee had sat till 2 a.m. not very usefully as Attlee had asked all the War Cabinet to attend and much time had been taken up by Bevin declaiming "We must have a victory. What the British Public wants is a victory!" As if we didn't all want one! A.E. spoke to P.M. on the telephone and told him he ought to come back at once. P.M. appeared peevish and reluctant and implied he was doing most important things over

1. The Battles of the Coral Sea, and Midway Island had ended in victory for the Americans on June 6, and are considered the turning point in the war against Japan.

there. Very little information yet about the disaster but A.E. thinks we were both outmanoeuvred and outweaponed. Yet this was the situation which Auchinleck wanted; he wanted to be attacked, not to attack.

The P.M. has sent a strong and stirring telegram to Auchinleck urging him to display the utmost vigour in holding the frontier and telling him he can count on full support of H.M.G. He has got Roosevelt to agree to send American armoured troops to reinforce. P.M. evidently just about to start home.

We discussed China today. For China proper there is little we can do at present. It was thought that a treaty *à la Russe* would not be desirable as we can do so little; we have already undertaken to waive territorial rights and unequal treaties so to make a treaty of that would be thank you for nothing. Until we can send more stuff in and that means until fresh communications across Asia are opened up, we had better keep quiet.

June 23

We gather from a side-wind that the Beaver is out to see A.E. Minister of Defence "to get us out of this jam". A.E. says he would love to do it more than anything, but the P.M. would never allow anyone to do it. I'm afraid he is right and in a way I think the P.M. is right. In a war the P.M. cannot be a puppet and must run the war himself. Actually on this occasion there has been no interference by the P.M., whatever the critics may think or say, in strategy. The generals did and had what they wanted. The small inner Cabinet is working well and the P.M. has been much less arbitrary of late. What wants seeing to is the cumbersome and obstructive working of the service departments and the Chiefs of Staff. Somebody is needed to watch the Chiefs of Staff all the time and see that they don't go to sleep and neglect to see carried out the decisions of the Defence Committee. The trouble in the battle, beside that of bad generalship, was the failure to have sufficient tanks with the heavier guns now proved necessary. This need should have been obvious months ago and yet nothing effective was done to remedy it quickly. How can we be sure that this neglect won't occur again? Here an active Vice-Minister of Defence might help, working under the P.M. as M. of D. and whole-time watching and hustling the Chiefs of Staff machine.

June 24

Auck, I hear, has offered the P.M. his resignation to facilitate reorganisation. I think both he and Ritchie will have to go. P.M., I believe, rather favours Alexander[1] to succeed. He is a fine fighting general who did very well in Burma, but A.E. says he has no armoured warfare experience or local knowledge, no great brain. An alternative, I hear, is Montgomery,[2] a most ruthless man, with pale steel blue eyes who would clean up Cairo and put the fear of God into the staff. You want two men, one to be C. in C. which is really a sort of C.I.G.S. job and one to fight the battle. A.E. would favour making Montgomery C. in C. and leaving him to choose his other general; either Alexander or Gott (whom A.E. swears by) could do the latter.

June 25
We have abandoned Sollum and are falling back slowly on Matruh lines. Reinforcements are being hurried out from here and America. But Egypt is in jeopardy.

I don't like the news tonight. A most unhappy evening full of bitter anticipations.

Long talk with Jim T. I warned him of how grave I thought military situation was and of what might follow a further disaster. He didn't know how bad it was. If things got no worse by next week, we agreed that Wardlaw Milne's motion of censure would fail, its supporters were already falling away and he was left with the cranks and scamps. But if things were worse, then the Government majority might fall by so much as in the Narvik vote which put Neville Chamberlain out. Then Winston would have to go too. Jim didn't think, nor did I, that the King could send for anyone else but A.E. now. Attlee out of the question, Cripps' stocks now much too low, Lyttelton not known and no experience, A.E. steadily rising and now since the Molotov visit on the crest of the wave. Lloyd-George would back him if consulted by the King, so perhaps would Baldwin; Beaver would support him in the press for what that is worth which is doubtful. But what a heritage it would be! Jim is going to see Bobbety and get his antennae out.

June 29
News still most disquieting. We are out of Matruh and still falling

1. General Sir Harold Alexander (later Field Marshal Lord Alexander) was Commander-in-Chief in Burma.
2. Sir Bernard Montgomery (later Viscount Montgomery) held the S.E. Command in England.

back. Air Force working hard over Rommel's columns and supplies. But where do we hope to stand and what have we to counter-attack with? P.M. back last Saturday "in excellent form". He has formed his conception of the state of opinion in this country. The debate is to be on Wednesday and Thursday. By then Alexandria may have fallen!

July 1

We are now back on Alamein position, the last line before Alexandria. The latter is being evacuated in a hurry by our ships. A problem is presented by the immobilised French ships of Admiral Godefroy;[1] it has been decided that they are to sail under supervision to Suez or to be scuttled, by force if necessary. Auck. has taken over direct command from Ritchie. The Germans captured 6,000 tons of petrol at Tobruk. P.M. has sent a flamboyant message to him about making every ditch a last ditch and every post a winning post. Yet Rommell's forces fully stretched and without a man to spare, should now be a perfect target for our bombers concentrated on this small area. We should be able to smash them.

I hear that project of replacing Halifax by Beaverbrook is by no means dead. P.M. very much under his spell again and has been consulting him about his speech. Beaver, for his part, must be anxious that criticism of supply doesn't go back to his period of office. Did I mention that we had had a message from Roosevelt sent indirectly through Frankfurter to say how very highly he appreciated Halifax, that he couldn't wish to have a better Ambassador, he found him better even than Lothian who was apt to lecture him on how to govern America? This is clearly intended as the real reply to the P.M.'s enquiry via Harry Hopkins about replacing H. by B.

No doubt Roosevelt likes H. who leaves him alone and doesn't press him on disagreeable subjects, whereas B. would never leave him alone.

July 2

Debate[2] yesterday went on till 4 a.m. Not a good day for the Government. Although Wardlaw Milne made a fool of himself by the fantastic suggestion that the Duke of Gloucester be made C. in C. practically all speakers were critical. Lyttelton, for lack of parliamentary experience, didn't do well tho' his speech was a meaty

1. Vichy Admiral in command of French Fleet at Alexandria.
2. On the vote of censure.

defence of the omissions of supply. In the Lords the Beaver came out
in defence of the supply position also. P.M. is to speak this afternoon.

Meanwhile there is an ominous silence from Cairo. The battle of
Alamein has been raging since yesterday but we have no news of it.

P.M. very worried and difficult when A.E. saw him this morning.

Lampson pressing for instructions as to whether to go or stay
(he wants to stay) if the Germans arrive. P.M. refuses to send any,
saying the battle is not yet lost and the Delta is a magnificent place
to stop tanks. He refuses to contemplate the worst.

July 3

P.M. made, as usual, a great speech yesterday and on the whole
seems to have won the sympathy of the House. All were rather over-
awed by the issues being fought out in Africa and slightly ashamed of
themselves.

A.E. dined with P.M. afterwards. He told me this morning he
found the P.M. "in the greatest heart" and planning to go off at
once to Egypt himself by aeroplane! He told A.E. he had got the
King's permission as well as that of Attlee and Bevin. A.E. and Bracken did their best to shake him out of such a mad idea which, tho'
admittedly most heartening to the troops, would only hinder General
Auchinleck. P.M. was like a naughty child. He went on to say to A.E.
he had prepared his political testament which he would leave behind.
"You may like to know what is in it. You are in it."

Battle yesterday still uncertain. Very hard fighting round Alamein.
Late last night our most secret sources said that Rommel was talking
of making "one more attempt" to take the place today. That is
encouraging.

July 4

Battle of Alamein still undecided. News a little better for us, enemy
attacks beaten off yesterday again.

Charles Peake gave a dinner for de Gaulle last night. Dick Law,
Harold Macmillan, Harry Crookshank, Neville Lytton[1] and me.
G. (who had none of his people with him) in very friendly mood
impressed everybody. In the last war, he said, France had had the
luck to have a Clemenceau, in this war we had had the luck to have a
Churchill. In the last war the general run of French statesmen was far

1. Later Lord Lytton.

higher than in this, the Poincarés, the Millerands, the Briands, as against the Daladiers, Blums and Reynauds. He thought Mandel was the only one of the former Ministers who might serve again. The Comte de Paris had missed a great opportunity by failing to come out on the side of resistance at the collapse. In answer to a suggestion of mine about the division of France into Right and Left, he said there were several different sections of the Right, there were sound sections such as the lower clergy, the professional and military classes, the *petite noblesse de campagne* who were neither pro-German nor corrupt, as well as the bad fifth column elements. The weakness of France before the war was due to the fatal division of economic interests between employers and workers which had never been reconciled. France had not had a real government since Poincaré. Speaking of the military situation the General expressed himself definitely against invasion of Europe this year; we couldn't do it this year with overwhelming strength, for we must be prepared for Germany calling back strong forces from the East, and a failure this year would gravely handicap operations for next year. Asked about the prospects for Anglo-French friendship the General said that at present French sympathy was divided equally between England, America and Russia but he thought we should eventually again become the favourite ally *"car les Américains deviendront trop fatigants et les Russes trop inquiétants"*.

July 7
Chiefs of Staff proving most obstructive over Madagascar and Free French cooperation and F.O. policy. They are a menace. The less successful their campaigns the more they seek to interfere in policy. We suspect Ismay as an obstructionist who fans the P.M.'s dislikes. We are anxious to get a F.O. political adviser attached to the G.O.C. and to arrange for a Gaullist representative to visit the place. It is an important part of our policy of winning De Gaulle's confidence and strengthening his position generally. But the soldiers (like the sailors) have a passion for appeasing their Vichy opposite numbers. This fatal line has got us into difficulty over the French ships at Alex, and it has landed the Americans in similar embarrassments with Admiral Robert in Martinique. We don't want the same thing in Madagascar – an untrustworthy Vichy French Government left in power and possible Jap landings. Vichy cannot be appeased. But the P.M. also shares these deplorable delusions. He is almost as tender to Vichy as Hull. Poor de Gaulle meets opposition on every side. A.E., I'm glad

to say, likes him more and supports him the more he is unfairly attacked.

July 8
It is feared a very heavy toll has been taken of the North Russian convoy[1] – scattered and bombed in detail.

July 9
The American General Staff have decided to attach a General and an Admiral to de Gaulle. Pétainist State Department will hate this as much as our own soldiers. The Americans are all extremes – poor us who try to keep in the middle of the road!

The position of the North Russian convoy is now this: 7 sunk, 7 arrived, 21 still unaccounted for. This route looks like growing impossible. The sea is so cold that survivors only live for two or three minutes in it.

P.M. has proposed to Roosevelt that Marshall should be supreme Commander-in-Chief for invasion in 1943. Meanwhile we like less and less the prospects for large-scale continental operations this year. We would prefer action in North Africa which the Americans at one time favoured. But this will horrify the Russians who are making the greatest play with a second front this year as foreseen in the Washington communiqué of the Roosevelt–Molotov talks. Winant is worried and so is Dill, both think it may cause the Americans to shy off the West and go all out for the Pacific. P.M. however has passed on these views of ours to the President.

July 11
It now looks as if about 17 ships out of 35 in the N. Russian convoy are safe. On this the P.M. has decided that the July convoy must go forward too.

Our new Cabinet Ministers are not proving a success. Grigg at the W.O. is very ineffective, quite unable to assert himself over his Generals. Casey in Cairo seems equally ineffective. A light-weight, I'm afraid. Cripps is now debunked as a serious statesman – he remains a brilliant and erratic amateur. One of the most pernicious influences in the Government is Kingsley Wood who consistently obstructs every progressive proposal, a pip-squeak in a big place, but he gets the ear of the P.M. because the latter is prejudiced about

1. The P.Q. 17 Convoy.

future affairs and ignorant of home affairs – Lyttelton, on the whole, is being successful but he is no parliamentarian yet.

July 13
It looks now as if the N. Russian convoy has lost even more ships than we thought. If much over half are sunk, it is useless to continue with it unless we can establish air bases in N. Norway.

July 14
Very bad news from Russia.[1] The convoy news also gets worse each day (19 now sunk definitely). Maisky called very anxious and begging us "to do something now". A second front or more bombing. The Libyan news better. We are holding and counter-attacking. That is after all a second front and if we could be only moderately successful there and threaten the German position in Africa, we should soon draw off forces from the East.

July 15
A difficult day with Maisky yesterday. M. dined with P.M. and A.E. joined them again after. A message to Stalin is being drafted to show how hopeless it is to continue the North Russian convoys at present when over 2/3 go to the bottom. It may be possible to resume them later with aircraft carriers. Meanwhile we are trying to send more via Persia but capacity is limited. P.M. very anxious that America should proceed with the N.W. Africa plan.[2] We learn that the President too is very keen but is being opposed by his soldiers – so like ours.

De Gaulle addressed a meeting of members of Parliament, with such success that they spontaneously burst into the Marseillaise! He is a great speaker. His stock is rising.

The W.O. are still unbelievably obstructive over Madagascar. The soldiers have got themselves into a complete tangle by agreeing to two different versions of the armistice conditions.

July 16
Still bad news from Russia, but in Libya there is an uneasy equilibrium.

1. German summer offensive in full swing.
2. Later known as Torch.

July 18
A.E. tells me P.M. is ringing him up every morning now to discuss the night's news. I say how excellent this is. It enables him to guide the old gentleman a good deal. He hates bringing Attlee and all into his inmost counsels.

Dined with Charles Peake. Long talk about Halifax and A.E. and question of latter's visit to U.S.A. This must be arranged very tactfully as we feel pretty sure the two old prima donnas will be jealous of A.E.'s appearance on the American stage. We must arrange for him to be invited from the other side. We discussed Roosevelt. Peake said there was no doubt of his ambition and determination to run the world, but he was on the side of the angels. Would he not therefore stand again for a fourth term in 1944 which would be a crucial moment in the peace settlement? C.P. thought he would do so.

Peake told me Halifax has been shocked on returning after a year to a meeting of the War Cabinet to find how proceedings had deteriorated. Nothing but endless monologues from the P.M. He was also struck by the poor display of Lyttelton and Cripps. I said I agreed about Cripps' falling off but I didn't believe the same of Lyttelton.

July 21
Dinner last night with Bruce Lockhart to meet Jan Masaryk[1] just back from America. Masaryk thought that Roosevelt would probably stand again – if he chose to, he would get in. We spoke of the problem of negro-American troops here. There will be 100,000 – or one in ten of the white Americans. Masaryk motoring up from Plymouth had passed through a whole black area. Whatever way we handled them we would be wrong. If we treated them naturally as equals, there would be trouble with the Southern officers (there had already been a scene in a club at Cheltenham). If we treated them differently, there would be trouble with the "North Americans". Both sides were angling for the negro vote in the coming autumn elections, hence the decision to send the negroes over here just as if they were whites. It is rather a scandal that the Americans should thus export their internal problem. We don't want to see lynching begin in England. I can't bear the typical Southern attitude towards the negroes. It is a great ulcer on the American civilisation and makes nonsense of half their claims.

1. Czech Foreign Minister, who died in Prague soon after the Communist coup in 1948.

July 22

A.E. dined with P.M. and Harry Hopkins last night till 2 a.m. Meanwhile the American soldiers (including General Marshall) are here discussing plans with our soldiers. This seems bad as our soldiers are negative and will produce an unpromising impression while both are ignorant of political repercussions. However ours hope to convince theirs that a second front in the West is impossible this year. The P.M., and our soldiers we believe favour an American landing this year at Dakar.[1]

P.M. on tenterhooks to know when Auck will launch his counteroffensive. Latter will never get more reinforcements than he has now, and Rommel will be getting more. P.M. wonders whether he should send A. a telegram, but fears to hustle him. A.E. had a long talk with Humphrey Butler who has just returned from Cairo, full of information about the battle. He confirmed A.E.'s view that Gott is the best general we've got and says that this is the general opinion of the troops too. But he has never been allowed to do more than a little. Gott had always beaten Rommel when he had met him and believed he had him beat this time too when however he had been ordered to retire.

I'm sure our line should be to concentrate now on Libya and aim at driving the Germans out of Africa by Xmas.

July 23

Auchinleck's attack began yesterday. No real news yet.

July 24

Maisky has delivered Stalin's reply to our last message in which we told him of the decision not to send the next convoy to N. Russia, and not to undertake any combined operation in N. Norway at present but to try and send more through Persia and to hammer away at Rommel. Our message was a long one, his is a short one. Feeling also no doubt the cold water we had previously been obliged to pour on Russian references to an early Second Front in the West, he says we mean neither to send convoys to Russia nor to fight in the West till 1943. He implies our handling of the last convoy was inefficient and wet, viz. the turning back of the escorting battleships and other ships and the order to the convoy to scatter. He refuses to acquiesce in the decision to defer the Second Front. Not an agreeable message, tho' one can understand S.'s feelings at such a ghastly moment for him.

1. These discussions ended in the decision taken on 24 July 1942 to go for Torch.

There is no good arguing our case with him. We shall not convince him.

What can be done more? The convoys at present must be out of the question although in winter with longer nights they should be possible again. The Second Front is the trouble. We shall never persuade the Russians that it cannot be done this year.

The battle in Libya has degenerated into a ding-dong in which we get as many knocks as we give. British generals seem to have a natural bias for this uninspired form of warfare making up for their lack of talent at the expense of the British soldier, like the Passchendales of the last war. The danger is that Rommel can get his reinforcements in fairly quickly, ours (after we have used up the present lot), take months to come. R. has only to hold out, inflict losses on us, then get a fresh reinforcement and go for us again. But I suppose we shall be told that we haven't troops or tanks enough for any encircling operation.

I hear that the Beaver is now constantly closetted with the P.M. at No. 10, Cripps, on the other hand, the leader of the H. of C. complains that he never sees the P.M. at all except in Cabinet and is never consulted: he is getting into a resigning mood.

I wish A.E. would see more of his colleagues. He ought to keep constant touch with Bobbety, Cripps, Lyttelton. For the four together could do more than one alone in influencing the P.M. As it is, the P.M. is apt to go into a huddle with A.E., if with anyone apart from the Beaver, and tho' I think A.E. can do more with him than anyone, it still isn't much. The relation of P.M. to A.E. is father to son and heir, but the others are left out in the cold and there is risk of A.E. becoming himself isolated from his own age group of colleagues. It was the same before when if only he had been in closer touch with some of his colleagues his resignation might have provoked theirs and the Government would have been overthrown. As it was, the colleagues were ill-informed and bewildered. It must not be the same again. Cripps wants a long heart-to-heart with him next week and that is good because C. recognises now, I hear, that he can't be P.M. himself and would willingly work under A.E. but he is an awkward man and if he resigned, it would not help matters. But the four together, with A.E. the leader of them, would be an immensely strong team with a hold over the Left (Cripps and Bevin who would work with A.E.) over the Conservatives (Bobbety) and over the City and business (Lyttelton). But he must weld them and lead them. He sees much of Hardinge, which is good. His relations with the press are close and good. But for his colleagues and the H. of C. he has an invincible distaste.

July 26

The Libya battle has now died down. Another failure. We didn't achieve what we set out to do. We gained only local objectives at heavy cost in men and machines. Rommel remains at the gate of Egypt.

We are having trouble with General Spears,[1] our Minister in Syria, who has succeeded in getting himself complained of by (i) the Syrian President, (ii) the Minister of State, (iii) the British G.O.C., (iv) the Americans and (v) General de Gaulle. He is a hopeless misfit but he is a protégé of the P.M. Any professional diplomat would have been sacked, and rightly, for a third of what he has done.

July 28

P.M. told A.E. last night he wanted him to go to America to discuss the political side of certain future operations with the President. We must agree on a common diplomatic line. It would mean going soon, in spite of the heat, and it is proposed to use post-war problems as cover.

This is a most unexpected development and most opportune. It will enable A.E. to make the contacts he wants in Washington and to exchange views with Roosevelt, Hull and Sumner Welles on the future.

July 29

Auchinleck has attacked again but has had another failure. P.M. and A.E. much depressed. As A.E. said to me, "This war is not being run the way it should be!"

A.E. had a long talk with Cripps on Monday night. Latter thinks the P.M. has outlived his usefulness as P.M. and he has evolved the strange idea that A.E. should be P.M. with Winston as M. of Defence. But it is just as M. of D. that Winston is failing.

Only in the air are we now successful. A fine broadcast by Harris of Bomber Command last night foretelling the increasing destruction of Germany. That is our strong suit. But we are held up because of dissipation of our air forces and because, so A.E. tells me, the American output is not up to expectation and American bombers are being

1. Major-General Sir E. Spears, Minister to Republics of Syria and the Lebanon 1942–1944.

kept back for American pilots who have as yet no night-flying training nor night-flying instruments.

We say too much about the American war effort which at present is modest so far as fighting goes. We give the world the impression that the Americans like the Australians, the New Zealanders etc. etc. are doing everything, ourselves nothing. This is most dangerous. The increasing popular demand not only in Russia but here and in America for a Second Front this year feeds on this false impression.

July 30

The King dined with War Cabinet last night. After he had gone – about 1 a.m. – P.M. suddenly called a Cabinet and announced that he was leaving for Egypt on Friday! All had been arranged, his doctor had agreed and an aeroplane laid on. Everyone was astounded and didn't know what to say. P.M. wishes to look into question of command on the spot. Brooke would go too.

This of course complicates A.E.'s plans for America. Both can't be away at once. P.M.'s trip would take at least 3 weeks, out and back via W. Africa. A.E. has never favoured these trips by P.M. which the country dislikes. But he has opposed him so often and he now feels he had better leave it. At least P.M. seems to be moving in direction of putting Gott in command for which reason he wishes to meet him. It is high time after these repeated failures that sweeping changes were made there, and perhaps this is the best way to do it.

At this point a telegram from Clark-Kerr came, strongly advocating a meeting between Stalin and Winston in view of the Second Front problem. He urges the great risks of leaving Stalin alone at this juncture when the heaviest strains are falling on him. Roosevelt has also telegraphed urging the vital need to *ménager* Stalin as much as possible and not discourage him by flat refusals. All this fits in with the P.M.'s visit to Egypt and A.E. now favours his doing both. He at once went over to see Winston and put it to him and the latter agrees. There is to be a Cabinet at 12.45 to decide. This will much lengthen the absence of the P.M.

Afternoon

It has now been decided that the P.M. should do both. He is to start tomorrow for Egypt, meanwhile to telegraph to Stalin proposing to visit him and to pick up Stalin's reply en route. A.E.'s visit to America must wait. But what energy and gallantry of the old gentleman, setting off at 65 across Africa in the heat of mid-summer!

July 31
A.E. has done his best to prime the P.M. about the generals in Libya
and Gott in particular. He has warned him against the line that "Gott
is so good but he is really rather tired", which is the line the military
opposition may take up. P.M. has himself been much disturbed by
reports his son Randolph has brought back of confusion and in-
competence at G.H.Q.

P.M. starts tomorrow with Alec Cadogan and the C.I.G.S.

August 2
P.M. and Co. got as far as Gibraltar this morning. Stalin has now
replied welcoming the visit and the party are to go to Moscow as
Stalin can't leave. Maisky is going too.

August 3
P.M.'s visit to Russia is announced on the German wireless! Where
the leak came from we are trying to discover. But the Germans seem
to think he has gone to Moscow direct or has even paid the visit. No
mention of Egypt.

August 4
Smuts in Cairo with P.M. too. That will be a steadying influence.

News Chronicle Gallup Poll on who should be P.M. if anything
happened to Winston puts A.E. at 34% and Cripps at 28%. The rest –
Attlee, Beaver, Bevin down in the 3%s. A.E. remarked on the absence
of any Right Winger and wondered how the Kingsley Woods thought
they were going to fare. I said I thought the axis of politics had slipped.
I believed the Labour Party was dying and its leaders realised they
could never form an independent Government. They represented the
steady aristocracy of trades unionists, firm supporters of the capitalist
system, and they had nothing to tempt the younger workers with.
They had failed, unlike the Conservatives, to do anything to rejuvenate themselves. In these conditions it was not surprising that
Bevin should be so anxious to stand in with A.E. now and after the
war. They ought, if parties signified, to be enemies. But Bevin knew
he couldn't stand alone. I thought the truth was that the left half of the
Conservatives and the right half of Labour showed signs of coalescing,
the Conservatives had caught up the laggard Labourites. Like the
Whigs and Tories before the rising Liberals and Radicals, like Conservative and Liberal before Labour, now Conservative and Labour
before Communism were drawing together for protection. The danger

146

is that the new coalition, tho' admirable from A.E.'s point of view, will allow a dangerously extremist opposition to grow up, led by who? Cripps, Aneurin Bevan,[1] Shinwell,[2] Pritt?[3]

August 6
Winant is throwing rather cold water on A.E.'s visit to America to discuss postwar. We are not sure whether this reflects the President's wishes – he is reported, like the P.M., not to be much interested in postwar planning yet. Owing to P.M.'s absence there can be no possibility of his going till September and by then operational reasons may necessitate the visit. I must say I hope so. I'm sure he should visit America soon for domestic political reasons here and for making contacts over there. It doesn't matter much what he is to discuss.

Winant much perturbed at Beaver's activities. He is convinced, and all the many American officers B. is entertaining are convinced, that he is out to down the P.M. in the autumn. With a view to what? An A.E. Government or a Beaver Government, first one and then the other?

August 7
P.M. telegraphed last night his proposals from Cairo. Smuts,[4] the C.I.G.S. and Casey all concur. They are indeed slashing, a massacre of generals, tho' not of innocents. He proposes that the Middle East should be divided up into two, Near East (Egypt, Syria and Palestine) Mid East (Iraq and Persia). Alexander to be C. in C. Near East; Auchinleck Mid-East, Gott to be Army Commander under Alexander, a number of consequential changes involving extensive removals of chiefs of staff and subordinate generals. A.E. told me about it this morning. He is pleased on the whole, especially about Gott. He wonders if Alexander carries brains enough to be C. in C. and whether his well-known fighting qualities won't make him interfere with Gott in the battle. But he is against the division of Mid. East into two, he says it is one zone and has one set of problems, two C. in Cs. would be

1. Aneurin Bevan, M.P. for Ebbw Vale 1929–1962. Later Minister of Health in Attlee's Government.
2. Emanual Shinwell, M.P. later Lord Shinwell. War Minister and Defence Minister in Labour Government after the war.
3. D. N. Pritt, Labour M.P. for Hammersmith 1935–1950, though in fact a Communist.
4. Field Marshal Smuts, Prime Minister and Minister of Defence of South Africa 1939–1948.

THE WAR DIARIES OF OLIVER HARVEY

squabbling all the time. He thinks P.M. only did it with a view to "cushioning" Auck and that Auck should go if he has been a failure. I said Cairo was a sink, it had been so in the last war and it was only when Allenby picked up G.H.Q. and put it in Palestine things got better.[1] I thought Alexander should now do the same.

I think these drastic changes are right, indeed long overdue. We've lost at least three Desert battles now for insufficient reasons. If we are now in difficulties with Soviet Russia over the Second Front, it is because of this. We have suspected for months that Cairo was rotten. I think here Lyttelton, from the Government's point of view, is much to blame. The Government sent him there as a member of War Cabinet to watch it and he should have reported more severely. The trades union of generals is very strong. It has taken three major defeats and a personal visit of the P.M. to break it. Meanwhile the British Army has lost the respect of the Americans, of the Russians and even to some extent of ourselves.

We are on the verge of removing and interning Gandhi. The old fox has us in a fix, he thinks. But after the Cripps offer, however bad our record up till then may have been, he has no excuse and even the Americans have begun to look on him as a hopeless twister. The real problem for Gandhi is the Moslems, not us.

I forgot to mention that A.E. had a minor triumph in the H. of C. last Thursday when he announced his exchange of notes with the Czechs liquidating Munich. "The death of Munich" was the signal for loud cheers from all sides, including most of those who had applauded equally loudly when it had been born.

August 10

I was away from the Office Sat. and Sun. and on returning today learnt the shocking news that Gott had been killed on Friday in an aeroplane crash. But this is something like a national disaster – our only first-class desert general killed like this, on the eve of his recognition and appointment. What frightful luck pursues us! Rapid decisions had to be taken and it is now decided that Montgomery is to be the general to take his place. He has the reputation of being an able and ruthless soldier and an unspeakable cad. However it is the ability and ruthlessness which count, but he has no desert experience. Otherwise the changes so remain, Alexander as C. in C. Mid East and Auck C. in C. Iraq and Persia.

1. Oliver Harvey had served in Cairo during the last part of the first War.

P.M. goes on to Moscow via Tehran today plus Wavell. I expect he will get killed in a crash next.

Gandhi and co. locked up yesterday. Some disturbances. He is not being removed from India.

August 12
A.E. told me he, Attlee and Lyttelton had talked together after Defence Committee last night, much worried over outcome of P.M.'s action in Cairo. Owing to death of Gott, new appointments have got the wrong way round. Alexander should be commanding the battle as the fighting general, and someone else, even old Wilson, should be C. in C. Alex. had fighting qualities but not a strategic mind. Montgomery was admittedly a very fine soldier but had no desert experience, no more than Alexander. To make matters worse the P.M. had written a directive for Alex. full of resounding phrases about destroying Rommel which would encourage Alex. to fight the battle himself and interfere with Montgomery. The two were not likely to get on, they were too much alike. A contrast was wanted, a calm detached, strategic mind as C. in C. and a fighter at the Front. If Gott had lived, such was his experience and prestige in the desert that Alexander would have been less tempted to interfere. But we may be doing Alex. an injustice. He may be much more of a brain than we think. I still think he should now be in command of the battle vice Gott. But this is impossible as he has already been given the larger post.

August 13
Winterton[1] came to see A.E. to-day, worried about the future of the Conservative Party and of the Government. He said he thought P.M. would have to go sooner or later and A.E. should take his place. Was A.E. prepared to do so? A.E. said he would do nothing against Winston, now or ever, and he would be ready to serve under any of his colleagues.

I took him to task rather for this passive attitude, but he said he didn't wish to appear in any way as intriguing. He thought his position was pretty secure in actual fact in the country and also owing to the P.M.'s famous testament which he had left with Alec Hardinge recommending that the King should send for him if anything happened to himself.

I said I thought he might be a little more positive about his position. His enemies and his critics said he wouldn't lead and he was

1. Lord Winterton, M.P. Chancellor of Duchy of Lancaster 1937–39.

weak and imprecise. He should certainly not, when the moment came, agree to serve under anyone of his colleagues. He must then stand out and insist on being P.M. or nothing.

He feels himself he hasn't any serious rival. Cripps no party and no experience, Lyttelton no experience, Anderson ridiculous, Attlee or Bevin unthinkable. He may be right but as I rubbed in, the Party caucus, Kingsley Wood and James Stuart, will work against him, blinded to the interests of the party at the elections by their prejudices against him.

This fits in with a conversation I had yesterday with Ned Grigg, a good friend of A.E.'s too. He said there was much dissatisfaction at A.E.'s alleged lack of leadership. He and the other members of the War Cabinet were all becoming discredited as well as the P.M. If the War Cabinet became discredited, there was no-one left except the Beaver. There were three tendencies in the Conservative Party among young members – one to back O. Lyttelton, another to back O. Stanley, a third to back Cripps.

P.M. in Moscow. He had his first conversation with Stalin within 2 hours of his arrival. He began by explaining why we could not make a second front in France this year. Stalin remained unconvinced but agreed that it was for us to decide. P.M. then spoke of our policy of intensive bombing of Germany, at which Stalin cheered up a little. Finally he brought out our plans for Torch at which Stalin became definitely interested. P.M. and Stalin agreed as to need for earliest possible beginning and as to vast consequences which might ensue from success. S. anxious about effects in France.

A good beginning evidently after a sticky start. P.M. clearly much taken by Stalin. He is installed in a Soviet Government villa in a wood.

August 15
Both Roosevelt and Chiang-Kai-Shek are showing a tendency to intervene in India. Chiang is anxious for American or "United Nations" mediation and an underwriting of the Cripps' offer of independence at the end of the war. This is most distasteful to Winston and indeed to all here. We have made our offer and it stands. Gandhi has tried to twist us into immediate independence. Jinnah, the Moslem says he won't have a Gandhi solution at any price. Rioting is still sporadic and not too serious.

August 17
Long tel. from P.M. giving account of his second encounter with

Stalin. Not nearly so good as the first. Indeed Stalin was most unpleasant and recriminatory, speaking of broken promises and failure over supplies and second front. P.M. took him up firmly and vigorously over this, pointing out that we had fulfilled all our promises and that we had never concealed our views about the Second Front. No suggestion from Stalin of not fighting on.

This stiffening up after the earlier interview was curious. Much the same thing happened when we were in Moscow. P.M. was to have one final dinner alone with Stalin before leaving.

At this final dinner, we now hear, the atmosphere was more cordial and familiar again. It took place in Stalin's private flat and his little daughter appeared. P.M. believes he has established real personal relations with him. The party wasn't over till 2.30 a.m. – hardly unaccustomed for the P.M. – and he left at 5 again by air for Tehran.

August 20
P.M. very anxious to help Russians by air support in S. Caucasus and wishes to build this up as soon as Rommel has been driven back. But Chiefs of Staff here fear this will weaken Torch and so don't like it. It is the old story with the P.M. He can never have one plan and leave it alone. He immediately makes another plan, anticipates the success of the first, and then fatally weakens its chances by preparations for plan 2. High time he came back.

August 22
P.M. getting home on Monday or Tuesday. He has been round the Libyan battlefields. It is clear from his reports that his visit and the changes in command came not a day too soon. A fine old mess there. A disheartened army being messed about by incompetent and un-inspiring commanders. Evidently the spirit of our new generals, Alex and Montgomery, is quite different and already percolating down to the troops. Wilson is being made C. in C. Persia and Iraq – a separate command which may prove important if things go wrong for the Russians in the Caucasus. He is said to be a very wise old general.

August 24
Lunch and talk with A.E. who has been in the country resting for the last week. He had seen Ronnie Tree back from America and been much pleased to hear that what struck him most here was the marked change in A.E.'s position. Six months' ago A.E. was only one of several alternatives; now all agreed, whether they liked it or not, that

he only could succeed Winston. As a consequence all the tadpoles and tapers were turning to him (which I know is true)'

As I have noted, A.E.'s interest in the premiership is increasing all the time. As he said to me, "I feel I could do it now". I said that if the P.M. were suddenly to collapse, I thought all would go smoothly and only he could succeed. But if the P.M. went on and his powers declined, then a very different and complicated situation would arise. A.E. would make no move against him and there would be great opportunities for the Beavers and the rest of the malcontents.

We discussed A.E.'s future speeches. He has been thinking it over on his leave and is now keen to make a series beginning with the Mansion House luncheon at the beginning of September and a big public meeting at the end of it. I said (as I always do) the future belonged to the man who first fired popular imagination about the possibilities of the post-war. Opinion was starving for it.

August 25

P.M. arrived at 11. He kept A.E. and Attlee up till 1.30 telling them about it all.

A.E. had previously had a most useful dinner with Bobbety who was most sympathetic to his ideas. He too spoke of the importance of drawing the younger men together as a nucleus for a future party – R. A. Butler, Lyttelton (who might otherwise go back to the City and would make a good Chancellor of Exchequer); he undertook to tackle Oliver Stanley himself, and hold out hopes for the future; he thought they should work with Labour (Bevin and Co.) and leave the opposition to the Communists. This is also an idea of A.E.'s. When he recounted this, I said I thought it was right. Labour was so conservative and he A.E. so progressive that the two could never make a two-party system between them. Labour was losing their supporters in the country and it would be natural and normal for a Communist Party to arise now, especially after our alliance with Moscow, which would again constitute a real opposition to the Labour-Conservative group.

All this is most encouraging. I'm delighted at A.E.'s new zeal for politics. All due to a week off.

Visit from Sam Hoare today, just back on leave, very affable. Long talk about Spain. Franco régime loathed by all except office-holders and Falange gunmen, but no one dares to overthrow it yet for fear of bringing Germans in. Chaotic conditions in the country with 400,000 politicals in gaol. Sam thinks the only hope is a sort of General

1942

Monck regency to bring in the young King. I wonder! I still believe
the future belongs to our Republican friends who alone would fight
for us and whose stock must rise with the victory of the democracies.
All now, however, hate the Germans who infest the country.

August 27
Spears is busy bedevilling our relations with de Gaulle and the
Syrians in the Middle East. The P.M. alone sticks up for him. De
Gaulle is difficult enough in all conscience but that is one more reason
for having a skilled and tactful diplomat to handle him.

Torch is a great confusion. P.M. has begged A.E. to go to Chequers
tomorrow night when C.I.G.S. and U.S. Generals will be there to
straighten it out, namely where the landings are to be and how many
and how soon. It is very difficult to make plans on two sides of the
Atlantic and expect them to coincide. We are in favour of two prongs
– U.S. think they will only have enough for one. We don't like the
E. prong without the W. Behind and above all this are Winston and
Roosevelt goading each other on to fix dates etc. while all is vague.
And the American sailors don't like this war in the West so much as
the Pacific and want to starve it.

August 28
More obstruction over the publication of our British Diplomatic
Documents. A.E. recently again circulated a paper to the Cabinet
urging publication and contradicting Simon's specious arguments for
indefinite postponement. Now Kingsley Wood pipes up in another
paper and urges more delay but particularly because of the infamous
Horace Wilson record of Munich which it contains and should contain.

I hear the P.M. was much shocked in Cairo by the slovenly dress of
the Generals – all in shorts cut like ballet dancers' skirts and open-neck
shirts and no sleeves, in which they went out to dinner! He gave
orders at once for this to be stopped. I also hear that Alexander has
already moved G.H.Q. into the desert – like Allenby did in the last
war.

August 30
Week-end at Binderton with the Edens. Dill there on leave from
Washington where he represents us on the Joint Staff Mission. Dill has
high regard for Marshall[1] and the American soldiers and complains

1. General George C. Marshall, U.S. Chief of Staff 1939–1945.

153

that our soldiers here crab them too much. The American sailors more difficult than the soldiers, especially King who only wants to fight the war in the Pacific and to denude the Atlantic.

A.E. didn't arrive down till late from Chequers where P.M. and he had discussed Torch with C.I.G.S. and Eisenhower.[1] Rather inconclusively as Roosevelt hasn't yet replied to P.M.'s message asking that date of Oct. 14 be fixed and that decision be taken to do Algiers and Oran,[2] even if Casablanca is dropped.

We discussed it with Dill who told me "he hated it". He would prefer to concentrate in Egypt and Persia against German threats to the pipeline. The Americans, he said, both Marshall and Eisenhower, still prefer Sledgehammer[3] on the ground that operation, though difficult, is nearer home and our resources and reserves, which wouldn't be diminished by distant overseas commitment, and it would inevitably make Germany fight in the air. But nobody seems to think it likely that we could stay there and the last thing we can stand is another Dunkirk. But Torch, as D. says, is a very great gamble but with enormous stakes if successful – whole of North Africa in our hands.

P.M. had wanted to go and see Roosevelt but A.E. tried to dissuade him by offering to go himself.

If Torch fails, we are clearly in a frightful mess. P.M. has now promised Stalin that it shall be done – he is personally engaged. But it is very necessary that the plan should be studied from all angles and by the War Cabinet, which hasn't yet been done. Much will depend on the position in the Western Desert where Rommel (or his successor) is expected to attack very shortly. If we could defeat R., then the way would be open for Torch.

August 31
Rommel attacked this morning. No more news so far.

Meanwhile Roosevelt has replied to P.M. He thinks the two first landings must be entirely American as the French will be then less likely to attack. These should be Casablanca and Oran. He wants to do both sides at once and to establish communications across behind the mountains. Then he thinks the British should come in *a week*

1. General Eisenhower, Allied Commander in North Africa, later Supreme Commander SHAEF.
2. The Western Prong.
3. Plan for landing at Brest and Cherbourg in 1942.

later and go further East, i.e. Algiers and work eastwards. Difficulty is shipping for all three and this he promises to look into.

A.E. doesn't care for this plan at all. First of all, Americans will only have two divisions and that is not enough. Secondly, the British would have the dangerous end at Algiers and the Germans would have a week's warning to prepare. Algiers and still more Tunis are well within bombing range from Sardinia and Sicily. He has no belief in the acquiescence of French N. Africa in American landings. He wants three simultaneous landings with mixed forces.

September 1
Personal reply sent back to President urging risks of delay till November which changes may involve, and expressing strong preference for simultaneous assaults at Casablanca, Oran & Algiers as well as for mixed Anglo–American forces at each.

September 2
We hear P.M.'s heart is bad again. Sir C. Wilson[1] has said he really mustn't fly Atlantic again.

September 3
Roosevelt has now replied to P.M. about Torch. Not unsatisfactory, I think. He acquiesces in three simultaneous landings at Casablanca, Oran & Algiers, but with American troops only in first assault. The British would be in the background and come in for "follow up". He insists on his belief that French in N. Africa won't fight U.S. troops provided there are no British nor de Gaullists about. This assumption (which we don't share) is of course most important and would make whole difference to chances of operation. As Americans are not to be shaken in their faith in Vichy and its affection for America, it is best, I think, that the plan should be tried, as they suggest, in the circumstances most favourable to the American assumption. If the N. African French then do resist the U.S. troops, the eyes of the Americans will be opened. If, contrary to our view, they don't resist, then all the better.

Luncheon to American soldiers at Guildhall yesterday. A.E. cheered in the streets going and coming which pleased him very much. "That is where my strength lies, among the people."

1. Sir Charles Wilson, later Lord Moran, the Prime Minister's personal physician.

September 4 and 5
Before I left, (on leave) reply had been sent by P.M. to President accepting his revised plan, subject to adjustment of numbers for different landings, and party of admirals and generals concerned were going over to Washington to discuss final details.

Meanwhile Rommel's offensive for once seems to have been a failure and to-day, according to wireless, he is withdrawing slightly. So the first round goes to the new generals. I hope now we may attack soon.

September 14
Germans are on the N. Russian convoy again. 10 ships air-torpedoed today by a mass attack, 10 out of 40. But in Egypt the war goes better, Rommel having been heavily knocked in his last attack. The whole spirit different there. Also the Torch plans now seem reasonably settled and sound.

P.M. is becoming very exclusive again. No defence committees and nothing told to the War Cabinet. Cripps complained bitterly that he is told nothing.

A.E. mentioned the trouble he is having with Attlee over the future of Colonies. Attlee wants to internationalise them altogether, including international administration. A.E. and Bobbety favour national administration under the supervision and responsibility of an international authority – which will see to defence, economics etc.

Spears still a problem in Syria where he and de Gaulle have had a fine old row.[1] If only de Gaulle had controlled himself, we could have got Spears out by now thanks to the complaints we have received from all sides. But de G. has played into his hands and put more than enough rope round his own neck to hang himself with. De G. has now agreed to come home. We have told him we had intended to discuss handing over Madagascar to him but his attitude in Syria had made this extremely difficult. Once we get him back we can lead him back into sense again. But Spears, as the P.M.'s protégé, remains.

P.M. very dissatisfied with Grigg at W.O., I hear. He is right. He has been a failure, but so would any S. of S. for War who wasn't a superman. P.M. leaves him no position owing to his direct control of the war and direct dealings with C.I.G.S. (which are confidential to a large extent even from his Minister).

Great dissatisfaction at Cripps' leadership of House. He beat them

1. De Gaulle had threatened to force the British out of French territory, and demanded that control of Allied troops be put in French hands.

up the other day because they wouldn't stay on and make or listen to more speeches after the P.M. had made his. But it was just what the Government wanted. As Shinwell said "We are beaten up for not beating up the Government!" Added to this, Cripps himself is so dissatisfied with his position or lack of position in the councils of the P.M. that A.E. thinks he might walk out. If he did, and if the leadership were offered to A.E. now, he would take it, he says, but whilst keeping F.O. which he regards as essential if he is to keep his hold over policy. He is right, I'm sure. The leadership means less speech-making than I had thought when it came up before and I think now he could and should do both.

September 15
Winant told A.E. today that Roosevelt wanted him to return for a short leave about Thanksgiving Day and W. thought it would be a good idea for A.E. to go too. The elections would just be over.

September 17
A drive is being made, I'm glad to say, to intensify our bombing over Germany this winter. P.M. has appealed to Roosevelt to increase the American effort (which has not come up to promises given).

Madagascar operations proceeding well, at last almost a walk-over.[1] P.M. very tiresome over it, anxious to make terms with Anet, the Vichy Governor, and keep de Gaulle out. But Anet is unreliable and "wet". We could never trust any terms he signed; he would remain Vichy's man. Also we are practically committed to handing it over sooner or later to de G.

P.M., as always blinded by his passions to his interests, now hates de Gaulle. But he is increasingly difficult to deal with in such matters, fussing over little points, reopening questions, up one day down the next.

Maisky is being very active, rather improperly so, over the Second Front. He sees English and American journalists continually, disparaging our efforts and implying that we have run out on our promises. This we have never done. Whether Stalin agrees with our views or not, and he probably does not, we have never concealed from his our resources and our intentions. It is the Russians who have never taken *us* into their confidence over plans or methods.

1. In August, having failed to reach agreement with the Vichy Governor, the British Government had decided to occupy the whole island.

Maisky here and Litvinov in America are doing all they can to play us off against America. Maisky may feel he is under a cloud in Moscow because Stalin refused to allow him to accompany the P.M.'s party and summoned his counsellor Novikoff instead. (N. has never since been heard of!) When Cadogan mentioned Maisky to Stalin, the latter in fact looked as if he had never heard of him.

September 18
Anet, the Governor of Madagascar, has rejected our armistice terms and asks for conditions permitting of communication with Vichy, maintenance of Anet himself and his official administration, and "confidence in Vichy". Our operations are therefore proceeding. But what impudence! Confidence in Vichy means confidence in Laval (and in Hitler).

We discussed the future in the Office in view of the P.M.'s well known yearning after appeasement with Vichy. We all agreed that we were in any case practically committed to handing over the administration to de Gaulle, that de G.'s shares in France are rising with the resistance provoked by the Vichy Govt.'s handling of the Jewish question and that of labour conscription for Germany and that we should be wise to do nothing to discourage the Gaullist elements in France by such a snub as keeping him out of Madagascar. As for Torch, to put de G. into Madagascar was as likely to encourage capitulation in N. Africa as the reverse. The Americans could be counted on to make it clear to the French in N. Africa that they would not give it over to de Gaulle. If of course the French nonetheless resisted, this might bring de G. back again into the picture. Finally, to accept any terms leaving Anet in charge at Madagascar would mean that we could never withdraw troops and be sure against treachery – in fact the whole operation would have been unnecessary.

The Americans are determined to work with Vichy and Pétain if possible. Murphy,[1] their representative in N. Africa, has come over here in the greatest secrecy to confer with Eisenhower. I hear M. is moderately confident that although the naval guns in the harbours will go off, the soldiers will not offer much fight. The Americans have hopes of Giraud[2] and are in touch with him. I wonder how well founded these hopes will prove. I have no faith in old French generals.

1. Robert D. Murphy, U.S. Consul in Algiers became the President's special representative in N. Africa 1942–1943.
2. General Giraud had escaped to North Africa from a German POW camp in April.

September 20

We are running into difficulties with America over India. Opinion there was none too pleased with Winston's flat-footed statement in the H. of C. last week. The Americans were never too sure that the Cripps offer was genuine, or that if genuine, it was not wrecked by the die-hards from London. They have never been persuaded of the complexity of the problem and even Roosevelt clearly thinks we could do more and better. Winston has now convinced them of their fears. Halifax, who is wise about India, is clearly worried too and thinks Winston is mishandling it. Winston has a bad history over India: he led the diehards against the India Act and feels fiercely against Halifax personally for his part in it. And Amery is scarcely a help. The Labour Party are said to be none too happy. Nor should they be, though I suppose Attlee agreed to the Cabinet policy. But the blunt truth is we must get India straight ourselves or others will come and do it for us. Public opinion here, I suspect, is not much stirred about India and is certainly not in favour of repression. People here are tired of India and would thankfully welcome a settlement which would take it off their hands. It is no reply to the Americans, tempting as it is, that we can teach them how to look after their negroes. They are Hamiltonian at home and Jeffersonian abroad, and they see no inconsistency.

September 21

A.E. was at Chequers for the night for a conference with American generals. There is again question of the P.M. or A.E. going over to Washington shortly to reason the Americans out of the general stoppage which they have put on supplies of aircraft, troops or ships for the U.K. pending Torch. No more U.S. troops are to come here, no more aeroplanes. They have even given up building landing craft for us. A.E. is not keen to go at this moment on the eve of elections and on such subjects. But P.M. seems not very well. He is inditing a message to Roosevelt.

September 22

P.M. still being very difficult about admitting de Gaulle to Madagascar. The General is arriving from Syria on Thursday and he is then to be seen by the P.M. We hope that after the usual explosion there will be the usual reconciliation. But P.M. is very scratchy about him, hotted up by Spears' telegrams and the soldiers. I'm pretty certain that if A.E. can deal with him, he will reduce the General to sense over Syria, and we ought then to get him admitted to Madagascar. We ought to put him in quickly, getting Legentilhomme appointed for the purpose, well in advance of Torch. If only the General had not been such a fool as to behave as he did in Cairo and Syria (and as Charles Peake had begged him not to behave) his man would already have been on the way there.

Anglo–Russian relations are very sore at present. The Russians are distressed at our action in holding up certain aeroplanes which were to have gone there by convoy. The aeroplanes (which were American) were withdrawn at Eisenhower's request because of "Torch" requirements. But they will be still more cross when they hear we can't send any more convoys at all to N. Russia because of lack of shipping and escorts during Torch.

A.E. was called over to P.M. this evening and afterwards told me that there were Government changes in prospect. First of all, the Viceroyalty – the P.M. was thinking of sending Anderson there; secondly, Cripps was disgruntled and had written a letter to say so, the P.M. was thinking of offering him Anderson's work as L. Pres. of C.; thirdly, the leadership of H. of C., the P.M. was thinking of offering it to Oliver Stanley.[1] A.E.'s first reaction to the first was to press strongly Roger Lumley's[2] claims. The P.M. didn't know him but undertook to speak to Amery about him. As regards Cripps, he was inclined to think he had made up his mind to go altogether; the P.M. didn't think it would greatly matter if he did. As to the leadership, A.E. said he would be willing to take it on himself if he could have a deputy Foreign Secretary, i.e. Dick Law.

A.E. was to see the P.M. again after dinner and discuss this further. What did Dick Law and I think? I said I thought emphatically that it would be a great mistake to appoint Anderson Viceroy and not Lumley. A. was old and would arouse no enthusiasm in this country, still less in America, at a time when our handling of India was of enormous importance. Roger was young, of the most actual Indian experience, an associate of A.E.'s: he would be welcomed as a sign of a new deal there. Old A., even tho' no diehard, would be regarded as such. We were both dead against O. Stanley being given the leadership: it was another move by the Whips Office against A.E. and should be resisted. A.E. should insist on leading if it fell vacant. As for Cripps we felt it wouldn't matter if he left now. I said I thought he would

1. Oliver Stanley had been President of the Board of Trade in Chamberlain's Government, and Minister for War.
2. Later Lord Scarbrough. He had been Governor of Bombay.

make a good leader of the Opposition, better than Greenwood or Shinwell, and for the future working of Parliament it was necessary to think of this. We didn't want the future Opposition to be led by Pritt. A.E. said Winston favoured letting Cripps go, but he A.E. would be reluctant to lose him as he was an ally; but if he went, then he would try to get Bobbety into the War Cabinet. A.E. said that when he sees the P.M. again tonight, he would stake out his claim for the leadership. A.E. added that if Bobbety came into War Cabinet and vacated C.O. (which he said Bobbety wanted to do) then he wouldn't object to Stanley being given that.

The Beaver has been closeted with the P.M. and who knows what he is advising!

September 23
A.E. told me of last night's elucubrations with the P.M., the Beaver also being there. P.M. had shown him his reply to Cripps' letter; it was friendly and A.E. was satisfied with it, but he is pretty sure Cripps means to go. The P.M. had agreed that A.E. should have the leadership if he went, and A.E. had asked that Dick Law should be given more authority to enable him to take more F.O. work off his shoulders (the Beaver strongly backed this – "he is the son of my best friend[1]") and the P.M. had agreed to this also. About the Viceroy, A.E. said he was convinced that the appointment of Anderson would be as big a flop as sending H. to Washington. The P.M. turned to the Beaver who laughed and agreed. P.M. said he thought A. would be reliable and "safe". As regards Stanley, the idea came up of making him deputy leader of H. of C. to A.E., the latter said he wouldn't mind this. The alternative suggestion was Duff, which A.E. would also welcome. Finally A.E. had urged the P.M. to take Bobbety into the War Cabinet which the P.M. had taken fairly well, tho' he thought he suspected A.E. was trying to map out the key positions with his own men (Roger Lumley the other) and it would make things more difficult for him in the Cabinet.

A.E. was fairly happy with all this. I said I thought the Stanley proposal bad, as S. would have great opportunities in the H. of manoeuvring opinion and acquiring virtue for himself as No. 2 there. The stout Duff would be much better. If S. had to be given a post, he would surely be better in Bobbety's place at C.O. (if Bobbety gave it up and went into War Cabinet), where he would be fully and usefully occupied. I think A.E. was impressed and he may speak again to

1. Andrew Bonar Law, Prime Minister 1923.

P.M. He is satisfied however that the Whips had had nothing to do with it. The P.M. had said they didn't yet know that any changes were in view. The idea we think came from Bracken, a great friend of O.S.

A.E. is going to have a word with Bevin tonight – with P.M.'s authority. Unfortunately Bobbety is away today or he would have seen him.

Dick is much impressed with the idea of Cripps leading the Opposition, having in view the future ordering of parties. This is my view too – a National Tory–Labour party on one side, and a redder Socialist–Communist party on the other.

September 25

Jim Thomas came up last evening. Bobbety also came up and had a word with A.E. Jim was very much opposed to Stanley at any price as deputy leader: he said he was incapable of loyalty and would do infinite harm. Nor was he much in favour of Duff for the post either because of his unpopularity in the country. But why, he said, have a deputy at all? If A.E. is to have a deputy Foreign Secretary and then deputy leader of H. of C. as well, it will be ridiculous and everyone will laugh. Let there be no deputy leader but if A.E. has to be away, then Duff can take it on temporarily without any special title. This sounds sense. We all foregathered with A.E. after dinner – Dick, Jim and myself. A.E. told us it was practically settled that Anderson should go to India; he had got no support for the Lumley idea. P.M. had agreed that he, A.E., should have leadership and that Dick should be assistant Foreign Secretary here. We put to him Jim's point about no deputy leader, and he agreed. He decided to have a further word with the P.M. that night to clinch all this.

This morning he told us P.M. agreed about no deputy leader and also that if Bobbety went into War Cabinet it would be a good idea for Stanley to have C.O. Meanwhile Cripps was still with them and it looked more as if he meant to stay on.

September 26

A.E.'s speech at Leamington on Saturday with its references to future world order went well. But how cautious and timid he is when speaking of postwar, as hesitating as he is bold and certain when speaking of foreign affairs. We push and push and each time get him a little way but the time has long come for a big bold lead and damn the consequences. 1 want him to take the wind out of the sails of F.D.R. and

Wallace[1] and Perkins[2] but he still gives the impression of lagging behind.

September 28
Long talk tonight with Toby Martin. He doesn't agree with my view of a compact Communist opposition arising. He says Labour is too divided, no cohesion even among extreme Left and Cripps would not be welcome to them. Rooted mistrust of Labour for any class but their own prevents their using or trusting any one such as Cripps. Pritt likewise has no influence in H. of C.

T. thought the P.M.'s position much weaker now and personally he thought it would be better that he should now go, especially because of his resistance to planning for the future. He had heard Cripps was wobbly but thought he couldn't go just yet owing to his recent gaffe in H. of C. He rather questioned whether A.E. would be next P.M. rather than Cripps, which surprised me. I said C. was without party and without experience, a too unstable star to lead but very useful in Cabinet.

The Anglo–American war effort is having its full share of teething troubles. The American machine in Washington is not coordinated as ours now is – the War Department are supreme and demand this and that for an enormous American army which can never be shipped out of America, so upsetting production of tanks and aircraft for the forces now fighting or ready to fight in Europe. Departments in Washington are free and uncontrolled and the strongest takes what it wants and the rest what they can get. This doesn't suit us at all because we have severely rationalised our own production and our effort depends on this being integrated with American production, e.g. we make more fighters, they make more tanks and bombers. Again, the Americans in the Middle East find us haughty and unapproachable (which may be true), though those here find they like us very well. Willkie gave a disturbing account to Clark-Kerr in Moscow when he was there on his recent trip to the Middle East, Russia and China, of the dislike which all the Americans he met, of whatever sort, expressed for us.

October 1
De Gaulle had his long awaited interview with the P.M. yesterday. It couldn't have gone worse. A.E. was there and de Gaulle brought

1. Henry Wallace, Vice-President of U.S. 1941–1945.
2. Frances Perkins, U.S. Secretary of Labour 1933–1945.

Pleven.[1] De Gaulle was stiff and rude and arrogant, the P.M. was frank but patient. De Gaulle, if he had handled the P.M. right, could have got anything out of him. As it was, the P.M. said he was sorry for the man, he was such a fool. A.E. said afterwards he had never seen anything like it in the way of rudeness since Ribbentrop. Blank refusal to budge over Syrian questions,[2] insistence on our evil motives as proved by Madagascar. Behind all this stands the sinister influence of that charlatan Spears who has said "he is out to smash de Gaulle".

A deadlock but it must be removed. Yet even A.E. is discouraged by de G.'s behaviour. Palewsky[3] came to see me, and Henry Hopkinson saw de Gaulle's A.D.C., both very worried and anxious to know what the next step is to be. The General they said was *ulcéré* because he considered the P.M. had insulted him. We had an office discussion with A.E. who eventually agreed that Moley should see Dejean,[4] make it clear what exactly did pass at P.M.'s meeting because it seemed probable that both de Gaulle and Pleven were too excited to have taken clear note, and then suggest that the diplomats on both sides ought to get together and work out some proposal for settlement, linking up Syria with Madagascar.

Cripps came round to see A.E. this evening and told him that he had seen the P.M. last night about his letter. They had had quite a row. Cripps complained that he had only seen the P.M. once since the India visit; he knew nothing of what was going on; the Government machine was working badly, no planning, no coordination. This is of course exactly what A.E. and I have so often said. P.M. had accused him of trying to upset the Government and said he must have an answer as to whether he was going or staying within 24 hours.

Cripps was not disposed to go on. He said the Beaver was at the back of all this, poisoning the P.M.'s mind against him. He could now go into opposition or he might take on another job, such as coordination of Ministry of Supply work in Washington, where he would no longer be responsible for conduct of the war.

The question is how far Cripps' going now would upset the Government. He can certainly make a most damaging speech about the way Winston conducts business, and a most justified one. The

1. René Pleven, later French Prime Minister 1950–1951.
2. I.e. holding of elections or transferring some of the administration into Syrian hands.
3. Gaston Palewski, de Gaulle's *Chef de Cabinet*.
4. Maurice Dejean, French National Commissioner for Foreign Affairs 1940–1942.

pity is the opportunity can't be taken by the War Cabinet as a whole to make a frontal attack on the old man and the old system. But the P.M. is what he is and nothing will change his method in running the war. It always comes back to the same thing.

A.E. is uneasy himself because he agrees with much of Cripps' criticism. He says he feels like Halifax when A.E. came to resign. He thinks the P.M. foolish to try and force C. out. He is going to see Attlee and also the P.M. himself tonight.

October 2

A.E. had a busy night. He first saw Attlee, who was going to dine with P.M., and then he went across to No. 10 and joined them afterwards. He found the P.M. in a great state of anger, rolling out threats and invectives against C. and declaring it was a conspiracy. A.E. set about calming him and reasoning with him. When Winston started shouting, A.E. said "I thought we were fighting the Germans!" He said he must see that Cripps had a case and that it really was not a conspiracy. A.E. finally persuaded him, and it was no small business, that he should not try and drive C. out but should offer him either the Washington Supply job or the M.A.P. Lyttelton had joined them by this time and was apparently ready to have him at Ministry of Aircraft Production where Llewellyn had proved a failure. Then Cripps was summoned to No. 10 and seen by A.E. and Attlee in another room. C. finally agreed to think it over and was to see the P.M. again this morning. It was also urged that if he did agree, the change should be postponed for another month (until Torch had started) when the other changes will be made.

This morning A.E. feels more strongly than ever that it would be a mistake to let C. go out of the Government and that he was right to urge him to accept another post. He also feels as strongly that he must not go now on the eve of Torch. The P.M. himself said last night "if Torch fails, then I'm done for and must go and hand over to one of you."

What I can't understand is that Cripps, disagreeing with conduct of the war, as well he might, should yet be prepared to accept another post under the Government. His duty as a political leader in such a case is to go into opposition. However that is his affair. Meanwhile Attlee is objecting strongly to Anderson as Viceroy. He prefers R. A. Butler to Roger Lumley.

More talks this afternoon. Cripps to see A.E. to whom he said he was still undecided. A.E. pressed him strongly to defer everything for a month. C. asked if A.E. would then join with him in insisting on a change of method. A.E. declined to promise because, as he said to me afterwards, he couldn't enter into a bargain about this.

A.E. then saw P.M. again. Latter was very cross as he had been woken up in his afternoon sleep and inclined to go back on last night's offer. However, it has now been left that C. is to make up his mind whether he stays or goes by tomorrow. I hear he has a further grievance over the P.M.'s last Indian statement. C. did not approve it but the P.M., when he showed it to Attlee, said C. did approve it. This is pretty bad however it may be explained.

In the midst of all this the de Gaulle row rolls on. Dejean saw Moley this morning and had a satisfactory conversation. Moley said that after Wednesday's conversation it was not possible for the S. of S. to resume conversations with the General; they might be resumed on a lower official level. Dejean said the General, who was now in a much calmer frame of mind, was ready for this and would in fact agree to meet us over various Syrian points. Moley undertook to refer this to S. of S. and A.E. is speaking to P.M. If this is now agreed, common sense conversations can begin next week in the department. If once the professionals can get hold of this again and the prima donnas are kept out of the ring, we shall soon reach agreement. And Spears must go. As he is a politician, this means he must be found another job.

My own conviction has never wavered that we should put de G. into Madagascar as soon as possible, not only because of de Gaulle, to whom we practically promised it, but because it is to our advantage to do so. Only if Madagascar is in Free French hands can we be secure against treachery there, and only thus can we disprove French suspicion, which is ingrained, that we mean to keep it ourselves. But de Gaulle makes all this none too easy for us, whilst on our side things are made even more difficult by the multiplicity of busybodies who have a finger in this business: Desmond Morton[1] at No. 10, who has enthusiasm without wisdom and hots up the P.M., Spears, who is carrying out his own policy to smash de Gaulle, and our soldiers in the Middle East, who prefer to fraternise with our enemies, the Vichy people, to making friends with our allies, the Free French, and finally, certain ante-diluvians on the spot, who really would like to paint the map red. However we shall get it right in time, much as we got Abyssinia right which has been perfectly quiet since we got the Emperor in and our blimps out.

1. Sir Desmond Morton, Personal assistant to Winston Churchill 1940–1946.

October 5

A.E. told me today that Cripps had consented on Saturday to stay on as he is *pro tem* because of Torch. He had written P.M. a letter, expressing his dissatisfaction with the way in which things were done but saying that in the national interest he agreed to remain on for the present. P.M. has accepted this, and so all is closed till after Torch.

The Free French conversations have been making rapid progress between the F.O. and Dejean, General de Gaulle being kept out of the picture. A stern warning has been issued to Cabinet Ministers to mind their own business and not meddle in Free French affairs.

Stalin has sent an appeal to Winston and Roosevelt for more fighters, offering if necessary to go without tanks.

October 7

The de Gaulle business is still going well. P.M. has approved the course of the discussions and we are to begin now discussing Madagascar. A slightly tiresome element is the arrival of Bill Astor with violent pro-Spears opinions who has rushed to impart them to the ever-ready Morton.

The P.M. suddenly suggested to Lord Beaverbrook the day before last that he, B., should go to Moscow and explain our difficulties and problems to Stalin. B., correctly, telephoned A.E. (it was the first he had heard of it) to say he had refused.

Meanwhile great discussion between here and Washington as to the terms of the message to Stalin regarding future convoys and supplies. We propose to tell S. frankly that we cannot send another convoy till Torch is over and that meanwhile we will try and sail through single ships with volunteer crews. Roosevelt wants not to say this but to hedge and try and send very small convoys.

October 9

Beaverbrook came to see A.E. last night to tell him about the P.M.'s suggestion that he should go to Moscow. P.M. was hunting about for someone to send and mentioned Lyttelton and then A.E. himself and when Beaverbrook said he didn't think the first would do or A.E. could be spared from here, P.M. suggested that B. should go himself and told him to talk it over with A.E. B. made it quite clear to P.M. he didn't wish to go.

B. then went on to talk to A.E. about the future here. He said the P.M. was a "bent" man and couldn't be expected to last long. He had not been the same since his last journey. The future belonged to A.E.

"but be careful of the Tory Party. Don't be too hard on them. Say what you like about the brave new world, but don't talk too much about controls after the war."

A.E. was much intrigued and amused by this conversation and he asked me what I thought was the B.'s motive, which baffled him. I said I thought he had been looking round to see who would be the successor to Winston and found that A.E. was the best runner. He hated Cripps. He wishes therefore to pose as A.E.'s patron and backer, and then no doubt when A.E. became P.M., he would hope to run him.

October 13
Maisky has been behaving in a very odd and indeed alarming way. After speaking to all and sundry in and out of season to urge the opening of a Second Front, he is now letting it be known equally widely that no operations *outside Europe* would count as a Second Front. Finally, he has just told Cummings of the *News Chronicle*, who told Philip Jordan, who properly passed it on at once to the security authorities, all the details of Torch. This is extremely serious, hazarding as it might the lives of thousands. Has he gone off his head? Is he acting on instructions to do his utmost to wreck Torch, so that we may revert to Round-up[1] early next year which Torch would prevent?

October 15
A.E.'s interest in postwar questions is increasing steadily. We have on the stocks two important papers – one proposing adoption of the Four Power Plan for running the world after the war (England, America, Russia and China) and one dealing with colonial and Far Eastern questions in the sense of placing such areas as the Far East, Africa, the Caribbean, under regional councils responsible for pooled defence, economy and planning on which all the States holding territory there would sit, whilst leaving local administration in the hands of the existing authority, i.e. not internationalisation of colonial administration but international supervision. A.E. intended to discuss these with P.M. and Smuts over weekend and if they can be approved, we can then get on with discussing them with the Americans and the Russians.

A.E. has at last sensed the public need for post war planning. The chief obstacle remains the P.M.

1. Plan for liberating France in 1943.

October 16

A.E. saw Maisky yesterday and spoke to him severely about the leakage as regards Torch and his spreading about that only a Second Front in Europe would count. Maisky denied hotly that he had ever done either. It was a painful and awkward interview and A.E. doesn't know what to make of it. Maisky said sinister influences were at work and were spreading stories about him, as for instance that he was being moved.

The Free French questions are making good progress as between Carlton Gardens and the F.O. both on Syria and on Madagascar. On the former the solution we have worked out and regard as satisfactory is now being questioned by the Minister of State, Casey and by Moyne. Neither of these is well qualified in such matters and both have taken to the spell of Spears who works ceaselessly to wreck Anglo–Free French relations.

October 18

I was away yesterday and came back today to find a fresh crisis has arisen in Free French affairs. De Gaulle, fed up at delays over Madagascar and encouraged by something Morton had said to Palewsky (whom he had no business to see) which made him believe we weren't serious over Syria or Madagascar, had sacked Dejean and appointed Pleven instead as Commissioner for Foreign Affairs. Catroux[1] from Syria had also reported to him against the Syrian proposals – here I suspect the handiwork of Spears. So all the fat is in the fire again!

De Gaulle is nearly impossible. If we had the exclusive handling of him, we might get the thing to work. If all these Spears and Mortons are going to take a hand, it is impossible. Anyway Morton has had his head washed for interfering. I'm very sorry about Dejean. He has acted admirably throughout, fearlessly and faithfully in the true interests of the Free French movement. De Gaulle shows himself a fool to part with him.

But a formidable and important development has also taken place over Torch. Murphy, the U.S. representative in N. Africa, has just reported that he has been approached by an emissary on behalf of Giraud and Darlan[2] as they expect to be attacked by Germany and he has disclosed to them the Torch idea but not the date. As a result an

1. General Catroux, Free French Delegate-General Syria and Lebanon 1941–1943.
2. Admiral Darlan was Vice-President of the Council, Minister for Foreign Affairs and of the Interior in the Vichy Government. He was also C-in-C of Vichy French forces.

urgent Chiefs of Staff meeting took place last night. P.M., Smuts and A.E. returned from Chequers to London and Eisenhower was also there. It was decided to send the American general Clark[1] off to Algiers in a submarine to see the emissary and convince him of the imminence of Torch and its overwhelming strength.

I shall hear more tomorrow from A.E. but this is all I know at the moment. I don't feel easy about it. I don't trust Darlan when he says he wants to be with us again. I have little faith in the American diplomats who are handling Vichy and N. Africa. They are much too soft where Vichy is concerned. The P.M. too is much too eager to grasp after these alluring but unsubstantial prospects when they fit in with what he wants. Anyway Roosevelt means that Torch shall figure as an all-American operation and the part of the Royal Navy in getting it there and of the British troops who will follow it up, is going to be severely played down.

October 19

P.M., to whom A.E. handed a copy of his paper on Four Power post-war policy on Friday, has sent a foolish and denigrating minute, hoping that such matters be left to those who have nothing else to do. Unfortunately the three, the P.M., Smuts and A.E., weren't able to have the discussion about it I had hoped. Torch affairs intervened and they talked of little else. A.E. is much annoyed at this further example of the P.M.'s blockading of postwar questions and means to send a firm reply. We must get on with this.

October 21

Darlan is reported to have gone to Algiers. Here presumably he will now see the American general Clark. A.E. is very dubious of all this. He fears that Darlan will seek to delay the attack; he warned the P.M. and Chiefs of Staff of the danger of this. But, as he said to me, Winston was so excited by the prospect that he was already half way up the road from Marseilles to Paris.

De Gaulle affairs calmer again. We propose to hold our course of 1) Syrian settlement and then 2) Madagascar to Free French. The first was practically settled with Dejean and we have the P.M.'s approval to discuss Madagascar with Legentilhomme[2] as de Gaulle's

1. General Mark Clark was Chief of Staff U.S. Ground forces in Europe 1942, and later Commander of the U.S. 5th Army.
2. General P. Legentilhomme had commanded the Allied Forces in Syria which had taken Damascus in 1941.

governor and date of arrival for first or second week of November. If Pleven or de Gaulle wish to reopen Syria, then we hold up Madagascar, otherwise not.

October 22
France is clearly boiling up for a crisis. The Germans are becoming rougher with Laval as his failure to get labour for Germany is obvious. He, for his part, reiterates appeals, threats and bribes to the French who are stubbornly unresponsive. It looks as if the Germans were about to take over the rest of France and seize the labour they need. Darlan is off to Algiers and (we know) will meet there the American emissary. He will have large hopes of pro-Vichy America. One way or another Torch is likely to inflame the whole situation. Strong rumours of Torch are current now in France and must also reach Germany and Spain.

October 23
Mrs. Roosevelt arrived today at last. Winant and I went by plane from Hendon to Whitchurch to meet her. She is a giantess, but a most friendly and genial one. I talked to her for a little and was enchanted. She is niece of old Theodore Roosevelt and married her cousin Franklin, so indeed she should be doubly remarkable. We came back to London by special train – four special trains had been laid on with steam up at different points in England as till she landed no one knew which port the aeroplane would be able to make owing to the weather. King and Queen on the platform at Paddington to meet her.

Mrs. Roosevelt has evidently a full share of the Roosevelt energy and bounce. She is a stormy petrel in American politics and outrages half America by her outspoken Left-wing and far worse pro-negro opinions. She engaged a table from the White House at a smart Washington hotel for a party of six and arrived with five negresses! I call that grand.

P.M. has sent another foolish minute about our postwar paper. He wishes to put the clock back to the Congress of Vienna. With Roosevelt straining to put the British Empire into liquidation and Winston pulling in the opposite direction to put it back to pre-Boer War, we are in danger of losing both the Old and the New World. It is essential to get our Four Power Plan agreed and then start discussing it with the Americans.

Long articles in *The Times* by Wavell on "generalship". How some people lack a sense of humour! I mistrust these writing generals, it is

171

THE WAR DIARIES OF OLIVER HARVEY

too much like Ian Hamilton over again. Why can't they win the battles
and leave the writing to somebody else? What an occupation for a
general in war-time!

October 24
Our attack in Egypt began yesterday. We have an enormous
superiority of tanks and aircraft and if we don't beat Rommel this
time, we really had better give up.

October 26
The American general Clark has just returned from his secret trip to
N. Africa. He and an officer went from Gibraltar in a submarine which
landed them in or near Algiers where they met General Mast, a
French general who commands a division there, together with
Murphy, the American representative in North Africa. Mast told
Clark that General Giraud was at the head of his movement but that
Darlan was not in it as he wasn't trusted. Clark didn't disclose any
dates but said the Americans were coming, it might be sooner it might
be later, with very large forces. Mast urged that all should go inside
the Med. (and avoid Casablanca) and they should avoid the French
Navy. Mast was going to communicate with Giraud and send a
message to Clark via Murphy. He asked that he should be given 4 days
notice before operations began. I'm relieved that Darlan isn't in it:
I hope neither Pétain nor Weygand are either.

Meanwhile the Libyan battle has started well. Much hard fighting
in the forward position – heavy bombing by us.

Anglo–Russian relations almost as bad as they can be. Stalin has
only sent a brief "thank you" to the P.M.'s last message offering extra
aeroplanes, air cooperation in the South, and small convoys by the
North, though all of them require some measure of Soviet cooperation
to fulfil. We are baffled. Is it only the Second Front? Stalin knows all
our plans and approved specifically of Torch. We have been frank
with him. Maisky here continues to be as mischievous as possible,
giving tendentious interviews to the press. The presence of Hess here
is now being made a source of offence, regardless of the fact that he
came over here before Russia was in the war and has been shut up ever
since.[1] Do the Russians seriously think we are keeping him for some
anti-Soviet move? Hess is quite mad and useless for any purpose.

Dejean came to see me. He had come to say goodbye to the S. of S.
after his sacking by de Gaulle. He has worked well and hard. He told

1. *Pravda* had described Great Britain as a place of refuge for gangsters.

me the difficulties all arose he thought from the fact that General de Gaulle conceived of himself as C. in C. of the Fighting French and treated all questions, military or political, as such, arbitrarily. He ignored or overruled the Commissaires and the Comité on political questions of which he had not the least experience. We should insist, he said, in return for handing over Madagascar, that the General should become democratic and be guided by his committee.

October 28
General Giraud has now replied to Mast's message. He is "interested" in the U.S. plan; he would like an agreement about the command;[1] and he would like a U.S. submarine. Mast, for his part, urges that Eisenhower should push straight on to Bone. Eisenhower has now decided to tell Mast the date.

We don't care about Giraud's suggestion about the "command". G. cannot possibly take over any command of Allied troops. Also to tell Mast the date seems excessively risky; the Bone idea seems good. The British submarine already standing by is to be converted into a U.S. one but it will take 8 days to get him across.

October 29
Battle in Egypt seems rather stuck again. Alexander says it will be a week from the start before we can tell how it is going.

October 31
Our difficulties with Stalin have decided us to send Clark Kerr instructions to remonstrate and have it out with him. Stalin is to speak on November 7th, the Soviet anniversary, and we are anxious to forestall any irretrievable utterance he may think of making. A.E. thinks, and rightly, that it is up to us to try and prevent the Russians from deceiving themselves about us and our intentions, though whether this remonstrance will do any good is another matter. We propose to ask bluntly, what is it? Is it really Hess? Is it the Second Front or what? Do please tell us as between friends and allies in confidence and not shout it to our enemies from the housetops.

I fear the truth is there is so deep a gulf between British and Russian mentality that we never have and never will have confidence and understanding. The difference is due to centuries of totally

1. He had demanded command of the American troops.

different outlook and political experience and education, Russia at the dawn of sudden freedom and enlightenment, we in the midday of centuries of progressive enlightenment and freedom, and even yet the kind of freedom and enlightenment are of different characters. Finally, they mistrust Winston and his anti-Bolshevik past. And here they are right because he hates Russia and all it stands for, though he will do his utmost to help her in the war.

The Australians, after running screaming to America whom they contrasted with the mean and shabby England, are now finding that the presence of large numbers of Americans under MacArthur to defend them is not quite so good as they expected. The Americans are critical of the Australian war effort especially over conscription for overseas service, as well as of the interminable and petty party strife of the country. The Australians are critical of MacArthur.

November 2

A.E.'s visit to America must soon be decided. The last idea, Winant's, was that he should go with W. when the latter goes on leave at the end of November, the elections then being well over. A.E. recently mentioned this to Halifax who has replied, typically, with a long waffle about it being necessary to make sure that it would be welcome, and that it should be a great success and that perhaps it would be better to leave it till the New Year and that Winston will no doubt come again first. Meanwhile Harry Hopkins has told Lyttelton, who is now off there to discuss coordination of supply questions, that the President will want to discuss major questions of policy with him. Finally, Halifax has also written to Winston suggesting that *he* should go over again soon and discuss postwar planning with the President. Roosevelt has in fact said to Halifax that he would like to take up postwar settlement with the P.M. "soon". It is clear to me that A.E. and no one else, certainly not the P.M., should discuss postwar planning with Roosevelt. It is also clear that H. wants to postpone A.E. going over there and wants to get the P.M. over there first. It is also clear that Roosevelt is ready to discuss postwar (or if he isn't ready to discuss it, he is ready to make unilateral pronouncements about it which means that it is high time A.E. *did* get over there to discuss it). I also have a suspicion that Roosevelt is less keen on seeing A.E. than the P.M. who is no rival for the future whereas A.E. may be.

We discussed all this in the Office this afternoon. A.E. agreed that the first thing to do was to clear it up with the P.M. He has already spoken to the P.M. of his own visit and the P.M. approved. He doesn't believe the P.M. is particularly keen to go again now, and the P.M.'s doctor has urged strongly against any more flying. A.E. would go over after Torch and discuss both military operations and postwar, the former subject being obvious and unassailable, the latter to be kept secret if necessary.

About Torch. The Americans have now had a further message from Mast, to whom the date had been communicated. Mast is furious at not having been told when Clark was there how imminent the operation was. Giraud also says he must have at least 3 weeks to coordinate his plans in France before he can leave and come over to N. Africa. Therefore Murphy coolly asks on their behalf for a delay of 3 weeks! We gather that the Americans aren't having any, and a firm reply refusing any delay has been sent. The transports are piling up fast in Gibraltar or just outside, delay would be fatal to any surprise. We think the Americans will learn a lot about cooperation with the French before they are done.

November 3

Very good news of the battle in Egypt. Rommel, according to secret reports, is in great difficulties and says he may not be able to extricate himself.

Eisenhower and his staff flying to Gibraltar to-day. Giraud has had a sudden change of heart and is now asking to be flown there at once too. The Americans have told him that he had better come by submarine.

Row in the Cabinet today over postwar. There were two papers on the agenda, one about the Dutch–Norwegian proposal for establishing international bases in Europe, the other about relief for Europe after the war. These provoked the P.M. to the most obstreperous utterances. He said that the only way to run Europe after the war was for Gt. Britain and Russia to keep out, and for Europe to be run by a Grand Council of "Great" Powers, including Prussia, Italy, Spain and a Scandinavian Confederacy. He did not want America in Europe. A.E. said that in the past 20 years he had been at many international conferences and the one thing he had learnt was that unless Gt. Britain, Russia and America took a share in Europe in future there would most certainly be another war in 20 years. The P.M. was warmly supported by Amery and Kingsley Wood. Smuts said that the bases plan required to be coordinated with a general plan. A.E. said that he had been trying to circulate his general plan for weeks but the trouble was that the P.M. disagreed with it. This made the P.M. slightly uneasy and there was a general demand to see the plan. This is now to be circulated.

A.E. was furious and said that if the P.M. was going to take this line, he must find another Foreign Secretary. The trouble is that the P.M., when elated by good news from the front, becomes at once intolerable. If allowed to, he will win the war and lose us the peace as certain as certain. A.E. can't possibly acquiesce in such policies. He is the second man in the Government and with him on postwar is the bulk of the country.

On the other hand, we have President Roosevelt who has given vent to the view to Halifax that neither Poland nor France should have any army at all after the war!

November 4

P.M. returned to the charge again late last night when he rang up A.E. and raged at him about the King's speech, the draft of which had been settled by a Committee including A.E. "Why had he included all this about Education? Had he not read what Cardinal Hinsley had said? Why had he allowed a reference to a Catering Bill to pass? Did he not know that 200 Conservative M.P.s would vote against it? A.E. replied that the Education proposals were those of R. A. Butler and the Caterers' Bill was recommended by Bevin. How should he know that there was opposition to them unless the Chief Whip came and told him so instead of sneaking direct to the P.M.? The exchanges were pretty hot! I gather A.E. offered to leave the P.M. to govern with Kingsley Wood and James Stuart if he preferred it.

The P.M. is on edge with nerves over the battles and events to come. In this mood he is gingered up by that lickspittle Kingsley Wood on behalf of the Diehards.

A telegram has just come from Alexander to say we have broken through, and the enemy forces are in full retreat.

November 5

Good news from Eygpt continues. The whole German line in retreat, thousands of prisoners including the German general Von Thoma, in our hands.

Giraud, it is now arranged, is to come out of France at once, pick up a U.S. submarine off the coast, and then from that be taken on by seaplane to Gibraltar. All in order otherwise about Torch. Eisenhower, we hope, gets to Gibraltar today. Gibraltar is bursting with ships but the exact significance of their presence hasn't yet dawned on the enemy. They still seem to be thinking of Dakar. In any case they will be busy trying to bolster up Rommel and should not have much to spare for Tunis or Algeria.

Madagascar is also being tied up in the general enthusiasm. A.E., by agreement with the P.M., is to see de Gaulle tomorrow and let him know we agree to an announcement that General Legentilhomme is to be made Governor and will proceed there shortly. This is what the P.M. calls de Gaulle's consolation prize for the shock and disappointment to come from Torch and the appearance of Giraud in the ring. De G. is not to be told of Torch till Saturday night.

November 6

Torch only 36 hours off. Meanwhile the Egyptian battle continues to develop according to plan.

The Spaniards are getting nervous at the armada at Gibraltar. Sam Hoare is to wake up the Foreign Minister at zero hour in the middle of Saturday/Sunday night and give him the solemn announcement of H.M.G. and U.S. Government that we do not intend to touch Spanish territory. The danger of trouble between France and Spain remains but we will do our best to keep them apart.

Giraud is believed to be arriving at Gibraltar to-night. De Gaulle is only to be told of Torch on Sunday. We wanted to tell him the evening before but Roosevelt won't hear of it.

The armada is now well into the Mediterranean, the largest expedition that has ever set sail, 500,000 men. It has eluded the pack of German submarines lying off Gibraltar but it now comes within range of bombers from Sardina and Sicily. The Germans are concentrating all they can there but our ships have large forces of fighters in carriers.

November 7

Torch news this morning still good, though one ship has been torpedoed. No bombing at all yet. It is believed the Germans think we are out to reinforce Malta or land in Tripoli.

Giraud is still awaited at Gib. though whether he is yet in the submarine on the way is not known. Eisenhower proposes, if he arrives in time, to invite him to leave at once for North Africa, just in advance of zero hour, and raise the flag of revolt. I haven't much faith in old French generals and I suspect he'll prove thoroughly tiresome.

De Gaulle, his unsuspecting rival, is invited to lunch at No. 10 tomorrow when the news should have just broken. I'm afraid it will be a black day for him. De Gaulle was most unforthcoming when A.E.

saw him yesterday and proposed an immediate announcement of Legentilhomme's appointment to Madagascar. He refused to have it on a plate like that but preferred to wait until all the *modalités* had been discussed and agreed. Tho' he may well suspect some expedition is afoot, we believe he thinks it is Dakar. He has got wind of the American contacts with Giraud, we think, from sources of his own. When Giraud first escaped from Germany, de Gaulle sent him a message of friendship and loyalty but so far as we know, Giraud sent no reply.

The Egypt news magnificent. 20,000 prisoners. 300 tanks and 400 guns.

November 8
A day of excitements!

We first heard early that Oran and Algiers landings had been made without opposition. No news from Casablanca.

Giraud who had been got to Algiers in time was on the air first thing appealing to the French North African Army to rally to him along with the United Nations Forces. He had again assumed command, he said.

Meanwhile Pétain at 9 a.m. received from Tuck Roosevelt's sentimental appeal. He gave him a reply already made that he had learnt "with sadness and amazement of this aggression", and of the President's message, invoking pretexts which nothing justified. He would defend the Empire against any aggressor – "Darlan was on the spot".

According to reports Darlan is indeed on the spot at Algiers and in preventive custody.

No German reactions at all so far. Only one ship was torpedoed en route. No bombing yet. But the situation at Casablanca is obscure, and so indeed it is elsewhere in the interior. The Egyptian battle goes better and better. A rout is developing, the Germans having seized all the transport to escape, leaving the wretched Italians to be captured. Heavy bombing on all the German lines of retreat. Prisoners now between 30 and 40 thousand.

The Spanish situation is not without danger. The American Ambassador we learnt today, made the most clumsy intervention yesterday when he called on the Spanish M.F.A., Jordana (who is friendly compared with Suner). He told him bluntly that there was a report that Germany had asked to be allowed to pass German troops through Spain if the Allies attacked North Africa, and if that was so, compliance would mean immediate war. If however Spain resisted, the President of the U.S. authorised him to say he would extend all help to Spain. Jordana denied the report and said he had no fear that Germany would enter Spain unless French Morocco or Oran were invaded. Morocco was a unit and the Moors one people. Spain would adopt precautionary military measures and she might be unable to avoid accepting assistance from Germany. The U.S. Ambassador said this would mean war. Jordana made a special plea that the Allies should keep out of Oran and Morocco.

This clumsy performance might well push Spain into Germany's arms if she wanted her. Spain was well set to accept the *fait accompli*, and we think she probably will, but the time has not yet come for threats.

No one loves Franco Spain less than I do, but this is not the moment to threaten the well disposed Jordana. In any case it is hardly for America which has tried to appease Pétain, to threaten Franco. One good thing so far is the final debunking of Pétain, that wet defeatist who imposed on Leahy and through him on Roosevelt. He has come out in his true colours.

Latest news this afternoon is that there is resistance at Casablanca where the French ships made a sortie and attacked ours, and also at Oran where resistance has grown up since the landing, but at Algiers conditions are best. Noguès[1] and Juin[2] are said to be organising resistance. So it does not look like a walk-over.

A.E. has just come back from his luncheon at No. 10 with the P.M. and de Gaulle. The General was at his best. He said it was necessary to think of France and we were right to choose Giraud for this. He hoped we wouldn't encourage separate Free French movements, with America backing Giraud and ourselves backing de Gaulle; we should try to unify them. He is to broadcast tonight.

November 9
Algiers town has surrendered after negotiation with Darlan. What this exactly signified we don't yet know or what becomes of Darlan.

Naval action continues off Casablanca, and there is resistance still at Oran.

Giraud, we hear today, couldn't have been more tiresome. On arrival at Gib. he wrangled for three hours and declared that he must

1. General Noguès, French Resident-General Morocco (Vichy) 1936–43.
2. General Juin, French C-in-C North Africa 1941–42 (Vichy) later C-in-C French Forces in Tunisian Campaign.

be recognised as C. in C. of the whole N. African command including Allies and be independent to talk to troops where he chose, or he wouldn't have anything to do with it. He wanted to make an immediate landing in S. of France. Eisenhower reasoned with him as best he could and finally got him "to accept recognition as leader of the French in N. Africa and as Governor and C. in C. French Forces". G. was quite out of touch with realities. He was most disappointed.

November 10

N. African operations still confused. The Americans have not yet got inside Casablanca where opposition is severe. The U.S. fleet here has been dealing out drastic punishment to the French fleet which is resisting fiercely. At Oran fighting is also stiff and the Americans haven't yet got the town. At Algiers things are easier. The Americans have got the town and we and they are pushing towards Tunisia. The Darlan mystery persists. The American General Clark was to see Darlan yesterday (he had already agreed to surrender the town) and discuss the position.

Finally, Laval, we learn from secret sources, has left with Abetz[1] for Berchtesgaden. The Americans have broken off relations with Vichy.

The determined resistance at Casablanca is interesting because we were never in favour of an Allied landing on the Atlantic side where physical conditions are hardest and opposition, we estimated, was most probable. But the Americans insisted. The Americans, for their part, didn't want to land at Algiers, which we insisted on, where in fact it has turned out easiest of all.

A most important question is what is the next step after N. Africa. The P.M., A.E. tells me, is wildly in favour of roping Turkey in and of entering Europe from her end. He even mentioned this to Maisky yesterday. I told A.E. that after thinking it over, whatever the military merits, to bring in Turkey would involve enormous political troubles. It would arouse the worst suspicions of Soviet Russia and it would be doubtful if she and Turkey could be prevented from fighting each other. Russia is always suspicious of Turkey and would think we intended by this means to counteract her influence in the Balkans. On the other hand, the Greeks would be upset because they would fear for their islands. The Turks would prove grasping allies.

1. Otto Abetz, German Gauleiter of France.

A.E. said that Greece must certainly get her islands this time and it was the P.M.'s idea to give the Turks nothing at all. The origin of the proposal was the need for planning now where we were going to strike next year. The Chiefs of Staff had solemnly proposed that our war effort next year should be limited to occupying Sicily while the Russians were again left to do the rest of the fighting. Both the P.M. and A.E. were horrified at this. Hence the P.M.'s Turkey idea.

Egyptian battle now a rout. The Germans are beyond Matruh and it is very doubtful if any can get away; they are under heavy bombing all the time. There is a little too much "I", "I", in Montgomery's communiqués and interviews. He doesn't suffer from false modesty; but our more gentlemanly generals were not so successful.

November 11

In North Africa the armistice position is still obscure. We don't know yet what was decided at the Clark–Darlan talks. Casablanca and Oran have now been captured after considerable fighting. Germans are being poured into Tunisia to forestall us, men and aircraft. American and British forces are advancing there from the West. In France Hitler is occupying unoccupied France, as we expected he would. Pétain has protested at this. He protests too much.

A.E. laid up with a cold, and can't speak in the House tomorrow. Important talks are to take place at Chequers for the weekend on future operations. P.M. favours concentrating on Italy now as the weak link and bombing Rome. We hear tonight that an armistice has been signed between Clark & Darlan covering the whole of N. Africa. No details yet.

November 12

Darlan is trying hard to edge his way into the front row again. He agreed to the armistice but is claiming to maintain some role in N. Africa. Giraud is of course his rival here and the Americans are trying to get the two to meet. I'm afraid the Americans still have delusions about Darlan. Meanwhile Pétain has counterordered Darlan's armistice order with the inevitable result of disorder and confusion among the French. The French fleet remains an unknown factor but Darlan repeats (as he did to us in 1940) that it won't fall into German hands.

November 13

A race for Tunis. Germans are pushing in all they can. We are advancing as fast as we can from Algiers. The French are non-cooperative and as though dazed. If they only would cooperate, they have enough troops to stop all German infiltration till we come. On the Egyptian side we are making for Tobruk, the Germans are going westward as fast as they can.

Darlan has been prevailed upon to broadcast to the French Fleet in Toulon inviting them to join the Allies or to go to West Africa. So much and no more. We are getting little but obstruction from the French in our delivery of them.

We are horrified to hear this afternoon that Giraud and Darlan have come to an agreement to divide the N. African administration between them, G. to take military control and D. political. The Americans are quite green enough to fall for it, and we have sent a warning telegram to Halifax to speak to Hull or the President, pointing out that any such arrangement would go extremely badly in this country, besides making any hope of uniting French resistance illusory because the Gaullists would never accept it. As the P.M. has said himself, if Darlan could bring over the French fleet he might have a seat on the band waggon but if he fails to, as he has, he deserves nothing from us. All he has done is to kill British and American sailors.

November 14

Very worrying situations developing in North Africa out of American conversations with Darlan. Eisenhower and our Admiral Cunningham went to Algiers yesterday. According to Cunningham,[1] Darlan, Nogués, Juin and Giraud have come to agreement to work with us. What does this mean? How can we work with Darlan who is a traitor and who has failed either to deliver the French fleet or even to pacify N. Africa without fighting? Darlan is the slipperiest politician, in the Laval class, and Murphy, the American civil adviser, is infatuated with Vichy. Our Cunningham is the biggest old bloody fool off his ship, and the American generals are as simple as lambs.

A.E. is off today to Chequers for the meeting and we had some discussion here first. His view, and I understand, the P.M.'s view is that the first consideration is the military necessity of getting quick control of N. Africa including Tunis. If Darlan can help over this, well and good. Once we have military control, then Darlan and Co.

1. Admiral Cunningham (later Lord Cunningham), C-in-C of the British Mediterranean Fleet 1939–1942. Later First Sea Lord and Chief of Naval Staff.

must be told that they must either join us in the fight or we shall lock them up. We can't allow N. Africa to be neutral. There is sense in this but it is highly dangerous and problematical.

With these woolly admirals and Americans anything may be possible. A prolonged negotiation, which is most likely, can only benefit Vichy and embarrass us. It will arouse afresh all Stalin's mistrust of us. Again, our real friends in France, and the Fighting French outside France will think we've sold them to Darlan. Also, it is by no means excluded that Darlan's manoeuvre is not in collusion with Pétain and Laval and with Hitler himself in the background, to confuse France and so keep it quiet and to neutralise N. Africa.

I have not been so worried for a long time. I have written a note of my anxieties to A.E. down at Chequers. All here in the F.O. are alive to the danger. But the Admiralty and the Chiefs of Staff must be expected to hold the most foolish views. However, I think the P.M. himself can be relied on over this. But I fear our blind self-effacement before America over this whole business. We start thinking we have a clear-cut issue – it is rapidly confused in argumentation with clever negotiators and willing appeasers and then we discover too late we have sold the pass.

De Gaulle, in view of all this, has decided to hold up the emissaries he was proposing to send to Giraud.

The P.M. has already warned Roosevelt of our solemn commitments to de Gaulle.

Lyttelton is in America and to A.E.'s great annoyance he and Halifax have telegraphed to the P.M. urging him to go over at once to discuss future strategy. The P.M. mercifully does not want to go, and his doctor is dead against it. A.E. is offering to go himself and I hope he will be allowed to do so. Halifax has been working hard to get the P.M. over and to postpone A.E.'s visit. Why? What is the old appeaser up to now?

Tonight and tomorrow the P.M., A.E., Smuts and the Chiefs of Staff are to discuss future strategy. The Chiefs of Staff, as I have said, wish to do nothing till 1944 except carry out a few raids and give arms to Russia to carry on the fight. The Russian Army having played the allotted role of killing Germans, our Chiefs of Staff think by 1944 they could stage a general onslaught on the exhausted animal. Both the P.M. and A.E. reject these foolish military views and must now decide what we can do next year which the Chiefs of Staff can be made to accept. Of the ways of entry into Europe there is Turkey who is determined to keep out of the war, and whose entry would cause vast trouble with Russia and Greece. Then there is Italy, war-weary and unwilling partner of Hitler, to which we now have a bridge from N. Africa. Then there is France nearest to our base and our resources, with a friendly population but more heavily defended and occupied by the enemy than any other coast. France is thought the least favourable; Smuts believes this, tho' A.E. is not so sure. Italy is the easiest and weakest point, and in itself concentration on Italy would mean screams for help to Germany, withdrawal of Italian garrison forces from the Balkans (to be replaced by Germans taken from somewhere else), and sending of more Germans to Italy itself, thus relieving pressure on Russia.

It is obvious that we must develop another front in Europe next year. It is obvious that Russia can't be expected to fight alone through another year. And we must decide pretty quickly if we are going to do anything at all next spring. Connected with this is the question of hotting up our bombing against Italy at the expense of attacks on Germany.

The more I think of the Darlan business the more disturbed I am at its possible consequences. What will Parliament and the British public say? It may be a Hoare–Laval over again. After all Darlan has been represented to them by H.M.G., and rightly, as the archtraitor of France, second only to Laval, who betrayed our cause in 1940 and who has fired on British sailors, a man responsible with Laval for collaboration with Germany and for the overthrow of French democracy. He is now to be on our side. What can anyone believe in future?

NOTE TO S. OF S. DATED 14 NOVEMBER

I am becoming increasingly worried over the Darlan business. I quite see the advantage of using Darlan to get N. Africa cleared up and then saying either you now fight for us or we throw you out. But negotiations with this sort of Quisling don't in my experience take this clear-cut course. They become a long and discreditable waffle.

In the meanwhile, what are going to be the reactions of Stalin? All his suspicions will be awakened. He will say it is another Hess.

Then, France will be thrown into complete confusion – our friends in Occupied France who are sabotaging; and Herriot & Co. will say we have sold them to Darlan. Fighting France will say the same.

Finally, can we exclude the possibility that the whole Darlan game has been fixed up with Pétain and Laval, with Hitler in the background, in order to neutralise N. Africa and keep France quiet?

I know you feel all this as much as I do and you must forgive me for putting it down. But it smells to me so much like Appeasement again. Compromise with Darlans and Pétains never pays. I want to keep our war clean!

O.C.H.

November 15
Full account came in this morning from Eisenhower and I have seen nothing like it since Sam Hoare's telegram came from Paris advocating the Hoare–Laval agreement.

In short it is this. The position in N. Africa was quite different from what they expected to find (as we thought it would be). The name of Pétain was the only one that counted and Darlan the only one after him who could exercise any authority. Unless he could be got to play, neither Noguès nor Esteva would help. Giraud cut no ice at all, rather the reverse. (The French in N. Africa in fact are so reluctant to help that unless ordered to do so by Darlan they will resist their rescuers.) Both Esteva and Noguès promised to obey Darlan. Agreement has therefore been reached with Darlan by which the group will organise N. Africa for effective cooperation including use of selected troops for active participation in the war. It will also try to get the Fleet out of Toulon.

This was agreed to as without it the Americans couldn't quickly gain Tunis, and 60,000 men would be needed to hold the tribes quiet.

Eisenhower then says they are going to watch Darlan closely, as they evidently do not trust him. The Darlan appeal to the Toulon Fleet has fallen quite flat, but in spite of this Eisenhower maintains D. is not empty-handed (What has he in fact brought?). Eisenhower confesses that he is at the mercy of Darlan and therefore he is obliged to reach agreement with him. He says he is quite certain what he has done is right, Cunningham agrees with him and no one not on the spot can understand. What a document! What a confession! Appeasement and nothing else. What is this agreement worth? And what harm won't it do us everywhere else? Compromising with Frenchmen who have betrayed us and killed our men, for military necessity. It is Munich reasoning over again.

We are all very worried here, from Alec Cadogan downwards. P.M.[1] has sent a message to Roosevelt saying our doubts and fears

1. See Churchill IV 567.

have not been removed by this report, asking him to consult us about long-term arrangements and urging danger that we are being double-crossed.

November 16
Press very restive today. It is clearly going to hot up. American press, we hear, is full of outspoken comment, but this is not reaching us owing to rigid censorship in America.

P.M. and A.E. are seeing de Gaulle this morning before luncheon.

A.E. arrived only just before the de Gaulle meeting but there was no doubt of his now being alive to the crisis. He agrees it is like Hoare–Laval all over again and we are in for a first-class row. But what can we do? The P.M., in his chivalrous way, has publicly declared himself the President's lieutenant in N. Africa. There is the importance of the battle of Tunis – if the Germans can get two divisions in there before we arrive, it will make all the difference to the military situation. There is Eisenhower's opinion, the man on the spot. We all agreed that we must get rid of Darlan somehow. He must be thrown over after Tunis and the President must be told the British and the Allies cannot stomach him. The only way to put this across would be for A.E. to go himself to Washington. We don't believe Eisenhower's assumption is correct – that Darlan can do for us what he claims. There is no evidence yet that Esteva and his French at Tunis have done anything but acquiesce in German landings.

A.E. and I lunched together alone afterwards.

I put it to him at lunch. Would he, if he were in command of a force of 500,000 with all modern equipment, consent to be held up and bluffed by Darlan at Algiers? He said of course he wouldn't. I said if he went to Washington, he would go as the representative of all of Allies who would be behind him over this. De Gaulle, A.E. told me, behaved with great restraint and dignity when he saw P.M. and A.E. He would never, he said, have anything to do with a traitor like Darlan and he must issue a communiqué to that effect. The P.M. said to him "You have nothing to worry about. You aren't tarnished like we are!" If only de G. keeps cool, he will come out best out of all this.

Maisky called this afternoon to ask what was happening. He said he understood our using Darlan to get Tunis but after that we must get rid of him as quickly as possible.

After a further discussion in the Office A.E. proposes to urge P.M. to send another and firmer message to Roosevelt tonight stressing the effect on de Gaulle, the Fighting French and our supporters in France, on the occupied countries and finally on the British public who are fighting for decency, and making it quite clear that we cannot agree to any permanent arrangement in which Darlan figures. How could we trust him with any arms?

A.E. also told me under the seal of the greatest secrecy that the P.M. was now thinking of sending Dick Law to India as Viceroy. This is as surprising as it is excellent. He would be sadly missed here, a body-blow as A.E. said. He was wondering whom we could have as U.-S. instead. The P.M. apparently was much impressed by Dick's speech last week. It would be a most admirable choice, youth and imagination, just what we want.

A.E. disturbed at the differences between himself and the P.M. over foreign affairs, "just like with Neville Chamberlain again". He was annoyed because Kingsley Wood has had a paper written up in the Treasury against his Four Power Plan. K.W. plays up to the P.M. who doesn't discourage him.

A.E. spoke of going to India himself! I said that was nonsense. No one going to India now could ever be P.M. He could resign again if he must but he must remain in England. His future was to be P.M. of England and only someone who had been in this country in the next vital years would be P.M. He exaggerated his differences with the P.M. He should talk to him heart to heart. The P.M. loved him as a son and spoke of him as his successor. He alone of his colleagues was listened to by the P.M. in military matters. He should have it out with him and demand more support for himself in foreign affairs as against the K.W.s who were the P.M.'s enemies anyway.

November 17

The *affaire Darlan* becomes more incredible and discreditable every day. We heard today an account from a British officer on Eisenhower's staff who had returned from Algiers from which it was clear that Darlan had *roulé* the Americans completely. The landings at Oran and Algiers had gone fairly well but that at Casablanca was badly held up. In these circumstances it was felt essential to get Noguès to cease fire and only Darlan could order him to do it. Darlan consented at the price of recognition of himself and his fellow rascals and ordered Noguès to cease fire, which he did. We know, however, from secret sources that Noguès was at the end of his ammunition and would have had to do so anyway. Eisenhower only went over to Algiers for an hour to agree this "Pact of Algiers", and obviously did not know what his military position was, its strength and the fundamental weakness of the French.

Meanwhile A.E. spoke to the P.M. again last night and the latter is fully alive now to the impossibility of any long-term agreement with Darlan and Co. He is drafting a message in stronger terms to Roosevelt and another is to be sent to Halifax.

No reply yet from Roosevelt to the P.M.'s first message, but he is clearly having his difficulties. One of these must be how to disown Darlan without disowning Eisenhower.

It was typical that at the Cabinet earlier yesterday evening Bevin didn't see anything to worry about. Cripps didn't either, as he was quite quiet. And Attlee hardly uttered. What blimps!

What was decided last night was that Dick should be Viceroy. He doesn't know yet. It will be a blow to us here. I am not sure how good it is for Dick himself. It will take him out of politics for four years, but if he doesn't take a peerage, as A.E. will recommend him not to do, he should still be young enough to fit in again.

Two telegrams sent off this afternoon, one from P.M. to President and one from A.E. to Halifax expressing in strong terms our doubts and fears of Eisenhower–Darlan agreement and the impossibility of our peoples accepting Darlan as an ally. H. of C. very uneasy this afternoon.

November 18

Situation much better this morning thanks to clear statement issued by President Roosevelt that all arrangements with Darlan are of strictly local and temporary military character and can have no bearing on final political arrangements. With this on record we all feel clearer and happier. (Roosevelt replied also personally to P.M. that he too had felt the dangers of the situation and he had therefore decided to act at once as he had done.)

Eisenhower has now proposed that Cadogan should go out to Gibraltar to confer with him on these political questions, and both P.M. and A.E. are in favour of his going. The questions to discuss would be how soon and in what way Darlan can be eliminated. This is going to be hard enough to solve but anyway we are at least now in full agreement with Roosevelt again on policy, and what might have been a dangerous rift is stopped.

A.E. tells me that in connection with appointment of Dick as Viceroy, Cripps is to go to Ministry of Aircraft Production, Bobbety to leave C.O. and become Lord Privy Seal, and A.E. himself to become Leader of H. of C.

P.M. all eagerness now to compel Turkey to join us in the war. He is galloping ahead hard on that line.

Spain is mobilising. We cannot and are not raising objection. A.E. saw Alba[1] to-day and said we assumed that this step was being taken for the protection of her neutrality. We did not threaten her; we did not object; we supposed it must be directed at another party.

November 19

Now that we have Roosevelt's clear declaration about Darlan, the next thing is to get it carried out, and this means getting the American soldiers to carry it out. There are signs that American soldiers are no wiser than British in political matters and we still have the usual foolish obstruction. Our view is that Darlan should now be required to release all anti-Axis prisoners, French as well as Allied, and abrogate all restrictions imposed by the Vichy régime. If he refuses or jibs, he must then be thrown out. What D. of course will try to do is to agree to everything and to procrastinate over execution. This should not be allowed and it gives us our opportunity for throwing Darlan out. But the soldiers and the Vichy American Murphy are unlikely to be cooperative. American G.H.Q. are not allowing the President's anti-Darlan statement to be dropped as leaflets over Metropolitan France. We are broadcasting it from here.

Roosevelt has also sent a message to P.M. to say he has no objection to Cadogan going to Gibraltar for a conference with Eisenhower, but it must be understood that they do not discuss political aspects but only military aspects of situation. What then is the use of his going? A.E. and Cadogan discussed this with the P.M. this morning. It was decided that Cadogan should not go and it is proposed to take up the question of disposing of Darlan with Washington direct. All this is slightly disquieting. Meanwhile our moral position and our credit with the real anti-Quisling resisters in France and everywhere else hangs in the balance. Pucheu,[2] Darlan's man in the Vichy cabinet, has now turned up at Barcelona, eager to join the band waggon in Algiers.

November 20

There seems little doubt now from all the evidence that Darlan and

1. Duke of Alba, Spanish Ambassador in London 1939–1945.
2. P. Pucheu, Vichy French Minister of the Interior 1941–2, under Darlan.

Pétain are working in collusion. Darlan has admitted as much himself, and so the proclamations of Pétain disowning Darlan are nothing but play-acting. The game of course is to save Vichy whichever side wins. I'm afraid the Americans (Leahy, State Department, Eisenhower) will be tempted to fall for this. Hull has been consistently pro-Vichy. Although the President has made his declaration it is not going to prove so easy now to overthrow Darlan. First of all, D. will exaggerate his usefulness to the soldiers and sailors who will become his most powerful advocate – as they are already – (Cunningham sends nauseating telegrams about what D. is doing). Eisenhower is already discussing lightheartedly the rearmament of these turncoats. At the same time Darlan is being allowed to broadcast and mention Pétain in every other sentence. What are our friends in France to think?

However, a hopeful message has just come from the President to the P.M. suggesting that we both send a high civilian to N. Africa to act as an overriding authority over the French with powers of veto on legislation. This is now being considered.

Maisky called to enquire officially as to Anglo–American intentions as to Darlan. Whilst the Soviets understood immediate use of him over Tunis, any political arrangements involving Darlan, Flandin or Pucheu would have the worst effects. A.E. reassured him.

November 22
I was away yesterday but there was some activity because there was an unexpected Cabinet to consider a so-called Protocol which Eisenhower was proposing to sign with Darlan defining their relations and respective undertakings. Although this was essentially a military agreement defining what the French Authorities in N. Africa were required to do, it recognised Darlan as High Commissioner. The F.O. wished to cut out all reference to Darlan. President Roosevelt had already expressed his view that if possible there should be no Protocol or signed document at all as having too diplomatic and binding a character, but that Eisenhower should make a unilateral declaration of its terms in which Darlan would concur. The Cabinet eventually agreed with the President. The Cabinet's view was much influenced by Smuts who had passed through Gibraltar and reported on the military importance of keeping Darlan sweet and on the degree to which the French were in fact now helping. He even said that it would be necessary to envisage keeping Darlan for a fairly long period.

Exactly – this is what I had feared. It is difficult to counter the military argument once the military have committed themselves to, and based themselves on cooperation with Darlan. On the other hand, evidence shows how opportunist the nature of this help is – the maintenance of the link with Vichy and old Pétain by broadcast references, a threat by Nogués to resign if Darlan is thrown out. Now the soldiers are trying to get the President to pipe down even on his declaration about the temporary character of the deal with Darlan, whilst "temporary" is being interpreted as "for the duration of the war". All this is having calamitous effects on French resistance in Metropolitan France. I am sorry to say that P.M. is going anti-de Gaulle again. The poor General is in a frenzy and is anxious now to broadcast exactly what he thinks of Darlan. He has been prevented. We cannot obviously have a direct conflict with America over this; we have bigger fish to fry together, but it is unfair to de Gaulle, our only French friend in our darkest hour.

November 23
Government changes out today. Cripps to Aircraft Production, Bobbety to be Lord Privy Seal, A.E. to lead H. of C., Herbert Morrison to go into War Cabinet, Oliver Stanley to C.O. Nothing about the Viceroy yet. The appointment of Stanley is an appeasement. He is a disgruntled and disloyal critic outside; inside he will prove a flabby and timid Colonial Secretary. I'm sorry Bobbety has had to leave C.O., he was vigorous and imaginative. The C.O. is one of the most important and vulnerable of our Government departments; yet it is always a Cinderella. I understand though not members of the War Cabinet both Cripps and Bobbety will have access to it and the right to speak.

Dick Law, I hear, is jibbing at the Viceroyalty. From his own point of view it is certainly a doubtful proposition; the absence from England may gravely affect his political prospects at home. He is after all a potential P.M. From India's point of view his going would be of enormous advantage. He would be forceful and imaginative; he would impress America that we were trying.

Roosevelt's suggestion of appointing an American and an English civilian to control the French authorities in N. Africa is being explored. It is dangerous to leave this all to the soldiers but sending a civilian involves a degree of recognition of Darlan which is repugnant. But I think we must do so. Roosevelt has invited de Gaulle to Washington but he has taken the gilt off this by letting it be known that to win the war he is working with Darlan in N. Africa as he would work in Paris with Laval!

This is worrying. We obviously cannot divest ourselves of responsibility by simply saying it is an American affair. In a matter which cuts across all we are fighting for, decency and democracy, we must make our wishes felt. We must save the Americans from themselves. They could certainly blame us if they got into a mess and we did'nt help them out. But this involves participation with them in handling Darlan in N. Africa. I think therefore we should agree to Roosevelt's suggestion of two high-powered High Commissioners and they should be armed with powers of life and death over Darlan's administration. As the military situation clears up and our control becomes absolute, we should force Darlan and Co. out, whatever the soldiers think. But it is not a pretty situation.

November 24
Dick Law still very hesistant about Viceroyalty. He says he will go if he is ordered but he doesn't want it. A.E. very certain that he should not be pressed to go, and rather doubtful now about his qualifications. But who to send? I suppose there is no chance of sending Halifax back! He would be good with Americans, with the "Left" here, and with India.

Thanks to the leverage provided by Sumner Welles' speech the P.M. has agreed to the 4 Power Plan being taken at Thursday's Cabinet. He has also agreed (it seems) to A.E. going to Washington in consequence, provided he himself hasn't got to go on defence matters. A.E. doesn't wish to be there during Xmas. Winant now says he won't be going on leave till December 17th, and so A.E. proposes to go about the middle of January. Winant could prepare the way and still be over there. I hope all this will work out like that.

November 25
Darlan gets worse and worse. He is rapidly sealing his position by bringing in W. Africa – always in the name of the Marshal. We have agreed to Roosevelt's proposal for appointing each a high civilian. P.M. very anti-de Gaulle. Result no doubt of prickings of a bad conscience. De G. is to go over to Washington. I'm glad of this. He has a considerable public there and he will be able to air his case.

November 26
A.E. is intending to send the P.M. a note on the consequences and repercussions of dealing with Darlan. The P.M. is horrifying in his attitude. He was saying today to A.E. that D. had done more for us

than de G. He behaved shockingly to de G. the last time he saw him.

November 27
Cabinet restive today about Darlan. Also the Labour Party.

The search for a Viceroy goes on. Bobbety is now being again pressed to go, and he is consulting his doctor.

Late this evening came the news of the German entry into Toulon, in spite of their promise to respect it and of the scuttling of the French navy there. Thank goodness the ships are at the bottom of the sea. They can at least no longer be a threat to us and a temptation to the Germans. Darlan will of course get the credit.

November 28
P.M. and A.E. delighted over the scuttling of the French fleet, which they regard as the first sign of spontaneous resistance to Germany by the French in France. P.M. is getting more and more enthusiastic over Darlan and extracts great satisfaction from an article by Vernon Bartlett in *News Chronicle* today, describing him as a useful tool. V.B. is notoriously unstable in his impressions. But the P.M. is in that mood when he sees any straw which favours his own view and turns a blind eye to the massive opinion which is against it. I fear A.E. is infected too. But it is madness. It is playing with fire to play with Darlan.

This puts for instance our Spanish policy, an appeasement anyway, in a much more sinister light. The Spanish Government are putting pressure on us (strongly supported by Sam Hoare) to expel Negrin and Ascarate. I'm glad to say we are replying that we will do no such thing and reminding the Spanish government that in the past we have protected Spanish Whites as well as Reds – even Alba. The latter is still playing the clown here with his extravagant motor cars and his lavish entertainments, to which he has now added a demand for a preposterous number of clothing coupons.

Darlan also raises our policy towards Italy. Are we now to hold out hopes to the Cianos and Grandis and Badoglios? I hope not. We surely should not commit ourselves to any Quislings in order to gain a quick victory. If we do, it will be a short victory.

November 30
I'm afraid our Jewish policy is becoming more and more backward. After distinguishing ourselves in the last war with the Balfour Declaration as the pioneers of an enlightened policy, we have steadily fallen

behind till now the Jews are treated hardly better than enemy refugees. This is largely due to the blind pro-Arabism of the F.O. which A.E. has never resisted. Indeed he is a blind pro-Arab himself. The result of the last White Paper which niggled the Jewish position down to a hopeless one, has been that power has passed from the Zionist moderates to the extremists. Weizmann, who is our friend and the statesman of the movement, has had to give way to the American Jewish extremists who hate us.

I have often talked to A.E. about this but he is hopelessly prejudiced. The Arab myth clouds his mind. The only solution is a Jewish Palestine, which should be a British Palestine, the Arab inhabitants being transferred across the frontier and re-established there. There is plenty of room in Syria, Transjordan, Iraq and Arabia for the Palestine Arabs. There is no solution of the Jewish problem except in Palestine: it is nonsense to talk of Jewish states in Central Europe or Central Africa or Central America. If people would read their history they would understand that.

Why are we afraid of the Arabs? Why do we appease them? Why do we flatter ourselves they like us? It is on a par with the British penchant for Hungarian noblemen.

We risk getting at loggerheads with the Americans over our Jewish policy. It is to them another example of the old Adam in the British Empire. The American Jews are as powerful politically as the American Irish. I'm afraid I think American influence in the Middle East, which we are shy of, would be a breath of fresh air.

December 1

The U.S. Government are becoming very baffling to us, more and more secretive. They invited Madame Chiang kai Chek to visit Washington and *smuggled her by air through India, including a night en route* without letting either us or India know anything about it all! These are not the manners of a great Power. Then again they tell us and consult us less and less about N. Africa, letting Eisenhower fix up things locally as he wishes, without any regard to other than U.S. interests. He has made an extremely bad bargain over the French shipping in N. Africa which Darlan has succeeded in keeping out of a common pool. He has also involved himself in negotiations over French West Africa which seem to deny us any access at all.

Why? Don't the Americans trust us? Are they afraid of our disapproval? Or is it the American soldiers who are out of control of the State Department and the President? Over Darlan there is less and less indication that the President's promise of its temporary character will be observed, or was ever intended to be observed. Do they think they can run the war without us? There are also ugly cases of American commercial interests being pushed under military cover.

December 2

Worse news from Darlan who has now been allowed to declare himself Chef d'Etat and representative of French imperial interests whilst Metropolitan France is occupied. No word of warning of this from the Americans. At the same time Roosevelt has been singularly ungracious towards de Gaulle of whom he said in his press conference that he did not know whether he was coming to America, though if he did he would receive him. As a matter of fact Roosevelt has taken steps to prevent his going to America at all till January. A.E. has undertaken to give the H. of C. a secret session on Darlan, probably next week. I wish it could be an open one. The Americans are free to criticise our Indian policy openly. Our criticism of their Darlan policy is hushed and silenced.

Instructions have been sent to Halifax to insist on our being represented at the Dakar discussions in view of our immense interests in West Africa and of the fact that we are responsible for policing the Eastern Atlantic.

December 3

The Russian counter-offensive is assuming grand proportions. Pushes are developing near Moscow as well as round Stalingrad. Stalin is as reluctant as ever to see us cooperating with them in the Caucasus. We promised to send him bomber squadrons as part of our help instead of the Second Front in the West. Stalin, when things are bad in the Caucasus, would never admit that they could get worse as our offer to help implied and now that they are better, he doesn't want us there either. He asks for the aeroplanes themselves and not a British manned unit. We seem to him to have an unhealthy itch to get ourselves into the Caucasus.

It looks as if the Darlan proclamation may prove the last straw to the British Government and the British public. A.E. today is inspiring a P.Q. to make clear that we had no knowledge of it and did not recognise it. The secret session is laid on for Thursday next. Finally, there are some encouraging words from Hull himself. But we shall have trouble yet with Eisenhower and the American soldiers who are as dense in political matters as soldiers usually are. The obvious lesson is that soldiers (and sailors) must never be left free to conduct negotiations with the civil power.

Admiral Godefroy in Alexandria is still in the pangs of *crises de conscience*. He cannot make up his mind where his loyalty lies, with Pétain or with Darlan, the only thing clear being that he doesn't want to fight the Germans.

December 4

Darlan situation made yet worse by a fulsome message from Eisenhower congratulating Darlan on his cooperation and saying all worthy Frenchmen will now forget "their small differences". What a perfect fool Eisenhower must be. We are anxious to take up with Roosevelt the appointment of civilian high commissioners at once if the P.M. can be got to agree. Poor de Gaulle is naturally livid and anxious to broadcast a mouthful. A.E. has seen the script and favours permission being given but he has referred it to the P.M. (P.M. would not allow one particular passage and the General won't broadcast.)

December 7

Mack[1], who was summoned back from Algiers, arrived on Sunday and was immediately whisked down to Binderton with William Strang. A.E. says he is now at last beginning to see more clearly into this. Mack said it was really necessary to come to terms with D. as he was the only person who had any authority. Giraud himself gave way to Darlan. On the other hand, nearly all are agreed and many Frenchmen as well there that he must be got rid of. The best man of all is Béthouart[2] with whom the Americans were in touch before Torch, who rose before they arrived and actually arrested Noguès. He is now at Gib. without a job having been thrown over by the Americans in favour of Darlan. Mast, though a lighter weight, is also still without a job. Noguès is one of the worst of all. Béthouart would like to come to terms with de Gaulle. Unexpectedly enough, the British are far from unpopular in North Africa and at the recent parade got the loudest cheers of all from the public. A.E. thinks the solution is to work for the elimination of D. and his replacement by a group of sound generals (Béthouart and Co.) who would cooperate with de Gaulle. Béthouart favours this solution, urges that the French themselves be left to get rid of D. which would be much better than for us or the Americans to do so, and would like Catroux to become Resident General of

1. W. H. B. Mack, Political Liaison Officer with Gen. Eisenhower.
2. Pro-Allied French General in N. Africa.

Morocco. But all this will take time, meanwhile both the public here and de Gaulle will be impatient.

Wendell Willkie[1] has come out fiercely against Darlan and is attacking the President whom he lumps with Winston ("We shall hold what we have") for fighting the war for mean ends. The British press and the H. of C. show signs of increasing disquiet. Winston, on the other hand, half approves (being half-American) the gangster mentality which justified the use of Darlan and is wishing to postpone the secret session till next week. A.E. is having a row with him about this.

P.M. when in Moscow suggested to Stalin eventual meeting *à trois* with Roosevelt, possibly in Iceland. This idea has developed and the time is now thought ripe for a meeting in January on future strategy, perhaps in Khartoum. Roosevelt has accepted and wants to discuss both strategy and the beginnings of post war. Winston says he wants to bring A.E. but for some reason he fears Roosevelt may object because the latter doesn't propose to bring anyone from the State Department. A.E. feels that if postwar is to be discussed, he must certainly be there. Neither Winston nor Roosevelt understand Europe or its problems. Why should Roosevelt object? Because he doesn't want to bring either Hull or Sumner Welles? The dictatorial tendencies of Winston are flattered and gratified by meeting these dictators man to man, but as A.E. says, we haven't a dictatorship here whatever the P.M. may imagine.

December 8
Another prolonged row between A.E. and the P.M. last night. The old man is in the most intolerable state. The leadership of the House, in which the P.M. thinks A.E. is unduly soft, is responsible for these frequent clashes of arms. But A.E. won't stand it beyond a certain point and the P.M. will have to find another leader.

Catroux has held a press conference in which he roundly condemned Darlan as a man no one can trust and whose position on the Allied lines of communication must be a permanent danger. The secret session is now fixed for Thursday – much against the P.M.'s will.

December 9
A.E. had de Gaulle and Catroux to dine last night. The atmosphere was friendly and trustful, the two generals opened up and A.E.

1. Wendell Willkie had been Republican candidate in the 1940 Presidential Election.

showed clearly how much he was on their side. They practically said that they would be ready to cooperate with anyone in N. Africa except Darlan. Catroux insists on returning to Syria *pro tem*, but he will probably have a meeting with Béthouart en route at Gibraltar. A.E. told me that the more he saw of de Gaulle and Catroux the more he realised how superior they were. Neither a Vichy nor a communist France will help us in the future. We have to work for a France of non-extremes.

December 10
A telegram from our Consul-General at Algiers today confirms the general discouragement of our supporters in N. Africa at the steps being taken by Darlan to dig himself in and to maintain his semi-fascist gestapo bodies. The happy-go-lucky Americans are proving far too tolerant and trusting.

December 11
At the secret session yesterday on Darlan I gather the P.M. put up a brilliant performance but nonetheless this left an unpleasant taste in the mouth for the attack it contained on General de Gaulle.

The effect of the speech in pacifying the House was largely spoilt too by a venomous attack on Aneurin Bevan and his friends. The latter refused to take any further part in the debate and announced their intention of attacking the Government over Darlan, in public, in and out of the House. Apart from this, everybody present, from Right to Left, tho' admitting the military arguments, felt extreme disquiet at the continuance of Darlan. They insisted on the immediate release of pro-Ally prisoners and Gaullists, also of the International Brigade and Spanish refugees, as well as the rescinding of anti-Semitic legislation.

The P.M. is still unable to see the deep passions which have been aroused and has sent a reassuring letter to Roosevelt. But the Cabinet as a body is becoming more and more uneasy.

Hal Mack is returning to Gib. on Sunday. A.E. has impressed on him that whilst maintaining his admirable relationship which he has established with Eisenhower, he must work steadily and relentlessly for the removal of Darlan.

It is also proposed to take up with Roosevelt the appointment of high civilians to take political work off Eisenhower's shoulders. Harold Macmillan is a possible candidate and we would attach Roger Makins[1] to him.

1. Roger Makins, later Lord Sherfield, and Ambassador to U.S. 1953–1956.

The Dutch Government have now officially expressed their concern over Darlan which is bewildering sections of their own people in Holland. Clark-Kerr has warned us too of the risks of upsetting Russian confidence afresh.

The search for a Viceroy has been given up. Linlithgow has again been prolonged and meanwhile Roger Lumley is coming home and will be looked at.

December 12

Telegram has gone to Roosevelt from P.M. urging appointment of civilian representatives for N. Africa. Roosevelt has also repeated to Eisenhower the telegram sent to him earlier by the P.M. describing the confusion and lack of security along the Spanish/Moroccan frontier, the continuance of oppressive measures and the disquiet of our French supporters. Mack went down to Chequers for the night before going back to Algiers. We are all nervous that the P.M. will shake out of him the good instructions he has been given by the S. of S. The P.M. will belittle the strength of public feeling here and his views will go a good deal further with Eisenhower than A.E.'s However we are warning him, especially as it looks as if official opinion in America were at last becoming disturbed at what has been done. Up till now the State Department have been rigorously excluded by the War Department from any part in N. African affairs. Murphy reports direct to the President. There is no coordination in Washington between one department or minister and another; the President alone holds all the strings and the American soldiers loathe the State Dept. Hal tells me his American friends are amazed at the smoothness and efficiency with which our F.O. works.

Bobbety has drafted an admirable paper which he thinks of circulating to the Cabinet, on the moral issues raised by use of Darlan. I hope he will circulate it although it will infuriate the P.M. Bobbety is like a rock on these things.

Many peacefeelers are coming in from Italy. The only interesting one is indirectly from the Duke of Aosta (brother of the man who died a prisoner in East Africa) who, we are given to understand, would be ready to rise against the Fascist regime in conjunction with an Allied landing. This is a monarchist move aiming at restoration of the monarchy to its old pre-fascist position. There will be plenty ready to come over to us *à la Darlan* as the rot advances. I hope we shall refuse the help of any Fascist. Grandi[1] will be the obvious Darlan, and many

1. Count Dino Grandi, Italian Ambassador in London 1932–1939.

will be ready to excuse him. He is as deep a dyed Fascist as any, *di prima ora*, and his mission to London was used to throw dust in our eyes. Here I'm afraid I now trust the Americans less than ourselves.

December 14
Over the weekend we heard from Gibraltar of the Béthouart–Catroux meeting. This went well and the two generals agreed that cooperation would be easy but that Darlan was impossible and must be got rid of. Darlan had also sent an emissary of his own to Gibraltar and even he came clean and confessed that Darlan could not be allowed to remain. General Giraud wants to send Béthouart on a mission to Washington in January. Meanwhile Darlan *"fait patte de velours"* with Eisenhower, all smiles and helpfulness. But I am more hopeful now than I was of seeing him steered out by means of the "good" French themselves if they can keep together. Béthouart and Mast have both been reinstated, we hear this morning. Admiral Godefroy, however, remains adamant at Alexandria and will have nothing to do with the Darlanite messengers; he is for Pétain and nobody else; but his sailors, better men than he, are gradually deserting and soon he will have none left. The Agreement for our handing over Madagascar to de Gaulle is being signed to-day. This will further strengthen de Gaulle's position.

December 15
We are going ahead again in the Western Desert. Rommel has again been forced out of his positions and is retreating from Agheila. But in Tunis we are stuck.

We are boiling up for another attack of second-front trouble with Stalin. He is prodding us and our answers are evasive. We, that is H.M.G. and the U.S., haven't yet cleared our own minds about the second front. The P.M. and the American General Marshall are veering back to a second front in France next year, with increasing bombing against Germany, whilst leaving the Med. action limited to bombing of Italy, without invasion, opening the seaways to Egypt and bringing Turkey in if possible. Stalin is pressing to know what we intend but refuses to leave Russia to come to a conference with the P.M. and the President. The P.M. is hankering after a meeting with the President at any rate to discuss all this, whilst trying to keep Stalin reassured.

December 17
Darlan has issued a sort of apologia saying what wonderful things he

is doing for us now and how he couldn't have done other than he did before, all out of pure patriotism. He has also sent the P.M. a nauseating letter. *The Times* comments acidly on the apologia and says the sooner Darlan disappears the better.

Murphy, we hear, has been appointed U.S. civil representative in N. Africa. This is a bad appointment for us; M. is the nigger in the woodpile over Darlan and Vichy, and we would have preferred Biddle who was apparently offered the job. We must now appoint our man, Harold Macmillan, I hope, and attach Roger Makins to him.

The leadership of the House is proving more than A.E. can do without loss of efficiency in the Office. He must spend all day in the H. of C. three days a week, and mostly on the bench itself. He has no time to see Ambassadors or others, which it is part of his work to do, and paper work duly piles up all day and remains to be done later in the evening or at night. All office work has to be taken at the double. It may be and probably is good for him politically to gain this further experience and like him, having taken it on, he throws himself into it passionately and is loving it. But it is bad for the Office and for foreign affairs which do not get that care and reflection they require. The remedy is to make Dick Law Assistant Foreign Secretary. The P.M. is ready to approve but A.E. is still reluctant because he hates to let the controls go out of his hands even for a minute. But it is not possible to continue at pressure without a serious breakdown of health and efficiency.

December 18
The big news today was an appeal by the Pope to us to make Rome an open town not subject to bombing in return for which the Italian military authorities including Musso would leave Rome. The Fascist star is getting low on the horizon when the Duce offers to abandon his capital. We are consulting the Americans and suggesting conditions.

We had a horrifying telegram from our Consul General at Algiers saying that some dozen Frenchmen, including Jews, who had helped us, had been condemned to death and others were awaiting trial. A.E. at once authorised the C.G. to give them sanctuary on a British ship and brought it to the attention of the Americans.

December 20
Reply came today from the President to P.M.'s telegram proposing appointment of Harold Macmillan as Agent General in North Africa. P.M.'s proposal was that he should work in cooperation with Murphy

but remain a member of H.M.G. since he would have charge of British interests, Consuls etc. and not be on Eisenhower's staff. President doesn't like this but wants him in exactly same position as Murphy as part of Eisenhower's staff. But this is impossible position for a British Minister and would stultify him from the start. Mack is already on Eisenhower's staff. What we want is an independent civilian who would be directly under H.M.G. but who would of course cooperate closely with Allied C. in C.

Roosevelt seems determined to keep us out of effective say in N. Africa. It is disquieting for the future of Anglo–American cooperation. I gather that even P.M. is becoming slightly peeved at the Presidential methods.

December 21

P.M. is getting more and more restive. "How can I carry on a war with such people?" Obstruction over Darlan (in spite of the P.M.'s most chivalrous behaviour); obstruction over Dakar, obstruction over planning. Even over our suggestions for handling the Pope's proposal about Rome, Hull is making difficulties. Even Alec Cadogan, the imperturbable, is worried. They are just like the Russians, as full of prickles and just as inconsiderate themselves.

December 23

A.E. told me today in great secrecy when we were lunching together that the President's courier had arrived and brought with him a letter proposing a meeting between F.D.R. and the P.M. somewhere in Africa in the middle of January. This would be to discuss war plans; and F.D.R. would prefer no F.O. representation but to keep the meeting to themselves and Chiefs of Staff. As P.M. said, this meant that the President didn't want A.E. A.E. told P.M. he didn't wish to force himself on them but there were a number of postwar and other foreign matters which he wanted to discuss with them and would therefore the P.M. agree to his going to America independently after the African meeting? P.M. said he would.

P.M. has returned to the charge with the President over Macmillan. He has now suggested that he go to North Africa as H.M.G.'s political representative at Eisenhower's H.Q. reporting to P.M. direct. Eisenhower and Murphy are getting more and more involved with Darlan who is of course doing everything to make himself appear indispensable.

A.E. is more tired than I've seen him for a long time. The extra work of the H. of C. is proving too much and it is essential that he delegates F.O. matters more to Dick, but he hates letting go, and both his health and the work are suffering.

December 24

De Gaulle and we hope Catroux are leaving for America this week. Béthouart is also going there from North Africa.

Duncan Sandys has just returned from N. Africa and told A.E. that even Eisenhower himself saw that Darlan couldn't be kept on because he was too unpopular and mistrusted a leader for any effective cooperation there. This is comforting, but we still don't trust Murphy, his civil adviser, who seems to be working for his perpetuation for the duration of the war.

The P.M. now favours a Giraud solution which would be perfectly satisfactory from our point of view and from de Gaulle's. I hope Macmillan can get out there soon to get to work.

December 25

Darlan is dead! He was shot five times yesterday afternoon and died at once. We know no more except that we believe it was a Frenchman and Giraud has taken charge. A sigh of relief and satisfaction will run through the country and the European nations at the removal of this horrible quisling who deserted us in 1939, who fought us and denounced us while we were fighting alone and finally who fought even the Americans until they capitulated to his terms. I didn't hear the B.B.C. but I'm told it scarcely concealed a note of glee. The only false note is from President Roosevelt who described it as "murder of the first degree!"

Now again Providence has given us a chance of reuniting French resistance. The chief obstruction has been removed. But American pride and selfesteem will have been wounded. It is probable that the assassin was a Gaullist[1] and this, if we aren't careful, will be used to perpetuate the vendetta against de Gaulle. De Gaulle would undoubtedly have shot Darlan as a traitor, had he got him in his power, after a court martial. He cannot be expected to condemn it. Murphy, who is anti-British as well as anti-de Gaulle (whom he regards as subversive), will do his utmost to persuade the President that this is the case. If the French are now left alone, Giraud, Catroux and de Gaulle are likely to come together. De Gaulle was by way of starting for America tomorrow, being joined by Catroux. The only way to

1. Now believed to have been a Royalist.

handle the situation that I can see is for the P.M. to send a firm message to the President urging a fresh start to reunite the anti-Axis French under Giraud and de Gaulle. This is a foretaste of the forces which Quislingism has released in France and in Europe. A warning to the Americans not to play with fire.

From the information which reaches us of the North African operations I conclude that it is a mess, Eisenhower an admirable peace-time general overwhelmed by the realities and complexities of war. After all it has taken us all this time to work through our peacetime soldiers till we got to the Alexanders and Montgomeries. The Americans are at the beginning of this process. There has been the usual W.O. muddle as well. Our tanks are inferior to any German tanks; the American tanks are superior: but our crews are trained and superior to the American crews. Result the good American tanks can't be operated and our good crews have nothing effective to operate with.

Darlan, though dead, hasn't yet finished his deadly work. He will leave a nasty hang-over on Anglo–American relations. H.M.G. have been proved right, which is unforgiveable, and Roosevelt's first plunge in European politics has been a failure. This will be a weapon to the isolationists in the presidential campaign. Fortunately, Willkie has been right throughout over this.

December 26
I was horrified to hear on the wireless to-day that Darlan's assassin had been executed this morning after court martial. It was Darlan who should thus have been executed. It shows how wrong you get if once you compromise with evil. You find yourself shooting a good man for doing what you should have done yourself. It is horrible to think of that young man being shot after so hasty and panicky a trial by Vichy colonels. He has done more for France than most Frenchmen.

December 27
Off duty today and yesterday. I hear that de Gaulle was going to Chequers today to luncheon with the P.M. and that he had sent a message to Giraud offering collaboration. His trip to America is postponed. According to the tape, Giraud has been selected to succeed Darlan as High Commissioner. He is alleged to have said he was also ready to collaborate with de Gaulle. If now the Americans can keep their clumsy hands off, the French should unite. American H.Q. here held up de Gaulle's message to Giraud, which has to pass through

Allied G.H.Q. at Algiers for 24 hours "because they didn't think
General Eisenhower would want to be worried with it!" Moley tells
me there is a telegram from Murphy practically admitting that he had
miscalculated the opposition to Darlan and the strength of Gaullism.

December 28

I find President telegraphed to P.M. on 26th proposing in view of
Darlan's assassination and instability in N. Africa that de Gaulle
postpone his journey to U.S. and that Macmillan appointment should
also be delayed. P.M. replied that de G. had agreed to delay but that
H.M.G. attached great importance to getting Macmillan out as soon
as possible as we were quite unrepresented and yet our fortunes were
being committed by events there. He hoped therefore President would
agree to immediate announcement.

Murphy had telegraphed on 25th and 26th, saying Giraud was only
possible successor in his, M.'s, opinion and in that of other generals
including Bergeret and Noguès. The "Imperial Council" had met and
selected Giraud to succeed in virtue of a provision laid down a month
ago. Noguès had said now was the time to make a concerted effort to
reunite all French resistance including Gaullists and that Catroux
would form a very good bridge.

December 29

De Gaulle called on A.E. yesterday. He was quite prepared to cooperate with Giraud and even Noguès, though less willingly with
Boisson.[1] He favoured a single French Authority being formed which
would administer the French Empire. He had offered to meet Giraud
"in Africa". He doubts, however, if amalgamation will prove easy and
he has no opinion of Giraud's intelligence. He has a rooted mistrust of
the Americans.

P.M. has sent a further telegram to Roosevelt, saying he wishes to
announce Macmillan's appointment at once and an aeroplane has been
laid on for Thursday.

December 30

Roosevelt agrees to Macmillan's appointment and departure but
without enthusiasm.

Eisenhower's dispositions in Tunisia are causing our people concern. His forces are widely stretched on the front and far ahead of

1. Governor-General of French West Africa who had handed over Gaullist
   prisoners to the Germans.

reserves. The Germans can reinforce faster than we can and the delay of two months may enable the former to get in their attack first. Rommel is expected to abandon Tripoli and fall back on Tunis to join forces. Eisenhower seems to be too slow, too easy-going and too confident.

December 31

News comes today of a "plot" in N. Africa to murder Giraud, Murphy and others in the interests of Vichy. Giraud has accepted its authenticity and is arresting people who were known supporters of ours and the Americans before the landing took place. We believe it to be a plant by Vichy fifth-columnists to discredit the new movement, separate G. from de Gaulle, and embitter Anglo–American relations. It is a most disquieting situation, which Eisenhower, who seems more and more of an old woman, is in no way qualified to handle. Macmillan left to-day.

There are too many Vichyites about still, e.g. Brisson, Noguès and Chatel. Giraud is an old fool though an honourable one. He has now sent a reply to de Gaulle's message proposing that the latter send an emissary to discuss coordination of all French forces.

Eisenhower's H.Q. and methods of work, we hear, are chaotic. Snap decisions taken without thought; no privacy, everybody in and out. A complete contrast to the orderliness and efficiency of Montgomery's and Alexander's.

The P.M. and F.D.R. are due to meet in North Africa about 16th. After that the P.M. is going to look round. I hope he may clear it up, as he cleared up Cairo. It is a very serious situation, both militarily and politically.

Minor cabinet changes today. Harry Crookshank, P.M.G. (I believe he wouldn't take Housing and Planning), Cherwell, Winston's henchman, becomes Paymaster General. He is a somewhat sinister figure who under the guise of scientific adviser puts up a lot of reactionary stuff.

1943

January 2
Hull has complained to our Embassy that the British press is criticising his French policy. But we have a free press here, as in America itself which never fails to bring home to us our shortcomings in India etc. What about the Luce letter in *Life*?

Roosevelt persists in regarding de Gaulle as just another tiresome "local" Frenchman for all his having fought with us since the beginning.

But it is serious, this division between us over French affairs. We cannot however be dragged into support of Quislings even for America. The British people and the Allied Governments won't stand it. All this is having a noticeable effect in making Europe look to us rather more than to the Americans as their future saviours and protectors. We cannot afford to antagonise America without whose help we cannot win the war, or the peace. We cannot allow her to become disgruntled and isolationist. Her face must always be saved.

De Gaulle in reply to Giraud has offered to meet him personally in Africa. He doesn't wish to send an emissary.

January 5
A.E. told me last night that the P.M. had now definitely agreed to his going to Washington in February, immediately after his own meeting with the President in N. Africa. As to the latter his idea was to send for de Gaulle while he was out there and bring him and Giraud together. For this purpose he would send for A.E. to come out to North Africa too and help. P.M. said he would himself take over leadership of H. of C. while A.E. was in America. A.E. said he wanted to be in America about three weeks so as to be able to go about a little.

January 7
Giraud has now invited de Gaulle to visit him in Algiers at the end of January and proposes a meeting of military representatives meanwhile.

Macmillan seems to be making a good start. A kind of civil Allied Council has been set up on his initiative to deal with all political nations under him and Murphy with representatives of C. in C. and the Navy etc.

P.M. has caused a strong reply to be sent to Hull for his complaints about criticism by the British press of his French policy. He points out that we here have a free press and parliament which we can no more bridle than Hull can the Luces or Willkies. British public opinion was shocked and disgusted at the Darlan episode.

January 18

P.M. has reached his rendezvous with Roosevelt[1] and sent over the weekend an invitation to de Gaulle to go out and join them and meet Giraud with a view to union. A.E. saw de Gaulle on Sunday when he flatly refused. He wouldn't go to meet G. with the P.M. and the President but would go and meet G. alone anywhere the latter chose. He clearly suspected that he would be "muniched". His attitude is understandable but not helpful. It will enrage the P.M. and play into the hands of the President who hates him. I'm only afraid lest the P.M. under this provocation may do something foolish such as disavowing de Gaulle's leadership. But it was too sudden and brutal an approach for these complicated Frenchmen. De G. feels that he has more to offer than G., that G. in fact should join de G.'s movement. G. has a shrewd suspicion that de G. means to swallow him if he can, and he is right.

P.M. and F.D.R. have been having useful talks about the war in N. Africa. The timely advance of the British forces in Tripoli has brought Alexander and Montgomery into the picture at a moment when Eisenhower and Anderson are not doing so well.

January 19

I must record my view that with A.E. leading the House foreign affairs are bound to suffer. They are left to the fag end of the day or to hasty moments snatched between parliamentary business. He cannot give them first attention or adequate reflection. Yet he is quite unable to delegate work. All our plans for giving Dick more have come to nothing because A.E. won't do so. Half the business could be got through by delegation. Even so I am convinced that the Foreign Secretary should not be charged with parliamentary work. He will end by making a mess of both. Half an hour was wasted last night by drafting an eloquent testimony to Lloyd-George on his 80th birthday.

P.M. has sent his reply to de Gaulle's refusal. It is a reasoned

1. At Casablanca.

reiteration of the invitation but it conveys some obvious hints of trouble for de Gaulle if he persists in standing out – no invitation to America, change of attitude to movement by H.M.G. A.E. is to see de Gaulle this afternoon. In the meanwhile the message is being softened down a bit.

These veiled threats will have no effect on a man of de G.'s obstinacy. He is however sending an officer, Billotte, as an emissary to Giraud. There is only one way to bring the two movements together and that is to leave them alone. There can be discreet and useful work in the background but these clumsy methods of forcing G. and de G. together are doomed to failure. But neither the P.M. nor the President can see that. And it would be an ugly thing to apply threats to a man who stood by us in July 1940.

De G. is showing some reluctance to come and it is now decided to hold a cabinet before A.E. delivers the message. The Cabinet are a good deal steadier than the P.M. over this and don't like the idea of threats which it may be awkward to carry out. De Gaulle has a strong position with the British press and public, and any suggestions of "muniching" him would be strongly resented. Also there can be no doubt of the hold he has over occupied France, all the more since it was wholly occupied. He is the symbol of the pure uncontaminated anti-Axis French flame and if we repudiated him, the French would never forgive us. It would shatter French resistance. Even our own shares in France have gone up for our support of de Gaulle against Darlan and the Americans.

January 20
De G. finally declined to come to see A.E. last night when the latter would have handed to him the message from the P.M. as softened down by the Cabinet. Pleven[1] came to see William Strang[2] and told him that de G. did not trust himself not to say things which he would afterwards regret. Charles P. had a further talk with de G. himself when the latter showed that he was well aware that he couldn't stand up against P.M. and Pres. but that he nonetheless must keep his hands clean. G.'s action in appointing the dubious Peyrouton[3] has of course

1. Pleven had succeeded Dejean as de Gaulle's Commissioner for Foreign Affairs.
2. William Strang (later Lord Strang) was Assistant Under-Secretary at the Foreign Office.
3. Vichy French Minister of the Interior in 1940. He had come to N. Africa on Giraud's invitation, and been made Governor-General of Algiers.

increased de G.'s reluctance to go out. But there is still some hope that de G. would respond to an invitation from G. himself. What drives him wild is being invited to French territory by an Englishman and an American. He has already telegraphed to G. offering to meet him when and where he wishes, but G. has not replied.

I'm afraid there is going to be a fresh row here over Peyrouton. Both the H. of C. and the press are up in arms again. "Another blunder" etc.

P.M. seems otherwise to be having satisfactory military talks with Pres.

I talked to A.E. today about the H. of C. He sees himself that it is too much to combine this with F.O. But who is to be leader? Again this morning our de G. business has been rendered more difficult by A.E.'s inaccessibility in H. of C. where there is a row going on over Chairman of Ways and Means!

De G. has agreed to start for N. Africa with Catroux, d'Argenlieu and Palewsky tonight. The aeroplane is laid on but the weather is doubtful. He will miss the Pres. unless he arrives by Friday. He agreed reluctantly after prolonged discussion with his Committee. It is a great triumph for Charles Peake's diplomacy. In reporting this to P.M., A.E. suggested that if possible de G. should be given an opportunity of private talk with G. at outset.

January 22

De G. and company got off last night and should arrive by mid-day.

Cabinet agreed unanimously that it would be unwise for P.M. to go beetling after the Turks[1] and sent a tactfully worded telegram pointing out risks, British public's dislike of absence, probable embarrassment of Turks. To this P.M. has now returned a sorrowful reply: he is obviously disappointed but it looks as if he has given up the idea.

Military situation better and better. Three major successful offensives on Russian fronts, N., centre and S. Obviously the Caucasus is being cleared altogether of enemy, thus releasing all our partially built up Iraq–Persian army for other tasks. In Africa Montgomery's army is on the outskirts of Tripoli, the Rommel forces being bombed and battered as they retreat along the coast into Tunisia. Only in Tunisia itself are things held up – partly mud, partly muddle.

January 23

No news of the de G.–G. meeting in North Africa. But the P.M.–

1. He was proposing to do this after visiting Cairo.

President party is breaking up tomorrow and P.M. goes, we believe, to Cairo. We hope not to meet the Turks.

January 25

Yesterday Cabinet received further telegram from P.M. returning to the charge about Turkey and urging, nay almost insisting that he should go and meet Turkish P.M. at some secret rendezvous. Roosevelt, he said, also favoured this and he would speak on behalf of both. He didn't mind rebuffs. Now was the time etc. Cabinet hastily met at midday and sent back a further reasoned reply against this course. This has produced a further telegram from N. Africa which is to be considered today. We all hate this plan. First, it will alarm the Turks and make them go backwards. This would not matter in itself if it were no more than that, for we shall be better without the Turks in this war. It will however make an unpleasant effect on the Russians who will see in it an attempt to nip into the Balkans with their old enemy Turkey before they can get there themselves. The Turks, to defend their rearguard action, will probably ask for guarantees, territories and munitions. We can agree to none of these without embarrassment. We cannot guarantee Turkey against Russia which is what she wants – without gross offence. We cannot bribe her with territories which don't belong to us (? Syria, Dodecanese). We cannot or should not promise munitions which we cannot spare and which the Turks are incapable of using. This is a hairbrained scheme. No sooner has the P.M. achieved a triumph then he rushes into a folly which spoils it.

The Generals G. and de G. have met and shaken hands, we learn. A joint communiqué will be issued announcing their agreement on the necessity of union for the liberation of France. They have been photographed together in the presence of P.M. and President. De G. is now on the way home.

January 26

Cabinet agreed yesterday reluctantly to give way about P.M. and Turkey. Messages from him and President have been sent off to Turks proposing a meeting with P.M. at Cyprus. Cabinet thought it was hopeless to resist any longer as the P.M. was determined to go and had probably committed himself to the President. We rather hope Turks will refuse. Failing that, they will come with enormous lists of demands.

The famous communiqué of the Winston–Roosevelt meeting is now to come out tomorrow. It is a somewhat bombastic document, "nothing like this has ever occurred before", and will give Stalin a wry smile and Goebbels a laugh.

January 27

Turks have replied to P.M.'s proposal suggesting a visit to Angora if he wishes to see the President (who cannot constitutionally leave Turkish territory) or alternatively agreeing that Sarajoglu and the C. of Staff should meet the P.M. at Cyprus. Cabinet are considering this today. We here feel Angora far too risky on security grounds and best course would be Cyprus meeting with Sarajoglu and the soldiers.

Details of the G. and de G. meeting are coming to hand. It appears that P.M. was pretty rough with de G. but said that provided de G. played up and didn't let personalities affect him, he, the P.M., would not let him down. The President, on the other hand, charmed and impressed de G. enormously and was equally impressed by him. Giraud is a complete bonehead who understands nothing since about 1890. In the joint communiqué, on which P.M. and President insisted, G. refused to allow the words "democratic rights" to appear: it had to be changed to "human rights". De G. and G. were pretty stiff with each other. Catroux was the better solvent and got on well with G. whilst realising to the full that de G. was the only possible leader. Catroux is anxious to go to N. Africa as head of the de G. liaison mission which it was agreed to send.

But de G. is depressed. It is not going to be easy. N. Africa behind the façade of the bold and brave G. has a completely Vichy lay-out – Peyrouton, Noguès etc. – who are backed, *faute de mieux*, by Murphy and the Americans. There is no doubt a real shortage of Frenchmen of big enough calibre or experience to take responsibility and run the machine, but whilst we, like de G. realise how disastrous this will be for the future unless remedied somehow, the Americans regard it cynically and as of no future consequence.

Cabinet have replied to P.M. advising most strongly against visit to Angora. A visit to Turkish territory close to frontier would be less objectionable. This has crossed a telegram from P.M. saying the Turks are delighted and he is just starting off.

Mack brought a message for A.E. from Roosevelt saying "he looked forward to seeing him again somewhere soon". This is encouraging but there is nothing to show that P.M. has ever broached the question of his going over now.

January 28
P.M. has fixed his visit to Adana for 29th or 30th. It is very doubtful
if Alec Cadogan will catch him in time. He is evidently in the highest
spirits and maintains that he has been "cordially invited". We are all
much alarmed at what may now transpire. A.E. is distinctly nervous
and resentful at this intrusion into foreign affairs. Why cannot P.M.'s
be content to use their Foreign Secretaries? They are all alike in
fancying themselves.

January 29
P.M. beetling off to Adana, full of eager anticipation.
   Both Massigli[1] and Charbonnière, who have just arrived from
France, confirm and indeed more than confirm, go beyond our esti-
mates of the support which de G. enjoys there. M., we hear, may take
Pleven's place on the National Committee. We hope Catroux may go
back to N. Africa as head of the liaison mission which is to be sent.
He knows G. well and can work with him: he knows N. Africa; and he
is loyal to de G. We have some reason to fear Murphy may have done
some deal with G. behind our backs. Although his Vichy policy has
failed, he remains obstinately wedded to it.
   Are the Americans, like Alexander I, after being the great liberals,
going to become the reactionaries of the Peace Congress? There are
signs of it. "Bulwarks against Bolshevism" "Big Business'; "Law and
Order" etc. etc. If so, I hope, we, as then, will take the other side.

January 31
Our surmise was only too true. The P.M. and the President having
dispersed from Casablanca, Murphy has produced two documents –
one providing for supply of arms and aircraft to Giraud on a lavish
scale from American sources, the other recognising him to all intents
as the sole authority for French affairs not only in N. Africa but
everywhere else. No reference to our having any part in N. Africa or
any right to consultation. Murphy gives Macmillan to understand that
both the President and the P.M. had endorsed these documents. We
cannot believe this. In any case nothing whatever had been said of
them to Macmillan himself by Murphy. Macmillan has been told that
both must be held up pending reference to the P.M. We have telegraphed to the P.M. pointing out the grave embarrassment which
would be caused to H.M.G. if it were held to have approved the sidetracking of de G. in favour of G. Sharp work by Murphy!

1. René Massigli, later French Ambassador to Britain 1944–54.

It seems to be the American intention to build up Giraud with arms and authority so as to enable him to return to France with a conquering army and restore there a near-Vichy authority. De G. is too shrewd to be caught by that. But G. is an old fool.

However prospects of a G. de G. agreement are brighter. Catroux has been appointed to lead the de G. mission to N. Africa. Massigli is to become de G.'s foreign minister. G. himself is making a start with releasing communist deputies and de G. sympathisers. The French may yet get together and pull a surprise on their backers.

February 2
More details of the Adana talks are coming in. In particular a paper called "Morning Thoughts" which the P.M. left with the Turks and which gives them the main lines of our future military and political policy, including post-war plans. Most of this goes far beyond anything which the Cabinet or even the F.O. had ever proposed. The P.M. after obstructing any discussion of such plans, brings them out in a paper of his own and hands it to the Turks who aren't even fighting for us. Added to this, we have good reason to fear that the whole thing will have been read by the Germans owing to the P.M.'s staff sending it off in the local general's cypher.

Attlee can think of nothing better to do than to send each day a fulsome telegram of praise and flattery to the P.M. who is trampling on the Cabinet and doing everything they tried to prevent him doing. A.E. refuses to be associated with these messages.

One bright feature is that the P.M. has replied that he had never seen the French documents (recognising Giraud as the authority for all French interests outside France) which Murphy had alleged had been approved and that he strongly disapproves of them. He is going to look into this in Algiers on his way home.

A.E. gave a dinner last night to Massigli, de Gaulle, and Catroux. Bobbety Cranbourne and Moley were there and I got A.E. to ask Herbert Morrison (who is worth six of Attlee and deserves encouragement and guidance). De G. very pessimistic about the prospects of reunion. The mass of French opinion which alone counted was with him, de G. Giraud represented nothing except the Vichy elements and opportunists who surrounded and held him. G. was a stout opponent of the Axis but a reactionary old man. He instanced his refusal to accept the words "democratic rights" which de G. had put into his draft for the joint communiqué and which had had to be modified to "human rights". If G. returned to France at the head of these people and had not united with de G. there could only be civil war. A civil war in France would benefit only the Communists: its repercussions would be felt even in England. All present were impressed with his views, both Bobbety and Morrison being more Gaullist even than A.E. But all said that if this were so, then it was the duty of de G. to do all he could to prevent civil war by trying now to get hold of G. by means of a liaison mission and to guide and control his movements. On this de G. remained profoundly sceptical. Only if G. were given to understand by the British and U.S. Governments that they disapproved of Peyrouton and Co. would changes be made and public opinion orient itself accordingly.

Massigli confirmed that there would be civil war in France if Vichy elements returned with G. Only a de G. Government would have the authority and prestige to hold and control France during the transition period until regular forces could be set up again.

February 6
The papers announce today that Ciano has been sacked together with Grandi and others in what looks like a purge of the Fascist Government. Musso remains. They also say that Rosso, the former somewhat anti-Fascist Ambassador in Moscow, and a very decent man, has been appointed Ambassador to Turkey. One's first thought is that Ciano, Grandi and Co. are getting ready to be Darlans. With Papen as German Ambassador in Angora, also an obvious Darlan, we look to be in for some strong peace-feelers. I hope we can resist them. No good will come of any truck with such people who are steeped to the neck in Fascism and are in a way worse than Musso. himself. But Grandi would have many friends here.

Massigli's appointment as National Commissary for F.A. is out today with Catroux's appointment to head the mission to North Africa. We are getting on. With these two at work there is hope at last of a reunion. The French alone can get together and dish the Americans.

February 8
P.M. got back on Sunday a day later than expected owing to a breakdown of his aeroplane.

He confessed to A.E. that he had never said a word to the President about his visit to Washington but he was all in favour of his going in about a fortnight, and that he would telegraph to Roosevelt and propose it. A.E. wants to look at his agenda and see how soon he can start before the P.M. telegraphs.

P.M. in very belligerent mood, as usual on the return from these trips, and indignant at the Cabinet's attempts to restrain him from going to Turkey. His encounters with Roosevelt always have a bad effect. He dominates the President and at the same time envies him for being untrammelled by a Cabinet.

Meanwhile the P.M. on his way back through Algiers secured the modification of the famous Murphy Giraud documents in the sense we wanted, viz. confining Giraud's pretensions to North Africa. This change has now been referred to the President. But it transpires that the President, for all his championship of Giraud, has the oddest ideas of the future France. He talked airily of making Dakar an Allied base after the war and of sticking to the French islands in the Pacific which the U.S. are occupying, regardless of the fact that, unlike us, he has committed himself in documents to both Pleven and Giraud to restore the integrity of the French Empire. At one time he even said he didn't think France should have an army, though he agreed at Casablanca to rearm Giraud's forces on the most extravagant scale, far beyond reason or shipping capacity. Giraud himself is doing better, enlarging and liberalising his régime, giving rights to Jews, releasing Communists etc.

Now that the Eighth Army has cleared the enemy out of Tripoli and entered Tunisia, the time has come to put into force the new plan by which Eisenhower becomes C. in C. with Alexander as deputy. Although the idea behind this is that Alex and Monty will now run the battle which Eisenhower is making a mess of, the British public will not know this and criticism may be expected. The British people are critical of generals and now we've found a good one they won't see why our men should be put under a peacetime American. Oh! this face-saving!

February 9

The P.M. has come back even more anti-de Gaulle than when he left. He is outraged at de G.'s slowness in accepting the invitation to Casablanca when he had done everything he could to make him acceptable to the Americans. He now talks of breaking him. A.E. reasoned with him as usual, receiving, again as usual, no help from Attlee who could only nod his head in approval of whatever nonsense the P.M. said. What the P.M. doesn't realise is that de Gaulle is past breaking now. He can break him here but we cannot break him in

France where the bulk of his supporters are. All we should achieve by that would be to turn sound French opinion against us, whilst troubling profoundly the waters of public opinion here which are strongly pro-de Gaulle, anti-North African and beginning to be anti-American too. The P.M. is to see Massigli today and may take a more sober view.

February 10
Spectacular Russian victories continue[1] – Kursk, Rostov, wherever the Russians attack, the Germans give way. The impression created here among people at large is immense. I have the feeling that there is a slight gap between the enthusiasm of the masses and the attitude of some of the Government (not by any means all). To some of the Government it is incredible, unforgiveable, indeed inadmissible, that the Russians can be so successful. This is the attitude of the W.O. and of Grigg – to take an extreme case. The Russians are very tiresome allies, importunate, graceless, ungrateful, secretive, suspicious, ever asking for more, but they are delivering the goods.

A.E. hopes to start for Washington in about 10 days. He has now sent the P.M. the draft of a telegram for Roosevelt proposing the visit.

The announcement of the new military commands in N. Africa is about to be made. Roosevelt is anxious to stress Eisenhower's appointment as Allied C. in C. over all forces in N. Africa including 8th Army but to say nothing of the arrangement by which Alexander is to be deputy C. in C. with specific task of fighting the battle of Tunis with combined British, American and French forces. P.M. has very properly replied that there is much criticism of Eisenhower's generalship here which the M. of I. are having difficulty in repressing and that if this bald announcement now comes out, criticism will be uncontrollable and will react on Anglo–American relations. He urges strongly that the full plan should be divulged.

February 13
I've been laid up with a throat and haven't been to the Office for 2 days. I hear on the telephone that the President has replied to the P.M. agreeing to A.E.'s visit, but that the P.M. had altered the terms of our draft considerably before it went off. I suppose he has cut out all the references to postwar problems – the old rascal! Anyway I don't much mind so long as A.E. gets there. What he talks about when he

1. Von Paulus had surrendered at Stalingrad on February 2.

gets there cannot be controlled from No. 10. A.E. will have to do a sort of Canning and bring in the New World again to jockey along Downing Street.

A very good broadcast by the President last night, stating more completely than ever that there can be no future for quisling governments after the war, and no Fascist nor Nazi government can be set up after the war, nor can the Atlantic Charter be held to cover freedom to make war on neighbours or to enslave at home. Admirable and exactly what was needed to dispel the confusion in our ranks caused by the Darlan episode.

February 15
Returned to F.O. today and find we are set to start for America on Monday next.

February 16
Full of preparations for our trip.

P.M. is anxious to follow up Adana by pushing the Turks and the Soviets into each other's arms. The Turks, somewhat embarrassed, take the line that they are ready for a *rapprochement* provided it doesn't upset Germany. They suggest themselves as a go-between us and the Soviets in the Balkans for after the war. This is the last thing we want.

February 17
A.E. had a meeting after dinner last night with the Washington party to discuss our agenda. A useful talk which showed that A.E. had no definite proposals which he would have Cabinet authority to put forward. The chief value of the visit would be to enable him to put the screw on the Cabinet here by showing how far ahead the Americans were thinking.

February 18
A further set back on the American front in Tunis. The Germans have lashed out again and forced an American retreat with loss of 170 tanks and some airfields. The new Alexander set-up is coming to effect today, I believe. But it is the old story of untrained troops and peace-time generals. It takes three years to make an army.

On the Russian front all is going marvellously. Maisky, who had a message from Stalin, came last night to say the situation was so grave for the Germans in the East that there might even be a collapse, and to urge that we review our plans for the possibility of an earlier entry into Europe. The situation had changed even since Casablanca, and the plans they prepared for Husky [Sicilian landing] might no longer hold.

In the actual message which Maisky brought Stalin urged forcibly the need for action earlier than our plans implied. He drew attention to the delays in Tunis which, he alleged, had enabled the Germans to send more troops against Russia. He wants a general attack from all sides at once (including "The Second Front in Europe") as soon as possible, i.e. spring or early summer.

February 19

P.M. has asked A.E. to delay his journey for a week or so as owing to his cold he doesn't feel able to take on the extra work of F.O. and H. of C. P.M. still has a temperature of 101 and is feeling pretty low.

Gandhi has been fasting and now looks pretty bad. If he dies, it will be said we have killed him, though his confinement consists only in his living in the palatial villa of the Aga Khan. Roosevelt and Hull have sent the Viceroy a message direct, through Phillips, the President's personal representative in India, hoping that means may be found of preventing the situation deteriorating. This intervention hasn't gone well: it is indeed inadmissible, but nonetheless the Viceroy has a bad anti-American complex and the Government's record isn't so positive as they can be proud of it. The Viceroy gives the impression of being rigid and awkward in his handling of Gandhi. Halifax would have done it better.

The lavish American promises of rearmament and re-equipment to Giraud are coming home to roost. General Giraud has now complained that nothing has been done, French opinion in North Africa is discouraged and disillusioned, whilst the American reverses and losses have made even more doubtful the possibility of promised supplies and shipping being available. Roosevelt's conception, as it appears to us, is to maintain American control over the French administration, to prevent any central political authority being formed and to deal ad hoc with any French territories in his hands, using them himself now and deciding their future later. (He may want some for bases.) He doesn't seem to want France as a first-class power after the war. H.M.G.'s policy, on the other hand, is a strong France, starting now by the union of G. and de G. and of the N. African and Free French territories, under a single centralised authority which should become increasingly civilian and democratic in character by grouping round it as many Frenchmen of ability as possible.

February 22

P.M. rather better according to the bulletin though I hear Mrs. C. is very worried about him and it is clear that after such a persistent temperature he will take another week or two if not more to recover.

Gandhi is very near dying. The Government persist in refusing to release him. American opinion is disquieted. I think the Government are wrong. It is no answer to say, as the Viceroy does, he thinks he has the situation in hand.

A very difficult question of strategy is now arising. At Casablanca it was decided that after Tunis was cleared the Anglo–American forces should embark on Husky. This decision involves sending the assault landing craft in three weeks' time from England via the Cape to Egypt, a journey which will take two months. Now comes Stalin's and Maisky's pleas for quicker action against Germany by means of a second front, as well as our planners' report that the Germans have been so mauled by the Russians that a breakdown must be taken into account as well as the strong probability that they can no longer seriously reinforce W. Europe to resist landings. In fact a landing in France may be possible against diminished resistance this summer to put it no higher. Under the existing plan all our landing craft would be either wending their way beyond recall round the Cape or engaged in a big but not necessarily determining operation in Sicily. The Russians would like this plan scrapped and a new plan started to bring all available forces back to England immediately Tunis is clear in order to mount an attack on the continent from here. A middle course is to scrap Husky and go for Sardinia and Corsica instead. To do this, the landing craft could start from here and go direct into the Mediterranean via Gibraltar, a month's time would be gained, it would be easier to ship them or bring them home for operations in Northern France and alternatively they would be on the spot for landings in S. France if conditions of weakened German resistance promised success.

All this must be decided by the middle of March at latest.

P.M.'s health still stationary. He is taking no papers.

Tunisia is in a nasty mess. The Germans are hitting out against the soft places represented by the Americans and French in the centre, with consequent danger to the British First Army in the North. The British Eighth Army coming up from the South has still to overcome the Mareth defences. Eisenhower, like the unfortunate Auchinleck before Alamein, has got his forces all split up into bits and pieces and scattered; they are discouraged and worried. Alexander in fact has to try and repeat his feat at Alamein of reorganising and reinspiring a troubled and disorganised army, with the added complication of three nationalities, inexperienced American troops and ill-equipped French ones. And, finally, what is not sufficiently known, there is the scandalous muddle of the W.O. in sending out our best armoured division with two pounder tanks (no match against the Germans) instead of arranging for them to receive American Shermans in N. Africa. This is one of the worse things the W.O. has done and the C.I.G.S. must be held responsible.

Appeasement of Italy has begun to raise its ugly head. Ciano has taken up his position as Ambassador to Vatican where he will be well placed to pull the Pope's strings. Archbishop Spellman of New York, a former colleague of the Pope, has arrived in Rome. I don't think either the P.M. or Roosevelt is to be trusted where Italy is concerned. But the row over Darlan would be as nothing compared with the storm which any dealing with Ciano would raise.

February 24
P.M. better this morning. Normal temperature.

French affairs going rather better under the impulsion of Massigli as I knew they would. M. came to see A.E. and told him that the National Committee here was acting as a constitutional body whose approval had to be obtained for the general's decisions; this hadn't amounted to much check hitherto owing to poor quality of Free French commissioners but this was now improving as more men came out from France. The General, himself, wished to make a tour again to Syria, Central Africa and North Africa. We don't like the idea of his going off again to Syria where things are going well at present and where he would be certain to do impetuous and foolish things as he did before, but we see no harm in his going to North Africa to see Eisenhower and Giraud. (General de G. had sent a flattering telegram to Eisenhower which has evidently tickled the latter to death because he asked him to visit him.)

February 25
P.M. has come to life again with a vengeance. He has dictated, without reference to anyone, a telegram for despatch to Macmillan directing that he should take any opportunity of pushing Flandin[1] into the N.

1. Pierre-Etienne Flandin, former French P.M. and Foreign Minister, had been Vichy Foreign Minister for three months at the end of 1940, and was a noted collaborator.

African Government! He has, we suspect, been encouraged to do this by Randolph Churchill who is living in a farm next door to Flandin. A.E. at the same moment had directed that a telegram be sent warning Mack against any employment of Flandin because of the disastrous impression which the appearance of such a snake would have here. A.E. held up both telegrams and went to beard the P.M. this morning. The latter fell into a fury at his telegram being held up and said he would say what he liked. A.E. finally got him to wait for a dossier on F. which is being prepared. But from what the P.M. said it is doubtful if he will agree to drop it and violent and shattering storms must be expected on this and every other subject. The P.M. is getting more reactionary and more dictator-minded. He is in a mood to defy the Cabinet and public opinion. Naturally this is increased by his illness and weakness. But while he is ill, he really cannot expect to govern. When he is well, he can fight it out with his Cabinet. As usual this wrath falls mostly on A.E.'s head.

February 26
A.E. saw P.M. again last evening when he was very contrite, saying he was worried at delaying A.E.'s trip, showing him the little "V" sign ornament Beatrice had given him and so on. As for Flandin, he agreed to telegraph to Macmillan instructing him to refer home if there was any question of bringing F. into the administration. So it is going to be, I'm afraid, up and down, explosions and contritions. He is proving equally difficult to his other Ministers. Amery said his views on India were those of a subaltern at Poona in 1892!

February 28
P.M. has said A.E. can plan for his departure about March 12th. He will then be well enough to take over F.O. and H. of C.

The old boy is in a rage again with de G. He wishes force used if necessary to prevent his leaving the country to visit Syria, and Africa, declares that he is our "foe". What nonsense! De G. is a very difficult man, but he is incorruptible and anti-Axis. On that basis he has steadily increased in stature. Because he is awkward and not pliant is one of the reasons for his hold over his people. I don't believe he is a crypto-Fascist or would establish an authoritarian régime in France except for the purpose of holding elections. I believe we can rely on him to resist German blandishments now or hereafter. We cannot say the same of Pétain, or of the North Africans. Giraud, though honest and anti-Axis too, is weak, reactionary and old.

March 2

As a result of Russian refusal of the airforce unit to protect our convoys
in North Russia and of other acts of obstruction A.E. read Maisky a
lecture last Friday and Clark-Kerr has repeated it in Moscow ending
up by saying we must now reconsider our policy of sending convoys
to Russia at all. The Cabinet all felt it was time for a show-down.

March 3

Once again we look like a head-on collision with de G. The latter
asked some time ago for facilities to visit Syria, Central Africa and
North Africa. Hitherto we have succeeded in stalling on this by
urging Massigli to get him to postpone these plans; first, because it
was unnecessary to visit Syria at all now where all for once is going
smoothly, second, because the General should remain in London to
handle the negotiations with Giraud, and third, because it would be a
fatal mistake for de G. to visit N. Africa before Catroux's mission had
got to work there, and he couldn't visit Eisenhower in N. Africa
without seeing G. All this time the P.M. has been in increasing rage
with de G. whom he wished to prevent leaving by force because he has
come to regard him as our "foe". Now de G. who is never helpful to
his friends, has become suspicious and impatient and poor Massigli
has failed to head him off the planned visits. De G. sent for Charles
Peake[1] yesterday and asked him point blank to let him know in 24
hours when he could start or whether he was a prisoner – the consequences for which would be most grave!

A.E. is between the hammer and the anvil. For British interests we
are all convinced that we should work with de G. (who has stood by us,
who is anti-Axis and anti-Vichy and who has France behind him).
The P.M. is passionately persuaded that de G. is our enemy, that he
will work against us now and even after and that he means to bedevil
Anglo–American relations. De G. is convinced that he is Joan of Arc,
that Giraud's position is disintegrating and that he has only to sit back
and be rude to everybody for N. Africa now and France afterwards to
fall into his lap.

Now what are the facts and the British interests? First, the best of
France (the masses, labour, peasants, youth) are pro-de Gaulle.
Second, N. Africa is not pro-de Gaulle but pro-Vichy and Giraud is its
prisoner. Third, the Americans have put their money on G. and for
their prestige's sake won't let him "disintegrate". Fourth, de G. has a

1. Charles Peake had become British Representative with the French National
Committee in London.

very strong hold over British public opinion because he is anti-Vichy and the Government here is mistrusted because of Darlan. A row between de G. and H.M.G. would astonish and displease the British public. Fifth, de G. is a most bloody man in his obstinacy, vanity, ignorance and lack of diplomacy, but these very failings are part of his strength. Sixth, a wiser man would have known how to handle Winston, flatter the Americans (as he has flattered Eisenhower) and capture the Giraud position by infiltration. Seventh, now we are heading for a bust-up with him here in which we shall appear in a shabby role, and for a civil war in France afterwards which will revive the fires of the Spanish Civil war.

Cabinet considered de G.'s ultimatum this morning. It was decided it was intolerable that he should treat us so rough, that Charles Peake should see Massigli and not de G. in consequence and that he should convey to M. a reasoned reply setting out why H.M.G. thought it highly undesirable that de G. should absent himself from England at this moment and consequently they would not allow him facilities.

March 4

Massigli to whom Charles Peake handed this reply, begged to see A.E. before delivering it. A.E. saw him at once. M. begged that A.E. should see de G. himself but A.E. said this would be useless and would make matters worse. M. then said he feared reply would have worse effect and de G. would resign, declaring himself to be a prisoner.

March 5

The reply to de Gaulle hasn't as yet produced the catastrophic effects I feared. The General has retired to his mountain-top at Hampstead and has cancelled a luncheon party he was giving. He went to Admiral Stark,[1] the American liaison officer, and told him that H.M.G. had been unable to give facilities for his visit to N. Africa – for reasons which he quite understood; he was anxious to go to see Eisenhower for whom he had a profound admiration and to whom he felt sure he could be helpful in discussing the military situation in N. Africa. Could the Americans provide him with an aeroplane? Stark was deeply impressed and told Charles Peake that he thought we were quite wrong about the General. Stark has been told that we are most anxious for de Gaulle to visit N. Africa and see not only Eisenhower

1. Admiral H. R. Stark, commanding U.S. Naval Forces in Europe 1942–1945.

but Giraud, but that we are sure it is best for Catroux to go first and prepare the ground and that de G. should then go and clinch agreement.

March 8
Our trip is now fixed for Thursday.

March 11
At last we have started. Special train from Euston at 1.30 p.m. The party consists of William Strang, Gladwyn Jebb, Michael Wright, Robin Cruikshank (from M. of I.) myself and the detective.

A.E. came up from Chequers this morning. He said P.M. was in good spirits, but thinner and older looking for his illness. P.M. wouldn't agree to Bobbety taking on Foreign Office while A.E. was away. He said Dick Law and Moley must do it, referring to him if necessary. He laughed and said "You be careful offering the F.O. to others. There has already been one candidate who has offered himself, Herbert Morrison!"

P.M. warned A.E. against paying too much attention to the Republicans in America. He told him for his most confidential information that he understood F.D.R. would run again.

I hope P.M. won't take any desperate action against de Gaulle in our absence. It looks as if de G. himself had decided not to kick against the pricks for the present. Charles Peake has heard no more from him. We must keep our hands off the French. If there is to be a row with de G., let it come from the French themselves, from Catroux or Massigli resigning. It would be fatal for us to touch de G. or to try to remove him. It would be burning Joan of Arc all over again.

Arrived at Kilmarnock about 10.30 p.m. and drive in cars to the Prestwick Airport. It was the first time I'd flown at night. We seemed to slide into the air. Inside the aeroplane there were two berths at the further end which A.E. and Strang took, and six seats, 3 on each side. I took the last one.

We landed on Gander aerodrome about 3.30 (our time) 12.30 p.m. (local time) after 15 hours' flight. We clambered out of the hole in the aeroplane and staggered gratefully across the slippery frozen ground into the hangar where the Canadian Commandant took charge of us and brought us to breakfast in his own little house. What a breakfast – glasses of orange juice, cereals, bacon and eggs, butter, coffee. After two hours we started again for Washington, another six hours off.

We had a wonderful view of New York in the sun, the Hudson

River, and the skyscrapers looking from the height like the houses in an Italian town, all a warm brown colour. Finally, we flew over Baltimore and Washington itself landing exactly at 7 p.m. (local time), 23 hours after leaving Prestwick. Halifax and Sumner Welles were there to meet us and we drove to the Embassy.

We dined at the Embassy. A.E., Strang and me with Halifax and Ronnie Campbell and Brand – Harry Hopkins came in later to talk to A.E. about plans. He is the *éminence grise* of the President and is always helpful to us; a funny exhausted-looking little man of about 45, originally a social worker and then a New Dealer and now chief favourite. Halifax seemed more patrician, dynastic and aloof from reality than ever, ready in the most charming way to pour plenty of water into our wine. He is no representative of England in 1943; he is an old Whig.

The President, according to Hopkins, is eager for the fullest conversations with A.E. He has asked him to dine tomorrow and Sunday to begin with. He loves Winston as a man for the war, but is horrified at his reactionary attitude for after the war.

Next week is to be given to talks and contacts in Washington; the following week-end to New York to stay with the Ogden Reids[1] and have more contacts there. Then back to Washington with visits to Army and Navy during the second week.

Bed after further talks with Ronnie Campbell who put in a word of warning against taking the President *au pied de la lettre*. He tells us how cagey the State Department have recently become, rarely confiding in us or telling us even of what they are about to do.

March 13
Breakfast with William Strang. We discuss Halifax's tendency to keep us all away from A.E. and agree it must be firmly resisted. I have a feeling of isolation in this Embassy. There seems to be no human contact with the outside world or even with the staff except on the highest levels. Very Viceregal. A.E. rather fussed at thought of big press conference this morning. He thinks now it was a mistake to have it, says Winston never has them. I can only reply that everybody from Halifax downwards thinks we must hold one.

Press Conference duly took place in the Embassy ballroom. It was a great success. All very friendly; no difficulties or hostile questions and nothing about Gandhi or Beveridge! Snowing outside.

Winant came to the lunch. He told A.E. he couldn't come to meet

1. Of the *New York Herald Tribune*.

him at the aerodrome yesterday because Sumner Welles, who is jealous of him, wouldn't tell him when A.E. was arriving. Welles was furious because the President had asked Winant and not him to dine with him to meet A.E. tonight.

The Dominion Representatives came this afternoon when A.E. gave them an admirable account of the war situation. Both the Australian Dixon,[1] and Nash,[2] the New Zealander, spoke bitterly of the cavalier way in which the Americans behaved towards their countries in the Pacific. They urged strongly how important it was for Great Britain to increase her forces there.

A day of telephoning and of making appointments for the coming week.

Talked to A.E. while he was dressing before he went to dine at the White House. It will be a momentous conversation. Roosevelt clearly thinks little of Winston for the future. I hope this means he hopes to cooperate with A.E. I urged greatest frankness in his discussions. A.E. feels it is all rather like a mad house. He said to me he felt more at home in the Kremlin. There at least they meant business. Here all is confusion and woolliness. President jealous of Hull, Winant and Welles at cross purposes. It is not possible here, imagine, to discuss our problems with Roosevelt, Hull and Welles altogether. Each has to be addressed separately and it is doubtful if one will tell the other what he has said.

March 14

A.E. didn't get home from the White House till 12.30 a.m. – almost Winstonian hours. I saw him first thing. Much easier and happier in mind after the first fence. He says he begins to get the feel of the place and how things work. There must be no hurrying them. It will take time, but he is definitely hopeful of results. The President was most charming, "birds off the tree" and all that.

The President spoke of the draft Senate resolution which appeared this morning. It urges the U.S. Government to take initiative in setting up U.N. machinery for coordinating the war effort now, for policing Europe after the war, for preparing relief plans, for organising the administration of occupied territories on deliverance. This has been engineered by the President who believes it to be the best means of getting round the Senate difficulty. He looks forward to holding shortly a U.N. Conference on Food Production somewhere outside

1. Sir Owen Dixon, Australian Minister to U.S. 1942–1944.
2. Walter Nash, Minister of New Zealand to U.S. 1942–1944.

Washington when quiet work can be done. He hopes later on to have a conference with P.M. and Joe together at . . . . A.E. is to dine with him again tonight but this is to be a larger dinner with cinema after. So far all is *couleur de rose* – the press very friendly and indeed the press conference evidently exactly right.

A.E. saw both Stimson[1] and Knox[2] today. Latter very anxious for him to visit the Navy. If he were to see all that he is wanted to see he'd be here for years. We have already postponed our departure for Canada to about March 31.

A.E. saw Hopkins and Winant again before dinner. H.H. admitted that in his talks with President, Hull and Sumner Welles A.E. would find three quite different sets of views of the future. He must follow up what seemed the most promising.

March 15

A.E. saw Wallace[3] and Hull this morning and lunched with Knox at the Navy Department. The Hull meeting went well, I gather. Hull talked at length about his Vichy policy which is a fetish with him and complained of the attacks he had suffered from Gt. Britain. A.E. and Halifax did their best to persuade him of the groundlessness of his grievance. The British people felt intensely about Vichy and Pétain and Darlan, and no one, neither A.E. nor Winston himself, could have persuaded them of the contrary. On broader questions Hull was better. He said the future depended upon Gt. B. and U.S.A. understanding each other and working in collaboration with Russia. He believed there was here a drift against isolationism and he for his part was determined to avoid if possible the fiasco of Wilson.

I lunched with Harold Butler. Butler said that our stand over Darlan had immensely helped us in America. All those who attacked us over India were silenced because they were the anti-Darlanites here. When Gandhi failed to die after H.M.G. had made clear they didn't intend to release him they were again impressed by our successful toughness, and decided it was a phoney fast.

A.E. told me how embarrassing it was at his meetings with both Wallace and Hull when they had expatiated on their approval of his conduct in resigning over appeasement in the presence of Halifax. I said to him it was only because he had resigned that he was where he was and Halifax where he was. H. had only himself to blame.

1. H. Stimson, U.S. Secretary for War 1940–1945.
2. Colonel Frank Knox, U.S. Secretary for Navy 1940–1944.
3. Henry Wallace, U.S. Vice-President 1941–1945.

Poor H. is most helpful and yet he kills everything that comes near him. He devitalises his staff. Ronnie Campbell looks only half alive. Yet H. has a very good mind and has very attractive sides. He has a devastating simplicity but I remind myself that it conceals a harsh and ruthless nature. Lady H. is enchanting.

Roosevelt is developing a passion for A.E. *"On ne se quitte plus"*. He telephoned after lunch today to ask him to dine again with him tonight and the Embassy dinner which had been arranged was hastily cancelled. Nothing could be better. If these two men can really make friends almost anything is possible. A.E. is happier and easier every day. I think he may be doing immensely valuable work. We must not worry about the *means*, untidy or otherwise, which Roosevelt adopts to involve America in Europe. He knows the Senate and his people and how best he can tease them along.

March 16
A.E. didn't get back from White House till 12.30 a.m. He had had a most satisfactory evening again. Much fuller and more far-reaching discussions of political problems than ever before. His next date with the President is tea tomorrow. Hopkins told A.E. that he should carry on similar conversations with Hull and Welles, developing his ideas as he did to the President, but not repeating to them what the President's ideas were! It is an exhausting country where the President can, and insists on, discussing foreign policy without his Foreign Secretary being present and without even wishing him to know what his ideas are.

The President developed his view that after the war only the big Three Powers, U.S.A., U.S.S.R., and G.B., should have any armaments at all. A.E. pointed out some of the difficulties of this. The President spoke also of the importance of improving collaboration between the U.S. and U.S.S.R. Here we were in a better position. He returned to his idea of a meeting *à trois* with Stalin. At this point A.E. told him what we understood Russia's views of her frontiers to be. (Maisky saw A.E. just before we left, and speaking personally, said he believed the Soviet Government's policy was to absorb the Baltic States, give Poland E. Prussia, occupy the Curzon Line, and to insist on guarantee pacts with Roumania and Finland.) The President thought G.B. and U.S. and U.S.S.R. should agree a policy for Poland between themselves and then impose it. He made no difficulty over Baltic States or Curzon Line but spoke vaguely of plebiscites which are a favourite idea of his. He questioned whether it would be possible to work with Russia now and after. A.E. said we must try in virtue of the Anglo–Soviet Treaty. In any case we could be no worse off for trying. Turning to Germany, the President spoke strongly in favour of dismemberment – E. Prussia, W. Poland, Wurtenburg and Bavaria, the Rhineland. He thought the occupation should be so designed to make of Germany three or four separate zones within which every separatist tendency should be encouraged. The policing of Germany should be done by the big Three on behalf of the rest. The same principle could be applied elsewhere. A.E. spoke of the desirability of letting the Allied Governments take over responsibility for their own countries as soon as possible. This led the President to ask which Governments we thought would return. The Norwegians, Dutch, Czechs, Yugoslavs and Greeks, A.E. thought. The President was doubtful of Belgium and thought it might need an international authority. He developed his pet theory of "Wallonia" consisting of a new state composed of Belgium, Burgundy, Lorraine (and Holland, I think). A.E. expressed doubts of this. The President also favoured the creation of a separate Serbia, Croatia and Slovenia. A.E. represented the need for fewer rather than more states and the probability that, badly as it worked, Yugoslavia was yet better than any alternative. The President was doubtful too of the King of Greece's prospects.

The most doubtful idea in all this seems to me the dismemberment of Germany. That seems to me folly. But if the Americans are prepared to see it through, then I suppose we need not object. It would be fatal to impose dismemberment and then for America to expect the British and Russians to maintain it alone together.

A.E. saw Sumner Welles today. He was delighted to find a clear tidy mind to deal with but found S.W. himself still cold. He prefers Hull. They say Hull has the greatest influence in the country after the President and so far as the Senate goes his word is law. Indeed he enjoys more respect even than the President among the plain people for whom the President is a little too clever. S.W. is a man of immense ambition, vast wealth and great ability. He is a sort of squire of Maryland and is thought to aspire to being its Senator.

A.E. saw Hull again this afternoon and the latter dined at the Embassy when he spoke again of his grievances over French policy.

I saw Pertinax (Géraud) today.[1] Little changed but much concerned over French divisions. He said all his information convinced him that de Gaulle had the backing of the whole of France and that de G. was the only man strong enough to govern France in the interim

1. Andre Géraud, French political commentator.

period till elections could be held. Giraud was an old fool. He was worried over Léger[1] whom he said had great influence with S.W. and who had suddenly turned against de G. He put this down to a conversation Léger had had with the P.M. when he was over here and when the latter was alleged to have told Léger de G. was a *cagoulard*.

March 17
There is a very serious shipping crisis owing to military demands for Torch and Husky which are gravely threatening our own import programme. The Americans are building ships but keeping them for themselves and the safer waters. Our own losses are far heavier because of our dangerous European waters, while our building programme is of necessity extremely modest. A.E. is tackling our good friend Harry Hopkins about it. He does everything here. He is like the secretary to the Cabinet, the private secretary to the President and general coordinator all in one. He has this unique position because there is literally no contact between different departments or ministers and no Cabinet control as we have it. He is a most helpful and admirable man and knows exactly how to handle the President.

Dinner at Embassy. Frankfurter quite brilliant. He is a judge of the Supreme Court and a Jew. He gave his view of what A.E. should say at the joint luncheon which Senator Connally[2] and Rep. Sol Bloom[3] are giving him tomorrow at the Capitol. He thought A.E. should explain the spirit of England and how similar were the views and lives of the ordinary man in both countries. I talked to Frankfurter after and we discussed the great opportunity given us by the presence of American soldiers in England.

Lippmann[4] interested A.E. enormously by saying he thought opinion in the Senate was now ripe for an Anglo–American Treaty of Mutual assistance. The resolution put up by the four Senators for initiating action by the U.S. Government to form U.N. machinery has been rejected, but this was because, Lippmann thought, the Senate found it too vague. We talked this over afterwards and A.E. was so taken by it that he thinks of putting it to the President to see what he

1. Alexis Léger, Secretary-General French Ministry of Foreign Affairs 1933–1940.
2. Senator Connally was Chairman of the U.S. Senate Foreign Relations Committee 1941–1946.
3. Rep. Sol Bloom was Chairman of the Home Affairs Committee.
4. Walter Lippmann wrote for the *New York Herald Tribune* and was the most prestigious American political journalist.

says. We would offer a 20 years treaty like the Russian Treaty. I doubt myself whether it is practical with this awful American constitution. On the other hand, if it were possible, it would do more than anything to fix the future.

I find myself reacting violently against Halifax. He seems to have got more circumlocutionary than ever, using long woolly sentences to express the obvious.

March 19
A.E. went to see the President again this morning. He had had a telegram from the P.M. sending the text of a message from Stalin, a rough one about our failure to form a second front. All the usual complaints as well as new ones; for instance that N. Africa had led to an increase rather than a decrease of pressure on Russia. There was also another telegram from the P.M. to say that the German fleet, Tirpitz, Scharnhorst etc. were concentrated at Narvik and it would not be possible to sail the next convoy to Russia without detailing the British Home Fleet to act as escort; this would mean decreasing escorts in the Atlantic (where sinkings are already on the increase); and so it looked as if the convoy itself must be abandoned for the present.

The President asked A.E. to spend the next week-end at Hyde Park and when he said he thought this might be rather difficult as he would still have so much to do in Washington, the President insisted on his coming to the White House for the last three days. This is a great compliment and will form a fine finale to the visit.

After lunch we started for New York by train. Too foggy to fly. We arrived just in time for a dinner party including Willkie. Talk round the table after dinner. Willkie said he didn't think either we or they were doing enough to help and encourage Russia. The same was true of China. He didn't want Russia to have the Baltic States which would be contrary to the Atlantic Charter (though he said he didn't approve of the Atlantic Charter), and he thought Russia meant to go for China later.

March 20
We all went first thing this morning to call on La Guardia, the Mayor, at the City Hall. A.E. and he were photographed grasping each other by the hand, and swearing eternal cooperation. We then went on to the Waldorf Astoria for another press conference. A.E. did this in modest fashion, one or two tricky questions about Polish frontiers. He

got their confidence, made them laugh, told them he had no secret treaties this time, and they all rose up and cheered.

March 21
Mr. Hoover[1] came to lunch today looking like a caricature of himself, an enormous domelike head with a tiny crumpled face at the bottom of it, like a human embryo's. He said he had made investigations to test American opinion which showed (a) that people favoured Anglo–American cooperation after the war, (b) that most would agree to an Anglo–American police force but (c) that they were very doubtful of Russia. He didn't favour any fixing of frontiers now. Awkward questions often settled themselves if left alone. So it might be with the Polish frontiers.

P.M. broadcast today – quite a good broadcast mainly about domestic affairs including a blessing on the Beveridge Report. No mention of A.E.'s visit here. A.E. rather injured.

March 22
A.E. went to see Hull, then lunched at the White House and after that went off by air with old Dill and General Marshall to visit U.S. Forces. Two days off for me.

March 23
In Washington and New York, I feel that, as in Paris, I am living in a village – in a few weeks or months everyone would pass through one's acquaintance. Even in a few days I seem to have met all the Americans I have ever heard of. I doubt if "knowing America" is so much greater a proposition than knowing a European country. More space perhaps, but no more people who count.

March 24
A.E. away with the Army. I worked all the morning and then Hoppenot[2] lunched with me. Such a pleasure to see him. We rattled away in French in a crowded American restaurant and felt terribly European. Hoppenot, who is here with Béthouart representing Giraud, has all the sound ideas one would have expected of him, a high regard for de G. and what he stands for in France, a realistic idea of the necessity of uniting the two French movements, much mistrust of the amateurishness of the Americans in regard to Europe. I told him he

1. Herbert Hoover, President of the United States 1929–1933.
2. Previously Under-Sec. at the Quai d'Orsay.

must come to London as soon as he could and see Massigli and they must pull the thing together between them. I spoke of the danger of civil war in France – with which he agreed. He was rather apprehensive that de G. meant to play a political part in France after the war. I said I only thought he wished to maintain order till elections were held. We agreed about de G.'s lack of experience in politics, his foolish mishandling of America and of England, and about the lack of good men of experience and weight in both French camps.

A.E. is making his speech at Annapolis on Friday. A first draft of the speech had been prepared by the Embassy on lines suggested by us from London before we left. We worked on this draft ourselves last week and, thanks to the train journey to New York, I was able to get A.E. to work on it himself and dictate his own draft from it. This draft wasn't too bad. A.E. worked at it again on Monday when I hoped we would reach a final text. But I was thwarted because the Army insisted on taking him off early that afternoon so we had only this morning and only $\frac{1}{2}$ hour of that. Anyway we had a goodish draft most of which A.E. had made into his own. Monday afternoon Halifax started redrafting it and produced a new version – a watery version as was to be expected, rubbing down the salient passages, lengthening the sentences and the adjectives and putting in the shibboleth of appeasement. I knew A.E. wouldn't like it but my advice was very noticeably not asked. A.E. returned from the Army just before dinner when Sumner Welles was dining. When he had left about 11.30, Halifax produced his draft, saying "I wouldn't be ashamed now to deliver it myself", then, thank goodness, went to bed. A.E. then went through it with Robin Cruikshank and myself. As I expected, he rejected H.'s version almost *in toto*, "full of appeasement"; "this is not my policy"; and reverted to his own. At last by 1 a.m. we had got our final text. A.E. goes off at dawn after tomorrow to see the U.S. Navy at Norfolk. Meanwhile H. will discover the awful truth.

A.E. enjoyed his visit to the Army immensely. He went down far South into Georgia. General Marshall took him personally and they seem to have taken to each other thoroughly, M. discovering to his surprise that the British Foreign Secretary was as much (or more as he would say) interested in troops as in foreign affairs. The two days away have been to him like a weekend at Binderton. Instead of being exhausted as I feared he has returned bronzed and refreshed.

A.E. told me Welles at dinner had spoken at length about President Roosevelt's proposal[1] for a conference of several European nations

1. See Harvey Vol. I, *Diplomatic Diaries*, p. 67–71.

which Neville Chamberlain turned down because it would interfere with his own plan. S-W said, I think, he had been responsible for it and A.E. was able to tell him how it had been turned down while he was in the South of France without even reference to him.

March 25

A.E. went to Norfolk for the day to see the Navy. He got back at 6.30 when I had what I hoped was the final text of his speech tomorrow for him to look at. We were anxious to get it out at once so that the press will have it, including the papers in the Middle and Far East, in good time. He approved for despatch and I went to dinner. Hardly was my back turned than Halifax got at him about his rejected amendments and so shook him that he had everything held up again for further consideration after dinner. When I got back about 11, hoping to creep to bed, I found a full session of A.E., Winant, Halifax and Cruikshank going over all of it again. I was in despair. A.E. was deplorably weak with H. and should have insisted on his own text being left alone. We talked and argued, H. being most obstinate about inserting passages of appeasement. Winant was helpful and turned most of them down. Finally, we got a text at 1 a.m. with only two bits of Halifax inserted. They add nothing to the speech but words, and hours have been wasted.

At last night's dinner I learn Sumner Welles developed some interesting views about future world organisation. He would like to have 4 Policemen States, G.B., U.S.A., Russia and China, who alone would apply force. He would have a political council which would include these four plus representative states of Europe, Asia, Africa, S. America. This would be a sort of Council of the League of Nations where questions would be debated, solutions recommended but if in case of belligerency the Council's proposals were not accepted, then the matter would fall to the Police States to handle. In addition there might be a sort of world assembly for all. S.W. also expressed his belief that opinion was setting here strongly in favour of international cooperation and that some sort of Senate resolution to urge this would emerge in a few months' time. He also touched on Palestine and favoured a federation of Middle Eastern States, Palestine being under international trusteeship with another 500,000 Jews there.

March 26

We set off after tea for Annapolis in two large cars preceded by police cops on motor bicycles. We went hooting down the streets across the traffic lights. Rather shaming, we thought, clearing the public off the road, but they don't seem to mind it here, though we would never stand for it in London.

We reached Annapolis about 7. We stopped at the Governor's House a particularly fine Queen Anne redbrick house with white windows and doors. Here we were met by the Governor and his lady and by a number of State Senators and representatives.

After dinner we walked across to the General Assembly, a magnificent eighteenth century classical building, where the representatives' chamber was already crowded. This building had actually been built by Sir Robert Eden, A.E.'s great-great-grandfather whose portrait had been hung over the Speaker's chair.

A.E.'s speech, after all the trouble we had had with it, was excellent. He spoke extremely well, impressively and without intoning as he is apt to do. The atmosphere was tense with eager and friendly interest. It was also being broadcast all over America and 23 other State Legislatures had held special sessions to be linked up with it.

After it was over, A.E. held a sort of levee with the Governor in an upper room, some hundred people filing past. We didn't get away till nearly midnight or home till after 1, rather dead.

March 27
A.E. went off to White House before lunch. A.E., Halifax and Strang had a long more or less formal meeting with the President, Hull and S.W. this afternoon.

From all sides, American and British, we had good accounts of the speech.

March 28
I went to White House at 11 to see A.E. I found him in a large old-fashioned Victorian bedroom with a four-poster. While we were talking, in slopped Harry Hopkins in a dressing gown and pyjamas. They had been up with the President till 2 a.m. the night before with a cinema – very Winstonian.

After tea again to White House. Harry Hopkins appeared, dressed this time and whisky in hand. We discussed the issue of a further communique or agreed statement for when we leave. H.H. thought this would be wise and would give an opportunity of bringing Russia and China into the picture.

A.E. was to have a quiet dinner this evening with the President and H.H. and hoped to get down to real work again. What a way they

work here! No method, no organisation, working in bedrooms. And
how they drink! Incessant cocktails and "highballs" (whiskies and
soda) at all hours of the day between meals.

I went tonight to a buffet supper party given by Angus MacDonell
in his flat. Such a crowd, such a noise of shouting voices. Huge
quantities of food. We are very far from the war here. Afterwards a
man recited interminable nigger stories and a woman sang no less
interminable nigger songs.

March 29
A hectic day. I came to White House at 10 with papers, went back to
the Embassy at 10.30, and returned to the White House at 11.15.
A.E. then saw with me the Chinese Ambassador Dr. Wellington Koo
and the Chinese Foreign Secretary, Dr. Soong. With perfect politeness
they told us of Madame Chiang's pleasure at A.E.'s reference to
China in his speech. A.E. then said he hoped she would be able to
visit us soon. At this Koo said something which showed that she was
uncertain what kind of reception she would have if she came. A.E.
said he could promise her an overwhelming reception.

Then came my big moment. I was taken down to be presented to
the President. We went to the ground floor of the building where the
offices are, and then Harry Hopkins picked us up and took us along
to the Cabinet room. The President was then wheeled in on his little
wheeled chair. A.E. introduced me to him and he grasped my hand
with a friendly smile. He was then wheeled next door into his office
where we followed him. This was a pleasant circular room looking out
into a terraced garden. Here he was swiftly transferred from his
wheeled chair to the arm-chair behind his writing table. A magnificent torso of a man, head and neck and chest, and then the legs
which are powerless. Is it any compensation for these two useless legs
that he can make ten million other legs march?

Tonight Mr. Hull gave us a dinner at the Carlton Hotel, some 50
people. I sat next to Harry Hopkins. He said he had two obsessions,
prejudices and the P.M. The former were the opinions of officials
who decided policies and got them through the President because he
was too busy to read everything. Everybody had personal prejudices
which shaped their desires. The trouble for him was how to ensure the
President's own inclinations were not thus distorted by officials. He
said the same was the case in England with the F.O. His second worry
was the P.M., his age, his unteachability. He was not the man to make
the peace. Nor was Hull aged 73, nor Norman Davis nor Halifax

aged 63, all too old and too steeped in the past. They would never understand whatt he new world was about. H.H. has something of the Baptist missionary about him, earnest, ignorant, worried, determined to help, woolly, but he is a good friend to us. A remarkable absence was that of Sumner Welles but H.H. told A.E. that Hull never asked him to his parties because he disliked him so. They always gave separate official parties.

After dinner I repaired again to the White House with a typist. We sat alone together in A.E.'s bedroom for about 2 hours facing the four-poster while he had a further crack with the President. He appeared at last very sleepy about midnight, and dictated telegrams. Though tired, he was delighted by the obvious pleasure which his visit is giving the President. H.H. told him he had never known such a success. The President has promised to make a statement about it at his next Press Conference in lieu of a final communiqué. He says he will do us proud.

March 30

Off to the White House again at 10.30, then back to the Embassy to make my goodbyes and finally off to the airport at 12.30 when we took off for Canada. Our visit to America is over.

At 4 we landed at Ottawa after a journey spent entirely in the clouds. Snow everywhere. Mackenzie King[1] met us as we crawled in the most undignified way out of what Winston would call the underbelly of the aeroplane, the faithful Liberator, which had brought us from England, now provided with a British crew. We drove over bumpy snowy roads to Government House where we found ourselves at once in a royal atmosphere, the Athlones surrounded by A.D.C.s, Comptroller and lady-in-waiting as at a court to receive us – a contrast from the sloppy cosy bedroom atmosphere of the White House. We had tea, and then talked with Malcolm MacDonald, the High Commissioner.

March 31

Breakfast at 9 – went with A.E. to a press conference at Parliament House at 10. Mackenzie King met us and showed us round.

This evening we dined with the P.M. who gave us a Government Dinner at the country club. I drove with A.E. and the Governor General over wintry roads. About 50 people. Mackenzie King made a speech of 45 minutes to which A.E. made a perfect reply in about

1. W. L. Mackenzie King, Prime Minister of Canada.

15 minutes. Mackenzie King could not have been more flattering to
A.E. about the stand he had made over his resignation, though
Mackenzie King at the time was a thorough-going appeaser. He
asked A.E. what was the further reason which had led him to resign
but which he had not ever disclosed. He said he had always wondered.
When A.E. told him of Roosevelt's offer to call a conference, he was
horrified.

A.E. had this afternoon a long *tête-à-tête* with Mackenzie King.
The latter proved quite reasonable about the Four Power Plan for
Relief, saw our argument of the importance of not blocking an
American initiative and showed every readiness to agree provided he
received a letter to say that the acceptance by Canada of the secondary
position assigned to her on the Relief Plan did not constitute a precedent. Malcolm MacDonald was almost in hysterics over this and
told A.E. this morning he would be breaking up the British Empire if
he persisted. I must say I've seen nothing here to modify my previous
opinion that Malcolm is nothing more than a nice lightweight.

April 1
A killing day.

A.E. went off to see Air Training Units this morning and I went to
High Commissioner's office to work. We lunched at Government
House and then went off to Parliament House where A.E. spoke at
3.30. The H. of C. is exactly like ours in appearance, though bigger
and the members have desks. We all waited in the Speaker's Room
till the moment came and then filed in, A.E. being given a special
chair by the Government front bench and the rest of the party chairs
along the side. Mackenzie King could not resist giving us another
half hour's speech which was followed by the three leaders of the
Opposition parties. Then A.E. spoke, standing at the head of the
table with his back to the Speaker at a sort of desk which had been
prepared for him. Quite a good speech, better indeed than average,
part in French.

After that all the members filed past him and shook hands. Then
Malcolm gave a cocktail party which was rather fun, officials and
diplomats chiefly. Then we hastily put together a text for a broadcast
made up of excerpts from the speech and rushed off to dine with the
P.M. at Laurier House.

At 10.30 we dashed off again to the Chateau Laurier, the large
hotel here where the Canadian Broadcasting Station lives for A.E. to
broadcast to Canada.

April 2

Off to the airport where Mackenzie King was waiting. Goodbyes and off the ground at 9.30 for Montreal.

I liked Mackenzie King. No doubt he may be, as they say here, a very cunning politician. He is certainly a triton among minnows and if he has been in power for nine years, it is largely because Canada has not produced any other big men in politics. Rather like the States, the best men go into business. But M. King has great charm, old-wordly, cultured. He regards himself as the spiritual son and disciple of Laurier and the great nineteenth century liberals – pictures of Gladstone prominent on his walls. He has an enormous devotion for Roosevelt and would certainly never set himself against his policies. With this he combines, I think, an equal devotion to the King and Queen, Winston, and now, I hope, A.E. M.K. wants to figure conspicuously at the Peace. His problem now is to choose the best moment for his election (due in 1945) to ensure this.

We arrived at Montreal about 11. It was snowing. Air Marshal Bowhill, head of Ferry Command, a very fierce-looking man with eyebrows curled up like moustaches, took us under his wing. (That afternoon, after 3 attempts to take off had failed, the return trip was postponed till next day. Ed.)

We dined, the first quiet unworried evening we had had, in the restaurant and went up to bed.

A.E. is flat out but pleased. He feels, he told me tonight, that he had done himself good by the success of this visit after the visit to Russia. It brings him again before the public eye. It will please the Conservatives that he should go to America and still more to Canada. It strengthens his hand not only with the public, but with the P.M. and the Cabinet. He has put himself across everywhere here as the successor to the P.M. I entirely agreed. He had made personal friends of the President as well as of Mackenzie King. Also the idea of the United Nations as the organisation for the future has definitely taken shape in people's minds.

April 3

Off from the Hotel at 10.20. We finally got into the air at 12.45. We flew mostly over and along the St. Lawrence. It looked enormous and partly frozen. We had lunch in the air, sandwiches and coffee. At 5 we arrived at Goose, a new airport which is being made as an alternative to Gander where we stopped on our way out but which is subject to Newfoundland fogs.

At 6.45 we piled into our aeroplane again. We raced down the white runway and got easily off just after sunset about 7. At dawn we looked out on the sea and soon after that on to Northern Ireland. Very clear and steady. Then we crossed over to Scotland, very close to Ireland here, and came over the Clyde and Arran to Prestwick. We made a perfect landing at about 5.30 a.m. according to our time, at 10.30 according to British double summer time. About 10½ hours flight from Goose Bay. Two aeroplanes were waiting to take us to Hendon. A.E. rang up the P.M. who insisted on his going down to Chequers for the night. A pity! No rest for him and a late night.

Now, on looking back, what are the most important impressions I received?

First of all, of the very general realisation that America could not slide out again from international responsibilities when peace came. This was found on the Republican as well as on the Democrat side. A general belief that American security was bound up in maintaining the peace settlement.

As to how America was to do this there was great uncertainty, woolliness and naiveté.

Secondly, the realistic attitude to Russia. America is much more afraid of Communism than we are but there was a general acceptance of the view that there couldn't be a World or a European settlement without Russia being in it. Doubt as to whether it would prove possible to secure Russia's confidence and cooperation in a peace settlement but general agreement (both Democratic and Republican) that the greatest efforts must be made to secure it if possible.

Thirdly, the peculiar constitution of the U.S. and the chaotic working conditions it creates for us. Not only is the Executive separated in every way from the Legislature, but within the Executive itself the President works in a sort of vacuum, no Cabinet secretariat to keep the Departments in touch with him or coordinate his decisions, each Department working for itself and against the others, the President working through a series of court favourites, good or bad, (e.g. Harry Hopkins) without official status or permanence.

From such a system we must never expect to get treaties or tidy plans. We must allow the President to work it in his own way which means vague generalisation and indirect methods of approach. It is probable that the Ball–Hatch–Burton resolution may be followed by another put up by heavier senatorial guns in much the same terms, viz to urge the President to take the initiative in various international ways. If this happens, it will be tremendous for us, but still the method will have to be indirect. It is doubtful whether any Senate will ever ratify a direct treaty commitment to fight in Europe, but it is to be hoped that by a number of different approaches – none of which will require a treaty – e.g. Food, Currency, Production Conferences and others to come, the States may be tied up by the number and complexity of the interest these will involve.

April 6
A.E. arrived at F.O. about 4. His first engagement to see General de Gaulle over the latter's visit to Algiers, which had been laid on and then laid off at Eisenhower's request. De G. much upset. The fear in N. Africa is that if de G. arrives, there will be manifestations if not a landslide in his favour. Catroux is also anxious to postpone de G.'s arrival until the agreement between the two generals is nearer completion. De G. (and Massigli) have some suspicion of Catroux's motives now too. It has been agreed that Catroux should come home and report and de G. wait here meanwhile.

April 13
A.E. told me this morning he had had an unsatisfactory talk with the P.M. The latter told him Roosevelt had asked Beaverbrook to pay a visit and the P.M. thought he should stay there some time "and then eventually" take Halifax's place as Ambassador, H. returning to this country as Lord President and Anderson going to India as Viceroy. A.E. much troubled at this. The worst of all possible worlds. But what can the President want by inviting the Beaver? Does he like him? Does he want him as Ambassador? I suspect a Harriman intrigue. There must be no question of letting H. go in these circumstances. Fortunately H. realises the danger himself.

April 16
A.E. saw de Gaulle this evening, for once a satisfactory interview. De G. said Catroux was just going back to Algiers with further proposals. De G. was ready to accept an equal place with Giraud but he couldn't agree to Giraud being both military C. in C. and political chief. That would be too anti-democratic. But if Giraud would give up being C. in C., then he and de G. could occupy equal positions in a reconstructed National Committee. If he preferred to remain C. in C., then he must not be a political figure as well. (But who is to be No. 1 of the two generals? This is not clear. De G. should concede this to G.)
  What a fool that Admiral Cunningham is! He now wants to offer a

naval command to Admiral Esteva when Tunis falls. Esteva, who refused to resist the German landings at Tunis in spite of appeals by Giraud and Darlan, and is largely responsible for our still having to fight there. How true that sailors are always at sea on land.

Amery has written to the P.M. suggesting that A.E. should be next Viceroy, failing him old Anderson. I hope no one will take this seriously. For A.E. to go would be to lose all he has now gained – to miss the P.M.-ship, to miss the vital peace-making years, to confound his friends and confirm his critics. Anderson would be a disaster for India. But it seems impossible to think of Halifax going, even though he is willing, because I doubt if the P.M. would ever agree and because if once he left Washington we should have the Beaver slipped in if we weren't very careful. Therefore Roger Lumley becomes my next candidate.

April 19

I talked to Jim Thomas about all this. He didn't know that H. was ready to consider going back to India, and agreed he would be far the best. He thought Archie Sinclair should go to Washington.

He bemoaned to me, as often before, how bad A.E. was in keeping up with his friends; he never now saw his old H. of C. friends; he never asked them to dine or down to his home.

April 20

Maisky yesterday conveyed to A.E. Molotov's thanks for the full account which he had sent him of his talks in Washington. An interesting example of how forthcomingness may pay in that quarter. Clark Kerr also reports a warming-up of the atmosphere towards himself and and us generally in Moscow, and a greater appreciation of what we are doing in the war.

Russo–Polish relations, on the other hand, have taken a turn for the worse. A common grave[1] has been discovered at Smolensk full of the bodies of Polish officers murdered and buried there by the Russians, as the Poles allege, put there by the Germans as the Russians allege. A move is being made for Anglo–American representations in Moscow for a better understanding. There is also a further idea of Moley's

1. The Katyn massacre. The news was disclosed in a German accusation. The Poles who had previously reported large numbers of unaccounted-for Polish officers in Russia, whilst recognising the possibility of German fabrication, demanded an enquiry which the Russians refused, breaking off diplomatic relations with Poland.

for suggesting to Washington that we should now try to put across the President's own plan for a Russo–American–British agreement on Polish frontiers to be imposed on the Poles. The frontier question[1] is at the bottom of Polish Russian friction and until it is settled there is little hope of improvement.

April 21
A.E. told me this morning he had discussed with the P.M. the proposal that he should go to India.[2] The P.M. had raised it himself by saying "it would be very difficult". A.E. said that he would of course "do what he was told" and that "in wartime there was nothing else to be done!" The P.M. said that he understood the attraction of the post for A.E., that it was one of the posts he would have liked to hold himself, but that A.E. was the only possible successor to himself. This had come to be generally recognized – that he himself was an old man and accidents might happen etc., that A.E. would have to be available at short notice and no Viceroy could be in that position and, finally, that the British public would not understand it. He had talked it over at the Palace and there opinion had been final and against it. So that bogey is allayed! Anyway A.E. thinks much good will have come of it being brought up in this way as it will show the P.M. that he is not so eager to succeed him as he may think.

From this the P.M. went on to discuss his colleagues from which it appeared that he is developing an intense dislike of Herbert Morrison. The latter is throwing his weight about much too much to please the P.M. who infinitely prefers working with Bevin and Alexander. Yes, indeed, but I am not sure that isn't a tribute to Morrison.

I had a word with Charles Peake yesterday about Halifax. He is contemplating three months' leave this year. Even Charles thought this a bit hot and I warned him that the Beaver was on the warpath and *"qui va à la chasse perd sa place"*. C.P. quite saw this and told me that at all costs H. was determined to keep the Beaver out of the Embassy.

Much criticism beneath the surface over the refugee problem and the dilatory procedure of H.M.G. and the U.S. Government in tackling it. This is really more the fault of the Americans than of ourselves as we had to wait for them to call the Bermuda Conference which has just opened and which Dick Law is attending. But our own case is not a good one; it is more showy than substantial, because we

1. The Poles were still sticking out for their frontiers of September 1939.
2. Linlithgow had by this time been Viceroy since 1936.

sit on the one obvious outlet for these unfortunate Jews, viz. Palestine because of the White Paper and our weakness for the Arabs. We certainly cannot take more in the U.K. but Palestine should be made a Jewish reserve now, and the Arabs compensated.

Weizmann has just written to P.M. a fine letter recalling the broken pledges of the past and the attempt to clamp down the White Paper as a permanent settlement. The P.M. has written a note to say he never approved and never will approve the White Paper[1] which he regards as a gross breach of faith by the Chamberlain Government. Hence much fluster and agitation in the C.O. and F.O. dovecots. Unfortunately A.E. is immovable on the subject of Palestine. He loves Arabs and hates Jews. Our only hope is a firm Anglo–American agreement over Palestine – Sumner Welles and the President favour a Jewish State as Winston does.

April 22

To my horror A.E. told me today that the P.M. had reverted to his idea of India for A.E. He had had a midnight talk. The P.M. had been turning it over again in his mind, he said: he felt it might be the only chance of saving India. A.E. could also direct the Far Eastern war; he himself, barring accidents, hoped to go on some years yet. A.E. could always come back and meanwhile the war was pretty well running itself and so A.E.'s help here was no longer so needed, and much more in the same strain. A.E. had put forward various counter-arguments, but was evidently rather attracted by the idea. Bobbety would come to F.O. I reacted as vigorously and seriously as possible – losing touch here if he went, the importance of the approach to peace and of the peace negotiations, A.E.'s unique position of influence with Stalin and Roosevelt, danger of Winston himself if left alone, likelihood of Winston upsetting the boat here on home or foreign affairs if A.E.'s restraining hand were removed. I hope I made some impression. But it is awkward if the P.M. is now going to press him to go. I am as convinced as I could possibly be that it would be fatal to A.E.'s future as P.M. if he went, his stocks here would fall like a stone, and more than that, his absence now onwards from here would have catastrophic consequences on the future peace.

After A.E.'s midnight talk with the P.M. and our talk this morning, he had another go with the P.M. this afternoon when he went over to see him and Wavell who has just arrived. He told me he had been put to a good deal of pressure from both of them to go and take charge of

1. Of May 1939 which limited Jewish immigration to ⅓ of the population.

India and the Far Eastern War. The P.M. had decided to put it all to the King. This is worrying as A.E. himself is now getting more shakey as the pressure increases. I was glad therefore when he saw Bracken later in the afternoon and the latter took the line that the P.M. would get into such difficulties here with his Cabinet without A.E. I again said all I could to dissuade him from looking at it, especially the fact that he had now built himself up with his visits to Stalin and Roosevelt and his work at home on future peace plans as the man who could construct the peace. He himself saw that it would not be possible to spend less than two years in India, the next two years which would be the most vital years of all for future peace as I pointed out. But he is shaken, although when he left for the country about 7, he told me "not to worry!"

I was so worried that I got hold of Jim Thomas at once. A.E. had already discussed it with him so there was no breach of confidence. But Jim was not aware of the fresh pressure which was being applied. Jim was most alarmed, and we decided to ring up Beatrice at once and warn her of the position before A.E. reached home. We both spoke to her in parables on the open line and said we were both absolutely convinced acceptance would be fatal to A.E. She is on our side to some extent we know because she is horrified at being a Vicereine herself.

April 23
I didn't go to the Office this morning and Jim rang me up to say he had sat up late writing a letter to A.E. which he would send down today. He had spoken to Bobbety who was equally disturbed and as certain as we are of the disaster it would mean. Bobbety was going to ring him up from the country and also to get in touch with Alec Hardinge who unfortunately is laid up with flu and not with the King at present. The good Jim! He has written A.E. a most powerful and outspoken letter. Meanwhile Turnbull from the India Office is going down to Binderton tomorrow at A.E.'s request to explain the prospects of his pulling off an Indian settlement.

What a kettle of fish! All our plans and hard work in jeopardy. A.E. is now set for the highest position and he threatens to run out on us. He would not ever be able to get back to the same position. The country would drop him and would be right. Even India would be lost or saved in London. There is a perfectly good Viceroy available in Halifax – a better one than A.E. would ever be – and good enough Ambassador for Washington in Archie Sinclair. The P.M. clearly is the more enchanted with his plan the more he looks at it. (Is the Chief

Whip working on him too?) As is his wont, he is now running away with it. He sees A.E. fixing India and Japan, with himself running the war (and incidentally botching the peace) from here with no interference. I gathered from Jim that Bracken had also swung round or been swung round about it too. Jim will go down to see A.E. if need be and so will I. What lunacy it all is.

April 24
Jim rang up last evening to say he had had an unsatisfactory conversation with A.E. on the telephone; A.E. being flippant and Jim frank. Bobbety, he said, was working hard and was going to see Alec Hardinge. But the pressure on A.E. is very great. I see how A.E. feels himself. The East and India have an immense pull on him. He has so often said to me half longingly in jest that he believed India was his fate. At the same time now he feels the future closing in on him if he remains here, no escape from No. 10, and he shrinks from it, as well he may. But the combination of these two reactions, the lure of the East and escapism from the West, added to the P.M.'s pressure which makes it all look like duty, is very strong indeed.

April 25
I returned to Office this morning. A.E. rang up from the country to know if there was any news. He said nothing about India, nor did I. He will bring it up himself in time. Meanwhile better let frayed nerves calm.

The Polish–Soviet business has suddenly blown up into a flaming row. Stalin in a personal message to the P.M. complains bitterly of the way Sikorski, without reference to him, has publicised the alleged murder of Polish officers at Smolensk. He declares this a Nazi trap which Sikorski and his anti-Soviet Government here have deliberately and indeed collusively agreed to exhibit. He proposes therefore to break off relations with the Polish Government. A.E. got Sikorski down to Binderton on Saturday and with Moley he was got to agree to call off the enquiry by the International Red Cross which he had asked for and to damp down his newspapers. The P.M. has sent a soothing reply to Stalin, promising a further and more considered reply later. But the Poles have fairly upset the applecart. They will need very firm treatment if they are not to upset the peace settlement and wreck Anglo–Russian unity. All this brings us back to the necessity of settling Polish frontiers soon. This will mean a settlement which will have to be imposed. But until the frontiers are unchangeably fixed, we shall have no peace because no end to manoeuvring for position by both Poland and Russia.

The Tunis battle has started off again. All going well, it seems. A slow, methodical and, I fear, costly advance all along the line.

A.E. told Moley in the course of the afternoon and evening he spent at Binderton on Saturday all about the Viceroy question. Moley, who lunched with me today, who had known nothing about it at all and was quite unprompted, at once pointed out the difficulties. He told him in particular he didn't see how A.E. could ever get back again in case of emergency. How could the King send for the Viceroy to form a Government? How would the H. of C. like that? In fact he made it clear what a very bad plan he thought it would be. Moley told me that A.E. had said it had been referred back to the King who had objected to it before, and he gave the impression that he thought it would fall through.

A.E. never mentioned it to me throughout the day nor did I do so to him.

Jim told me this evening that Bobbety was working very hard and that Hardinge was also advising against it.

April 26
A.E. still in the country. When he rang me up this morning he referred laughing to the fact that the India Office official was going down there to lunch today. I thereupon groaned. He said it was all very worrying; it had now been put again to the King by the P.M. who was explaining why he had changed his mind. He said Hardinge was all against it and he himself had not agreed to anything, no decision would be taken in a hurry. I said that the more I thought over it the more I felt it would be impossible for him to come back from India to be P.M. If he went it would mean goodbye to that. He was inclined to agree though Winston, he said, denied this and maintained that we didn't realise how near India was now with flying. I made Moley's point that it would be very difficult for the King to send for the Viceroy to form a Government and that the H. of C. would object to that. He said the H. of C. would soon lose interest in him if he had once gone, though he didn't see who else they could find to be P.M. I said he mustn't be too sure they wouldn't find somebody. I then repeated what I had said before, that even if he came back as P.M. later, it was now that the critical period for foreign affairs was beginning for which he alone had the experience and position necessary to guide Winston, e.g. the present Polish–Soviet row. A.E. said that he

felt part of the P.M.'s eagerness to see A.E. Viceroy was due to his own growing desire to handle foreign affairs himself. I agreed – the well known disease which always appears in No. 10 after a year or two. A.E. felt it would mean increasing clashes with the old man and "he didn't want to have to resign again." I sympathised but said nonetheless the P.M., because of his affection for A.E. and his respect for his judgment, did listen to him and he alone could guide him at all.

Stalin has replied to the P.M.'s message by saying that he has broken off relations with the Poles and is announcing it tonight. This will be a gift for Goebbels. We must try and use it to get the remaining Polish families out of Russia and then perhaps we may be able to take up the Polish frontiers question and settle that. There can hardly be a return to normal relations now without a big and final settlement of Russo–Polish differences. But it will be very difficult and the Poles will manoeuvre to do the maximum harm to Russian relations with ourselves and America. Why must Stalin work like this?

April 29
Yesterday given up entirely to Polish Russian affairs. A.E. saw Sikorski in the morning and both saw P.M. in the afternoon. A further and rather stiffer message has gone to Stalin from the P.M. urging moderation, urging that the Poles in Russia be allowed to leave and saying that it is being suggested that the U.S.S.R. intend to set up a Left-Wing Polish Government in Russia and this we could not recognise. Sikorski has also put out a communiqué refuting Molotov's communiqué in which he accused the Polish Government of acting in collusion with the Germans.

A.E. saw Maisky this morning and washed his head over the Soviet War News, a publication of the Embassy here, which has been adding fuel to the flames. Maisky, for what it is worth, said he did not think Stalin meant to set up a rival Polish Government.

A.E. is at a loss to see what Stalin is up to. It is too like Hitler and Benes to be pleasant. Is it wounded self-respect at the Smolensk revelations just when Stalin thought he had become received into society? Is it the frontier question and the Russian method for bringing that up for final settlement? Is it fear of Sikorski's Poland as likely to be a spearhead against Russia in future? It is clear that Stalin means to have the Curzon Line and the Baltic States, but who is going to prevent him at the end of the war? However if like that other gangster Hitler, he has a passion for legality, then he may be wanting, even so, to get out of us now our official endorsement of those frontiers. But it is a dangerous game for all concerned. Poland is potential dynamite to Europe. She will always tend to divide feeling between Russia and Poland on ideological lines, both here and in America, and even between us and America.

Catroux has more or less completed his talks with Giraud and the latter is ready to meet de G. "at Marrakech or some other quiet spot". G. however wishes to remain as Generalissimo as well as President of the Council. In a conversation with Macmillan, Giraud clearly showed that he was suffering from *folie des grandeurs*. He took all the credit to himself for planning and directing the successful Tunisian operations and practically demanded for the future equal place with Eisenhower. As for de G. he was only a general *"de second grade"* and he didn't know if he would ever have him on his council. De G. is hesitant about going out. Catroux is urging him to go. We think on the whole he should go. The Americans won't let Giraud fail as de G. fondly hopes and by refusing to meet him and even accept an inferior position he plays into the hands of his American and other enemies.

I asked A.E. this morning what had happened about India. He said it was "in cold storage". I asked for how long? He said he thought for some time until the P.M. returned anyway. (The P.M. is off to Washington in greatest secrecy with Wavell.)

April 30
Clark Kerr has sent some suggestions for improving and indeed stiffening the P.M.'s message to Stalin. Stalin, he says, is susceptible to British public opinion and it is necessary to bring out more its displeasure at his behaviour. These points are being considered this morning by the P.M.

P.M. is seeing de Gaulle today to urge him to go and meet Giraud. He promises to be nice to him.

May 3
India has surged up again over the weekend owing to the P.M.'s imminent departure for America. A.E.'s answer is required before he goes. A.E. is terribly inclined to go and he is asking advice from everybody, who he thinks may urge him to do so. He hasn't had much luck, but he is pining to go all the same. I see only too clearly that it will be the end of him if he does.

He asked Alec and then me to lunch with him but neither of us could go as we were lunching at the Belgian Embassy. He then asked William Strang. I prompted William beforehand. He didn't need any prompting as to the line he should take. Afterwards he told me that A.E. was very drawn to it but that he had said all he could against it; notably that it was his duty to stay here rather than to go to India because of his knowledge of foreign affairs and the guidance he alone could give to the P.M.

I had a few words with A.E. at teatime. He said nothing had yet been decided but the P.M. was pressing him very hard. He wanted A.E.'s decision before he leaves for the U.S. tomorrow night. I said that I was appalled at the idea of his going and all that he had fought for in foreign affairs would be jeopardised if not lost if he left at this crucial time. And he would miss being P.M. He said he wanted to go to India and he didn't wish to be P.M. India, according to Wavell, was in the worst state, inefficiency, demoralisation, lack of fighting spirit, in fact very near a complete breakdown. He might be the means of saving it, while Bobbety could take his place here. I said Bobbety would be excellent but he had nothing like A.E.'s position in the country, the P.M. would quarrel with him and he would resign, and then the P.M. would install his own nominee. He said Beatrice was now in favour of it. I asked about the Palace. He said he hadn't seen the reply but that he understood it was against his going. I said the P.M. was a wicked old man to press him and it was partly for his own purposes that he was doing so. Even if A.E. were to go to India to run the war against Japan, I doubted if the P.M. would in fact allow him to do so. A.E. had no experience of India, all his training was for foreign affairs. Why could not Halifax go? He would be absolutely firstclass. A.E. said the P.M. would never agree to H.

Jim Thomas arrived from the country in the late afternoon when I told him what had passed. We felt sad and disillusioned. I said I thought Bobbety was the only one who could now influence him. Jim rang up Lady Cranborne and asked if we could come round and see Bobbety after dinner. She said we could and added that Bobbety had talked to A.E. yesterday and it had been decided that he should refuse. We were astonished at this because it was far from the impression I had got. Jim said he knew Bobbety and Hardinge had had a long talk.

After the Cabinet this evening A.E. had a further talk with the P.M. When he came back about 7.45 he said to me, "to put you out of your misery, I must tell you it is now much less likely!" I said I was immensely relieved. He told me the P.M. was no longer pressing it himself so hard and had said he wouldn't urge it unless he, A.E., was himself most eager to go.

May 4

A.E. told me this morning he had been up till 2 a.m. with the P.M. The latter had shown him both his own letter to the King and the King's reply. Both of these were in such terms as were immensely flattering and he was much moved by them. I gather that the King, while not definitely opposing it, had put forward all the objections. Anyway it had been decided to leave decision till after the P.M.'s return but Oliver Lyttelton had been brought into the picture as the alternative. Reason has begun to prevail! I said I thought the P.M. himself must begin to see how much he would miss A.E., and he said he had pointed out how difficult it would be for the P.M. to make his trips abroad if A.E. were not here to manage the House.

Polish–Soviet relations rather steadier. Stalin made us a magnificent speech on May Day refuting Goebbels and his hopes of wedgedriving between the U.S., ourselves and Russia, categorically repudiating any ideas of separate negotiation.

May 5

P.M. off at last.

Tunis battle looks better, much better. Indeed the Germans, according to our secret sources, look like preparing to quit.

May 6

De Gaulle is still holding out to meet Giraud at Algiers or not at all. General confusion again. I'm pretty sure de G. is right in thinking G.'s position is deteriorating. G. is becoming more and more ridiculous in his behaviour. But the Americans will never allow him to disintegrate, and this de G. forgets.

Stalin, in answer to an American press correspondent, has announced that he wants good relations with a strong Poland after the war. This olive branch has been or is being picked up by Sikorski who is sending a friendly response. I was rung up at 1.30 a.m. about it and urged that its terms should be considered in the morning but Sikorski wouldn't. I turned William Strang on to it and he judged the proposed message "not bad" – in any case Sikorski said he was informing us, not consulting us.

A.E. saw the King today. He told me the candidates now favoured for India were Lyttelton and himself. He also told me that the Chief Whip was against his going.

May 7

Tunisian battle still going well. Possibly the last stages.

Stalin has sent a reply to the P.M.'s message about the Poles. He reproaches us for not having warned him of the Polish anti-Soviet press offensive and for not having stopped it. He repudiates again any idea of setting up a new Polish Government but urges that G.B., U.S. and U.S.S.R. should set about improving present Polish Government; as regards Poles in Russia, Soviet Government "have never put obstacles in way of their exit"!

May 8
Bizerta and Tunis have fallen.

May 10
50,000 prisoners now in our hands in Tunisia.

I gather Viceroyship is now resting between Lyttelton and Anderson, with balance in favour of youth and energy of the former.

May 11
More trouble over the Viceroyalty. It has all blown up again owing to O. Lyttelton having political ambitions and wishing to remain here and because of some minor retreat of our forces in Burma. Lyttelton anyway knows what going to India means! Amery has been at it again. A.E. and Jim Thomas had a long talk about it last night and A.E. spoke to me during our morning walk. He is feeling tired and defeatist and full of self-pity. The P.M. refreshed by the sea breezes and egged on no doubt by Beaverbrook who is on the ship with him, has been sending out a stream of messages contemplating actions of various kinds which have annoyed A.E. intensely. P.M. wants to seize the Azores. He wants to beat up Sikorski for provoking Stalin. A.E. agrees with none of this. He says he is exhausted and will be dead in three months if he has to go on like this as well as with H. of C. and F.O. Let the P.M. and the Beaver run the show as they wish and he be out of it. And much more.

He is certainly tired out and needs a rest. It is his own fault if he hasn't got more parliamentary help. He won't delegate. The truth is he quails before continuous battling with the P.M. He fondly believes India will be a rest-cure from which a grateful country and H. of C. will summon him back to take over in two or three years' time.

May 12
Further but calmer talk with A.E. about India. Lyttelton doesn't want it because he wishes to stay in politics here. (It is believed he would like to be Chancellor of the Exchequer.) Anderson, on the other hand,

would be a deplorable choice. Grigg (who had been Financial Secretary to Government of India) told him the Indian machine would drive him mad – its slowness; they did no work there at all and looked on the war as merely a tiresome interruption of peacetime life. Grigg doubted if O.L. would be good, too much of the City man, also Chairman of Burma Corporation. (The same applies, as A.E. said, to his being a Chancellor of Exchequer.) A.E. thought the Labour leaders must be brought into the question. They haven't been consulted at all yet. Evidently "orders would have to be given" to the person upon whom the Cabinet decided. He repeated all over again his own wish to go – a show of his own at last, an end to battling with the P.M., his dislike of "politics" as against "administration". I repeated my usual arguments.

A.E. is anxious to see Lord Baldwin. This is being arranged for Monday. We ought to be able to count on sense from that quarter. Meanwhile Tommy Dugdale, now the Chairman of the Party, has tackled A.E. and protested strongly against any idea of departure.

May 13
Complete enemy collapse in Tunisia. Well over 150,000 prisoners.

P.M. has sent a message to Stalin, revised in accordance with A.E.'s suggestions, about the Poles. He says he is taking steps to discipline the Polish press, points out difficulty of Sikorski reforming his government under threat but promises to urge him to do so in due course. Finally he expresses satisfaction at hearing that Stalin doesn't intend to prevent Poles leaving Russia.

May 17
De G. and G. have still not met. De G. has appointed an unspecified M. "X" as leader of the resistance movement in France, to be a member of the National Committee – a shrewd move to emphasise his close connection with the mother country. Cambon and Comert, who were hurried out to N. Africa by the Americans to lend weight and respectability to the Giraud party, have come home again, disabused, I hear.

Polish–Soviet relations slightly calmer. Public opinion here pro-Soviet rather than pro-Polish.

May 18
A.E. told me something of his talk with Baldwin yesterday. He was rather "snorty – just what one would have expected! Of course the old

man only thinks of the H. of C. His candidate for India was Sam Hoare – it shows he has learnt nothing!" Jim had previously given me S.B.'s account of the conversation. B. had been very fatherly but had made it quite clear that if he went to India, he would never come back to be P.M. A.E. had pleaded it was so difficult to know what was his duty. To this S.B. had replied, "when in doubt between two duties, it is wise to choose the most unpleasant".

A.E. told me he had also discussed it with O. Lyttelton and Bobbety at dinner afterwards. O.L. wants to stay on as he believes he understands finance and economics. As A.E. says, he puts a high valuation on himself.

Again according to Jim, Bobbety had been very outspoken. He had told A.E. that if he went to India, his friends here would never understand it and would think it was "desertion". "And what is more, I should think so too." A.E. was much hurt at this.

A.E. then went on to say he felt that if he stayed on here, then he must give up the leadership of the H. of C. He couldn't do both. I said I saw no reason why he shouldn't do this. He had done it and shown that he could do it. The public would well understand that his F.O. work was too heavy to permit of his continuing to do it. Indeed they would derive satisfaction from this because they would suppose it meant more attention to postwar planning. He said he loathed the H. of C. and hated the thought of years more of it combined now with battling with the P.M. "I should love to go to India and have a show of my own."

Though we are far from out of the wood, I rather sense that he may be turning away from it now, reluctantly and rather bitterly, as the last glimpse of fresh air and freedom. Probably Baldwin affected him more than he admits. But, if firmly pressed, he still would give way and go. He has sent some message to the P.M. which I haven't seen in reply to his about the choice being between O.L. and Anderson.

Who could be leader of the H. of C.? He thought the P.M. should do it himself with aid from a deputy, e.g. Harry Crookshank, who would do it well, but not Duff, whom P.M. would want but who would be less good.

Charles Peake told me today that he had heard from Desmond Morton, who cannot keep his mouth shut, that the P.M. in going to the U.S. with the Beaver intended to offer Halifax India if he would go and let B. take his place. I knew the Beaver wanted the Embassy but I never thought the P.M. would ever admit of H. going back to India. It only shows how strong the pressure is. C.P. thought H. would hesitate long before accepting if it meant B. becoming Ambassador. Another case of conflict of duty. I am certain H. is the right man to be Viceroy – to complete his work in India – but it would be unthinkable to have B. Ambassador in Washington. Will the P.M. hope to come back with H.'s acceptance in his pocket? And what about all this pressure on A.E.? I don't believe the Cabinet would agree to have B. in Washington. And if that is so, I suppose Winston would refuse to let H. go to India, and then we come back to A.E. Blast the Beaver – he will ruin us yet.

A.E. has to address the Conservative Party Conference on Thursday in the P.M.'s absence. He takes less than no interest in it. In better days he would have loved this opportunity.

A fresh development on the French front. Giraud has replied to de Gaulle that he will agree to a meeting in Algiers provided de G. accepts principle of collective Cabinet responsibility and election of a provisional government according to French Constitution after liberation of France. He proposes that the two movements should be amalgamated at once under a reformed executive Committee over which Giraud and de G. should preside in turn. "All other questions at issue, (including presumably that of G. being C. in C. as well as President of Committee) to be discussed and decided by the new Committee." A bold step forward by old G. I hope de G. will accept.

May 19
A.E.'s doctor tells him that he has a poisoned tonsil and he is surprised that he should not feel worse than he does. This may account for the lamentable escapism he has been suffering from too. At this discovery he is rather relieved. I think he was genuinely fussed, as he always is over his health, at his tiredness and general exhaustion. He now has a reason for it, and not a serious one, and feels better for it. *Sursum corda*! Meanwhile Bobbety's outspoken remarks at dinner the night before last are working. Speaking of his speech to the Conservative Party tomorrow, he said "I dislike speaking to the Conservative Party. That is not where my supporters come from. The Conservative Party only has me because it must!" I agreed and said his supporters lay among the general mass of opinion in this country which was not strongly party-minded. To those people he had become a sort of symbol of the kind of future they wanted and that was why I was so horrified at any idea of India. They would regard him as having abandoned them and would be bewildered and disillusioned. It would have very embittering effects on politics here. He didn't reject this.

May 20
We are getting a fresh spate of proofs of de G.'s hold over the French. From France a message from Herriot expressing readiness to form part of his movement; from N. Africa report of the low stocks of Giraud; the support for de Gaulle among both soldiers and lesser civilians; troops in G.'s forces longing to go over to de G.'s; respect for the clarity of de G.'s policies as against the wobbling and compromising of G., the old Vichy officials, Noguès and Co. still playing their old tricks under G.'s nose; from French sailors all over the world on Giraud ships who desert to de G. – to the fury of the Americans. De G. has the people on his side and even Cambon and Comert confess that G. is hopeless. No reactions yet to G.'s last invitation, but Catroux is coming back himself to try and sell it.

May 21
P.M. telephoned to A.E. this morning from Washington to tell him of the intense feeling against de Gaulle he had found, both with President and with Hull. A document of indictment of de G. was being sent for us to see. The feeling threatened to jeopardise far bigger things and the P.M. wanted the Cabinet "to break with de G.". A.E. expressed some scepticism but the P.M. said he asked him to believe what he said with all earnestness was true.

Macmillan and Catroux are arriving over the weekend, and so will the document from Washington and it must all be gone into on Monday. We had a little meeting this morning, A.E., Hal Mack and myself. A.E. took a very sensible line and said that just when de G. looked like joining up with G., it would be impossible to break with him. Even Eisenhower didn't now want to stop him coming. A.E. thought, as we all did, that the Americans see the deterioration in G.'s position and are intensely annoyed at it; they think the two generals will meet, and they will have to deal with de G. who, with some excuse, hates them. They also fondly suppose that it is we with our superior cleverness who have rigged this.

I'm afraid this is the only construction to put upon it. We have done little enough to build up de G. of late. We know how he treats us. But the evidence of his prestige is overwhelming. It is all that old fool Hull who is smarting under the attacks brought on himself ever since Darlan. We have been right over France; the Murphys, Matthews, Starks, Leahys and Hulls have been wrong. But the storm over Darlan in America as here would be nothing to that which the breaking of de G. would rouse. Nor would it "break" him. We would "make" him and make an enemy of him at the same time. What fools these Americans are! I hope the P.M. will not be more than usually headstrong and impulsive over this. He has come himself to feel about de G. almost as Hull does, although he has done more than anyone to build him up. The American atmosphere goes to his head.

The P.M. has also warned us that he and the President are strongly in favour of the seizure of the Azores. The Chiefs of Staff (after blowing cold, now blowing hot) have persuaded themselves or been ordered to persuade themselves that the occupation of the islands and the control over submarine activity which would result, would mean an immense saving of shipping and of sailors' lives. The P.M. does not favour invoking the Anglo–Portuguese Alliance and asking Salazar's consent: he wishes to step in, only warning Salazar the night before. He says, rightly, we are fighting for the small nations and we are entitled to take what is necessary for us to do so. I strongly agree with this line of argument. But, to my mind, it all turns on the facts, is it or is it not militarily necessary? If so, there should be no doubt about it. I mistrust the Chiefs of Staff's objectivity; we went into it all a month or so ago and they then said it wasn't necessary.

May 24
The threatened de G. indictment turned up yesterday in the form of 3 telegrams from the P.M. containing a piece from the President, a piece from the State Department, a miscellaneous collection of "dirt" which covers a number of minor cases of tiresomeness none of them new, none of them of much importance. The P.M. in his covering telegram commends these to the attention of the Cabinet by a set of the most shaming *ex parte* arguments I have ever seen. From anyone else it would be the telegram of a cad. He has been "got at" by the Americans who are staging a last moment attempt to prevent the union of the two French movements and the arrival of de G. in N. Africa. The P.M. claims that he could defend the breaking with de G. on the basis of these flimsy complaints, but he is greatly mistaken.

The question was considered at a special Cabinet on Sunday night. As a result 3 extremely wise telegrams were sent then and there in reply, disposing effectively of the odds and ends brought up against de G., drawing attention to the number of solemn agreements entered into between H.M.G. and de G., including letters from the P.M. himself, and to the harm which would follow a break involving confusion in Central Africa, the Free French Navy (with which the Admiralty is now extremely satisfied), the Free French Army, and to the fact that they followed on de G.'s placing himself on our side when we stood alone, eighteen months before the U.S.A. came into the war, and lastly pointing out that union between G. and de G. had never been nearer than at present, that de G.'s position had never been higher in France and elsewhere, and that a breach now would have incalculable effects on French resistance, and on French opinion towards us both now and after the war.

It is high time the old man came home. The American atmosphere, the dictatorial powers of the President and the adulation which surrounds him there, have gone to his head.

This morning de G. has asked for facilities to go to Algiers, for Friday. Catroux wants to go on ahead. This means that union has been agreed on the basis of G.'s offer and any action taken by us now to stop de G. would make us responsible for defeating it.

Much curiosity over the decision to abolish the Comintern. The Labour Party couldn't be more perturbed. Bevin suspects a ruse to insinuate Communists into the T.U. and Labour movement. In reality the Comintern has been moribund for years, and this is only a development of Stalin's policy of nationalism. As Maisky once said to me, Lenin thought the Russian revolution could only survive if there were world revolution; Stalin thought Russia big enough to make the experiment alone and if she succeeded that would be the best pro-paganda for communism. I only hope Stalin isn't going to abolish Communism itself next and instead put a crown on his head. Anyway, outwardly, it will dispel distrust and facilitate postwar cooperation.

But the dilemma for the British Labour Party and the T.U.C. remains. They can no longer refuse affiliation to the Communists on the grounds of their connection with Moscow. They must accept them or reject them on their merits. They are scared of being pepped up from within; they equally dislike proclaiming their conservative tendencies by excluding them. The Labour ministers refused to agree to a Government statement welcoming the decision.

May 25
A sour telegram from P.M. acquiescing with ill grace in the departure of de G. for Algiers. A.E. and even Attlee are fed up at this lecturing and hectoring from across the Atlantic.

May 26
Both Eisenhower and Giraud now formally agree to de G.'s departure so the stage is set for his leaving on Saturday.

The P.M. is returning home via N. Africa and will be due there about the same date as de G. What will then happen Heaven knows!

The Washington staff talks developed into a friendly wrangle between U.S. and British as to what to do after Husky. U.S. want us to lay off in that quarter and concentrate on building up here for cross-Channel operations early next year. British want to exploit Husky further by subsequent action against Italy and in the Mediterranean generally. We say that unless German forces can be weakened and dispersed between now and next year, cross-Channel operations won't be possible. They say if we go on plunging ahead in the Mediterranean during the summer and autumn, we won't have forces enough for any cross-Channel operations next spring. In our view Russia alone can severely maul German land forces and we must do all we can, from now onwards, to help her in this by drawing off and engaging German forces in the Mediterranean area. Under the American plan the Germans would have a truce from us till next spring and so could concentrate against Russia. I think our view prevailed and I must say our arguments seemed the stronger.

A.E. saw de G. today to say goodbye. He gave him some good advice about the importance of working with us and of getting on good terms with the Americans. De G. said he intended to stay now in North Africa but to leave a strong delegation here which he would visit from time to time. A.E. said he hoped he would not take away with him any too bitter memories. De G. replied *"Le peuple anglais a été merveilleux"* (No compliments to H.M.G.!)

May 30
De G., Massigli, Philippe and Palewski duly arrived in Algiers yesterday. I regret that General Georges[1] has also arrived there having been extricated from France itself at P.M.'s invitation. He and the P.M. are already getting together. Old Georges is about as much use as old Gamelin, two broken generals who were no good in 1939–1940 and are certainly no good, military or political, now. Georges will, I imagine, join the Giraud party.

The P.M. telegraphed yesterday asking A.E. to go out and join him in Algiers for a few days consultation. A.E. is off this afternoon and should arrive tomorrow. In one sense this is all to the good. A.E. will help the P.M. over the Husky and post-Husky operations which he no doubt wants to discuss with him on the ground and with the com-

1. General Georges had been Gamelin's Chief of Staff in 1939, and Commander of the French Armies in the North East 1940.

manders. A.E. will also curb the P.M.'s impetuosity over Giraud–de Gaulle affair, (in which the less intervention the better) and over the Azores problem. Finally, it is a useful and timely proof of how necessary A.E. is to the P.M. and what nonsense the idea of his going to India would make.

A.E. made a good little speech at Portsmouth on Friday and administered a slap to Franco who had dared to express horror at our bombing campaign. Franco of all people who bombed his way to power via Guernica! A.E. also said some tough things for Musso and the Fascists. All this was just what the British public felt like.

The P.M. is determined to oust Wavell from his command in India and Burma. He has never thought highly of W. and now he says he is shocked at the lifelessness of our command there. He wants to put Wavell on the shelf as Governor General of Australia and appoint Auckinleck C. in C. India with a younger fighting general to do the operations. A.E. has always had the highest opinion of Wavell. I have never shared his enthusiasm, though I have little to judge on. I know by experience A.E. is not always a good judge of men, e.g. Nevile Henderson, Casey, J.G. Grigg for whose appointments he was largely responsible. And he hadn't much opinion of Alexander or Montgomery before they had proved their outstanding merit in Egypt and Libya. But it strikes me as odd that Auchinleck should be given fresh work. He was a monumental failure. But that makes little difference in the Army.

June 2
Ominous rumblings from the de Gaulle–Giraud meeting. Peyrouton has resigned from Governor-General of Algiers.

June 4
New French Committee formed[1] and explosions – Nogués and Peyrouton both to go.

June 5
I met P.M. and A.E. at Northolt at 6 a.m. after a, for me, interrupted night of messages and counter-messages as to the time of arrival. I got there just as their aeroplane was circling round to land. Pound, Portal and Nye were already there. One single aeroplane contained the P.M., A.E., Brooke and Alexander. They looked strangely brown in the grey morning.

1. General de Gaulle and General Giraud were co-presidents.

A.E. had enjoyed himself immensely and looked much better for the trip. He reported that all the commanders were highly confident of the success of Husky. The P.M. had been quite dead when he first arrived from America and could hardly move but the sun and the bathing had gradually revived him.

The P.M. had wanted to intervene in the French squabbles, but A.E. wisely restrained him and in the end they both kept out. Before leaving, both attended a luncheon given by Admiral Cunningham to all the members of the new united French Committee amid general cordiality. P.M. was much taken up with his old friend Georges, whom A.E. had no use for. The P.M. continues to be violently anti-de G. and is joining President Roosevelt in representations against the removal of Boisson, the ex-Vichyite Governor-General of West Africa. He is also annoyed with the pro-de G. turn of the news from N. Africa. The P.M. and the President have little conception of modern France.

A.E. told me this afternoon he had talked with Bobbety (with whom he lunched) about India and that Bobbety now thought it lay between A.E. and Lyttelton and that he (Bobbety) inclined to L., but that if L. did go, then A.E. should give up the leadership of the H. of C. and concentrate on the F.O. With this I heartily agreed. F.O. work is being neglected and we are getting behindhand under the present arrangement.

The Food Conference[1] contrary to all expectation, has ended as a considerable success. Dick Law evidently did brilliantly by his handling of our own delegation and of the Americans and Russians. This was the first of the conferences which the President intends to call to make the American public internationally-minded. It is the means by which he hopes "to involve" his people in world affairs without arousing their suspicions and without the necessity of getting Senate consent to a Treaty. It was most important that it should not be a failure.

The military conversations in Algiers just terminated have tied up, more or less satisfactorily, the conclusion of the earlier Washington conversations. Broadly speaking, the U.S. Navy (Ad. King) only want to fight in the Pacific, the U.S. Army (General Marshall) only want to fight in N. France. We want to finish the Germans before we seriously take on the Japs, but we want to fight in the Mediterranean before we fight across the Channel. Our views have generally prevailed and it is decided that we go ahead with Husky now, and then follow up either

1. The Hot Springs Conference on Food and Agriculture.

with invasion of toe, heel and leg of Italy itself or with occupation of Sardinia and Corsica, according as resistance in Italy after Husky shapes. P.M. is very anxious for invasion of Italy and capture of Rome. Russians are shy of this as a commitment which will prejudice and even prevent the cross-Channel operations next year.

A.E. is dining with P.M. tonight when there will be a fresh on-slaught about India. I am afraid A.E. is still v. wobbly. Much pressure was applied in Algiers. A.E. either doesn't know his own mind or wants to go and is pathetically anxious to canvas opinion accordingly. He asked his detective his opinion (no bad judge for "the man in the street") and he answered at once, "If you went to India, you would be forgotten here in 2 years!" A very good reply for the detective, but a shocking state of mind for a future P.M.

June 7

On our morning walk A.E. told me that "it was still undecided" but he had had a further long talk with the P.M. about it. I asked whether the P.M. was pressing him; he said no, he was torn too. P.M. was very worried about India and the Far Eastern war and felt how bad it would be if after doing so well in the West we lost India and bogged the war against Japan. He felt that A.E. was the best man to pull it together but at the same time realised how he would miss him here if he went. A.E. was the only colleague with whom he was on really intimate terms. A.E. said he thought the P.M. wanted him to say that he him-self felt he should go, but A.E. declined to do that and said it was a matter for the P.M. to decide, and that embarrassed the P.M. very much. Apart from himself, P.M. now was veering to Anderson rather than Lyttelton.

A.E. discussed it very calmly and admitted readily to strong argu-ments against going. I went through them again. (1) his previous training and experience for the future work in F.O. (2) the general expectation of the country that he would succeed P.M. and the jolt to public confidence if he went off to India, incalculable consequences of jolts to public opinion of this kind; (3) by remaining now he would save P.M. from many fatal gaffes; (4) even though Cranborne and Law between them would be a strong pair at F.O., C. would not have influence with P.M. which A.E. had and might easily be driven to resignation when the field would be open to disastrous innovations.

June 8

A.E. had another grilling from the P.M. late last night about India.

He told me this morning he had been subjected to a lot of pressure, but he was resisting. But who should go? P.M. was now off Lyttelton and thinking again of Lampson. He wished to bring the Beaver back again as part of the shuffle. I put in my word for Halifax and then for Dick Law. A.E. went to see the P.M. again at 10.30 to look at "six alternative solutions". Late this afternoon A.E. told me "it was definitely off!" P.M. has now decided to recommend Wavell. Thank God! But it is a funny choice. Halifax would have been best. This arrangement has the virtue of leaving the Cabinet undisturbed and so, I trust, leaving Beaverbrook out.

June 11

Explosions from N. Africa where de G. has presented his resignation from the new Committee because it won't accept his terms. P.M. and Roosevelt naturally are both straining to rush in. We hope it will blow over.

The Azores project has come forward again owing to a telegram from Ronnie Campbell indicating an unusually receptive frame of mind in Salazar. It is proposed to invoke the Alliance and ask him if we may use the Islands in return for guarantees of their retrocession and of integrity of the Portuguese colonies (which should be a powerful lever) and for a supply of anti-aircraft guns to protect Lisbon. If he refuses, we shall think again and probably act on our own.

June 14

P.M. is wild over de G.'s activity in N. Africa where he is rapidly taking command of the new Committee. By a mixture of push and threats he has scared the old generals who are actually in a minority now over his army proposals. De G. wishes to be Commissioner of Defence responsible for reform of the army. He favours a purge of senior officers and a smaller *armée de métier* which would be split up and attached to appropriate units of the Allied Armies. He would however leave Giraud as titular C. in C.

Roosevelt is determined not to let de G. control the French Army and to keep Boisson at Dakar. The P.M. is supporting him in this and has sent a stream of angry telegrams to Macmillan in this sense. A.E. is much annoyed at this intervention in foreign affairs. ("I gave up India so as to be Foreign Secretary!")

It is rather shaming to see the P.M. taking this line. He would do anything now to blacken de G. He will not face the fact that Giraud, Georges and Boisson mean nothing to the French. Giraud and Boisson are marked off as American puppets. Giraud and Georges are silly old fools and Boisson is a Vichyite who employs a private Gestapo, but the Americans find him easy and wish in any case to make a postwar base of Dakar. We must leave the French alone and let them fight out their quarrels now they are united on French soil. De G. is powerful because he is the only modern man France has thrown up and because his personal record is impeccable. France is our nearest neighbour and we must continue to live with her and work with her whatever the Americans do. We cannot afford to allow our French policy to be dictated from Washington.

The P.M. has been so successful in putting our strategic plans across the President that he feels no doubt bound, in return, to accept the latter's French policy. One could wish de G. was a more diplomatic man and would set out to woo the Americans, but he is not that sort of man and it is because of this that he has France behind him.

But the U.S. approach to Europe is disturbing. The Darlan and Giraud frame of mind must be expected to reappear everywhere else. The State Dept. are ill-informed about Europe as their diplomatists have rarely been more than amateurs. Added to that, their own views are reactionary. They want a "comfortable" pre-war Europe of Pétains. America is an old-fashioned country itself, fearful of political and economic change, and its bankers, business men and politicians side naturally with the Right and Right Centre in Europe. Yet, under the stimulus of Russia and of a strong Leftward wind in England, Europe is moving Leftwards. The "comfortable" capitalist régimes of pre-war are doomed. Unless it is to be communist, it must at least be Beveridge. The bitterness against the Pétains and Quislings has not penetrated to America.

Stalin has sent the P.M. and Roosevelt a dusty message in reply to theirs about our strategic plans. In these he sees only the postponement again of the Second Front from 1943 to 1944. But this is grossly unfair. The Mediterranean victories have immensely relieved Russia. There has been no German offensive in the East yet because of them.

June 16
Roosevelt and the Dominions having all agreed to our tackling Salazar over the Azores, Ronnie Campbell has now been instructed to go ahead.

June 18
What I can only describe as a hysterical diatribe against de G. has

arrived from President R. addressed to P.M. "The time has come to break with de G. We cannot trust him" etc. etc. Why can't R. leave him alone just now when the Committee is pulling together and when Eisenhower, Murphy and Macmillan are reporting not unsatisfactory progress?

A.E. is alive to the danger of a break with de G. which would be resented in the U.S. quite as much as here. P.M., I gather, was fairly calm though he doesn't need much to touch him off on that subject. I hope a reasoned reply might be sent. But what are we to think of President R. backing defeatism and reaction in France? Who won't he wish to back in Italy or Germany?

We should concentrate on making the Committee work. If de G. then kicks over the Committee, we should be on sound ground. Only Frenchmen should liquidate de G. The more we and the U.S. take a hand the more we consolidate him. But why don't we concentrate more on making de G. our friend? He is the only Frenchman France has thrown up in the war.

June 21

President R. and the P.M. have gone into action against de G. by instructing Eisenhower to tell him we must insist on Giraud being C. in C. and having full control of the French Army on military grounds. Eisenhower conveyed this to both generals meeting him together. He did it tactfully and reasonably (Eisenhower is a big man in his way. He has come out a figure of great dignity in all this.) De G. rather blew up and enquired what would be said if the Committee approved of his appointment as C. in C. He finally stalked off in a rage. We are now waiting to see what line the Committee will take when this Allied decision is conveyed to them. Will they approve, will de G. resign?

This is interference with French affairs, though with Eisenhower as Allied C. in C. we are not on such bad ground. With a man of de G.'s unpredictable temper it is even not unreasonable. The rub will come if he resigns and tries to set up a separate court at Brazzaville.

June 23

The French Committee in Algiers has now produced an agreed settlement between the two Generals providing that Giraud should be C. in C. of N. and W. Africa and de G. C. in C. of all the rest of the French possessions (Syria, Central Africa, Madagascar etc.). This the two generals have accepted. It also meets Roosevelt's and the P.M.'s point of not allowing de G. to control the forces in N. Africa. Macmillan strongly urges acceptance and tells us confidentially that Eisenhower is himself alarmed at the presidential tendency to intervene on grounds of military security to obtain political ends. Eisenhower and Macmillan are showing great wisdom and skill in handling this. They realise that de G. can cause far more military insecurity if he breaks with the Committee than if he can be kept in it.

A.E. had a long talk with the P.M. who has also reluctantly agreed, with many growls, to give this new arrangement a chance, and what is more, is telegraphing to Roosevelt advising this.

June 26

Stalin has sent us another ugly message in reply to the P.M.'s own reasoned reply to the previous one over our failure to attack across Channel this year. It has a nasty taste. Stalin quotes all the passages from previous messages of the P.M. in which action was foreshadowed. The man has clearly no conception of what cross-Channel operations involve and he refuses to admit that the Mediterranean operations are any substitute. A further reply is being prepared.

Slight lowering of temperature in French affairs. The new arrangement appears to have been accepted by the Generals and the Committee and acquiesced in by President R. A steady purge of Vichy or near-Vichy officers and officials is going on. Also the remaining anti-republican laws and decrees are being quashed. Giraud wished to dart off to America but Pres. R. at our instigation, has wisely discouraged this. There is also hope of getting rid of the unhealthy Boisson at Dakar. B. actually sent in his resignation and G. accepted it; G. was then told by Eisenhower that he mustn't do this. So G. suppressed his acceptance. But it is believed B. may still go and the presidential veto be got round.

June 28

The Germans are trickling troops pretty steadily into S. Italy and Sicily, now thought much hampered by our bombing raids on communications. But they are also reinforcing Sardinia and Greece and must be still in doubt where the blow will fall. We are pretty near the date now.

June 29

France again. The Associated Press in Washington has put out a flat-footed statement, with obvious State Department instigation, telling the whole story how Eisenhower had been ordered to tell de Gaulle that the American and British Governments would not tolerate "interference" by de G. in Allied affairs in N. Africa. Another inspired leakage in an American paper said that British officials had now been told "to drop" de G. in favour of G. The effect of these clumsy efforts has been to rouse Lippmann to write a scathing article on the folly of the State Department's pro-Giraud policy and a fresh attack on Hull and Co. has been started up. This is being echoed in the British press who are already resentful at the idea that British policy to France is being dictated from Washington. The final effect of all this is to strengthen de G.'s position enormously. Giraud is now in French eyes an American puppet. The next is to necessitate our restating our own attitude which the Americans, in their eagerness to get us behind their mistakes, have mis-stated. Our attitude is to support the Committee, not this General or that, but the corporate body, as we did when it was the Free French Committee and as we do now it is the combined French Committee. We have never "dropped" de G. though the P.M. has only been narrowly restrained from doing so at Roosevelt's behest. But we must now formally recognise the new Committee. Yet this both the President and the P.M. are now jibbing at because it includes de G. They have got themselves into an absurd position. A.E. will urge this course at the Cabinet. If we recognise the Committee we strengthen the civilian elements there and we may hope to reduce the influence of the generals, but this will mean converting the P.M. and getting him to tackle the President. I'm afraid however the President, if not the P.M., has ideas of keeping France in leading strings for a long time to come. But if the President is pro-Giraud, Stalin is as stubbornly pro-Gaulle – we in the middle as usual.

June 30

A P.Q. is being asked tomorrow about our policy to the French. The P.M. is answering it himself. We have sent him a good draft reply accentuating our support of the Committee rather than of individuals. It remains to be seen if he will use it. We hear, however, that even he is becoming impressed by the growing hostility of opinion here (as shown by the press and his letter bag) to American ideas on France.

I hear that the Beaver (who has now returned here) never went near the Embassy all the time he was in Washington and that he had been putting it about there that we or even perhaps "the P.M." thought that Roosevelt should be allowed to run again. As Willkie put it, if we worked this line hard enough, we should ensure a Republican victory.

July 4
French affairs quieter. P.M. made a most satisfactory statement in the House last Thursday, stressing the importance of the Committee as against the Generals. We now must concentrate on recognising the Committee and getting the President to do so. A Cabinet Paper has been prepared but we are waiting for Massigli who arrives tomorrow to get the layout clear. Meanwhile that old fool Giraud has hopped off to Washington in spite of the President's efforts to put him off. He will thus miss Husky and look more foolish than ever.

The Pope is getting more and more agitated at the prospect of our bombing Rome. The Americans, unexpectedly, are even tougher about this than we are. Personally, I hate the idea of bombing Italy, not out of love for Mussolini or the Pope, but because I feel Italy belongs to *me*, as a citizen of the world! They are *my* art treasures. Fortunately, we needn't worry about Germany. There is nothing in Berlin or the Ruhr we shall miss. But when it is the lives of our troops, every military objective whose existence increases their peril, is legitimate.

July 5
We heard this morning that Sikorski and his party including Victor Cazalet had crashed last night taking off from Gibraltar on their way home to England. Only three survivors, Sikorski not being one of them. This is a heavy blow for the Poles and even for us. He was far the most sensible Pole and the best about Russia.

July 6
Poles will probably have Mikolajczyk as their new P.M., a peasant leader and a civilian. The new C. in C. may be either Sosnkowski or Anders. They wish to separate the command from the premiership and build up the civilians. Obviously wise.

P.M. is being unbelievably tiresome over the French. He is now seeking to prevent early recognition of the combined Committee as untimely. He is getting crazy on the subject. There is no alternative committee in sight. The smaller Allies have mostly recognised already. Russia will recognise next, and, as A.E. said to me, the U.S. will probably recognise now that Giraud is in Washington, without even warning us. Spears is here on leave, intriguing and spreading poison. A.E. is fed up with the way French policy is taken out of his hands.

July 7
Slight advance on the French front. A.E. had a further but this time

friendly argument with the P.M. over recognition in the watches of the night. P.M., in mellow mood, agreed good humouredly that recognition should be given "in about a month". A.E. said "that it is too long". "Oh then, in a fortnight!" Meanwhile we hear today from Macmillan that Eisenhower (that wise American) has telegraphed to Marshall in Washington strongly urging immediate recognition before Husky. This is a great help and has enabled us this morning to get the P.M. to telegraph to Roosevelt the draft terms of recognition which we favour if and when he is ready to proceed. Giraud is there now and the White House is quite capable of recognising on their own, leaving us on a limb, in terms which would be too wide or too narrow. A.E. has Massigli to lunch today when he will go into it all.

July 8
German attacks on the Russian front now begun. This is good from our angle, within a week of Husky, but it weakens our claim to have held up the Germans, though we have certainly delayed them.

I hear the P.M. is playing with the idea of an early return to party politics with himself going to the country as head of the Tory Party – in fact soon after the German war is over. This would be a disaster because whether on peace-making or reconstruction he would rapidly split the country. But easier said than done, because I doubt if it will be easy to shake off the Bevins and Attlees who are now wedded to National Government or to get the younger Conservatives to agree either. The former are afraid to stand alone and the latter are afraid of their party.

We are suddenly precipitated into a Polish crisis. Raczyinski, as M.F.A. and Ambassador, has been telling of the difficulties. Mikolajczyk is the best man for P.M.; for C. in C. they wanted either Sosnkowski or Anders.[1] Our advice was that the new Government should not be such as to antagonise the Soviets more than necessary and after discreet consultation with Clark Kerr, we recommended Sosnkowski rather than Anders. A.E. agreed that it was a good thing to separate the functions of P.M. from those of C. in C. and for the latter not to be in the Cabinet. It now appears what the Polies did not make clear that under the Polish Constitution it is the President and not the P.M. who appoints the C. in C. who takes his order from the President and isn't under the P.M. at all. Mikolajczyk refuses to be P.M. at all in

1. General Anders was Commander of the Polish forces in Italy and the Middle East 1942–1943.

these circumstances if Sosnkowski is appointed and the President has put down a fast one by appointing S. without waiting till he had a Government. A good example of Polish ineptitude in politics. A.E. saw Raczyinski again today and urged that this appointment be witheld from publication until after Sikorski's funeral next Wednesday and that in the meanwhile efforts should be made to form a government so that both can be announced together. He is also exploring how far the constitutional point is valid as he feels, as everyone in this country will, that no self-respecting P.M. would consent to form a government which had not the C. in C. under its orders. But the Polish President, Raczkiewicz, is old and weak, and his entourage, notably Zalewski, is reactionary and violently anti-Russian. Sikorski alone held all together, soldiers and civilians, Right and Left, by his personality. The Polish forces are the largest element in the Polish emigration and require a strong general to hold them, but Poland can only hold her own place among the Allied nations if she has a decent democratically constituted government. All this makes things too easy for the Russians.

July 12
Landings in Sicily, which began at dawn on Saturday, so far successful. Too early yet to make anticipations. It is Alexander's show and majority of troops as well as air force and of course Navy are British.

A.E. has sent a further minute to P.M., urging necessity for us to recognise new French Committee in view of the many legal instruments which bound us to the old. In Washington the President, even with Giraud there, went on record as saying the question of recognition has not come up! "There is no France now." The P.M. more than half shares the President's prejudices and, exalted by the battle, will no doubt be even more obstinate than usual. F.O. are preparing a Cabinet Paper on our relations with France and the necessity for us, if not for the U.S., to have a strong France after the war.

July 13
A.E. dined last night at No. 10 because Winant and Stimson were there. He went full of misgiving as the P.M. has been intolerable of late. Apart from the perpetual row over the French, the P.M. has maddened him by writing an ill-tempered and foolish minute about King Peter's affairs. The last straw was a minute in praise of a report by Spears on Syria. This had been written at our request for internal consideration in the Office and Spears had sent it direct to the P.M.

The paper is in flat disagreement with our Syrian policy. A.E. was so furious that I feared an explosion at the dinner.

However, the dinner passed off all right and then after the guests had left, he and the P.M. had a set-to till 2.15 a.m. I gathered the broadsides were pretty hot! On French affairs, A.E. had got the P.M. to agree that as a long-term policy he could not accept the American ideas of keeping France in leading-strings and demoting her to a second-class Power. It was our interest that France should be restored and strong. The P.M. said he would be prepared eventually to have a showdown with the President on this. But on the question of immediate recognition, he was adamant and said menacingly, "I will fight you to the death. You may get some support, but it won't last long!" The P.M. was in a crazy state of exultation. The battle has gone to the old man's head. The quantities of liquor he consumed – champagne, brandies, whiskies – were incredible.

The question for A.E. is whether to have a show-down in the Cabinet over French recognition or to proceed "by sapping and mining". The Cabinet are behind A.E. but a direct attack might precipitate a crisis and would anyway leave a stink. On the whole, A.E. favours "sapping and mining", which is the method usually successful in the end. But meanwhile we risk an explosion in the H. of C. and in the press over the shocking subservience of our French policy to America. We are getting the worst of it in both countries. For in America we have lost all the goodwill of the Liberal quarters which we had gained by our anti-Darlan stand, while in France itself we are beginning to share the bitter resentment felt for the Americans.

July 14

A reconciliation! I'm beginning to know the form now. Frightful rows, nervous exhaustion on both sides, then next day a rather contrite P.M. seeking to make up, like a schoolboy who knows he's been naughty, rather shamefaced, needing much face-saving. Rather winning.

Anyway it proves the policy of "sapping and mining" to be right. P.M. said "I dislike having to argue with you in Cabinet. I'd much rather fight it out with you like this in private". Yes, but at the cost of what nervous exhaustion!

However, as a result of all this, the P.M. has agreed to A.E. answering in good forthcoming terms a P.Q. by Toby Martin[1] about

1. J. H. Martin, Labour M.P. for Southwark 1940–50.

recognition. He has also agreed to A.E. taking up with Winant the question of recognition on the basis of the F.O. formula which he says he likes. He has also agreed to his complaining to Winant about the tone of the American press and the use which the State Department have made of the confidential document on guidance to the British press which the P.M. gave Winant. The State Department have "leaked" this document to the press and said it proves our change of heart as regards de G.

All this is good going. I remarked to A.E. what a triumph this was for him, that it was the artistic temperament in the P.M. which made him react in these contradictory ways. He said "yes – but there is a bit of artistic temperament on both sides!"

This is not the only quarter in which we have done well. Salazar has now practically agreed to our minimum desiderata in the Azores and the P.M. has agreed to close on it. He admitted that he hadn't believed that we should get it. If it hadn't been for A.E., the P.M. would have insisted on raping Portugal and I doubt if anyone else could have stopped him.

Sam Hoare is as usual in a fright and conjures up all sorts of false alarms of what the Spaniards may not do to the Portuguese at the instigation of the Germans. Old wive's tales.

I hear that Alec Hardinge is resigning.[1] This is a most serious thing. H. was the perfect Private Secretary for the King. He had a mind of his own and didn't hesitate to state it. But there has been friction for some time (beginning from Munich and Neville Chamberlain), largely caused by the Queen who was determined to get him out. He had seen the King through difficult times and would have been a wise guide in the even more difficult times ahead. He was like old Ponsonby to Queen Victoria. The King is fundamentally a weak character and certainly a rather stupid one. The Queen is a strong one out of a rather reactionary stable. A strong sensible progressive-minded Private Secretary is therefore needed. With Hardinge one could be sure that robust modern views would be expressed at the same time as a perfect conception of the position of the monarchy in England today, its limitations and its strength. Alec Hardinge's departure is also a grave loss to A.E., of whom he was the stoutest supporter.

I talked again to A.E. today about his giving up the leadership of the H. of C. at the end of the session. He would have to visit Moscow again soon and probably Washington to discuss peace plans. He would

1. The Hon. Sir Alexander Hardinge, Private Secretary to the King since 1936.

have to travel more and more and his work here would increase more and more. He agreed, but I feel when it comes to the point he won't.

July 15
A.E. had his talk with Winant last evening about French affairs. He spoke seriously of the press campaign in the U.S.A. and the misuse of the P.M.'s confidential document. Winant had little to say in defence and confessed that he too was worried at the length to which the controversy was going. He had himself on his own initiative already telegraphed to the President about it and was most anxious to find a way out. A.E. then urged upon him the advantages of our formula of recognition of the Committee and the Ambassador promised to telegraph to Washington. Winant at any rate now sees the dangers of the policy. The P.M., however, spoilt the effect of this by a further bitter outburst in Winant's presence against de G., in which he declared, "I entirely share your President's views about him."

Meanwhile we have had two unusually clear and definite telegrams from our Embassy in Washington on the foolish and shortsighted behaviour of the State Department, Hull and the President over this and the harm which in the long run acquiescence by us will do not only to Anglo–French but even to Anglo–American relations.

I'm engaging in a minor skirmish with Halifax myself over the crowd of people he wishes to bring on leave with him by air at Government expense. However flabby he is in his political opinions, he is like iron in pushing his private interests.

The battle continues well. Extraordinarily feeble reactions so far. In the Balkans we have Italian divisional commanders offering to surrender to our secret agents! In Russia the new German attacks have been brought to a standstill after no appreciable gains. What is happening to the enemy? P.M. is eagerly exploring chances of a direct assault on Naples or Rome without waiting for the rest of Sicily.

July 16
I must say the P.M. doesn't let the grass grow under his feet. He now proposes that he and A.E. should meet Roosevelt at Quebec early next month. (Roosevelt had suggested early September) to discuss the next stage of operations in view of the unexpected feebleness of Axis resistance in Sicily. He is anxious to pin the Americans down before their well-known dislike of European operations except cross-Channel gets the better of them again, and they pull out their landing craft and send off their ships to the Pacific.

July 17

We may be on the very eve of an Italian collapse. Resistance to our invasion couldn't be more lifeless. Even the Germans are half-hearted. A bold advance on Naples or even Rome might bring us enormous dividends. Smuts is pressing this and so is the P.M.

The Poles seem to have wobbled out of their crisis for the moment. Mikolajczyk, the Peasant leader, becomes P.M., and he has agreed to Sosnkowski as C. in C., whom the President had already appointed. Sosnkowski is anathema to the Russians and is a survivor of Pilsudski's régime, which is doubly bad, but he is the best soldier and most likely to hold in the obstreperous Polish armies. Romer is M.F.A. instead of Raczinski who was both that and Ambassador.

July 20

A.E. discussed with me today his plans in connection with the P.M.'s visit to Quebec. This is now agreed between the P.M. and the President and the party will go by boat about – A.E. hasn't yet decided whether to go with the P.M. or to follow later by air and catch him up at Q for the talks. His idea would be to go after Q down south and across to N. Africa and Sicily and so home.

What is not yet decided is whether Joe should be invited to go to Q or to send a representative. On general grounds this is clearly desirable. There is however a complication.

The Americans are, as always, anxious for cross-Channel operations next year. To do this, it would be necessary to strip our forces in Sicily and N. Africa and in fact renounce the exploitation of our success in Sicily, since the build-up for next spring must begin this autumn. To the P.M., and A.E., (and indeed to everyone here) it seems madness not to push on from the South, the famous "soft underbelly" which now shows signs of disintegrating. If we lay off now, we give the Italians time to recover and then engage the Germans on the ground most favourable to themselves (i.e. N. French coast). But this is what the Americans want, and unfortunately the Russians share their views. The P.M. hopes that at Q he will be able to persuade the Americans to agree to opening up our operations in Italy at the expense of future operations cross-Channel and he believes he will be able to persuade the President. If, however, the Russians are there, not necessarily Uncle Joe, but Molotov, or even only a Russian general, who would support steadily American views, the P.M. feels he might well be overwhelmed.

P.M. in repentant mood. He told A.E. last night that a) A.E. had been right about Portugal and b) right about King Peter and c) we ought now to recognise the French Committee and he was prepared to tell the President so.

July 21

The P.M. has at long last sent an excellent telegram to Pres. R. giving all the reasons why H.M.G. cannot defer recognition of the French Committee much longer. He hopes the President will agree to recognise with us in the terms of our suggested formula; alternatively, he asks if the President would object to our acting alone. All this should of course have been sent weeks ago.

Winant is a curious man. He never seems to invite anyone to his house. In some ways he is rather a great man. He is certainly an unorthodox man. No one knows how much, if any influence he wields with the President, though the State Dept. dislike him. He is untidy in his mind and in his ways. His Embassy is unbelievably inefficient. He (or his staff) loses papers, doesn't acknowledge letters, doesn't answer invitations or requests. He has a shyness which is superficially attractive and a Lincoln caste of countenance but we still ask ourselves what it conceals. By his record, a self-made man who set out to strike and did strike oil (he is now a rich man), as a former State politician and Governor of his native state of New Hampshire, he can't be a tyro to public life and must be "a tough guy". His record as Director General of the I.L.O. and early New Dealer is another side. He left the Republican Party, I believe, to join President Roosevelt. Where does astuteness begin and Lincoln end?

July 24

The President has sent us another petulant and childish telegram about recognition of the French Committee. He boggles now at "recognition" and would prefer "acceptance" instead. We are not sure whether he had already had the P.M.'s telegram giving our formula, or not. What petty nonsense this is! We have done irreparable harm to our joint relations with France by this behaviour, strengthening Soviet influence, since Stalin is known to be ready to recognise and is only waiting for us, weakening the Committee itself to benefit of de G. in his autocratic capacity and causing confusion in the underground movement in France. For all this, Winston, Roosevelt and Hull bear sole responsibility.

Such unreal ideas are not encouraging when other countries as well as France have to be considered. Old Hull is clearly almost mental on the subject. Now we have old Stimson (aged 75) who is over here, passionately advocating an early shock offensive across the Channel. On this, I'm thankful to say, the P.M. will refuse absolutely to budge. On military matters he is instinctively right as he is wrong on foreign affairs. As a war minister he is superb, driving our own Chiefs of Staff, guiding them like a coach and four, applying whip or brake as necessary, with the confidence and touch of genius.

The Americans have cut across and captured Palermo, and two-thirds of the island are occupied. The Germans are still fighting desperately in front of Catania but even here we are forging ahead.

Jacques Kayser[1] dined with us. He arrived here 10 days ago from N. Africa, having got there through Portugal and Spain. We asked him about the future in France. He thought it would depend much on whether the war ended with fighting in France or as a result of a collapse in the East. If there were no fighting, the Communist element would be much strengthened as Russia would be regarded as the liberators. If the Germans were driven out of France after a victorious Allied campaign in which the French took part, the Western and democratic influences would gain. He thought it most important that the French Committee should be brought into the picture from the start, being made responsible for the government of the areas as they were liberated. A strong and authoritative government was necessary if civil war and local vendetta were to be prevented. Only the Committee would have the authority to impose itself and purge the local administrations. Whilst the French would understand the necessity for submitting to Allied military regulations in France, they would not tolerate outside interference in civil affairs. Vichy and the Germans have revolted them with imposed authorities. From the French internal point of view invasion couldn't begin too soon. The French expected it almost hourly. The longer it were postponed, the less French powers of resistance would become from sheer physical weakening by starvation and the gradual rounding-up of all able-bodied for work in Germany.

July 26
Musso has resigned and the King and Badoglio[2] have taken over. We heard it last night on the midnight news. So the first of the dictators and the father of the whole evil system has been the first to fall. What happens next? Badoglio declares "The war goes on". But those can

1. Previously Chef de Cabinet to Daladier.
2. Chief of the Italian General Staff.

only be brave words. Like Pétain when France fell, he will be anxious to make peace as fast as possible to save what he can from the wreck. We shall insist, I hope, on "unconditional surrender", as laid down at Casablanca.

A special cabinet is called for this evening.

July 27
We are eagerly awaiting developments but nothing clear has yet emerged. Badoglio has formed a government of completely unknown Italians except for Guariglia, Italian Ambassador in Angora, who becomes M.F.A. All sorts of rumours of riots and peace demonstrations in Italian cities. Musso said to be in house arrest and the Fascist Government shut up too.

P.M. and Pres. have exchanged first thoughts and both are tough. "No negotiation", "unconditional surrender". We have sent to the Americans our proposed armistice terms. We intend to use Italian territory, aerodromes, railways etc. ruthlessly for pursuing the onslaught on Germany. All expect an early offer from Badoglio. This is obviously the Pétain–Laval stage.

The next stage will be tricky. What are our relations to be with the King of Italy and Badoglio? Both are compromised by the past, Abyssinia etc. The idea at present is that although some such authority must be required to sign the surrender, it need not be regarded as the future administration with which we should deal. The trouble is all prominent Italians are compromised in Fascism and it will be hard to find any reputable régime. On the other hand, we hardly want to have the responsibility for administering Italy ourselves while the war is on. Hence it looks like a Pétain régime which would carry out Allied requirements.

No news yet of how the crack came. Presumably at Verona Musso asked Hitler for more help which Hitler refused. Musso then chucked his hand in or was ordered out by Badoglio. The last straw was of course the failure of the Italians to fight in Sicily and their tumultuous welcome to the Americans in Palermo.

Bothers over French recognition persist. We learn that Roosevelt *had* seen the P.M.'s telegram urging recognition in terms of our formula when he sent his last foolish message about "acceptance". Winant is at a loss what to do and says "he is in the dog-kennel", which apparently means that he is in disgrace for having advocated recognition. He believes Hull drafted the President's message and says even Harry Hopkins, who agrees with us, can do nothing. The question is, are we to go ahead without America or wait till Quebec to fix it? Dangerous and damaging to wait. Uncle Joe may go ahead; an evil precedent for us to take action independently of the Americans.

July 29
Italian situation still obscure though cracking is clearly going on. Riots in Milan. The Fascist Party abolished amid general rejoicing. "The war still goes on." We think Badoglio must be trying to get the Italian divisions back out of the Balkans before he asks us for terms. No news of Musso's whereabouts. We are getting our armistice terms ready with the Americans. General agreement that we must require fullest use of all Italian facilities for prosecution of war against Germany. We would accept Badoglio's and the King's signature for this but would in no way commit ourselves to recognise them as the future government of the country.

We are getting seriously worried about relations with Stalin. We get no replies to our telegrams. No response to A.E.'s offer to go to Moscow, nor to Roosevelt's invitation to meet in Alaska, no word of pleasure over Sicily nor now the collapse of Musso. Now we have the news of Maisky's retention in Moscow as Vice-Commissioner for F.A. and his replacement here by Gusev, Soviet Minister in Ottawa. The latter is a dim personality, about 40, formerly head of European Department in Moscow, a junior to Sobolev, the Counsellor-Minister now here. I cannot see him becoming an intimate collaborator with A.E. such as Maisky was.

July 30
No more news from Italy except that it becomes clearer that Hitler was insisting on a retreat to the North. Guariglia, the new M.F.A., spoke to the Turkish M.F.A. before he left Angora and clearly indicated Italy couldn't remain in the war. But G. hoped the Allies would adopt a policy of "understanding" and allow her to remain openly the ally of Germany whilst secretly preparing to pass over to us. "In other words", as the Turk said, "a policy of treachery".

Much telegraphing and counter-telegraphing between the P.M., Roosevelt and Eisenhower about armistice terms. Eisenhower keeps on making broadcast appeals to surrender only more or less approximate to the official terms. We wish to stop this because we don't think it is the right method and also we don't wish to be charged later with having induced the Italians to surrender on false pretences.

During these very busy days A.E. is still tied to spending a number of hours daily in the H. of C. The greatest folly, exhausting for the man and bad for the work. He can do neither the H. of C. nor the F.O. adequately. He is very tired and sleeping badly. Yet he refuses to give up the H. of C. because he hates leaving it to anyone else.

I really despair of our ever getting French recognition through. The P.M. has now turned round again and thinks the Roosevelt formula not too bad. He wishes to be quite certain de Gaulle is the prisoner of the Committee before he recognises, wishes to have more proofs of the way the French are working. In fact, "no hurry". It will take years to undo the harm already done to Anglo–French relations by this ungenerous and haggling attitude of Winston's. The British public is in no way approving of it and the dangerous feeling is growing that we have no policy of our own on this or other questions but defer always to the Americans.

August 3

No more developments yet from Italy. Efforts, largely vain, are being made to stop Eisenhower coming out with a fresh broadcast appeal every morning. As the P.M. says, "Action, not words is what is expected from a C.-in-C." There is also a slight sign of wobble by the President from the severe line of unconditional surrender. Several more telegrams have been exchanged between him and the P.M. on this. One has the impression of three people trying to drive a motor at the same time.

August 4

More confusion between Washington and London over Italy. Roosevelt has received proposal to make Rome an open city which he has approved in principle without any reference to us. P.M., much upset, and justifiably, begs that decision be deferred till Cabinet can consider. We are against it because acceptance now will look like weakening and will stiffen Italian resistance to unconditional surrender and because we wish to be sure we can use the Rome railway system ourselves when we occupy Italy. It would play straight into German hands and is doubtless encouraged if not prompted by them.

These Americans! They are so excitable and they over-simplify so. They are incapable of sitting quietly and thinking out the implications of a proposal. They rush off at once, in a high state of excitement, and commit themselves.

Meanwhile we have heard from Ronnie Campbell that the Italian Counsellor at Lisbon has asked to be received by him. We have told him to do so, but only to listen to what he says. Is this a peace offer?

Public opinion here is turning decisively against Badoglio. He was responsible for gassing the Abyssinians and is regarded as a Darlan. It will be difficult to accept him as the future government of Italy. This however is not intended. It is hoped to get him and the King to sign the surrender and after that to drop them.

Roosevelt has now asked that we shall defer further consideration of French recognition till he meets the P.M. at Quebec. Meanwhile the Committee themselves are making good progress in unifying their affairs. The President's attitude could not be more short-sighted.

August 5
P.M. off at last by ship last night. A.E. with Alec Cadogan and Nicholas is to follow by air next Saturday week.

A peace-feeler has reached Lisbon in the person of a new Italian counsellor, Marchese D'Ayala, who comes in the name of Badoglio to get in touch with our Ambassador. He claims that the King and B. are the only alternative to Bolshevism, no middle-classes having been left after 20 years of Fascism. The Germans are livid with the Italians and will shoot them up if they give in. K. and B. therefore have to make a show of going on with the war, but the whole country really wants peace. K. and B. want us to come in and drive out the Germans.

Not quite good enough. To begin with, I don't for a moment believe that K. and B. are the only alternative to Bolshevism – that is obvious propaganda. Secondly, this emissary is known to be a Ciano man. In other words it means the younger Fascists are hoping to get in again under cover of a K. and B. régime.

August 6
An Italian emissary with exactly similar tale has arrived at Tangier and seen Joe Gascoigne, our Consul General there.

Another has come to Barcelona with a different story. He says he represents the old Liberal parties of Bonomi[1] and Orlando[2] who wish to get in touch with us and call themselves "The Committee of Action of Free Italy". They declare Badoglio doesn't represent the people and is doomed to fail and ask for recognition of their Committee as Allies and as a Provisional Government.

P.M. has drafted a quite admirable telegram to Macmillan, which is to be sent in two or three days time when the old boy is in safer

1. Ivanoe Bonomi, Italian Prime Minister 1921–1922.
2. Orlando had been Prime Minister of Italy during the first War.

waters, telling him to tell the French Committee of his impending meeting with Roosevelt at which he hopes to secure satisfactory recognition, asking them to help him by continued wise and constructive action meanwhile and declaring it his view that "Committee should take its place" with other United Nations. This is most important and should help a lot to mitigate the damage already done.

Dick Law asked me to meet one of the leaders of the French Resistance Movement who is a pre-war friend of his. A most interesting man,[1] about 55, a banker and a Jew, he is only over here for 2 or 3 weeks and is then to be dropped in again. He spoke, as Kayser did, of the absolute necessity of recognising the Committee as a provisional Government which would take over as French territory is freed. All France, or rather 95% of France, was resistant and looked to the Committee as its authority. Unless that authority was installed officially and quickly, chaos and revolution would result. There was no danger of de G. becoming dictator. The French people would have no dictators. I am becoming convinced myself that this is what we must work for. There is no alternative government in France except that of Vichy. The new French political elements will take time to show themselves. Above all, we, the Anglo–Americans, must avoid having to govern France ourselves. We must never get pushed into Stulpnagel's[2] shoes.

August 8

Still nothing more from Italy. The Badoglio Government is busy sucking up to Germany, and the Germans are pouring troops through the Brenner into N. Italy, while cautiously withdrawing from Sicily. Genoa, Turin and Milan bombed last night.

August 9

A further enquiry about terms from Badoglio's emissary[3] at Tangier. P.M. is on the sea, Roosevelt is on holiday. A.E. is in the country. Not easy to consider and coordinate decisions. A.E. wants to reply that Badoglio must first offer unconditional surrender and after that we will communicate our terms.

1. Albert Kohan. He returned to France but was killed in an aircrash on his way out the second time.
2. German Military Governor of France.
3. Signor Berio, of the Italian Foreign Office.

Macmillan over here. Also Swinton.[1] A.E. as usual most reluctant to see either or for that matter even Jim and Dick who want to lecture him about giving up the leadership of the H. of C. Dick and Jim want him either to do this or else to appoint an Assistant Foreign Secretary, who should be Dick, to take more of the burden off him. But A.E. won't give up anything, he won't share anything and he hates even discussing it with his colleagues, all of whom bore him!

August 11
A message for the P.M. came from Stalin last night. This breaking of silence after such an ominous interval is a matter for relief. Stalin refers to the P.M.'s last message in which he told him of the impending meeting at Quebec, says he has been away at the front and cannot absent himself from the country but is anxious for a meeting of representatives of the three Powers soon. Finally, he congratulates us on Sicily and the overthrow of Musso.

This is encouraging and we feel we should take it up at once and fix an early meeting. This we have put to the P.M.

August 23
I have been away on leave and only came back to the office today. Much has been going on. Italy first of all. An Italian general[2] turned up at Lisbon with an introduction from Osborne[3] at the Vatican to Ronnie Campbell. He said he came from Badoglio (this is confirmed) to say the Italian Government would surrender unconditionally if they could join the Allies in turning out the Germans. All this had to be passed back to Quebec as a result of which a British and an American staff officer were sent from Eisenhower's H.Q. to see him and inform him of our surrender terms. We refused to commit ourselves to taking them on as allies but said we would judge them by results. They must resist and sabotage the Germans and afford us unopposed landings. This conversation took place on 19th, after which the Italians were to return to Rome as soon as they could and send Eisenhower a secret wireless message if Badoglio accepted. We would then give him a few hours' notice of our landing whereupon he must announce the surrender and aid our advance. The Italian General,

1. Lord Swinton, Cabinet Minister resident in West Africa. Later Minister for Civil Aviation. He had been Air Minister in Chamberlain's Government.
2. General Castellano, of the Italian General Staff.
3. Sir D'Arcy Osborne, British Minister to the Vatican.

who gave us all the German dispositions, said the Germans were threatening frightful reprisals on the Italians and intended to form a line from Genoa to Ravenna, setting up a Fascist Quisling Government under Farinacci.[1]

Meanwhile Portugal is in the bag, Salazar having finally agreed on our terms for the use of the Azores as from Oct. 8. This is very satisfactory and a tribute to Ronnie's painstaking diplomacy. Alone he did it.

I know nothing of the military decisions which have been taken at Quebec but A.E. and Hull have been talking about French recognition. Here no progress has been made, Hull being unwilling to recognise the French Committee in terms sufficiently positive for us to accept or indeed for good rather than harm to come of it. It looks as if Canada and H.M.G. may have to recognise independently in terms of their own. Recognition by us is now absolutely essential.

Finally, Finland wants to get out of the war and Hungary is ready to surrender unconditionally.

August 24

Quebec conference breaking up. No reply yet from Stalin about a meeting *à trois*. P.M. is staying on in Washington. A.E.'s movements uncertain.

It has been decided to appoint Mountbatten C. in C. of S.E. Asia Command with Wingate as a good second. People here are doubtful of M. being up to this, but the P.M. and the Americans are het up on it. Mountbatten–Wingate is at least a refreshing contrast to Wavell–Auchinleck.

It appears to have been decided that we and the Canadians are to go ahead with French recognition. *Tant pis* for Lafayette and all that!

The really important thing now is to have early and profound discussions with the Russians. We must discuss not only immediate military but political and postwar plans. We should try to reach definite agreement now on what we intend after the war as regards Eastern frontiers and postwar European controls. If Stalin won't come to meet us, then Molotov and Maisky (who is coming next month anyway to say goodbye) should be invited to come here, or A.E. and Sumner Welles should go to Moscow.

But Sumner Welles is on such bad terms with Hull (everywhere we now come across Hull's deadening influence) that he won't in all probability be allowed to undertake such a mission. There is no other

1. Roberto Farinacci, one of the early hard-line Fascists.

American who has the clear head or the experience to do it so well. A.E. himself has as yet only superficial ideas of what our future plans are and is not anxious to commit himself. Owing to that wretched H. of C. these subjects have been insufficiently studied by him and we are not ready. Brilliant empiricism and improvisation, which has served him so well in the turmoil of the war, cannot here replace solid work and thought.

August 25
Stalin has replied to the P.M.'s and President's messages and proposes the setting up of a tripartite armistice commission in Sicily at once, to study the Italians' and any other armistice terms which come along. This is something and should be welcomed and adopted at once. Russia must be brought into Italy just as or rather just because we want to be in the Polish, Czech, Roumanian pictures.

It seems now that the P.M. will be back (by ship) by the end of next week, and A.E. by Clipper at the end of this. I hope so, for thus only can we got on with all these decisions. As regards French recognition it is now definitely decided that we all recognise separately in our own terms – ourselves, Canada and U.S.A. Our recognition is reasonably full and generous in terms. The U.S. formula is grudging and sour.

The Quebec Conference on military matters has apparently gone well. We have held our own about the necessity of exploiting Italy well up into the leg of the country now, so that we can bomb Germany from the South, the more vulnerable angle, and make her spread out her forces on a new front. By this means we shall weaken her, we hope, sufficiently to make cross-Channel operations a reasonable risk for next year.

At long last, after 4 years of it, I feel we are really in our stride and know how to run this war. By sea, land and air, we are now efficient and up-to-date, both in men, methods and materials. The Americans are still amateurish in their approach. If the Western war is to be won quickly, it must be run by our strategy and our people.

August 27
Further Italian developments occurred during the night. Another Italian general[1] escorted by General Carton de Wiart (who had been taken prisoner in Italy) arrived at Lisbon, as Italian General No. 1

1. General Zanussi.

THE WAR DIARIES OF OLIVER HARVEY

hadn't returned. The latter had in fact just left but opportunity was taken to give the new Italian general the text of our latest and most comprehensive armistice document which hadn't been ready before. This he is to take back to Rome and say General Eisenhower will have it also at Palermo if the Italians send an emissary there. We hope therefore the Italians may come prepared to sign it.

What is amusing is that Grandi came on the same plane as this general, apparently doing a get-away.

French recognition is published today. Although we informed Stalin of our intentions, we gave him scarcely any time to conform and his recognition has come out this afternoon. He had wanted to recognise ages ago but at our appeal agreed to defer till we were ready. Having taken so long ourselves, we might have given him another day or two. The Russian recognition, in revenge, is more comprehensive even than ours.

All this makes it the more necessary to accept at once Stalin's proposals for an Armistice Commission in Sicily and for tripartite political talks. The Quebec military decisions can only bring him cold comfort.

August 28

From Lisbon we hear the second Italian general is to be sent back now via Gibraltar and Sicily as no more direct route to Italy is available or safe. There won't be much time for him to deliver his message and get us a reply before our landing starts. The Naples area is being plastered with bombs, but even so the operation will be hazardous. German troops are steadily pouring into Northern Italy.

August 30

A.E. came up after lunch. He has had frightful tussles with the P.M. and F.D.R. over Stalin whose rude messages have infuriated them. The P.M., he thinks, is now getting dangerously anti-Russian. A.E. had no idea of the strength of the anti-French recognition opposition. He had battle after battle with Hull whom he found quite hopeless. The old man went off in a very sour mood at the end. He was certainly responsible for driving out Sumner Welles and when the President had tentatively suggested using S.W. for visiting Moscow, he looked even sourer than usual. On the other hand, we seem to have got what we wanted on strategic questions and indeed the opposition to our views was less than anticipated.

August 31

All hands are being turned on to prepare the proposed tripartite conversations.[1] Long talks between A.E. and Maisky and A.E. and Winant. Maisky not discouraging.

Some confusion over the two Italian emissaries owing to Macmillan in Algiers butting in and holding up General No. 2 on security grounds and preventing him taking back the longer surrender document. But Gen. No. 1 has intimated his arrival in Rome and his plans to return to Sicily today or tomorrow. Our first landing is timed for September 3rd and the second for a week later.

Ciano and Edda[2] have escaped from Rome but we know not where. Grandi, we do know, arrived at Lisbon with the connivance of the Pope and Badoglio. He would like to come to London but we will have no truck with him!

September 1

Macmillan and Eisenhower are being incredibly wooden and obstructive over the armistice arrangements. They have held back Italian General No. 2 and sent on his companion only with a note saying the longer terms are only of relative importance. Eisenhower is in a fright over his operations and seems now to think the Italians must be won over to us. We are heading for a new Darlanism and what a row it will cause. We blame Macmillan for being stupid over this. He at least should have more sense. The only way to get anything out of the Italians is to go on hammering them.

September 2

General Castellano has returned to Sicily and met U.S. general Bedell Smith[3] again. Former was full of whines, the Italian Government were no longer free agents, they would like to sign but couldn't, they couldn't come out in the open with an announcement until after we had invaded; in fact the Italians were much more frightened of the Germans who were pouring in, than of us whose forces for invasion he clearly thought inadequate. Smith was commendably tough and said whatever the Italians did we were going to turn Italy into a battleground and we could accept nothing less than surrender. Eisenhower however has decided that Italian acquiescence is so needed for our operations that he will agree in principle to drop an airborne division

1. On future political decisions.
2. Edda Ciano, Mussolini's daughter.
3. General Bedell Smith was Chief of Staff to General Eisenhower.

in the Rome area "as a good gamble", to hearten and stiffen the Italians to resist there, provided the latter undertake to announce their surrender before our main landing and to get the Italian divisions near Rome to cooperate with us.

A.E. had Winant and Maisky to lunch *à trois*. This was my idea to get started the principle of 3-party discussion here. It worked excellently and Maisky explained to Winant the similarity of the Russian and British attitudes towards Europe, both countries are on the fringes, neither wished to dominate but neither would tolerate domination by anyone else. The advantages of conversations in London are becoming more evident, especially as there is a chance of Hull coming here.

September 3

Italian General Castellano has returned to Italy and replied that he is authorised to agree to our proposals and he would arrive again in Sicily on 2nd to discuss details.

The minor operation, called "Baytown" to establish a bridgehead on the toe of Italy opposite Sicily, was carried out this morning, It was not expected that they would encounter great enemy force. The Germans are believed to be evacuating northwards in order to form a strong line to keep us out of Lombardy and its aerodromes – v. heavy opposition however is expected for part 2 of our invasion ("Avalanche")[1] as both German divisions and airpower can be concentrated there quicker than we can. Much depends on the Italians, if they cease to fight the Germans will probably make their main line much further to the North, if they go on fighting, they may try to hold Rome.

September 6

Much has happened over the weekend. First, our operation against the toe of Italy has started well. Little or no opposition. Second, General Castellano returned to Sicily and signed the short armistice terms on the dotted line on September 3. The armistice is to be announced to-day before zero day for the big operation. The Italians are to do their utmost to fight and embarrass the Germans. It was made clear that thereafter they would be regarded no longer as enemies, but not as allies.

This involves us in telling them something of our future plans which is alarming. All the elements are here for Italian *combinazioni*. The Airborne Division to be dropped in the Rome area will be a

1. The Salerno landing.

horrid pledge to fortune. In any case, in the most favourable conditions, it will be a formidable task for it to hold out while our main forces are landing and painfully ploughing their way up from Naples.

Replies have also gone to Stalin about the meeting of Foreign Ministers and the setting up of the joint Armistice Control Commission. The P.M. accepts the former, says he will send A.E. if Molotov comes and suggests England as the meeting place and October as the date. Roosevelt also accepts in a separate message, offers Hull or Welles, but prefers Casablanca or Tunis.

As regards the Commission of Control, P.M. agrees too, though somewhat tepidly, suggests Algiers or Tunis as better than Sicily and proposes political representatives to whom soldiers could if necessary be attached. Roosevelt rather rides off the proposal by suggesting that a Russian soldier should be sent at once to sit at Eisenhower's H.Q. (This is bad and not at all what is wanted. It is essential that it should be a political body: if we try to keep the Russians out of Italy they will be able to keep us out of Eastern Europe.)

The P.M. is now settling down in Washington and does not intend to leave till September 14th. Whilst his influence on the President in military matters may be excellent, the President's influence on him in political matters is disastrous. The P.M.'s American half comes up more and more.

September 7

A reassuring telegram from Alexander about "Avalanche". The plans are being so laid that they can hardly be compromised if Italians don't play. Badoglio's announcement of the armistice is to be made tomorrow afternoon by wireless, telephone, proclamation and every possible form of publicity. Our airborne operation in Rome is timed to take place at a number of hours after the announcement sufficient to cancel the whole operation if the agreed announcement hasn't been made. But it will still remain a most hazardous business because no one can say what if anything Italian assistance to us will amount to.

A complication is that it will be difficult if not impossible to announce the terms of the surrender for some time owing the fact that it refers to various operational moves of the Italian Fleet etc. which the Germans mustn't know. But to keep the terms dark will awaken suspicion here of some Darlanlike deal with Badoglio.

September 8

All was set this morning for zero hour. A.E. was to see Maisky,

Wellington Koo, and the Allied Foreign Ministers this afternoon to tell them of what Eisenhower was announcing at 5.30. A.E. was giving a farewell lunch to Maisky and when he returned at 3, we heard there had been a hitch, Eisenhower had sent a telegram from which it appeared the Italians had run out. A War Cabinet had been summoned for 3.15 to consider it. What the telegram actually says, I haven't yet seen. "Avalanche" is due to start tonight and is not dependent on Italian cooperation. The despatch of the Airborne Division is dependent and must now I presume be suspended. I suspect the Italians are saying "We can't announce now as the Germans are watching but if you come as arranged we will help". Not good enough.

Later – Cabinet met. Facts are roughly that Eisenhower has had a message from Badoglio that he can't fulfil the terms of the armistice or guarantee the aerodromes for our airborne division as the Germans will seize Rome. He wishes therefore to call the whole thing off. Eisenhower has decided to go ahead with "Avalanche", to call off the airborne division operation (thank goodness!) but to announce the armistice and publicly commit Badoglio to it. What will happen in Rome or Italy we simply do not know. General confusion probably which will be helpful to us. Anyway it proves once again, for those who still do not know, how unreliable the Italians are, whether as enemies or allies. The P.M. is already harbouring visions of large Italian forces joining us in the destruction of Germans and Japs.

From 5.30 onwards we awaited eagerly for what the ether might yield. Eisenhower's piece came over at 5.30 according to plan. After that confusion and rumour. Some reports said Badoglio had spoken but these were unconfirmed.

September 9

Badoglio finally did broadcast, though apparently rather late. Eisenhower after receipt of his message sent a very rough reply to the effect that, although calling off airborne operations, he meant to make his broadcast as agreed and pin Badoglio to it. Whether Badoglio really meant to run out altogether or whether he only wished to disclaim ability to guarantee the safety of the Rome aerodromes, we do not know.

The Salerno landings are making good progress, and we heard at midday that the Italian fleet was steaming in the right direction.[1]

1. To surrender at Malta.

Stalin has now replied to the P.M.'s and President's messages. He is cross at the slowness and lack of warmth in our response about the Armistice Control Commission, (as well he might be), repudiates the idea of just sending a military officer and requests that the Commission be set up at once as requested. As regards the meeting of foreign ministers he plumps for Moscow early Oct. As regards the P.M.–Pres.–Stalin meeting he proposes Tehran.

Bevin told A.E. yesterday that there had been a secret meeting of the T.U.C. leaders at which they agreed that if anything happened to the P.M., they would back A.E. A.E. much flattered at this.

September 10
Operations proceeding at Salerno Bay all right so far. We hear Badoglio Government may be fleeing to Taranto. The Germans are attacking Rome, according to Osborne, and may be in today. The Italian fleet is steaming towards our ports.

A.E. in the country, the P.M. in Washington, everybody telephoning and telegraphing at cross-purposes. Why cannot these people stay quietly in their offices and do their work where it can be handled most efficiently and expeditiously?

P.M. has replied to Stalin's message agreeing to set-up as Stalin proposed of Armistice Control Commission in Sicily or Algiers, agreeing that Foreign Office representatives should meet in Moscow early Oct. and that A.E. should go, and agreeing to meeting of Big 3 themselves for Nov. or Dec. at Tehran.

F.D.R. has done likewise.

A.E. not best pleased at this prompt acquiescence in Moscow as against London, feels he is cast for a very undignified role which could be better filled by an official. The P.M. and F.D.R. indeed are keeping the best role for themselves to play personally with Stalin, while poor A.E. would have only stonewalling with Molotov.

September 11
Rome captured and occupied by the Germans. We don't know what is happening to the Pope. Nothing definite about Badoglio's whereabouts or the King's. There are reports of the latter's abdication. At Salerno our landings are going ahead but it is still ticklish. The Germans are moving up there and our build-up is slow.

The P.M. is still full of delusions at the help the Italians will give us. It is clear that their moral and physical collapse is pretty complete and, except for the ships (which we will have to run ourselves), we shall get nothing from them. They are just going to lie down. In N. Italy the Germans are rounding up and disarming the troops just as we are doing in the South. But this in itself is a great deal, because Germans (though not so many!) will have to be where Italians were before, in the Balkans, in S. France and of course in Italy itself. Heavy fresh calls on German manpower.

September 12

Heavy fighting in Salerno area. Easier going in Calabria where Germans are retreating under cover of demolitions. They are being bombed. Taranto is ours and now a British naval base. The Italian battle fleet is at anchor in Malta harbour. A few Italian ships have taken refuge in the Balearics. We hope to prise them out of the Spaniards.

It looks as if Badoglio was making for Taranto himself. Mason Macfarlane has been lifted out of Gibraltar[1] to meet him as Head of a Military Mission.

No more news from Rome. General reports from the frontiers show that the Italians are being rounded up and disarmed without much resistance.

I foresee we are going to find ourselves torn between the needs of the front in Italy and the build-up of "Overlord" [cross-Channel operation] for 1944.

September 13

Battle situation much the same. Germans claim to have rescued Musso. I have no regret about that. He will be another dead-weight round their necks. A skeleton at Hitler's feasts.

An interesting report based on secret information obtained from clerical sources in France. Even Pétain himself only puts his supporters at 50% but it is stated that Giraud and Georges are in touch with him and he believes that with their aid and that of the Americans his régime can be preserved when the French and Allied armies land. I can quite believe about Giraud and Georges being in touch with P. I can also believe that the State Department and possibly the President would wish to see Giraud succeed Pétain and not de Gaulle.

The Americans if they are not prevented will return to Europe as the leaders of reaction. The U.S. would like to see Europe back under the liberal royalist régimes of 1910. They have no conception of how

1. Where he had been Governor.

far all that is behind us. Are we to expect another Congress of Vienna with Roosevelt as a new Metternich and Gt. Britain supporting the new forces of Russia and France against reaction? I hope it may not come to that but the Americans may drive us to it. The natural American tendency to mass hysteria is heightened by the coming election year.

Lunch with A.E. who is much annoyed at P.M.'s prolonged absence. So too is the rest of the Cabinet. A.E. says he is even thinking of setting off again at the end of October for Italy. There is much public criticism, scarcely suppressed, that our policy is too much under American influence now.

A.E. says he can't be ready to go to Moscow before the middle of October. We must get the agenda cleared first. We sent our draft agenda to Washington weeks ago and we now hear only today that it hasn't yet been studied and that the Americans in any case favour keeping the talks "on more general lines". That is useless. We must proceed alone on our own agenda if necessary and leave the Americans out. In no other way can we have any talks at all with the Russians.

September 14
Salerno battle going badly. But Alexander is confessedly out of touch as there is no landing ground available yet and he must remain in contact with Navy and Air. I have no confidence in the American General Clark who is an advertiser and has never commanded anything in battle before. Montgomery should have been put in charge of this. The troops concerned are about half and half British and American.

P.M. should be starting back today by sea. We have proposed to him that we send our agenda to Moscow now without further delay. The conference is more or less fixed for October 15.

The President and the P.M. are to meet Stalin a month or so later in Tehran, if Stalin can't be got any further West.

September 15
News from Salerno not reassuring. Alexander was going there personally today and then we shall have a reliable report. The Germans are making a desperate and determined attempt to throw us into the sea before we can build up and before Montgomery and the Taranto force can arrive from the South.

We have telegraphed to Macmillan to urge that Badoglio, now at Taranto, should be required to sign the comprehensive surrender terms at once. This will forestall criticism in Parliament next week and tidy up the position. But I fear we shall have obstruction from both Macmillan and Eisenhower over this. Macmillan is a wooden-headed pedant.

Stalin has appointed Vyshynski[1] as his representative on Armistice Control Commission, which is a sign of the importance he attaches to it. This will be the first Anglo–Russo–American political body set up.

We have now had an outline of the American agenda for Moscow. Not bad and not inconsistent with ours. We still await authority from P.M. (now on the high seas)[2] to hand ours in to Moscow.

We hear that Musso is forming a new Italian Fascist Republican Government.[3] The King has apparently escaped with Badoglio to Taranto, though our people there have not reported it. So Musso will have his Hundred Days.

September 16

Alexander has now visited the Salerno front and reported. It looks pretty grave but not irremediable. Fresh troops are being flown in, including parachutists dropped behind the enemy lines. Montgomery is pushing on fast. All possible air support is being given.

It is important to know quickly what authority Badoglio still possesses and whether the King is with him. Now that Musso has declared a republic I rather think "*Casa Savoia*" may be our strongest card. The Italian monarchy has a great hold, much more like our own monarchy, over the people, a hold to some extent independent of the personality of the King.

A most interesting straw in the wind. The Jap Government have asked the Soviet Government to receive a special Mission which after visiting Moscow would go on via Turkey to Hungary, Germany and France, and then return to Moscow where it might be able to discuss matters of interest to all parties. A Jap peace feeler in fact, very possibly inspired by Germany. The Soviet Government have turned it down flat, refused to agree to such a Mission coming at all and have, most correctly, told the Americans and ourselves.

September 17

News from Salerno more encouraging. The approach of the Eighth

1. He was No. 2 to Molotoff.
2. Actually still in Washington.
3. Absolving Badoglio Government of taint of Darlanism.

Army is making itself felt. The enemy has not resumed his counter-attacks.

We hear at last from Mason Macfarlane that he has seen Badoglio and the King of Italy who are both at Taranto. They are anxious to be helpful but hold out little prospect of effective help by the Italians. No doubt the Italians will rally to the King as the battle goes in our favour.

September 20

P.M. back last night. Very busy with H. of C. debate tomorrow and preparations for our Moscow trip.

Question of status to be accorded to Badoglio and King of Italy under discussion. We favour "co-belligerent", but not "Allies". As P.M. says "They must work their passage". From all accounts they are a pretty dim lot. It is also thought they should be required to sign the famous comprehensive surrender terms for sake of tidiness and legality. Signature will greatly facilitate our subsequent operations in Italy. Apart from this, it is proposed to build up the King and B. as far as possible and gather round them as representative a set of men, from Right to Left including Communists, as possible. At present they have no army, no provinces and no government (which was left behind in Rome in the *"sauve qui peut"*). Admiral Leahy is still bleating about making Rome an open city, but we are dead against this as it would hamstring our future operations.

Germans seem to be falling back on Naples.

September 21

Battle of Salerno goes on well. Free French are fighting well in Corsica and the Germans seem to be clearing out. Sardinia has become ours for a song. In Russia the general advance along the whole line continues.

Kingsley Wood died of heart in the night. I'm afraid it cannot be said that he is a great loss to progress.

The Badoglio–King business is going slowly forward. The President has now weighed in and is opposed to the signature of the longer armistice terms – which we have already recommended to Eisenhower. Eisenhower and Macmillan are incredibly wooden and obstinate over it all. They hold up everything in order to argue.

September 23

Yesterday was a hellish day from the point of view of work. A debate in the H. of C. following the P.M.'s statement on Tuesday. A.E. on the bench all day and winding up finally in the evening. Every other consideration set aside.

We have given way to the President over the armistice terms. The comprehensive document is not now to be signed, and endless trouble will be caused us.

Preparations for our departure in full swing. Zero hour probably Sunday Oct. 3rd.

The intention of appointing Marshall as C. in C. of the European operations in London is leaking out in the U.S. where strangely enough it is criticised as a British manoeuvre to winkle him out of being Chief of the Combined Staffs in Washington where he is alleged to be obnoxious to us because he opposes our plans. If only the Americans realised how disagreeable the appointment will be to the British public when it is announced! We don't like inexperienced American generals taking command of British troops over the heads of Alexanders and Montgomerys. Against Marshall himself there is nothing personal and his work at Washington has not been at all unhelpful. It is the "Pacific First" Admiral King who is tiresome.

After lunch today A.E. called in Alec C. and myself to tell us, most confidentially, that a major reconstruction was to take place as a result of Kingsley Wood's death. The P.M.'s idea was this: Lyttelton to become Chancellor of the Exchequer, Anderson to become M. of Production, Attlee to become Lord President of Council and nothing else, Cranborne to return to Dominions Office where Attlee was a failure, Beaverbrook to be Lord Privy Seal and Leader of the Lords, Bracken to go to War Office, Dick Law to be M. of Information, and Duff Cooper to be Assistant Minister at F.O.

A.E. asked us what we thought of this. We both immediately shook our heads at the idea of Duff coming and Dick going. We both said we liked Duff but he was far too lazy and indeed incapable now of hard work at the F.O., whereas Dick was invaluable here. Nor would Dick be likely to prove a good M. of I. Could not Bracken remain at M. of I. and Dick become the Assistant Minister here? Here A.E. explained that the insufferable Grigg was to be demoted to a civil servant again and made Head of the Civil Service, and Bracken, who had been ill, wanted a change from the M. of I. Incidentally we thought Bracken who is good at the M. of I. would be deplorable at the W.O.

A.E. said he wished to have Jim T. here to take Dick's place as Under Secretary, though Alec thought this might cause trouble with Labour. But we kept returning to the waste it would be to let Dick go out of foreign affairs just now when he has got well into them and was proving such a success at international conferences on reconstruction. This led me to suggest that Dick might be promoted to take Jowitt's job at Minister without Portfolio in charge of reconstruction. Originally Jowitt was intended to do all reconstruction both home and foreign, but he proved such a failure that the foreign side lapsed back to Dick doing it entirely at the F.O. under A.E. If Dick took this on, he could do both. He was extremely interested in it and the foreign and the home dovetailed into each other. A.E. liked this idea which had the additional advantage of avoiding a second cabinet post in the F.O. as such. Dick could do the F.O. side of reconstruction he was doing now, as M. of Reconstruction, and would of course work through our departments here.

But what about the M. of Information? If A.E. was to put this to the P.M., he must have a name ready as alternative for M. of I. We thought of all the alternatives we could. It is a most difficult and thankless post. Duff had failed at it already. R.A. Butler couldn't be taken from his educational reforms. Finally, I said why shouldn't a newspaper proprietor do it? Bracken himself was a newspaper proprietor and the Ministry itself now was organised and only needed routine direction. Why not Camrose, who was respectable and respected among his fellows? A.E. was attracted by this and so was Alec and he agreed to put it to the P.M. in order to keep Dick for us as M. of Reconstruction, and to get Jim as U.S. If Dick is not Assistant Foreign Secretary and only M. of Reconstruction, it is easy on party lines to argue that Jim can succeed Dick as U.S. (The P.M. has apparently got it into his head that Mrs. Dick is a Communist!)

A.E. is to see the P.M. again at 5.15. One doesn't have long to think on these occasions. But the Beaver appointment will go very badly indeed. The P.M. says he wants to liven up the Government. It will liven up the critics too.

September 24
I hadn't another chance of a word with A.E. last evening after he had again seen the P.M. as he had to rush off to a dinner at Greenwich in honour of the American Colonel Knox. Jim T. had a word with him, however, (he didn't know any of the general plan and I of course didn't tell him) from which he gathered there was obstruction to his own appointment as U.S. and the P.M. wanted George Hall[1] (Labour aged 65) to come here and Jim to take his place as U.S. at the Admi-

1. George Hall, M.P. for Merthyr Tydfil since 1922, was Financial Secretary to the Admiralty 1942–1943.

ralty. Jim was much perturbed at this idea as he doesn't particularly want promotion to the Admiralty, he would like to come here and he believes he can do more for A.E. in the H. of C., if he is working closely with him. Jim even said to me he would prefer to resign from the Whips' Office and become A.E.'s PPS again sooner than bury himself in the Admiralty. I said it would be far best if he was U.S. here and I should feel A.E. would be very out of touch, dangerously so, on the parliamentary side without him. I couldn't tell Jim of the idea of making Dick M. of Reconstruction which of course further strengthens the argument for Jim taking his place here as U.S.

This morning I tackled A.E. again. He had had a long night session with the P.M. after his dinner. It is now proposed that Lyttelton should not be Chancellor but should remain at M. of Production. (This is probably wise – O.L. too much the smart City man to go well with the country.) Anderson is to be Chancellor. The appointment of Dick as M. of Reconstruction *vice* Jowitt is approved. Camrose as M. of Infn. is approved (my appointment!) A.E. told these ideas to the P.M. who now is quite persuaded they were his own. But the P.M. is opposing Jim T. as U.S. here because he wants George Hall to come from the Admiralty and to insert Duff Cooper as an Asst. Foreign Sec. P.M. does not like Jim for some reason (?his loyalty to Baldwin) and adores Duff.

Meanwhile the battle rolls on. The King of Italy is being urged to broadcast to rally his people and especially his Embassies abroad. Stalin has expressed a strong preference for getting the long terms of surrender signed now, and so has Macmillan and the American General Bedell Smith. The latter say we could get them signed now, but if we wait we shall have a haggle. We are trying to get the P.M. to urge this upon the President.

A.E. told me this evening after a further talk with the P.M. that Labour were now demanding a larger share of seats and this had upset the plan again. Attlee had also vetoed Duff Cooper. As a result it had been decided not to move Jowitt or Simon, as we had hoped, but to make Dick Law Assistant Foreign Sec. In consequence of this, it was not possible to have 3 Tory Ministers in the F.O. and it was intended to put George Hall here (unless we could think of a better Labour man) and give Jim his place at the Admiralty. On the whole this is not bad but it is very disappointing about Jim. He will be a great loss here, though with Dick remaining in the F.O. we can no doubt carry Hall. Hall himself will have a value as carrying an insight into the F.O. into the Labour Party.

September 25
List of new appointments out today including the Beaver,[1] Anderson
as Ch. Excheq., Attlee as Ld. P. of C., Bobbety at D.O. It is now
fixed that Jim goes to the Admiralty as U.S. and George Hall comes
to F.O. But all the rest of the changes – Grigg, Bracken, Jowitt,
Simon – are postponed or abandoned because of Labour difficulties.

A last minute change may occur in our Moscow plans. Hopkins
telephoned to A.E. during the Cabinet last night to say Hull wanted
now to take part in the conversations but couldn't go as far as Moscow. They proposed to suggest Washington. A.E. replied urging that
they really couldn't suggest Washington because of the double journey
for Molotov involved but they should propose London as half-way.
H.H. apparently agreed to try this. So we may be off to Washington or
we may stay here. It would be a triumph if we get it here.

P.M. is now anxious to send Duff Cooper as diplomatic representative to the Badoglio Government or alternatively Van! A.E. is
opposed to this and wants to have a professional diplomat. He discussed with Alec Cadogan and myself. I suggested Noel Charles as our
best qualified man, young, recent experience of Italy, already 2 years
Amb. Cadogan and A.E. agreed to this and A.E. will try it on the
P.M.

Whoever is chosen, the policy is a good one, to get our future
relations with Italy back on to the traditional lines of friendship.
Italian foreign policy was always based on friendship with Gt.
Britain until Musso and Fascism perverted it. This must now be
built up again on the basis of a democratic Italy, (monarchist or
republican is for her to decide), shorn of her empire and reduced to
her natural national proportions.

Roosevelt has now agreed that the comprehensive armistice terms
should be signed[2] and Eisenhower is being told to secure this. That
will close the old chapter and avoid future cavil. It is hoped to
broaden the basis of the Badoglio Government by getting Sforza[3] and
any other elements from Right to Left to join. This Government will
have "co-belligerent" but not "Allied" status, and it will have "to
work its passage". To the extent it can exercise authority over the
liberated regions of Italy, the administration will be handed over and

1. As Lord Privy Seal.
2. See Churchill V 171–2.
3. Count Sforza, pre-fascist Italian Foreign Minister, had been in exile in
   America.

Amgot (Allied military government) become merely supervisory. When we get to Rome, it will return there.

Roosevelt has sent his telegram to Stalin proposing England as our meeting place and Oct. 15 as date because Hull is anxious to attend. No reply yet. Sumner Welles has formally resigned and been replaced by Stettinius.

September 29

Still no reply from Moscow. An ominous silence. Nor have we yet received the Russian agenda for the Cfce altho ours & the Americans were sent in some time ago. As regards Italy, Stalin has sent a message to say he wishes the Politico–Military Commission, on which Vyshynski is his representative and which is to sit at Algiers, to deal with the whole armistice administration and to replace the Anglo–American Control Commission which we were proposing to set up. This is going to cause trouble. It is also confusing two things. What we now want is a Supreme Allied Council, U.S.A., U.S.S.R., and Gt. B., sitting in London as a clearing house on the highest level for all non-military issues which crop up. This is what we hoped the Politico–Military Committee could become, having been moved from Algiers to London. We also need an Allied Control Commission in Italy on which the Russians and others should be represented. This would only be concerned with Italian matters on the spot. We shall have to clear this up at the Moscow Meeting or wherever it is to be.

September 30

We have now had a reply from Stalin about the agenda but not about the place of meeting. He growls over the agenda, says he wants to discuss the Second Front, but still doesn't send his agenda.

A.E. spoke to me today about the Noel Charles' appointment which he wants to couple with a similar appointment to Algiers. The P.M. was still anxious to find a post for Duff. A.E. had discussed our own candidates with William Strang who had suggested a) Ronnie Campbell in Washington and b) me as the best. A.E. told Strang that he didn't think I would want it, and he then asked me if this was so. "You can have it of course if you want it." I said I thought this was really a post which Duff could hold. There would be advantages in this because of the P.M.'s affection for him which would enable him to stand up to the P.M. over our French policy far better than any professional. Duff knew France and the French extremely well. He was stout and Gaullist. His lack of activity was also rather an advantage. He would leave the French alone. A.E. said he didn't want always to be standing in Duff's way.

October 1
The full armistice terms were signed by Badoglio on board a British battleship at Malta yesterday. He begged that they should be kept secret as otherwise they would lose him all his support. The King of Italy was anxious for Grandi to join the Badoglio Government. Eisenhower did not favour this, and I'm glad to say both the Americans and ourselves agree that G. would be impossible. The King did not want Sforza.[1] The latter is leaving for Italy[2] but seems to intend taking up an independent position in politics there. I fancy he is rather a crook besides being quite out of date.

October 3
Stalin replied on Saturday to the President expressing a firm but polite preference for Moscow on 15th because he couldn't spare both Molotov and Vyshynski away at the same time. A conference in London would have to be without Molotov. To this the President has now replied that Hull will go to Moscow and be there by 15th. So that is something settled. We now have to coordinate our plans with Hull's as we want a preliminary talk with him on the way. It looks like starting next Friday or Saturday.

Sforza is arriving here today en route for Italy. We hope to make him consent to joining the Badoglio Government. (I personally think he is nothing but a slippery intriguer who won't get us anywhere.) The King and Badoglio are jibbing at declaring war on Germany. We are taking the line that until they do this, there can be no question of making Italy "co-belligerent", which will be most unpopular here anyway. But the P.M. and President have said flatly they will have nothing to do with Grandi.

Brig. Myers, who has been working with the Greek Guerillas, is over here. He speaks in the strongest terms of the republican feelings of the resistance groups and of the importance of keeping the King out until an election on the future Greek régime has been held. The whole trouble is that whoever holds elections in Greece, usually wins them. The poor King is never going to be a best seller. He has compromised himself irretrievably by acquiescence in the Metaxas

1. Sforza was anti-monarchist.
2. Before leaving America he said he would support the Badoglio Government.

dictatorship. He has no son and only a brother[1] (who is a complete dud) with a German wife. Greece is better as a republic. But it is difficult for us to bow off the King who represents for us the resistance of Greece to Italy and Germany.

October 5

Dates more and more definite – departure Sat.

Duff business is in progress. P.M. first reacted against the idea of putting him with the French and held that Italy was more important. A.E., provided with arguments by me, returned to the charge with the P.M. who has now agreed that this alternative should be put to Duff. A.E. is to see him tomorrow. He says he won't stand for Duff in Italy anyway. He is right. It would immensely complicate our task. The Left is already suspicious, and with reason, of apparent attempts to build up the Badoglio Government into allies and have discovered it contains several generals notably Roatta wanted by the Yugoslavs as war criminals.

Duff's arrival as Amb. would confirm all fears. He was an appeaser of Italy. In French affairs his record is unimpeachable by Left or Right. P.M. is determined to get Duff some job of this sort and he wants his government post to dispose of.

I had heart-searchings over my own position. Should I have offered to go to Algiers, should I have said I would have liked it when A.E. mentioned the possibility to me? I then just passed it by. I don't want to leave London. I have professional qualifications for the post but I feel that in view of the conflicts between us and the Americans and even between the P.M. and A.E. over French policy it is for a politican rather than a professional to handle.

October 6

A.E. had a long Cabinet last night when his Moscow briefs were to have been approved. The P.M. spoke for 3 hours, not having read any of the papers; he talked great nonsense and A.E. was furious. The P.M. kept saying such things as "We don't know in what condition Germany will be after the war". "We mustn't weaken Germany too much – we may need her against Russia" (Hear, hear, from Smuts). "We must destroy Prussianism". The Cabinet colleagues were horrified at all this. A.E. evidently got pretty hot and said he must have approval for his briefs or he wouldn't go at all.

I'm afraid this is the usual picture before a conference. The P.M.

1. Later King Paul.

has no understanding of the peace issues, and is a very old man with outdated ideas.

October 8

A.E. put the offer of Algiers to Duff and he liked it very much. I gather he will probably accept. I'm pretty sure this is best for all.

Full of preparations for the trip. We still hope to start on Saturday. Macmillan has suddenly appeared to A.E.'s fury! We wanted him the other end to prepare for us in Algiers. He is being packed off again. Macmillan is anxious to maintain a sort of *droit de regard* over all our French and Italian relations from his post at Eisenhower H.Q. A.E. does not wish to encourage this and part of the idea of the appointments of Duff and Charles to the French and the Italians is to cut him out of the picture. I can't think why he dislikes Macmillan (though he is certainly a bore) and is even jealous of him. I'm afraid both he and Dick Law have incurred this fantastic jealousy of his.

I rang up Duff who has now accepted. He said he believed he really could do good work with the French. So do I.

October 9

After fussing and changing, the P.M. has now decided not to go with us chiefly because the President weighed in and objected to the one going without the other. A.E. now feels he had better keep out of the Tunis military conference too. We are now to go to Algiers.

The Cos operations are going to cause a row. Undue risks were taken by Wilson under strong pressure from the P.M. Now the Germans have counter-attacked with unexpected speed and strength and we are being pushed out of Cos and other such islands we had occupied, banking rashly on strong Italian support.

Sforza passed through here yesterday on the way to Italy. He won't join the Badoglio Government. He believes the dynasty is sunk. He seems to think a kind of liberal régime under himself to be possible.

The King of Greece is also in trouble. The strong anti-monarchical feeling of the resistance movement in Greece itself has now infected the King's Government in Egypt who wish him to stand down or at least to say he won't come to Greece till Greece has decided about him. We shall hear plenty of all this from Rex[1] in Cairo next week.

Later

Left F.O. 7 p.m. for Northolt. Found the P.M.'s York waiting for us on the aerodrome, a super machine with berths and a dining room.

1. Sir R. Leeper, Ambassador to Greece 1943–46.

P.M. has suggested to A.E. that he should go to Brindisi and see the King of Italy to make him declare war on Germany. I'm doubtful of the wisdom of this. Anyway Eisenhower wishes to see us at Tunis we hear, so after a short halt at Algiers we shall go on there for the night.

October 10
Landed at Maison Blanche[1] about 7.30. Roger Makins met us and drove us into town. The Minister's house is a villa on a hill looking down on the harbour – rather frightful – dripping palms.

Discussions at once at the villa. The military conference at Tunis ended last night with unanimous agreement that nothing could be done with the Dodecanese. In these circumstances should A.E. still go to Tunis to see Eisenhower who wishes to go on to Italy? The decision will make the P.M. mad, but I daresay it is right.

Our plans have been made and unmade a score of times but finally we decided to stay here the night and go to Cairo tomorrow, and not to Tunis because the weather was doubtful for landing there.

October 11
Off early at 8. We drove through the town on the way to Maison Blanche. Landed at 6.15 at Cairo West – an airfield out near the Pyramids. A.E. and I are staying with the Caseys at Mena where he has a villa. Jumbo Wilson was waiting for A.E. and they went into a huddle at once.

October 12
Drove into Cairo early and left A.E. at G.H.Q. where he was meeting Wilson, Cunningham etc. to discuss the consequences of the decision about the Dodecanese. I went on to the Embassy.

October 13
Jumbo Wilson came to fetch A.E. here at Mena at 10.15 and took him away for a whole day's outing with the troops which he loves. A day off for me.

October 14
A heavy day of work. The heat is appalling! We went into Cairo early. A.E. to see King of Greece and King of Yugoslavia, and I to Embassy.

1. Macmillan's HQ.

306

The Embassy machinery is slow and antiquated. I got the impression that the whole set up is out of date and out of touch with the times. This is not the fault of the Secretaries but that of the Ambassador. Old Miles [Lampson] leads here a completely peacetime existence, a satrap. He does no work at all and keeps a crowd of A.D.C.s and secretaries hanging about. The secretaries have all complained to me that they want more work or to be moved. I am going to see that this is done.

A.E. and I lunched with Shone[1] to meet Nahas, the P.M., and Amin Pasha. N. was a most voluble little man. He took his tarboosh off for lunch to my surprise. He talked bad French. He defended himself heartily against the charge of xenophobia and gave the impression of a vain, noisy politician who however had a great respect for A.E. by whom he could always be beaten up, thanks to their treaty connection[2] of which he was extremely proud.

After that, A.E. saw Wavell who has followed us here in our tracks, and King Farouk. The latter is a difficult, tortuous and embittered young man who hates us and also hates Nahas and the Wafd government. Miles has not been successful with Farouk and the battering-in of the front door of Abdin Palace with a tank was a clumsy, rude and unnecessary way of getting what we wanted, which will never be forgotten nor forgiven. Nor should it be. The soldiers were against it. It was pure Miles. But this is not to say it is easy to get on with Farouk or that he is a nice young man.

I went to tea with Dorothea Russell.[3] I had hardly been there 5 minutes when Wavell walked in. He is really the most silent man I've ever seen. I don't think he uttered more than 3 words on any subject while he was there, and those of the most banal. A.E. afterwards told me exactly the same of his own interview for which Wavell had told his A.D.C. he feared an hour would not be long enough. A.E. doesn't even now know what he wanted to talk about. Silence or monosyllables. Dorothea plied him with questions as if he were a schoolboy. Pug Ismay told me he had also tried to get him to talk. He thought he would be interested in what Pug could tell him of the Indian Army (Pug was in the Indian Army). But no, not a word. Pug asked who he thought of making his military secretary. W. replied "my son-in-law" (who is a boy of 25). What is there really in W.? On paper he is very good. He produced a very good note on the Indian scene

1. Terence Shone, Minister in Cairo.
2. The Anglo–Egyptian Treaty of 1936.
3. Lady Russell, wife of Sir Thomas Russell (Russell Pasha).

and his personal views before he left London. But he remains a question mark. He is too old for the job anyway. His later time here at G.H.Q. showed he had lost grip.

No news of old Hull at all. Even Kirk,[1] the American Macmillan, doesn't know if he has even landed in Africa yet. A.E. doesn't want to hang about in Moscow waiting for him, so we decided to put off our departure another 24 hours to Sat.

October 15

Montgomery has announced his arrival for tonight, much to A.E.'s indignation. ("Why is he coming here? Isn't there a battle going on in Italy?")

October 16

Off to airport at 6.45 a.m. and airborne by 8.30. We are in a Liberator this time, the York being discarded reluctantly by A.E. as the P.M. had promised it to the First Sea Lord to take him to America.

Still no news of Hull though Harriman[2] is supposed to arrive in Cairo tonight.

Reached Habanayah about midday. Heat indescribable as we got lower and lower and landed. Cornwallis and the Air C. in C. to meet us. Lunch in the R.A.F. mess, a very nice well-designed place, cool and roomy. Took off again about 1.30 p.m. Heat like hell. 14,000 ft. oxygen masks. Then gradually lower again till the Elburz Mountain appeared with Tehran at the foot and we landed.

(At Teheran) I am staying with Adrian[3] at Gulheck which is the summer residence about 7 miles out. We drove out after tea and there was another great white Persian house enclosed in an enchanting garden of pools and trees and running water courses.

October 17

Adrian has succeeded in making quite friends with the young Shah. He goes and calls on him once a week and they have a chat. A. says he speaks frankly and openly with him about everything, what is going on, the talk of the town. He tells him he must make his Egyptian wife learn Persian. The Shah takes this all in v. good part and evidently

1. A. C. Kirk, U.S. Minister to Egypt 1941–1944. Afterwards U.S. Ambassador to Italy.
2. Averell Harriman, U.S. Ambassador to Russia 1943–1946.
3. Sir Adrian Holman, then Counsellor at Teheran.

welcomes having a disinterested friend to talk to. Robin Hankey[1] when he was here, did it too and played tennis with him. The Shah is almost Wimbledon form. A. gives a better account of the Shah than most. He says of course he makes mistakes like we all did when young but is intelligent and well read and seems to have the interest of the country at heart. These young sovereigns, the Shah and the King of Egypt, have great opportunities if they know how to take them. The peasants could be led if they had a leader. The Shah should take the wind out of the sails of the politicians by raising the standard of the peasants, encouraging health centres and so on. Farouk likewise.

Hull and Harriman have arrived this evening and A.E. went off to see them.

October 18
Teheran. Off early to airfield. Took off at 8 a.m. A perfect morning, no wind, no cloud.

A.E. had a very satisfactory talk with Hull last night. He found him much clearer and more precise than ever before, and that just after a whole day's flight. We hear the old man has actually started off for Moscow ahead of us this morning. He has a doctor travelling with him.

Landed at Moscow airfield at 3.30 p.m. Molotov and Litvinov[2] were there with Clark Kerr to meet us. A guard of honour played God Save the King and the Internationale and then did a little march up and down, terrific smartness and precision including goose-step. I thought they looked very German.

A.E. and Hull went to call on Molotov at 6 p.m. Molotov insists on A.E. riding everywhere in his bullet-proof car.

Dined with Clark Kerr. Harriman came in after to discuss the best way to handle the military side of the conversations. The complication is that Hull, unlike A.E. or Harriman himself, is not in on any American military affairs and so cannot usefully discuss them.

October 20
The meeting yesterday was unexpectedly serene, although it was devoted to the Second Front. Molotov seemed satisfied with the

1. Hon R. M. A. Hankey, later Ambassador to Sweden and U.K. delegate to O.E.E.C. and O.E.C.D.
2. Russian Ambassador to U.S.

account of our plans and only anxious to be sure that we should do in 1944 what we had promised to do.

Luncheon with Molotov at the Guest House. We were about a dozen English, a dozen American and a dozen Russian. Molotov, Vyshynski, Mikoyan[1], Voroshilov, Litvinov, Hull, Harriman, and Dunn;[2] A.E. and Ismay, William Strang, Douglas Howard.[3] Lunch was in a fair sized room in what used to be a largish private house, not in the Kremlin.

We began the usual series of toasts almost with the caviar and from then till the end we were hopping up and down drinking toasts and listening to pretty little speeches.

A really barbarous custom which makes any conversation impossible. Lunch began at 2 and lasted till 3.30. We then had a breather in the garden, before the next conference began at 4.

October 21

I can't describe how depressing and colourless is the aspect of the Moscow people in spite of the tidiness and cleanliness of the wide streets and squares. The only smart ones are the soldiers, especially the officers in their well-cut uniforms. Everything clearly goes to them. The only cheerful ones are the children.

October 22

I slipped off to the ballet last night with Douglas Howard.

The performance seemed to me quite perfect. the prime ballerina was Semianova, formerly wife of Karakhan, the Minister who was liquidated in the purge. The setting was completely conventional and we might have been looking at a show under the Tsars. A lovely performance. But even more exciting than the ballet was the audience. The opera was practically full for the greater part with officers and soldiers in uniform with their families. The officers are smart and striking-looking. So much more striking and impressive than the women. The women are all lumps and puddings. It is not only their dreary ill-made dowdy clothes and lack of lipstick and make-up. Their bodies are all the wrong shapes. Why is this?

Meanwhile A.E. had been to see Stalin at 10 p.m. to talk about convoys and did not get back till 11.30 p.m. He was on the whole well

1. A. I. Mikoyan, Soviet Minister for Foreign Trade 1938–1949.
2. James Dunn, State Department adviser on political relations. Later U.S. Ambassador in Rome.
3. Sir Douglas Howard, Counsellor at F.O., later Minister to the Vatican.

satisfied with his interview. Stalin began by being bearish but mel-
lowed. He wore a Marshal's uniform of mustard colour with heavy
epaulettes instead of his simple peasant blouse tunic. He expressed
most emphatic views about the effectiveness of bombing. He wanted
to see Turkey forced into the war at once and Sweden compelled to
give us air bases like Portugal. He said definitely he could not go
beyond Tehran to meet the P.M. and the President as he must be in
continuous touch with his G.H.Q. which was only possible from
there: Habanaya would not do. (Roosevelt had sent a message to
say he could not go beyond Habanaya as at Teheran he might get
weatherbound and for constitutional reasons he could not risk being
forced to extend his stay outside the States. So because of that comparatively tiny distance compared with the enormous journeys involved, it is unlikely that the Big Three will meet this year. This may
be a good thing if it enables the present conference to take more
decisions.

The ordinary meeting of the conference took place at 4 p.m. and
discussed the Four Power Declaration.[1] Here too no serious snags
were met. Hull takes little part in the discussion, but when he does, he
is helpful and even to the point – quite a new Hull. A.E. does practically all. We are carrying the American Delegation. Harriman is
unimpressive.

October 23
Yesterday A.E. had a satisfactory follow-up meeting with Molotov
about convoys.[2] He agreed to all his requirements about personnel to
handle them, but only insisted that our men be instructed to treat the
Russians there "as equals". As a matter of fact, it is our men who
complain of not being treated as equals or as allies by the Russians
there.

At the later Conference meeting good progress was again made and
we developed our ideas about the so-called Politico–Military Commission, our proposal to transfer it from Algiers to London and make
it a real clearing-house for Anglo–American–Russian policies and to
set up in Italy instead an advisory council of High Commissioners
(including a Russian) to supervise Italian affairs only.

We received today the text of a message from Stalin to Roosevelt

1. On war aims and post war international co-operation.
2. There had been an acrimonious exchange of letters between Mr. Churchill
   and Stalin on this subject, and Stalin's last letter had been returned
   unanswered to him.

explaining why he couldn't go beyond Tehran and of a reply from Roosevelt saying why he couldn't go beyond Basrah or Habanaya. He suggests as alternatives Asmara or even Turkey! These grotesque notions have no relation to Stalin's difficulty which is the necessity for direct telephonic communication with his troops who owing to the exceptional weather are being able to carry forward their summer offensive straight on into the winter. I doubt if the meeting takes place now, or is necessary, but it will be a pity to spoil our atmosphere with a wrangle over it.

We've also read a very disturbing telegram from the P.M. who has had second thoughts about the wisdom of Overlord next spring and of weakening the Italian front now for the sake of its build-up. We suspect this is due to Smuts' influence who has always been pro-Mediterranean. The strategic arguments are very sound indeed and probably right. The trouble is that the P.M. himself sold the pass at Quebec when he agreed to Overlord in consequence of American pressure. Both Americans and Russians are together over this in pressing us to undertake Overlord. Neither of course understand the implications of the operation. But after A.E. has just assured and reassured both Molotov and Stalin of the firmness of our intention (which both are suspicious of) to carry out Overlord next spring, it will be absolutely fatal if we now break our promise and wriggle out of it.

The Russians have put in a claim to a share of the Italian navy. So too have the Greeks, Jugs, and French. I hope we can satisfy them. A.E. is urging this but Eisenhower, Cunningham and Macmillan have made such a mess of the armistice terms that we aren't even sure that we have legal possession of it.

October 24

A.E. suddenly asked if he could go to church today. There is no church.

We received today copies of messages exchanged between the P.M. and Roosevelt. The P.M. proposed to the latter an early meeting of Combined Chiefs of Staff to consider changes since Quadrant[1] and suggested he and F.D.R. should meet on the way to the meeting with Stalin. Roosevelt replied, questioning the timeliness of this without Russian participation while the Moscow conference was taking place and proposed they should first await the results of Moscow. The P.M. replied to this by blurting out to the President all the doubts he had

1. The Quebec Conference of August.

312

developed to A.E. about Overlord and the risk of weakening our position in Italy if we start now moving away divisions, and again pressing for an immediate meeting.

A.E. discussed all this with me yesterday. He is profoundly disturbed at the P.M.'s sudden changes. It was obvious that it would make his own position vis-à-vis the Russians impossible if we again ran out on the Second Front. He had absolutely committed himself to a Second Front in certain conditions for 1944 during the recent conversations, as he had been authorised to do before he started in accordance with the Quadrant decisions. Any deviation would crack our conference immediately just when it looks like achieving most substantial results. He said that the only thing for him to do was to go on, and if later the P.M. decided to try and wriggle out of the promise for a Second Front, to resign. The Americans of course would be as horrified as the Soviets and it was probable that they would in any case refuse to agree. It was also true that the Germans were v. stretched and their morale possibly worse than we suspected (Stalin thinks so) and that the risks involved in dividing our forces could be taken. It was possible that they might collapse anyway as the result of the winter Russian campaign and of our bombing before Overlord could happen.

October 25
Molotov has sent to A.E. a draft treaty which he and Benes have just agreed. It is a pact of mutual assistance for 20 years and contains a protocol leaving it open to subsequent signature by neighbours (i.e. Poland). We cannot object to the terms themselves, although we do dislike the principle of such treaties between a Great Power and a small. But we have failed to prevent it and have incurred odium with the Soviets by doing so.

Our impression is, and it is confirmed by our press people, that the Soviets are determined that this conference shall be a success. No suggestion that difficulties are being encountered is allowed to pass the Censor. Individual Russians all express confidence and pleasure in conversation. For the first time they feel that they are being treated as equals and that we are bringing our troubles to them for unprejudiced discussion.

October 27
This morning we received a telegram from the P.M. saying he was repeating a message from General Alexander on the position in Italy.

This message increased his determination not to be hidebound by "a lawyers' agreement" to carry out Overlord next spring regardless of the military situation; the Italian battle must not be jeopardised for its sake and A.E. must show Alexanders' report to Stalin and make all reserves for the future. These instructions could scarcely have come at a worse moment when the political side of the conference is going well, largely we believe because of our assurance to Stalin about the Second Front. This very afternoon the Second Front problem was to be tackled again when we suspected the Russians intended to ask us to sign a resolution about it.

A.E. proposes to ask Molotov to take this off the agenda for today because of further information just received and to ask for an interview with Stalin tonight. It is v. awkward to handle because the Americans have no similar instructions and Alexander is under Eisenhower's orders. Also the President is as second-frontist as Stalin.

The burden of Alexander's report is that the German build-up in N. Italy is faster and greater than expected, while ours, because of lack of boats etc. is belated. The Germans mean to fight for Rome to keep us off the N. Italian airfields, and we shall have a slogging and costly battle to drive them back. This may leave us exhausted and exposed to the fresher German reserves.[1] The immediate argument from this, although it is not mentioned by Alexander, but is what the P.M. derives from it, is that we cannot now send back home the divisions and landing craft due to return now for Overlord.

The P.M. is set on not carrying out Overlord. He is almost certainly right on military grounds and to back his case, he uses every weapon. We suspect he has prompted Alexander to send his pessimistic message. How will Stalin take this? Will he explode or will he take the reasonable view that the common objective is to pin down and destroy German divisions and it doesn't matter whether this is done in Italy or in France? A.E. is expecting to see him late tonight.

We have had no more as to what Roosevelt's further reaction has been to this sudden change from the Quebec decisions and the plea for a meeting of Staffs. Nor have we yet heard Stalin's final reply to his request for a meeting in Basra. It would be absolutely fatal to have now an Anglo–American meeting without Russia.

A.E. discussed yesterday who should be our representative on the Advisory Council for Europe if it finally takes shape. I said Alec

1. According to the appreciation the Allies actually had fewer divisions to attack with in Italy than the Germans facing them.

Cadogan, Moley Sargent, or William Strang. A.E. rather fancies the last and suggested I might take his place in the Office if he did. I said that I would be very pleased to try and do this if he thought it a good plan.

October 28

A.E. went to see Stalin at 11.30 p.m. He read to him Alexander's report and the P.M.'s message but Stalin took it with surprising calm. He asked, did this mean the postponement of Overlord? A.E. said that it might but that every effort would be made to carry out Overlord as soon as possible. Stalin was in benign mood and no harsh words were uttered. It is a great relief and a great triumph to have got this over so successfully.

October 29

This morning Pug Ismay heard that the P.M. had invited the President to meet him near Casablanca about November 20th to discuss military matters, that the President had agreed and had urged that the Russians should be invited to send a general too, but that the P.M. had objected to this.

A.E. is aghast at this. The P.M. has deliberately refrained from letting A.E. know of his intentions. To exclude the Russians from a military conference now would torpedo all the results of our present conference and make A.E.'s position impossible. Public opinion in Russia, as at home, would be outraged at an exclusive Anglo–American meeting fixed up behind A.E.'s back while he was at Moscow and he could not possibly defend it. He purposes to send a telegram to the P.M. tonight. He cannot refer to the tel. to Pug, but he can insist on the necessity of inviting the Russians to all future meetings in view of the v. forthcoming attitude adopted here including Stalin's reaction to the postponement of Overlord.

The P.M. is untameable. He cannot leave well alone and he loathes the Russians. He would torpedo A.E.'s conference light-heartedly. His restless energy makes him tear down his own handiwork as soon as it is completed.

At this conference the Russians have been doing all the giving. They have acquiesced in our plans, broadly, both military and political. But London has not yet authorised us to give them a share in the Italian fleet. A.E. telegraphed last night to urge this again. A few Italian ships handed over would have a disproportionate effect psychologically to their naval value. That wicked old P.M. will bring our labours to nought yet. How little team-spirit there is in the government.

October 30

We are wondering whether we can get off tomorrow. The work won't be properly tidied up by then and it is doubtful if weather will permit. A.E. is determined to go even though it is spoiling the ship for a ha'pworth of tar. This is very silly. Once the conference disperses, nothing more will be settled by subsequent correspondence. But he is very prima donnaish today and has lain in bed all the morning wasting 3 good hours for work.

Finally, by 5.30 p.m. we heard definitely from the air people that it would be possible to fly tomorrow. Meanwhile A.E. had discovered, what we all knew, that it was not possible to finish the work tonight. So all is postponed for 24 hours.

Off to the Kremlin at 8.30. I remembered the rooms from last time, where we assembled, the Americans and ourselves. Last of all came Stalin advancing down the room with a group of officers, I thought instinctively of pictures of Napoleon surrounded by his marshals. Marshal Stalin was in a mustard-coloured uniform, breeches and boots, with medals, a very militarist figure compared with the Russian peasant effect he gave 18 months ago in his simple linen tunic. I recognised some of his entourage from last time in particular an enormously fat young man, then in black, now in full general's uniform and with a startling resemblance to Goering.[1] But in spite of the uniform, Stalin appeared as genial and kindly, the friendly bear, as before.

Dinner was interminable, a gargantuan repast with many wines. Toasts began at once and went on without stopping. We next moved on to the cinema where we saw an interminable film about Japanese intervention and atrocities in Siberia at the beginning of the Red Revolution, a very anti-Japanese film which must have gladdened Mr. Hull's heart. After the cinema 3 opera singers appeared and sang songs for another hour. Finally about 2.30 a.m. we got away.

October 31

Rain and low cloud. No flying for us tomorrow. Busy with work tidying up the conference.

1. G. Malenkov, Chairman of Council of Ministers of Soviet Union 1953–1955.

P.M., we discover, in sending Alexander's gloomy report on Italy, suppressed Eisenhower's covering report which did not support it and said only some more landing craft were needed. Pretty hot! Fortunately A.E. had taken Harriman into his confidence and the latter showed him the Eisenhower report. But the P.M.'s action might have wrecked our conference, if Stalin had chosen.

Hull has now been pressed into the task of ensuring the Russians are not excluded from the P.M.'s military conference. He has telegraphed to the President to urge that the meeting be delayed until he has returned. A.E. has telegraphed to the P.M. to insist on the importance, if the results of this conference are not to be jeopardised, of inviting a Russian representative to any future military discussions. The P.M. is set on keeping them out if he can and he is quite unscrupulous in his methods, but I think he will be prevented. Hull is also urging that unless the President can go to Teheran to meet Stalin for one day, the meeting of the three big men should be called off. It is in any case now unnecessary and would only be an occasion for showing off.

November 1
Although Hull has taken little active part in the conference, his having come here and put his impression on it will be of immense value. He stands in America for Right Wing respectability and he, far more than the President, can swing opinion in favour of cooperation with Russia hereafter.

The P.M.'s attempts to torpedo us continue. Pug Ismay heard today privately from Hollis that the P.M. was planning a combined staff conference in Cairo about Nov. 20 which he and the President would attend. No question of inviting Russians and the first item on the agenda was Overlord versus Avalanche. The P.M. has not revealed one single word of this to A.E., who only knows of it through Pug. Such a conference without the Russians would be indefensible, it could never be explained away either here or at home where the H. of C. and the press would be in an uproar. A.E. could not survive it. I wish he could get home quickly, but we are going to be stuck in Cairo talking to the Turkish M.F.A.

The Russians want us to press the Turks to come into the war at once. The Turk himself has suggested coming to see A.E. in Cairo. We want the Turks in but favour a more gradual method as in Portugal of getting certain facilities first – airfields for use against the Dodacanese and so on. A.E. will see the Turks and try out the ground.

We are due to start tomorrow as the weather seemed favourable. The results of the conference are being published this morning and we went to the ballet with easy hearts, a new Russian ballet called Lola. In the middle of the first act Johnnie Dashwood came and got me out of the box to say the Russian Air General in charge had telephoned that the weather was too bad to go, but that our own pilots thought it would be all right. We held a hasty conference and after consulting A.E., it was decided that Pug should go and discuss the prospects with the Soviet general.

A.E., the Amb. and I returned to the Embassy after the ballet while Pug went on to the Air General. On reaching the Embassy, we were told that the B.B.C. 6 o'clock news had duly published the conclusions of the conference, but this has been followed by a communiqué from No. 10 referring to some statement in the press implying that Pug Ismay's presence here had for the first time enabled Stalin to have a firsthand appreciation of the military situation and saying that this was quite untrue as the P.M. had sent over 100 messages to him! We were all horrified and took this to mean that the P.M. was in a foul temper and his anti-Russian feelings had got the better of him. A.E. said there could have been no more ungracious way of commenting on the conference. It is also a clear case of jealousy at A.E.'s success.

We also received 2 further telegrams from the P.M. opposing the invitation to a Russian general to participate in the next meeting, one being a copy of a telegram to Roosevelt in the same sense on the ground that they were "Anglo–American operations". In other words we are still fighting a different war from the Russians.

My God! The P.M. will lose us the war yet. His passionate and unscrupulous obstinacy is terrible and he is as jealous as a ballerina. A.E. takes it – or professes to take it – fairly calmly and says he will be able to persuade him round when he sees him. I daresay he may, but I don't know when we shall get home if we have to stay in Cairo wrangling with the Turks. Our best hope is now Roosevelt who is being strongly reinforced by Hull from here.

Pug got back about 11 p.m. and said the flight was definitely off for another 24 hours.

November 2

Further telegram from P.M. today. He has given way! He now proposes that he and F.D.R. should meet at Gib. and then proceed to Cairo for a conference at which a Russian should be invited to be present. The two staffs could have first met together and cleared their ideas, then at Cairo the great men could explain the position to the Russian. Chiang Kai Shek is also being invited to join. They would all fly to Tehran for a day, if this can be arranged, to meet Stalin. Otherwise Molotov should be invited to Cairo. A.E. very relieved.

A.E. proposes to go home first and make a statement in H. of C. next week before it rises. He could then come out to Cairo again to back up P.M.

November 3
Fly off at 8. V. low clouds.

About 4 we are flying out of Persia into Iraq and the desert plains begin. We cross the Tigris, and then the Euphrates, and land about 5 at Habanaya. We are to sleep at R.A.F. H.Q.

November 4
Cornwallis and Nuri came out early to meet us. R.A.F. camp a complete bit of England abroad. Church, football, cinema and a pack of hounds. All very Poona. Food atrocious – not the food itself but the cooking.

Off again at 11.30 for Cairo. Arrive at 4 p.m. Talk with C. in C. and Casey about Turkey. A.E. will see Turkish M.F.A. tomorrow and propose to him to give us airbases at once and to bring Turkey into the war before the end of the year.

November 5
Very busy day. Turkish talks began at 11.30 and were resumed at 5. Turks v. tough and not giving anything away. They hate and fear Russia and expect to get fair treatment from us. Turks won't look at giving us bases now and say this would certainly involve them in war. They prefer to consider coming into the war altogether or not at all. We point out that there is little danger for them in this. They are not convinced.

November 6
More Turkish talks in the morning. This was the end of them and the Turks who refused to budge are to go away and think it over.

Fitzroy Maclean[1] has turned up, just back from Yugoslavia. He reports that the Partisans under Tito are 200,000 strong as against 10,000 or so Chetniks under Mihaelovic. We should put all our money on Tito,

1. Brigadier Fitzroy Maclean, M.P. (later Sir Fitzroy Maclean), Head of British Mission to Tito 1943–1945.

who represents the future of Yugoslavia whether we like it or not. All this is being discussed today.

November 7

A busy day with Greeks and Jugs. It has now dawned on everyone that the King of Greece is a hopeless proposition, or rather his only hope is to say now he won't return after the war unless he is invited. But like most Kings he is not v. intelligent. His presence in the field divides the moderates and leaves the way clear for the Communists who are a virulant minority of brigands, anti-British. Meanwhile our military persist in wishing to back the Communists and supply them with arms. The Communists are not fighting the Germans. They are fighting the moderates, and they are accumulating the arms to seize Athens when the day comes and to set up a Communist dictatorship there. The military claim that without the Communists we could not blow up bridges etc. behind the German lines and the Germans would save 2 divisions. We much doubt this. But the political aftermath of giving the Communists free sway in Greece will be far worse than the comparatively small disadvantage of a slight increase of German military strength in this area where operations by us are not contemplated. Our policy therefore is to withdraw all support from the Communist bands, to back the smaller moderate bands, and to get the King to make his statement about not returning. Rex has had a hard job.

As for the Jugs, we propose to increase supplies to the partisans (Fitzroy's friends) and to allow a deputation of 6 to come out to Alexandria and see the C. in C. King Peter has agreed to see them himself if they will see him, and we think we should try to reconcile them thus to the monarchy. Fitzroy is sure that Tito represents the future government of Yugoslavia, whether we like it or not, a sort of peasant communism, and we should be wise to come to terms and try to guide them. This also has been more or less agreed upon.

November 9

Left Cairo at 8 for Algiers. Long and boring flight. Reached Maison Blanche ¾ hour late.

November 13

Back again since Wednesday and straight into fresh trouble.[1]

1. Giraud had resigned from the French National Committee on 9 Nov.

The French in Syria have arrested the Lebanon Government[1] and produced an uproar there. This has inflamed afresh all the P.M.'s latent jealousy and hatred of de G. whose handiwork he sees here. A.E. has also let himself go. (How everybody hates de G.!)

The French have behaved badly in precipitating this coup in an area close to military operations without any warning to us. We are much to blame for leaving Spears there as our representative. But he is a politician and a friend of the P.M. and so he can do no wrong. Finally, the Lebanese themselves are a cartload of monkeys, alive to all the tricks of playing off the French against the English and so on. It would be folly to allow a Syrian squabble to queer our relations with de G. But this is what we risk doing. Yet, in Algiers, everybody was saying how much de G. had developed. We should do our utmost to establish relations of confidence with this remarkable man who holds the future of France in his hand. Now even the Duff Cooper appointment is held up.

The P.M. has now started off to meet Roosevelt in Cairo. The latter, much to his annoyance, short-circuited him by inviting Stalin to send Molotov to meet them in Cairo on the first day, instead of, as the P.M. wished, only at the end of the first Anglo–American military talks. Fortunately Hull had seen Roosevelt and warned him against leaving the Russians to come in late. So now we have been saved from that calamity. The whole party is to go on to Tehran about 26th and meet Stalin who has agreed to come.

Late this evening came a telegram for P.M. from Stalin to say Molotov could not be spared after all to go to Cairo for meeting on November 22nd but he and Stalin himself would expect P.M. and F.D.R. at Tehran "at end of November". We think this change is due to Chiang K.S. coming to Cairo whom the Russians would be embarrassed to meet. So the P.M. gets his way and there will be an Anglo–American military meeting without the Russians. I am sorry, but anyway the Russians can't now complain.

November 16

Turks have now replied. They can't do anything before the spring. They haven't enough arms and they would only prove a liability to the Allies. This with a great deal of palaver of what they've already done for us by doing nothing.

1. Elections had been held in the Lebanon at the end of August. The new Government had thereupon taken action to reduce French powers.

November 17
Lebanon still in a mess. P.M.'s ire is rising and he will soon be capable of any folly. I regard the whole thing as due to Spears, who has never established proper relations of confidence with the French.

The most important development has been an approach by the Poles. Before we went to Moscow, A.E. asked the Poles if they wished him to take any action on their behalf in Moscow. The Polish Government begged him not to. Now today Raczinski and Mikolajczyk came with a memo and asked if the latter could fly out to discuss it with the P.M. The memo contains nothing but the old *non possumus* attitude about frontiers; they would expect to receive E. Prussia etc. from the Germans, but there would be no question of giving up E. Poland. Raczynski, however, talking after to Moley, practically went so far as to say that the Poles would put themselves in our hands if we would *impose* a settlement on them which the Russians would accept. The Polish Government could not take any initiative. They are evidently scared and, at the eleventh hour, before the Russians arrive in Poland, are anxious to find a solution. This is the only solution, an imposed solution, and I hope we shall pursue it.

November 18
William Strang is appointed our representative on the London Committee and I am to succeed him as U.S. here. I feel glad and sorry, glad to have new work, rather sorry that it will be such hard and difficult work. I want a rest. I think Bob Dixon succeeds me; he is my candidate, the best, I think.

Lebanon still troublesome. The French have a good case but they have behaved with foolish precipitancy. Our own record in Egypt and Iraq, in similar circumstances is not too good, though we forget it now. Our worst blunder has been to keep Spears there. Spears continues to exaggerate the situation, to irritate the French and to encourage the local politicians. Macmillan at Algiers is doing well. Casey, as usual, weak and undecided.

December 4
I have begun my new official life. I am responsible for France, Spain, Portugal, Germany, Poland, Czechoslovakia, Holland and Belgium!

No news from Teheran as to whether the Polish question has been taken up with the Russians.

Closer knowledge shows how very seriously our relations with France are being endangered. First of all, by Spears in Syria whose intrigues and passions have got us into an impasse where we find ourselves backing the Lebanese against the French, instead of agreeing with the French our policy to the Lebanese. The French position vis à vis Syria must be in line with ours in Iraq, Egypt and Palestine. We cannot afford to oust or weaken French influence without weakening our own. The Syrians hate us as much as they hate the French, but they think they can use us. Our long term interests and those of the French are identical.

Then there is the determined American policy of denigration of the French National Committee and General de Gaulle. The President is personally behind this, and harbours fantastic ideas of administering France with Anglo–American forces under an American C. in C. up till and including elections. I am glad to say here we are doing what we can to resist and to bring the French Committee[1] more and more into the foreground as a Provisional Govt. But the P.M. is lukewarm. The point has come to a head over the planning for Overlord. We want to discuss the French part with the French Committee (questions of local civil administration, selection of prefects etc. etc.). The Americans want to exclude the Committee and confine discussion to a French mission appointed by Giraud. They seem to be aiming at a new Darlanism.

The French Committee and de G. have come to stay, whether we like it or not. We can make them dislike us and compromise our future relations with France, but we cannot destroy them. The first important things are to get Duff out to Algiers and to get Spears removed from Syria.

December 13
A.E. & Co. back again.[2] P.M. still in Med.

A.E. talked to Stalin and Molotov about the Polish frontier. The latter said they wanted the Curzon Line with its Southern extension giving Lvov to Russia. (This is the correct ethnographic line.) To the North, in addition to Vilna, they wish for Koenigsberg. The remainder of E. Prussia should go to the Poles, and in the West the Poles might go as far as the Oder.

It is just that the Russians should have Lvov in spite of Polish claims. But the demand for Koenigsberg as an open port, seems excessive. It would take half the E. Prussian coastline from Poland. To

1. It was proposed to include representatives of French parties and of the Resistance.
2. From the Teheran Conference. He had left on 23 November.

encourage the Poles to go up to the Oder line in the West would be criminal. It is not yet decided how this is to be put to the Poles, who naturally are very nervous.

Both Stalin and the P.M. have come out in favour of the forcible dismemberment of Germany into separate federal states. This is madness, but it must be studied. I hope this will prove how mad it is. Meanwhile *The Times* has come out with a leading article, in ignorance of these views, insisting on the necessity of treating Germany as a unit.

On the strategic issue the P.M. has only had a modified success. Overlord is still on: there is to be a lesser Overlord from the South.

December 15

The great question now is whether Hitler's secret weapon exists and whether it is going to be used now. As to the first, it is clear preparations are being made for something on the N. French coast; over 100 sites have been observed which are believed to be for rocket guns or self-propelled aircraft. It is also now thought they will be ready by January. They would all aim at London and would be the reply to the bombing of Berlin. They would hardly be more than that, for Germany can't win the war now by destroying London. On the other hand, if held till April, the new weapon could be used far more effectively to stop Overlord. As for Overlord, I fear Tehran was a failure. The P.M. was unable to put across his sound conception of dropping it in favour of the Med. offensive in face of Stalin and Roosevelt who for different reasons prefer the Channel[1] (S. because he wants to see us well-blooded, and R. because he speaks as a fool – he least of all in his election year can stand heavy casualties).

A.E. thought Roosevelt much deteriorated. As an instance of this, I can only quote his strange intervention in Greek affairs. In Cairo, as a result of A.E.'s investigations, it was agreed that the only hope for the King was to say now he would not return to Greece until invited by the people. A.E. had with difficulty convinced the P.M., who is romantic about kings, of this truth. The P.M. had agreed and the King had been persuaded to write a letter to this effect. The King then had a private talk with Roosevelt, apparently on the way to the airport, when the latter completely turned round and advised the King to stick to his throne and pay no attention to such suggestions. The consequence was the King backed out and will now only make a very oblique reference in the letter to his awaiting the decision of his

1. For a description of the strategic arguments at Tehran, see Ehrman, *History of 2nd World War*, Vol. V.

Government. Anyway Roosevelt's conduct is shocking. He had agreed in Cairo to the new policy, and had told A.E. in Washington that he thought little of the prospects of the King of Greece and was in general much opposed to all the exiled Allied Governments.

About French affairs, Roosevelt has at last proposed, in the interests of Anglo–French and so of Anglo–French–American relations, that we should take over responsibility for occupying France and that Overlord should be rearranged so as to put the British on the right and the Americans on the left of the line of advance into Europe. This would bring us into France or S. Germany, the Americans into Belgium, Holland, Norway, and N. Germany. This is a flash of sense, but alas! the military complications of the changeover look like being insuperable.

I have seen Weizmann – the first time for some months. He had been immensely encouraged by a long and recent conversation he had had with the P.M. The latter had shown himself a determined Zionist and had urged W. to persist. "I know the Arabs" he said, "We owe them nothing". W. thought he was moving in favour of partition as a first step to a Jewish State. We are also being pressed from America now by Hull to say something for the Jews.

December 28
A.E. saw the Polish P.M. and M.F.A. before Xmas and put to them in vague terms that as a result of Tehran discussions he gathered Stalin favoured a strong Poland but one pushed further to the West, i.e. Curzon line as E. frontier and something towards the Oder on the West. He did not mention Stalin's demand for Koenigsberg. On the other hand, he urged the Poles to produce a statement of what their underground warfare organisation was doing so as to reassure Stalin that it was not to be used against the Russians.

The Poles undertook to consider this. It is unfortunate that the P.M., who is laid up in N. Africa, could not also have put this to the Poles as they regard him rather than A.E. as their real friend.

1944

February 1

Back at work again after a perfectly wretched month. We heard on December 31 John was missing, the next day I fell ill of a relapse of flu.

All the old problems are with us.

France. The Pres. and the P.M. still violently anti-de G. and liable to obstruct any reasonable way of handling the French Committee. Fortunately Eisenhower, who is now here, is sensible on this subject and is insisting that in his Overlord plans he be allowed to deal with the Committee as the French authority.

The Poles. Their offer to coordinate plans between the Polish underground movement[1] and the U.S.S.R. did not move the Russians who now demand the Curzon Line and a new pro-Russian Polish Government. The P.M. on his return from N. Africa spoke severely to Mikolajczyk and told him he should accept the Curzon Line frankly and he, the P.M., would tackle Stalin about interference with the Polish government. M. is to think this over and is also consulting the Poles in Poland. The P.M. has also sent a message to Stalin to tell him of this.

February 8

Poles. Much activity but not necessarily progress on this front. Clark Kerr, who had meanwhile returned to Moscow, has reported a long conversation with Stalin in which he professed that, provided he got Curzon Line and a new Polish Govt., he would resume diplomatic relations and allow Polish Gt. to return to Warsaw and be free and independent there just as the C.-S. Government.

P.M. greatly encouraged by this, immediately asked Mikolajczyk to lunch last Sunday at Chequers "to soften him up". Before Sunday came, we received Stalin's reply to the P.M.'s message. It demanded (a) Curzon Line (b) Koenigsberg (c) changes in Polish Government.[2]

1. The Russians had ordered Polish Underground units to be disarmed.
2. Including the removal of General Sosnkowski, the C-in-C, General Kukiel, and Professor Kot.

A.E. went to P.M.'s lunch party as well as O'Malley;[1] our Ambassador to Poles. The P.M. spoke pretty straight to Mikolajczyk (who had Romer, his M.F.A., and Raczynski, his Ambassador, with him) and said this was the one and only chance for the Poles to take Stalin's offer of a Poland between the Curzon Line and the Oder. The Russians alone could liberate Poland. Nobody else could do anything. If the Poles accepted, they had a decent prospect before them. If they refused, the Russian steamroller would go over them. He, the P.M., did not intend to allow Anglo–Russian relations to be wrecked by the Polish Government if they refused what he regarded as a reasonable offer and he would then conclude a direct agreement with Stalin without them.

The Poles, impressed and shaken, went away to think it over.

The Poles must accept the Curzon Line, and indeed they should on every ground of justice and ethnography. What is hard is that they must change their Government at Stalin's behest. But it is not yet certain that Polish Government will accept. If they refuse, Stalin will see to it that there is a Polish Government in Warsaw to suit him when he gets there.

February 10

Pressure on the Poles continues. They are v. dubious of the advantages of the cold bath proposed for them. But what alternative is there? The Curzon Line ought to be their frontier anyway. The Russians can alone free them from the Germans. The Russians offer what on the face of it is a fair deal. The Poles say the Russians don't mean to play fair. We say we think they do mean to play fair, but supposing even the Poles are right, what do they lose by accepting a fair offer and appearing reasonable? If they don't accept, opinion will be against them and the Russians will be free from any restraint to set up a puppet Polish Government.[2]

The more I look at it, the less I like the idea of the transfers of German territory which is in view – E. Prussia, Upper Silesia and even further up to the Oder as compensation for the Poles. Only as a reprisal and a punishment can the seizure of German territory be defended – as a sort of military sanction in fact. We must be careful not to create a new German Alsace–Lorraine in Poland. Because she had too much Russian territory before is no reason for giving her too

1. Sir Owen O'Malley, Ambassador to Poland 1942–45.
2. The Communist Party had set up in Warsaw a "National Council of the Homeland".

much German territory now. I think every safeguard justified on German soil against German militarism but we should be wrong to allow annexations of purely German territory.

Nor can we promise anything to the Poles now in the way of German territory. That must be left to the Peace Conference. I doubt if American and British opinion would countenance serious truncation of German territory – even if it did at the moment of peace, it would cease to do so 10 years after. We should be giving the Germans just the ammunition they want for their "Poor Germany" campaign.

February 13
We hear from O'Malley the Poles are going to refuse to accept the Curzon Line. They couldn't be more foolish and they will have no sympathy on this. If they had accepted the Line but refused to drop members of the Polish cabinet at Stalin's dictation they would be on strong ground.

The whole offer including quotations from Stalin's message appears in *Observer* this morning. A leak which can only have come from official sources. Which? Russian unlikely because it was not in any case passed through Soviet Embassy here. Polish more possible, though it is interesting that the description is objective and not markedly pro-one side or the other. The facts are stated fully and tomorrow we shall have a public discussion in the press of merits and demerits. This may be the leaker's intention so opinion can express itself, e.g. about transfers of German territory, changes in Polish Government. I don't exclude some Polish or pro-Polish trick – it is more like them than the Soviets who have less to gain by exposure of these terms.

February 15
Poles are now writing their apologia for the archives of Poland and have begged the P.M. to give them more time before he receives them. The P.M. is straining to get off his telegram to Stalin reporting his efforts to reach a settlement. The Poles still determined to do their usual suicide act.

Later – we hear there is dissension in the Polish Government over Mikolajczyk making even a half offer to the P.M., his own Peasant Party ministers alone out of the Four Parties represented in the Government supporting this.

February 17
P.M. and A.E. met the Polish P.M. and M.F.A. last evening. The

latter brought a paper which expressed readiness to discuss all questions with the Soviets but inability to accept the Curzon Line as the future frontier.

The P.M. made it quite clear that this was no good. The Poles insisted that they couldn't agree to more than a provisional administrative line leaving Vilna and Lvov to Poland. The P.M. spoke emphatically and picturesquely of the unreality of their attitude. Finally, the Poles agreed to think again and see if they could work out any advance on these terms which the P.M. could put to Stalin with any hope of acceptance.

February 19

Roosevelt is jumping us into a conference on oil in the Middle East – rather outrageously. We hate it, though we should welcome it. We cannot bear anyone to touch us in that part of the world – even our friends. As though we had made such a success of it! Our trouble is that we aren't strong enough to impose a proper settlement of Palestine and so our policy of necessity is one of appeasement of the Arabs who respond by revolting against us regularly. But if the Americans are taking oil for the Navy from the Middle East they must share in its security. They can share the burden of a proper settlement, and that will mean in the end a Jewish Palestine. I have always thought that it must be an Anglo–American solution. What a fight Palestine has been! Everybody's anti-Semitism coming out. But Palestine, as Weizman said to me long ago, should be a bastion of defence for us against the doubtful Arab states.

February 21

During weekend some progress was made on Soviet–Polish affairs. The Poles (Romer, Mikolajczyk and Raczynski) agreed to a revised version of the P.M.'s proposed message to Stalin. That is to say, they had no objection to his sending this version to Stalin on the understanding that they had seen it and approved his doing so, although at this point they could not say they accepted it. If Stalin accepted it, then the 3 Poles would put it to the Government as a whole for acceptance and if necessary resign on it. This was thought good enough and the P.M. has sent his message to Stalin.

The message now says the P.G. would accept a new line of demarcation based on ethnographic considerations but would like to keep Vilna and Lvov. Then it goes on that as no announcement can be made of what Poland is to receive in compensation at Germany's expense now, P. can't make any declaration about cession of territory on E. frontiers as it would appear too one-sided. Moreover it is all part of general peace settlement and must await armistice. Polish Government must consult Polish people before abdicating its rights and must therefore first return to Warsaw. It is hoped Soviets will facilitate return of P.G. to Poland – areas being handed over to their civil administration as freed. The P.G. would like in particular to include Vilna and Lvov. P.M. here puts in that he had told them Stalin would not agree to this but he would like to assure the P.G. they would have all areas West of Curzon Line. As to final frontier P.G. would favour an ethnographic line – this, adds P.M., would inevitably lead to the line which Stalin desires. Meanwhile P.G. have given orders to Underground Movement to cooperate with Soviet forces. P.M. expresses his agreement with Soviets having Koenigsberg. As to composition of P.G. this must await return to Warsaw when it would be found P.G. would only include men ready to cooperate with Soviets. Finally, would Stalin agree to join H.M.G. and Poland in recognizing Polish independence and integration as reconstituted, do their best to secure for Poland Danzig, Upper Silesia, E. Prussia minus Koenigsberg and "as much territory up to the Oder" as P.G. see fit to accept! H.M.G. would guarantee such a settlement to best of their ability.

This is of course a face-saving way of putting it for the Poles. But I'm not very hopeful of Stalin agreeing to these indirect methods. The important point is that we ourselves recognise the Curzon Line as the correct frontier.

What I'm far more disturbed about is the German territory which is being offered so lightheartedly in exchange.

February 25
Polish Government have put out a foolish semi-official statement refuting the P.M.'s speech (about the Polish Soviet question) and affirming that they refuse the Curzon Line.

February 27
Further leakage in *Observer* today which in addition to giving circumstantial account of further negotiations between P.M. and Polish P.M. and M.F.A. leading up to despatch of message to Stalin, reports that a new Polish C. in C. has been appointed in Poland by the pro-Soviet National Council there. This is news to us, though we knew already of the existence of the National Council.

We have now got evidence that Kot, the Polish M. of Interior, is the leaker. He is of course one of the two Polish Ministers to go if a settlement is reached. He is a twister anyway and his purpose presumably is to show up the futility of Miko. negotiating at all with the Soviet Government.

All this makes any serious negotiation almost impossible. The situation is slipping and the P.G. by their slowness to grasp at the offer, have enabled Stalin to push on with plans for a pro-Soviet Poland independent of the P.G. in London.

It is really believed at last that the bombing offensive against Germany is breaking down her aircraft production. This is due to the American daylight precision bombing, which is now coming into its own, rather than to the blanketing night raids of our bomber force over German towns. The Americans believe that given fair weather they can destroy the aircraft industry to an extent that Germany would have no fighter protection at all but only flak against us.

February 29
We had the first account today of Clark-Kerr's talk with Stalin over the P.M.'s message. It did not go well. Stalin poohpoohed the whole proposal, held the P.G. up to ridicule and said he only wanted two things – Curzon Line and reconstructed P.G. He feared Poles were determined to wreck Anglo–Soviet cooperation and his own relations with P.M. The official reply is to follow.

As we thought, the Polish offer did not go far enough and the Polish leakages and qualifying statements in the press have undermined the value of even their own offer. Our first reaction is that we shall get no further with the P.G. and we must fall back on direct Anglo–Soviet Agreement about Poland for duration of war. This would define future frontiers for Peace Conference and take note of Stalin's promises of future independence. It is the beginning of the end of this P.G. in London which will merely control Polish forces in the West; there will be a new P.G. when Warsaw is reached, set up by the Soviets, and we shall have to recognise it and unrecognise this Government, at best getting one or two of its members into the new Government.

March 2
Stalin's formal reply not yet received. P.M. meanwhile is reacting dangerously to Clark-Kerr's account. He wants to wash his hands of the Russians! However we must hope these alarming views will evaporate. We must not allow the Poles to wreck Anglo–Russian

relations. We must not forget the folly and provocative behaviour of the Poles since 1920.

I hear Alexander wants another division for the bridgehead[1] and this is causing a tremendous row.

March 6
Much happened over week-end. Stalin's reply came – much as expected, he says it is useless to deal with P.G. and question isn't "mature" yet.

President has told P.M. he has torn up the French civil affairs directive and rewritten it so as to leave everything in the hands of the generals on the spot.

In answer to the former a further message has now gone to Stalin, expressing disappointment, urging the risks to the Alliance of no-agreement with the Poles, and hoping that he will after all agree to a working agreement.

In answer to the latter A.E. has sent a minute to P.M. to say how fatal this waste of time is proving and how necessary to have the French Committee recognised as the proper authority for Eisenhower to deal with. Whether the P.M. will agree to say any more to the President we don't know, for the P.M. is really as demented as the Pres. about France – "Power corrupts . . ." How true of F.D.R. who becomes more and more arbitrary and unaccountable in his acts.

March 10
The idea is on foot again for A.E. to give up F.O. but keep leadership of H. of C. and his War Cabinet work and for Bobbety to take his place here. The P.M. doesn't like the idea at all and offered to take on the F.O. himself! But it is being persisted in and seems likely to come off in the end.

P.M. and A.E. both in very anti-Soviet mood – rather dangerously so, I think. We mustn't wed ourselves too much to this P.G. which after all is an exile Government out of touch since 4 years with opinion in Poland. Anyway we have pinned ourselves publicly now to the Curzon Line. We have next to no information of our own of what is position in Poland, only Russian or Polish information. There may be more genuine pro-Soviet feeling than we suspect.

March 11
Smuts has weighed in with a telegram of warning to the P.M. against

1. The Anzio landing.

going too far with the P.G. in antagonising S.R. Why should Poland be compensated for what she never should have had by promising her German territory which was never Polish, he asks. Very wise. The P.M. may listen to him, though at present I think he is going much too far with the Poles.

But it is a problem which looks like solving itself. This P.G. won't accept the Curzon Line and the Soviet G. won't deal with them. When the Soviets clear Poland, they will set up a new Government. Meanwhile this Government shows signs of disintegration General Anders in command of Polish troops is talking about disowning Mikolajczyk if he as much as mentions the Curzon Line. General Sosnkovski, Polish C. in C., is suspect to both Miko and Anders. Poor M. himself represents a minority in his own Cabinet. Time is working for Stalin.

March 20
Another rough reply from Stalin has come in. He says that as his last confidential message to the P.M. has appeared in the British press, he cannot continue the correspondence about Poland any more. This has enraged the P.M. and A.E. Although the Poles began the leaking, this particular message was leaked by the Soviet Embassy here and it was unknown to the Poles. We hope to get discussions off this dangerous high-level of P.M.–Stalin down to a Molotov–Clark-Kerr level. If we can keep the old prima donnas off the stage, we believe we might make progress.

Roosevelt, our other prima donna, has now lashed out again at the French Committee. The long-deferred French directive has appeared from the presidential press.[1] It is an extraordinary outburst which would leave Eisenhower sole and absolute arbiter of French affairs, all over France, without reference to anybody. At the same time the President is always insisting that France is our baby and we must make ourselves responsible for her. P.M., who is almost as demented as the President about France, thinks it a grand piece of work.

March 27
Stalin has sent us a further reply. This time he takes the P.M. to task

1. The French had produced in the autumn proposals for the National Committee to administer the liberated areas outside the zone of operations. No decision had been reached because of Roosevelt's refusal to deal with the Committee, in spite of the State Department having come round to the British view.

for "threatening" him, accuses us of backing out of Tehran agreement about Curzon Line, which he says he still stands by himself, and says his quarrel is not with Poland, an ally, but with the P.G. in London.

We think it is time to give up these exchanges of messages and to drop our ill-starred attempts at mediation. But I am sure we should make it clear we still abide by the Tehran plan and the Curzon Line (which has become like the Baltic States a sort of symbol of good faith with Stalin). We are certain to have the P.G. left on our hands. The moment Warsaw is freed a fresh P.G. will be formed based outwardly at least on popular support. The position of the P.G. in London will then be impossible. The problem is to obtain a decent transition.

French affairs still in a mess because of the personal prejudices of F.D.R. and W.C.

March 28
A.E. dined with us last night at the Ritz. He told us it was now decided that he should give up F.O. and keep leadership of H. of C. Bobbety would come to F.O. But to make it clear that H. of C. only was not a step-down for him it was intended that he should become First Lord of the Treasury (i.e. half the P.M.'s post) and so become the obvious coadjutor and successor. He said he couldn't possibly go on with F.O. and H. of C. I agreed about that. He then said the P.M. was really tired out now, "he doubted if it could last till the end of the year".

On the whole A.E. was pleased at the decision, I think, though he knows he will miss the F.O. work as soon as he is away from it. He thinks the H. of C. plus work on the Lord President's Committee of Home Affairs will be valuable training. I mentioned my doubt about Bobbety and the P.M. hitting it off. He admitted the risk but said the P.M. was really easier to handle now because he was so very tired.

I still doubt the wisdom of A.E. giving up F.O. I also doubt whether the P.M. is so near his end as all that.

April 7
Contrary to what was decided last week, A.E. is now *not* going to give up F.O. but will keep F.O. and H. of C. This is because the P.M. doesn't want a change and suspects that he and Bobbety will not get on, which is Bobbety's view too. As to H. of C. they profess that there is no one else but A.E. who can do it. I don't believe this. R. A. Butler or Stanley could do it or try to do it. But they don't want them to try in case they succeed.

I'm very sorry about this H. of C. business because it means F.O. is not going to get its fair share of A.E.

April 8

A surprisingly good bit of Polish news. The O.C. Polish Underground Movement in Volhynia has reached agreement with the Soviet General for converting his force into a regular Polish Division under Soviet Command, but still under the P.G. in London. This seems, as the Polish Ambassador said to me, too good to be true. If it is followed up by further such contacts, the best results may ensue. Does this mean that Poles and Soviets get on better if we don't interfere? It looks rather like it.

April 10

P.M. still holding out over France. All planning impossible.

There is a slight chance of Roumania betraying the Germans and going over to the Russians. We are in contact with the Roumanian Government and the Russians are offering practically cobelligerent status if their divisions surrender. They also agree to their keeping Transylvania or the major part of it. It remains to be seen if the Antonescus will agree. It is their only hope.

All this makes more maddening our inability to plan at all with France, our natural ally and neighbour who can help enormously with our own campaign – so meagre so far.

April 17

Bobbety and I had our talk about the question of A.E. and F.O. which has now been put in cold storage till Whitsun. I think Bobbety felt quite sure if he went to F.O. it wouldn't work with P.M., and he feels that the P.M. thinks so too. He heartily agrees that A.E. should give up H. of C. and thinks, as I do, that R.A.B. should be given the chance of doing it.

Bobbety would make a very great Foreign Minister, but I think he might break himself by an unsuccessful term now. I mean that if it came to a resignation over some point of foreign affairs on which he and P.M. disagreed, this might prejudice his prospects for a much more fruitful period later with A.E. as P.M.

April 26

No further progress with France. A.E. now back refuses absolutely to agree to President's directive. On other hand, we are assured President will never agree to alter it. We now propose a plan to do without any directive and merely to tell Eisenhower to negotiate with the French. This is rather a shaming subterfuge but the only way to advance. But the P.M. hasn't agreed to it yet. We shall have to explain all this to the Russians who will pass it on to the French. Duff[1] is standing up to the P.M. well, as I expected he would.

However Koenig,[2] the French military representative, and Bedell Smith, Eisenhower's C. of S., are already talking, and that is something. But what folly all this behaviour is!

Molotov denies flatly that the Poles and the Soviet force commanders have had any contacts whatsoever. This can't be true as a Pole has just come out of Poland who took part in the talks. There also seems to be some contact between the London Poles and the Moscow Poles. I am glad to say we are sitting back and taking no further part.

May 1

A.E. inclines more to keeping F.O. and giving up H. of C. He gives a very bad account of P.M.'s health – up one day down the next. P.M. interferes and meddles in everything, sending personal messages usually with unfortunate results.

French problem now to be dealt with entirely by P.Q. and Answer. P.M. won't send any message to Pres. to approve or to modify Pres.'s directive. P.M. and A.E. have agreed to let it be in abeyance and for A.E. to announce in H. of C. that conversations are in progress between Eisenhower and Koenig, head of French Military Mission here, and to leave it at that. It is not proposed to warn the U.S. Government in advance.

May 8

I am in despair about French affairs. A.E. made his announcement in H. of C. last week. Eisenhower meanwhile had asked for formal authority to conduct his conversations with Koenig on a tentative basis! H.M.G. at once agreed through our chiefs of staff. The Washington Chiefs of Staff, who were also disposed to agree, were pulled up by the Pres. who said Eisenhower must tell Koenig that he, Eisenhower, was nonetheless free to deal with any other group of

1. He had become British representative with the French Committee on January 1 1944.
2. Appointed by French National Committee to the command of the French resistance in February.

Frenchmen – the very point on which we refused to accept the President's directive. Meanwhile the conversations, thus unofficially begun, had come to a full stop any way owing to our ban[1] on any communications going out of the U.K. since Koenig could not consult his Committee. To start again, we must a) get the ban lifted for a Frenchman to go to Algiers or for a French cypher and b) get the P.M. to move the President.

De Gaulle, maddened as well he might be by all this, has just let out one of his usual outbursts, saying conversations are held up and implying he prefers Russia to us.

We can do nothing more on official level nor can Eisenhower do more on a military level. The politicians must accept responsibility for the mess, since the President means to hold up all dealing with de G. unless the P.M. can shift him. P.M. is of course as bad as the Pres. in his unreasoning hatred of de G. All this on the eve of Overlord when French good-will, which means de G., can be so helpful. There could be no clearer case of cutting off noses.

The last idea, thrown out by the P.M., is that A.E. should go to Algiers and "negotiate a settlement". But *anyone* can negotiate a settlement once the P.M. and the President are agreed that it should take the form of recognising the Committee as the Provisional Government of France. We have Duff who could do it or a mission could go from S.C.A.E.F., or Koenig could do it here. It seems a mad idea for A.E. to go, though it appeals to him as a jaunt in the limelight.

May 22

After many twists and turns we've now got to this position. The P.M., after consulting the President, has decided to invite de G. on D day to come here to discuss civil affairs for France. He has now telegraphed to Duff to tell this to de G. with a friendly reference to French share in battles in Italy.

Meanwhile French Committee look like declaring themselves the Provisional Government of France following on a resolution to this effect from Consultative Assembly. This of course has shocked P.M. and President, though F.O. see no harm and every advantage in recognising Committee as such. In fact it would not change anything since we already deal with Committee as a Provisional Government. Most surprising of all the Soviet Government have now endorsed the President's draft directive to give Eisenhower authority to deal with French Committee *or any other French body* which we have always

1. Because of the approach of D-day.

refused to do. However we hope we've side tracked and buried the President's directive anyway.

Soviet Government have asked the Polish Government, not through us but through some indirect channel, to meet an intermediary. We have now also heard the report of Lange, the American pro-Soviet Pole, who has been visiting Moscow. He speaks highly of Berling and Polish Patriots who appear as genuine patriotic Poles anxious for good relations with S.-R. but not for Communism, ready to accept Curzon Line but difficult over Lvov, and with much respect for Mikolajczyk but for no other London Pole. Lange also saw Stalin who repeated his readiness for a strong independent but friendly Poland and also spoke well of Mikolajczyk. Again, here in London, Miko. is beginning to consider changes in his Government and especially in status of Sosnkowski, who is the biggest single obstacle to resumption of relations. Finally, on underground front, we are trying discreetly to promote coordination of operations between Polish Commanders and Soviet Forces. All slightly more satisfactory therefore.

May 31

De G. has accepted to come. Meanwhile President has become more and more obstructive in all French matters and the P.M. runs away from them. He asks de G. here but he refuses to face the fact that de G. will expect a full civil affairs agreement if he comes. This the President at present flatly refuses. The President declines to allow Eisenhower to make any reference to the French Committee in his proclamation to French on D day. By his obstinacy he is increasing the difficulties of our troops for the more resistance is stimulated the worse for the Germans.

June 3

De G., after accepting, suddenly developed doubts because we couldn't guarantee U.S. participation in talks. He delayed a day and put it to French Committee. Latter by majority vote agreed he should come nonetheless. He leaves accordingly tonight. President has told P.M. he will have no political discussions in London.

When he arrives tomorrow, he and Massigli are to be taken at once to P.M. who is at advanced G.H.Q., for the day and the night. I am to meet him at dawn.

June 4

I met de G. this morning at 6 a.m. He came without Massigli, simply in his military capacity to see troops etc., since he thought it useless to bring civilian ministers in circumstances with no tripartite talks in view. Duff who came too, told me he had had the greatest tussle to get him to come at all. He told him it would be the end so far as he, de G., and the P.M. were concerned if he now refused, a situation from which the President alone would benefit.

Duff and we think the President has been trying to go behind our backs because he sent Ad. Ferrard back from Washington to Algiers with a fulsome but mysterious message to say how much the President really liked him and would wish him to visit him. This has completely mystified de G. – tripartite talks are refused here, but yet he is invited to Washington.

June 5
Rome fell last night.

De G. quite firm that he will have no civil discussions with us unless U.S. participate. Otherwise talks yesterday friendly between him and P.M. but not intimate.

De G. now refuses to broadcast because having been shown Eisenhower's broadcast and invited most foolishly by Bedell Smith to make any amendments, although it was in fact too late to make any changes at all, he wished to strike out the reference to the French people choosing their own Government when they were free, on the ground that this was not for General Eisenhower to say. When this was refused, he said he wouldn't then broadcast either.

Finally, he has now asked that his French liaison officers be withdrawn from their units as they have no orders! (This on D – 1!!) This is a fatal mistake of de G. and if insisted on could be used to ruin him with the British public. More than that it could have the worst effect on Anglo–French relations. I want to get Duff instructed to see him at once.

De G. couldn't be in more bloody mood. Everybody is under strain of the nervous tension which can be felt in the air. The P.M. has mishandled the whole affair and de G. can not be blamed. Whether he is wise is another matter. He certainly thinks he has got us because the press and H. of C. are on his side.

June 7
Second Front began yesterday at dawn.

Meanwhile continual rows over and with de G. He finally agreed to broadcast yesterday afternoon, a very good broadcast too. He also withdrew his order about the officers. Then, during the night, A.E. and Vienot[1] had a scene with the P.M. who was most abusive about de G. and said he would have nothing more to do with him. A.E. is now seeking to get relations by insisting that we must either break with de G. which means breaking with France, or conclude an agreement with him. There is no middle course. He wishes P.M. to put this to the President and say we must back De G.

Now the chief trouble is the Allied military currency which in default of any agreement with de G. Eisenhower is to proclaim in France. De G. says he will have nothing to do with it and will return to Algiers if the proclamation is made. He refuses to endorse by his presence here what he regards as an act of AMGOT.

June 9
After yesterday's Cabinet dinner it was agreed that A.E. should write to Vienot inviting conversations on civil affairs, suggesting that de G. should send for Massigli and Co., and offering to tell the U.S. Government of this and to ask the latter to be represented at the talks, after which U.S.–French talks could take place in Washington to which we would send an observer.

De G. quite firm that he must be recognised to represent France, and that he will not remain here to cover an AMGOT.

P.M. is almost insane at times in his hatred of de G., only less insane than the Pres.

Meanwhile on the currency de G. has offered to issue a decree accepting and fathering Eisenhower's currency. But this involves recognition of the sovereignty of the Committee, and neither the P.M. nor the President will have it.

I'm sick and tired of the tergiversations and dishonesty of the P.M. and President over this. Either the currency is issued by Eisenhower in which case it is AMGOT, or it is issued by de G. in which case it is French. There is no middle course. De G. will not recognise Eisenhower's AMGOT currency. We deal with de G. and the Committee as sovereign over every sort of question. We boggle at this. Yet it is the French treasury whom we expect eventually to father and repay these notes. Could any situation be more grotesque? I hope there will be an explosion in the H. of C. as over Darlan to expose all this criminal perversity.

1. Pierre Vienot previously as Under-Sec. at the Quai d'Orsay had become Diplomatic Representative of the French National Committee the previous October.

Today we hear de G. is replying to our letter by offering to allow Vienot to open negotiations, to return to Algiers himself and to send the Commissioners (Massigli and Co.) later if necessary. We don't think this is enough and wish to insist on Massigli & Co. coming at once. This will make it easier to impress the President with their importance.

Meanwhile de G. has asked to see the King and to be allowed to go across to the beaches. On both of these we are stalling on the P.M.'s instructions "to wait and see how he behaves" – very shabby.

June 11

No further progress whatever. Vienot says that de G. and Committee won't agree to Commissioners coming and he is ready to start negotiations with us at once. (The negotiations themselves should not be difficult – it is only the principle of negotiating at all which is the difficulty). P.M. and A.E. refuse to be interested in this.

Meanwhile, de G. has informed the press that the currency is being issued "without agreement or guarantee of the French authorities". The P.M. has wired to the President to ask him whether he will accept de G.'s offer to father the currency in return for recognition or whether the currency should be backed by U.S. and H.M.G. till the peace conference. The currency issue is going to boil up this week, as P.Q.s are already put down. It may make or break the whole thing. If we agree to Vienot's offer to negotiate and accept de G.'s currency proclamation, all can be settled. If we refuse, nothing remains except AMGOT for France and that will cause a first-rate row, here in Parliament and press, in U.S.A. and in Algiers. All this because of Roosevelt and our pusillanimity in standing up to him.

June 12

Second Front making slow but I gather satisfactory progress.

P.M. interferes more and more with foreign affairs. In fact while A.E. is leading the H. of C., P.M. is dealing with Italy, Greece, Tito and France, in all cases with unfortunate results. This is reacting on A.E.'s position, as we thought it would, and he is beginning to appear to the public as a *fainéant* where the F.O. is concerned.

In Italy there has been a quick and unexpected turn. No sooner did Badoglio reach Rome[1] than it was found the Italian politicians there would not accept him as P.M. as we had planned. They bowled Mason

1. By previous agreement, on the fall of Rome, the King had abdicated and Umberto had become "Lieutenant-General of the Realm".

344

Macfarlane[1] a fast one and Bonomi bobbed up as P.M. with Orlando and other ancients of former days. The P.M. is livid! But this is a healthy move. Badoglio was a bad man, a war criminal, a man who had worked with Fascism and a general. Now at least we have a return to parliamentarians who, though old are anti-Fascist, and they can decently carry on till the North is free and the new democratic forces can be released and consulted. Democracy is not dead in Italy.

June 13

No progress over de G. Pres. won't give way about currency and quite calmly contemplates an AMGOT currency. Chancellor of Exchequer v. alarmed at consequences of this.

Meanwhile at last it is agreed that de G. should go over to France tomorrow.

De G. dines with A.E. tonight. What a jolly party it will be! I shall be there too.

Meanwhile first reports from Normandy show that everyone wants de G.

June 14

Last night's dinner was grim. I have never seen de G. look so worn, *"martyrisé"*. Vienot alone was in good spirits because he was going with the party to France this morning.

But some progress has been made. The Cabinet decided last night to accept negotiations with Vienot for a civil affairs agreement. As regards the currency there was a great wrangle and a further telegram has been sent to Pres. We are still of course quite stuck by the Pres. but it will be something if we get an Anglo–French agreement.

June 17

French affairs rather brighter. De G. had a most successful visit to Normandy on Thursday. All went well – people relieved and delighted to see him. He went to Bayeux though he wasn't allowed to sleep there as he wanted. He brought with him two of his own officials – the civil commissioner for Normandy and his military equivalent – and left them. It is hoped that these will oil the wheels and make cooperation easier – much depends on their tact and that of our own people.

Talks are to begin on Monday between Vienot and officials.

1. General Mason Macfarlane had become Head of Allied Military Mission to Italian Government, and then Deputy President of Control Commission.

De G. left next night for Algiers. He didn't see the P.M. again, but he and A.E. had a more mellow discussion. There is no doubt the unanimity of the press and of parliament had shaken the P.M.

The famous secret weapon has come into action. We get it each day and night. It screeches overhead like a rocket and the great object is to hit it in the air so that it disintegrates before falling. It seems an extravagant form of weapon and can't go on for long. Mainly propaganda for Germans. One hit the Guards' Chapel at 11 o'clock this morning when everyone was in church.

June 25
French official talks going on well. A general lessening of temperature about France. But still no signs of sanity in the Pres.

Pilotless bombs go on. Most of the old women have left London. The only other escapees have been the Soviet Embassy who have demanded a special train to evacuate their women and children to Blackpool and the generals at SHAPE who have decided to seek safety at Portsmouth.

June 28
I lunched with A.E. alone yesterday. He told me he thought he had decided to give up leadership of H. of C. to R. A. Butler after this session and do F.O. only. I could only applaud this. He said he hadn't put it to P.M. yet. I shan't believe it till I see it.

A.E. very hopeful about war. He thought the Germans might crack in 2 months.

French affairs a little easier. Signs of change in the President over currency. A.E. very pleased at the way we had handled it here. He paid me a nice little tribute.

July 5
De G. in Washington – no word yet of the reaction to our texts, although the President is turning on all his synthetic charm.

A.E. wants to propose to recognise French Committee as Provisional Government from July 14th if he can get P.M. and Cabinet to agree.

July 10
Still no definite news of what happened with de G. in Washington. He has now gone on to Canada. But all accounts are very rosy.

July 15
On leave.

As we rather expected, Pres. received de G. all smiles said he was

346

"my friend" and there was very little between them. He subsequently announced at his Press Conference that he was ready to treat Committee as *de facto* authority for governing France and to accept British texts of agreement as basis for final agreement. De G. for his part played up well and created the best impression. As a result French and U.S. officials are to try and agree final text.

Both P.M. and A.E. rather bitter at this sudden volte face without any warning. As P.M. said to A.E. "The President has treated you badly", making it appear that it has been himself and nobody else who got us all out of the jam, when it was he and he alone who had created the jam in order to acquire for himself credit by removing it. What a slippery politician he is. Vienot, our good friend, in a great stew when he heard what the President had done. He came round to see me at once and urged the great need to put things in their right perspective through the radio and the press as otherwise French opinion in France which had been kept deliberately in the dark during the long Anglo–American wrangle would really suppose it was the Americans and not us who had done all the work. *"J'ai peur que vous ne soyez cocu!"* We laughed and thanked him but told him we thought the French and everybody else would see through these electoral manoeuvres in America.

A.E. however was seriously annoyed and at once amplified what he had been intending to say in answer to a P.Q. in order to put the whole course of events clear – our previous attitude about dealing with French Committee only, our invitation to de G. to come here, his visit, the start of conversations here, the agreement on texts here, acceptance of which by H.M.G. he now for the first time announced, and thereafter visit of de G. to Washington and hope of tripartite agreement on basis of our texts.

However we are not out of the wood yet. The U.S. officials are trying to stiffen up our texts in a way more offensive to the French. We are sitting back and say if they can agree, we can probably accept. But the French position is now a good deal stronger because of A.E.'s announcement in the H. of C. when faced by the President's volte face and because Roosevelt has made such a splash of his de G. conversation that he can hardly now afford to admit a fresh deadlock over the texts, when we have said we accept them.

A.E. has also now invited Massigli to come here for the signature of the agreement and also for a general talk. M. very anxious to talk about policy towards Germany from which both Stalin and Roosevelt wish to exclude France at present.

A.E. has also talked to Vienot, Kleffens,[1] Spaak[2] and Lie about his hope of concluding some closer arrangement with France, Belgium, Holland and Norway after the war "within the framework of any new world order which may be established and in support of the Anglo–Soviet Alliance which with U.S. collaboration is basis of our policy. These countries have been pressing us for many months to indicate our interest in the Western bloc idea, and now, I'm glad to say, after much hesitation and heart-searching we have given them this crumb of comfort. A.E. is getting fed up at referring everything to the U.S.A. "Can't we really have a foreign policy of our own?" Anything referred to U.S.A. is at once blocked by Hull or President who are afraid of anything being done at all except by themselves. But under any system we should and must have special relations with our Western neighbours. Stalin has no objection to what would be the counterpart of his own position towards States of E. Europe – Czechoslovakia, Poland etc., both positions being covered by A–S Alliance. If there is a world order, then all this is a useful scaffolding while the world order is being built.

July 21
Poor Vienot is dead. It was in the papers today. I left him last week seemingly quite well and recovered from the throat he had been having. Poor man, I am sorry. He has certainly died for his work just when it was getting straight.

We hear today on the wireless the news of the generals' revolt against Hitler.

July 30
No more news about Germany except what's in the papers. I am convinced that it was to our interest that this coup has failed. If Hitler had died, we would have had a surge to make peace with the generals. The rot must proceed further yet. Our enemies are both the Nazis and the generals. We should make peace with neither.

Poles.[3] At long last Mikolajczyk has been persuaded and bundled off to Moscow. Stalin to whom we proposed it, gave a grudging con-

1. Dutch Foreign Minister.
2. Belgian Foreign Minister.
3. During June there had been inconclusive discussions between Mikolajczyk and Lebedev, the Russian representative to the Allied governments in London, ending with a re-statement of Soviet demands on the London Poles.

sent. He had meanwhile given a provisional recognition to the P.N.G. of Liberation under Moravski which has formed a National Committee *à la* de Gaulle with whom Stalin has signed a Civil Affairs Agreement for liberated Polish territory.[1] But he assures us this is only provisional and the Government can only be formed after Poland is freed. I fear Mick is too late. He was never big enough or bold enough to take the jump in time – viz. accept Curzon Line and make Government changes. There is still a chance that he himself may be worked into a new Government but the rest of the London Government is out of the running. The Russians are now at the gates of Warsaw. But there is no evidence that Stalin does not still intend "a strong, independent and democratic Poland" under a Government he can trust. I wonder sometimes if any P.G. can be trusted.

August 5
Hitler is pursuing his purge of generals. A court of "honour" has been set up to enable the generals to purge themselves, a charming spectacle. Germans are incapable of loyalty even to each other. I despise the generals more than Hitler who deserves better treatment from them.

August 13
I've been lazy about my diary.
Mick in Moscow has had a series of talks with Stalin, Molotov and the Polish National Committee. They were all friendly and well-disposed. The P.N.C. offered Mick to be P.M. of a combined Government in which Mick's peasant party should have 4 seats. The P.N.C. delegation was headed by an entirely new and hitherto unheard of Pole called "Berut"[2] – a pseudonym – whom Mick described as a sort of Polish Tito. Finally Mick decided he must come back to London to report. We have thought this a mistake and telegraphed to urge him to stop on and have his party leaders out to Tehran if necessary. But he had already started and in fact reached London today. I fear now all the good work be undone because those opposed to settlement in Moscow as in London will work against it, the situation will slip

1. This had grown out of the National Council of the Homeland. The Committee known as the Lublin Committee immediately denounced the London Polish Government, and disassociated itself from the Underground movement directed by the London Poles.
2. Krasnodewski, a Communist Soviet agent imprisoned in Poland and exchanged in 1927.

again, Warsaw will fall and a new Government be set up in M.'s absence.

Meanwhile the Poles in London who control the underground movement in Poland have set off a general rising in Warsaw.[1] They had not timed this with Russian plans and we had told them we could accept no responsibility for advising them for such operation in the Russian sphere.[2] The Russian forces have been held up outside Warsaw by heavy German reinforcements and the Poles are now blaming everybody – us, the Russians – for not sending them help in parachutists and arms. As usual, they impute sinister motives to the Russians such as that they are deliberately not helping and not pressing their assault on Warsaw, because they wish the Poles to be exterminated. To send arms from England or Bari is now a most hazardous operation in the short nights and cannot be undertaken on a large-scale. We had heavy losses on one operation and now the Air Staff have decided wisely that it is too risky to justify. As a result of further Polish insistence, a Polish flight has been allowed to undertake it and it has been successful.

Now a fresh contretemps has occurred between the P.M. and de G. P.M. in passing through Algiers on his way to Italy asked de G. to meet him. De G. has refused, causing great annoyance to P.M. who characteristically sent for General Georges. The last fortunately couldn't be found. Here de G. was clearly in the wrong – just as the P.M. was in the wrong in his rude treatment of de G. while he was here.

August 15
My gloomy prognostications have come only too true. The Warsaw business has become magnified into the acid test of Soviet–Polish–British relations. We have made two more sorties from Bari to drop arms, as a result of Polish appeals and pressure, and have lost heavily from flak over Warsaw, 33% the last time, and now our Chiefs of Staff have said flatly they will do no more. Stalin, who was also pressed, has replied that he had tried to drop a Russian officer into Warsaw, that he was killed and now he must wash his hands of the whole business. It is not serious war and it was not coordinated with Moscow. Finally, he will not allow U.S. aeroplanes to drop arms on Warsaw on a shuttle service touching Soviet soil.

1. It began on August 1. The Russians had reached the outskirts on July 29.
2. Previous to the rising we had told the Poles we could not help.

This in spite of appeals by the P.M., and Stalin has told the Poles so. Obviously it is comparatively easy for the Russians to drop supplies on Warsaw from only 100 miles and it is in any case indefensible for them not to allow the Americans to attempt it. This is clearly going to make progress on the political talks impossible because Mick will either refuse to proceed with them or would be disavowed if he did.

Yet progress there had seemed possible and we had worked out ideas of a new Polish Government based on 50:50 of London and Moscow Poles with Mick as P.M. and a new President to be agreed to by both sides to hold elections in Poland. Mick and Romer lunched with A.E. last Monday (I was there) and Mick had said he personally favoured some such course (though not 50:50). He told us he got on better with the Russians than with the Poles and seemed fairly confident that Stalin meant business "because he realised how strong the Polish Government was". I have always doubted this myself, but I think Stalin finds Mick a type of Pole he could get on with, a Peasant who unlike the Socialists is not anti-Russian. Anyway it is difficult to square any of this now with the position created by Warsaw.

I believe Mick was wrong to leave Moscow. He could have held the situation better there. I also believe he overestimates his strength in Poland, so that if Warsaw is freed without agreement, it will be possible for Stalin to find an adequate Polish Government. So why need Stalin bother? The Poles here will be left high and dry, filling Christendom with their anti-Soviet cries. And if there is civil war in Poland, or if the Soviets adopt repressive measures, or can be represented by Polish propaganda as doing so, Anglo–Soviet relations will be gravely injured. One must confess Stalin is not helpful. By doing a little, he could help us so much in making Anglo–Soviet Alliance work.

August 18
Motored down to Binderton with A.E. and Nicolas this evening. We are to start at 9 tomorrow for Thorney Island from where we are to fly to France. We all feel like schoolboys having half-term holiday.

General Morgan, Deputy Chief of Staff, waiting for us to dine at Binderton. It was he who planned the Normandy landing, as C.O.O.S.C. Quite sound about the necessity of rooting out the German General Staff and thankful Hitler wasn't bumped off the other day.

A.E. very happy to be going but obviously very tired. We discussed the future of SHAEF after the war. Morgan rather pro-continuance of

SHAEF. We rather doubtful because of blurring of Anglo–American spheres.

Repercussions of Polish Soviet trouble pursue us. A telegram from P.M. proposing a tel. to Roosevelt suggesting a joint telegram to Stalin which A.E. agreed should be sent off to Washington.

August 19

Left for Thorney Island where Charles Peake and Col. Lash (U.S.) met us. Flew off at 10 in a Dakota with a fighter escort.

We first drove to see a refugee camp, then lunched with General Naylor. After that we went and saw the famous artificial port at Arromanches – most remarkable.

We then went to Caen and called on the Préfet, a former rector of the University and leader of the resistance movement. Poor Caen, ⅔ of it quite flat. The spire of one of the churches was taken off by a shell from the Rodney. We dined at Bayeux with Coulet, the Regional Commissioner and a former diplomat, with his staff.

August 20

Start at 9 from camp for General Crerar's HQ.[1] Long dusty drive through Bayeux to Caen again. The general was in his caravan and showed us all the maps, the Falaise pocket now closed and the remaining Germans outside falling back on the Seine. He has under him the Poles. He told us they had messed up one operation by their peculiarly Polish behaviour. When required to push ahead fast to engage and hustle the retreating Germans, they had become committed to a terrific and quite unnecessary fight against some Germans in a wood who should have been bypassed and sealed off. As a result the main advance was held up. They were always, he said, in a great state of excitement, very brave and very foolish. Just like their politics and at Warsaw! A perpetual series of Balaklavas.

After that, we left to try and find Monty's H.Q. but got hopelessly lost on the roads and so gave it up as we were due to lunch with General Eisenhower at 1.30. The latter was in camp too. No chateau life for generals in this war. He had just received Gen. de Gaulle who had arrived that morning. He had at once taken the initiative with de G., told him that the Leclerc Division should go first into Paris as a token of the Allies, that Gen. de G. should go in too and that he would make Gen. Koenig military governor. General de G. was evidently quite overcome by this and when Gen. Eisenhower followed it up by

1. Canadian Army Commander.

saying that de G. in turn must help him by explaining to the French that they would only get little food to begin with because all transport must be kept for the advancing armies, he took it quite well. "They shan't starve, but I'm darned if they are going to have cream with their dinner!" A big grandfather of a man, simple and large in ideas. He knows how to handle de G. better than the clever ones.

He told A.E. he wanted to keep SHAEF going during the armistice period as he thought like that it would be easier to keep his country-men in Europe, and that when they did leave, we could slip the French into their places.

Bedell Smith also there – a rougher, tougher, cleverer man, but much less attractive.

After having tea with the Guards Armoured Divn. HQ in a pleasant orchard, we drove off to General Montgomery's Advanced H.Q. A long drive on dusty roads crowded with transport and through vil-lages some destroyed altogether, but most more or less intact. The H.Q. were on the side of a road on a sloping hill looking across a wide valley. Here were the general's caravan and two or three tents. He came out to meet us. He carried A.E. off straight away for a talk; they sat on two chairs looking out at the view.

After A.E. and M. had had a good hour's talk we went into dinner in another open tent. 8 of us, A.E. and I on each side of M., de G., Dawnay, and A.D.C.

The Gen. sat up like a little bird with his head on one side, sharp as a needle and with very bright eyes. He was in most genial mood and kept putting questions to A.E., such as "What are the statesmen going to do when the soldiers have done?" "Is there going to be an election?" "What are you going to do with Germany?"

Speaking of the war, he said we really were on the eve of a very big thing. After the pocket had been cleared up, (which contained ele-ments of 14 divisions) he intended to make another scoop with his right wing against the Seine, and after that there really would be nothing left. (He told A.E. he meant to go on to Antwerp and then straight into the Ruhr.) He said the soldiers must be able to vote in the elections or there would be trouble. They must also get more pay if they were to go on fighting the Japs. "My soldiers will probably vote as I tell them." "They will vote *sensibly*," though what that would be he didn't say. He said he was working on them through his padres and he thrust out two hands "One hand, he said, was what you wanted to do, the other was what it was your duty to do. It was necessary to bring the two together. It may be your duty to go to Japan!"

A most striking little man with his bright eyes and long beaky nose. I daresay he is pretty ruthless with his generals.

He told A.E. how much he had found the P.M. aged, so slow now in reaching decisions. A.E. said to me afterwards he thought they had got on well and he had never seen M. so mellow. I told A.E. I was certain it was a most useful talk for them both to have, to know each other's mind. M. would have great influence after the war and I felt A.E. could probably guide him. M. is evidently a bit *naïf* in political matters.

August 24

Paris reported yesterday freed by the F.F.I. No entry from outside yet. The bells of St. Paul's were rung today, and tomorrow we are having a Thanksgiving Service in the crypt.

A good background for Massigli's visit.

Warsaw very bad. Fighting still going on, according to the Poles whose accounts we feel may well be exaggerated. Joe has sent a harsh reply to the joint message from the P.M. and the President asking him to help. He will have nothing to do with it, and regards the leaders as criminals who have needlessly sacrificed the people.

August 26

Paris at last "officially" freed yesterday and de G. himself there. SHAEF very stuffy about it – so like Stalin over Warsaw! Anyway de G. now wants his government to go there at once. This is asking a lot of the slow-moving military mind of SHAEF, But Massigli told me last night that he thought de G. wanted to have at once a *remaniement* of his government. And he is right. The situation in Paris cannot drift or there might be a commune. The sooner de G. reforms his government with the resistance leaders, the sooner he will establish his authority in Paris and France. There must be no *flottement*. That will be to no one's interest, least of all to SHAEF's. I told Charles Peake to pass this on to SHAEF.

But a more disturbing thing is that Eisenhower, doubtless on orders from Washington, has put through an order depriving Montgomery of single command of the battle and setting up a Northern Army under M. and a Central Army under Bradley, both under Eisenhower, who for all his virtues is unqualified for military command and had to be prevented in Tunisia. This is American jealousy and electioneering, I suppose, but it is hard and serious that the British general who has organised and led the assault should now be removed from sole control over the rout. Talk of swopping horses in the middle of the stream. The P.M. instead of fooling about in Italy,[1] should have stopped it.

August 31
P.M. ill.

September 1
P.M. better and seeing the Polish P.M. this evening.

Montgomery made a F.M. in recognition of his great military services and as some consolation for having the command of the whole force taken from him in the middle of the rout. Eisenhower and the press have published explanations of this decision which could not be more laboured or unconvincing. The truth is that Americans in an election year must be commanded by an American general so that it can be an American victory. The two great Allied commanders have been British, Montgomery and Alexander. The hardest fighting against the seasoned German troops has been by the British in Africa, in Italy and in Normandy. The major naval part has been British.

Adrian Holman[2] and the advance party of the Embassy go to Paris tomorrow. How I wish I was going with them! General de G. is reported to be making a *remaniement* of his government which we still call a Committee. What silly fools we look over that because of the P.M.'s embitterment against de G.!

Poles still screaming about Warsaw but nonetheless Mick has put to Moscow his political proposals for a compromise arrangement with the Polish National Committee. I suspect they will miss the bus – "too late and not enough" might be the motto of Polish politics. If the Poles had said 6 months' ago what they say now an arrangement might have been possible.

September 5
Poles still trying to occupy centre of the stage. Sosnkowski has come out with a flaming order of the day to Polish forces accusing us of doing nothing to help Warsaw. Mick says he will resign because S. took this action without any reference to him. P.M. (who has now left for Quebec) told Mick that he was the only Pole here whom he would support. If Mick went, he would wash his hands of the lot. A.E. saw

1. He had gone to Italy on August 9.
2. Who had become Minister at the Embassy.

Mick today – position obscure. Meanwhile and just before this P.M. had sent a further message to Stalin protesting against it.

September 6

Dined with Bruce Lockhart to say farewell to French and Belgian broadcasting teams now going back to their countries. A.E. there. He made a charming speech.

When A.E. saw the P.M. on his return, he was shocked at his appearance and had insisting on his not going to the Cabinet, but to bed. The P.M. had been bathing in Italy and had spent over 35 minutes in the water. He had even dived in! After that had come a baddish flight from Italy to N. Africa. Now the P.M. had started off again, by sea, to Quebec. A.E. had insisted on 5 doctors signing a note that he was fit to travel, and that if he went, he should take an M. & B. specialist with him. P.M. had said it was quite unnecessary. He would have the ship's surgeon! "I shall live much longer than you!" Moran had said he wouldn't have allowed anyone else to travel, but he might pick up on the sea voyage. A.E. had squared Cunningham to make the ship take a day and a half longer. P.M. had rung up C. in A.E.'s presence and complained of the slowness of the crossing and asked how long a battleship would take. "At least a day and a half longer" C. had said. P.M. was furious.

September 9

In the midst of all our victories V2 has arrived! Two rocket shells fell last evening with a terrific double explosion which fairly shook the Office.

Poles still hold out in Warsaw. Polish Government still not resigning.

September 10

Reply today from Molotov to last message about Poles. A long rigmarole pointing out that the whole Warsaw episode was hopelessly inept and never coordinated with Soviets, that latter had tried to drop supplies but realised that most fell into enemy hands, but that if we thought it so useful, they would agree to our attempting operation if we discussed it with them, i.e. the old idea of U.S. aircraft dropping supplies and landing on Soviet airfields. This is rather more hopeful and we are taking it up urgently with Americans. We ourselves can do no more either from Bari or from here as it is not regarded by our Air

Staff as a worthwhile military operation – too many losses for too little result.

September 16
V2 bombs still coming, one or two a day but with the wildest aiming.
Stalin has agreed as a result of the P.M./President appeal to allow U.S. aircraft to attempt to drop arms on Warsaw by flying from here to Russian airfields. Warsaw still holds out, that is the Polish Underground are still holding out in parts of the city, and the Russian offensive against Warsaw has resumed. Mick is being told he must get rid of the impossible Sosnkowski, which the Polish Pres. is holding up. Mick wants to get rid of him and naturally wishes to do it himself rather than through us. He is going to insist after the U.S. bombing operation has taken place. If the Pres. still refuses, then H.M.G. will intervene and insist. Both P.M. and A.E. have let it be understood it is Mick or nobody for us. The Polish parties are playing politics, jockeying for position. Mick is far the best and his party the Peasants are least anti-Russian. The Polish Socialists are the worst.

A.E. went off to join P.M. at Quebec. We hope they will finally settle there "the Zones" question, i.e. that we should take N.W. Germany and the Americans S.W. Germany for occupation. This was all settled at Quebec last time, since then the President has been trying to reverse it.

P.M. still being childish about recognising the Provisional French Government. Massigli is to come here as Ambassador. Bidault,[1] the resistance leader, has taken his place at Quai. First impressions seem that B. is hardly up to it. Duff and Diana went to Paris last week.

September 24
Quebec over. A.E. got back early last week and P.M. will be back on Tues. We won over the "Zones" question. We are to have the N.W. and the Americans the S.W. of Germany. But both P.M. and Pres. were adamant against recognition of French Committee. A.E. pressed and the more he pressed the more adamant they became. So this absurd pinprick will go on – what foolish diplomacy!

Massigli arrives tomorrow as Ambassador. He will press us at once for full membership for France of E.A.C. [European Advisory Council][2] and also for a zone in Germany to occupy. Bidault has

1. Georges Bidault, the French resistance leader 1943–1944, later Foreign Minister and Prime Minister.
2. Set up at the Moscow Conference 1943.

already told Duff he doesn't want a part of some one else's zone *sous-loué*!

The Poles continue to talk and to do nothing. Both Sosnkowski and Mick still remain. The Polish Pres. is refusing to let S. go, although the whole P.G. have demanded his resignation. Mick has some fear lest the Socialists rat on him and agree to form a government with the Pres. behind his back. The Pres. is hoping to secure a reconstruction of the government in return for dropping Sosnkowski by which the Sosnkowski influence would come in by the back door. All this time Stalin has been recovering ground by dropping supplies himself on Warsaw, by renewing his offensive there and by dealing direct with General Bor, the Polish Commander. Mick's stocks are falling. Unless he can show himself strong enough to throw S. out, he will have no chance of linking up again with Moscow and the other Poles. I was sure he made a fatal mistake by ever leaving Moscow. Now he has to get back. Meanwhile Warsaw may be freed and Stalin may justifiably set up a new P.G. Perhaps it would be the best solution.

Inside Germany there is a reign of terror. Himmler everywhere. A Nazi "underground" movement is being busily organised. No more peace feelers from there.

October 4
Sosnkowski gone at length. The Polish President finally agreed to drop him without any government changes, but with messages of obvious reluctance. Bor, Polish General in Warsaw, appointed instead, very ill received by Polish National Council who say he hasn't been in Warsaw at all!

But Warsaw itself has now fallen, owing to failure of further Russian offensive and general inability to supply them with arms and food.

Now however the P.M. and A.E. are off to Moscow mainly to discuss Russia coming into the Far East war but also "to settle the Polish problem". A.E. has asked me to go too. Of course I have agreed but it is a weary journey to undertake for the third time, and I had just arranged for myself a weekend in Paris. But what energy and what gallantry of the P.M. who is only just back from Quebec!

October 7
Off to Moscow again.

Train from Paddington at 6.30 to Lyneham. Pug Ismay, Bob Dixon and me. We are to join A.E. and Guy at the airfield at midnight.

October 8
Wake up at 6 over Italy – 6 hours! We landed at 7 near Naples just before a tremendous downpour. The P.M. had landed just before us and looked as fresh as paint in a tropical suit. Wilson, Alexander and Macmillan to meet the party. Rex Leeper there with his Greek P.M. Papandreou whom he wanted to introduce to A.E. We drove on to Naples and Posilippo where Macmillan and Wilson have their villas.

Start off again at 11.30 for Cairo. 3 aeroplanes. Landed at Cairo West airfield about 6.30 in the dark. Dinner party at Moyne's. P.M., A.E., C.I.G.S., Pug, Paget, Terence Shone and Moran. The electric light went out just as we started but it came on again. P.M. in his boiler suit.

Drove back to the airfield again in time to start at midnight. Here we found the P.M.'s York had injured itself in landing in the dark and it was *hors de combat*. Hasty reshuffle as a result of which P.M. and party came into our York and four of us had to go separately.

October 9
Slept late – flying very high above the clouds when I woke about 9 – rather bumpy. Landed at Moscow at 4.

October 10
Up at 9. A luncheon party for us at 2.30. Stalin and Molotov hosts, P.M. and A.E. principal guests, about 40 people in all. P.M. in khaki, Stalin in khaki too, sat side by side. Stalin thinner and sprucer than last year. His uniform better fitting. All the Soviet diplomats and commissars in uniform now – grey uniforms with gold epaulettes. I liked them better in their drab suits. Toasts began with the caviare, incessant toasts and over-long speeches by P.M., Stalin and Molotov. We hadn't got to the principal dish by 4.30!

At 7, A.E., the Ambassador and I went to Kremlin for our first talk on the Balkans. It lasted till 9. A.E. then went and dined with P.M. at his dacha and I to the Embassy.

October 11
A.E., Archie Clark-Kerr and I went to see Molotov again at 3 to continue our discussion on Bulgaria, Hungary and Yugoslavia. Conversation was markedly easier than yesterday and we got broadly what we wanted. This was presumably the result of A.E.'s plain speaking then.[1]

1. See Eden, *The Reckoning* p. 482–483. The P.M. had made his percentage proposals over the Balkans the day before.

We hear the Poles are arriving tomorrow in response to the invitation sent them from here yesterday.

Dinner at 9 at the Embassy. Stalin dining here for the first time ever to meet the P.M. and A.E. About 30 people. P.M. and Stalin both in their khaki uniforms.

After dinner Stalin spoke to P.M. about Warsaw and said, almost pleading, how it had been military difficulties and nothing else which had prevented it being freed. It was quite untrue that he had deliberately desisted. P.M. accepted this and said he had never believed the reports to this effect. Stalin said he could not say this publicly while the battle was on. P.M. then urged necessity for real Polish settlement because of effects on Anglo–Soviet relations. If two sets of Poles could not agree, then G.B. and Russia should impose a settlement. We had gone into war because of Poland though we had no sordid or material interest: British people would not understand if we abandoned Polish people.

October 12
Poles arrived this morning. Mick, Romer and Grabski.[1] They called this evening for a preliminary talk. Further talks at Kremlin with Molotov about Bulgaria and Yugoslavia. Much better going than the previous day.

October 13
P.M. and A.E., Stalin and Molotov saw London Poles together. At later meeting they saw Lublin Poles. Former were stubborn and refused to make even the proposals they had already made through Lebedev in London. Latter [Lublin Poles] produced a poor impression on P.M.[2] and A.E. (I wasn't there).

October 14
P.M. summoned the Poles to the Embassy at 12 and addressed them on the previous night's proceedings. He told them he was convinced the Curzon Line was the main issue and if the Poles would accept that he would get compensation for them in the West and the general help and support both of the Soviet Government and of H.M.G. If the Poles refused, he could do nothing more for them. He then proceeded to draft a document which should be agreed for this purpose by the three parties and undertook to show it as from himself to Stalin that

1. Stanislaw Grabski, President of Polish National Council.
2. The Prime Minister described them as "inverted Quislings".

afternoon. He would ask Stalin if he could get the Poles to accept it, would Stalin? The meeting broke up without any conclusion.

Early in the afternoon the Poles called on the P.M. and he again warned them in the strongest terms of the consequences of refusal to accept a settlement on the lines of the Memorandum. He then went off to see Stalin who, rather grudgingly, agreed to it.

October 15
We repaired to P.M.'s town house for a further meeting with Poles. On arrival we learned P.M. unwell. At 12.30 Poles arrived and P.M. appeared in his boiler suit. There ensued a terrific conversation. We first went through the document which P.M. had shown Stalin guaranteeing to Poland E. Prussia, Danzig, Oppeln and up to Oder in West in return for acceptance of Curzon Line in East, together with a united Polish Government in Lublin, with which both H.M.G. and Soviet Government would deal. This document the P.M. now wished to be authorised to give to Stalin as having been accepted by the Poles. Poles first asked for Stettin. P.M. was ready to give this, but A.E. demurred because of British opinion and effect on Germany. But the final blow came when Mick said he could not agree to P.M. giving the document to Stalin unless it gave the Poles Lvov too. P.M. blew up and rated Mick most soundly as unrealistic, as sacrificing his people and his country for a single town, as irresponsibly sowing the seeds of future wars. Nothing would move Mick who sat impassive while the P.M. raged. From time to time things were calmer but then the storm blew up again until the P.M. lost his temper. Up and down the room he paced, threatening and cursing. "I will have nothing more to do with you." "I don't care where you go." "You only deserve to be in your Pripet marshes." "I shall indict you." All through this Mick remained firm and impassive. He said he could agree to nothing which did not include Lvov. Finally the P.M. left the room, and we showed the Poles to their car.

A painful scene to witness – the P.M. so right and the Poles so foolish – like Bourbons expecting everything to come back to them.

After lunch A.E. had another go with them at the Embassy. They didn't move. All they asked was that P.M. should appeal to Stalin about Lvov but not hand him in the document.

All pretty hopeless.

Now this evening we hear the P.M. has a temperature and wasn't able to attend the second conversation with Stalin on military plans which A.E. went to instead.

A.E. spoke again to Stalin and Molotov about Lvov without handing the document. S. and M. firmly declined, saying they could not cede Lvov because it belonged to the Ukraine which was now to be set up as an independent State. All very friendly but unmovable – as we expected.

P.M.'s temperature now 101 and he seems to be heading for fresh bout of illness. Doctors and nurses being summoned from Cairo.

October 16
First news this morning is that P.M. is better and temperature normal again. Lord Moran's M. & B. pills have cured him as they cured me.

The Poles came to the Embassy at 12.30 and we talked to them on the terrace in the sunshine. They seemed to budge a little. Mick agreed that if the Curzon Line could be described in the document not as a frontier but as a demarcation line, they would agree to accept it. We doubted if Stalin would agree since what he wants is finality but it was agreed to speak to the P.M. about it. Mick admitted that in fact it would mean the same and imply a final settlement but it would be easier for his people.

At 3.30 we all went to the P.M.'s villa when he appeared again, just as before in his boiler suit, but he was much more kindly to the Poles. He agreed to put the revised document to Stalin with the word demarcation and to do his best. Mick said if this were agreed he would ask to see Stalin alone and ask him who was the leading Polish communist in order that he might meet him and discuss the new united government. Altogether a more promising attitude.

P.M. is to see Stalin this evening. A.E. is seeing Molotov about odds and ends.

The military talks have been most satisfactory. Our soldiers delighted at the extent the Russians have disclosed all their plans – a thing they have never done before. A.E. enormously impressed by Stalin's mastery of these military matters.

We heard tonight result of P.M.'s further talk with Stalin about the Curzon Line and Lvov. Stalin refused to accept the proposed description as a demarcation line. This was passed on to the Poles by the P.M. and A.E. later. They were urged to reflect again over the full acceptance of the word "frontier" as proposed before.

October 17
Poles came round at 12 to say that they could not agree to accept the word "frontier" for the Curzon Line. Mick however was prepared to

do this. He had asked to see Berut with whom he was ready to discuss the formation of the united Polish Govt. and he wanted to see Stalin alone to tell him of his plans. If he could get a satisfactory agreement out of Berut and Stalin about the future Government he would return at once to London, get his government to accept and then return to Moscow and go on to Lublin.

This is certainly a step forward and A.E. will recommend it to Molotov at luncheon. He and P.M. see Stalin again at 10 to-night.

October 18
Mick has seen Berut, Pres. of P.N.C., who while urging need for union, asked for absolute majority in new government.

A.E. and P.M. saw Stalin last night at 10 – stayed till 4! P.M. very garrulous and repetitive, A.E. said. Stalin said he had no intention of making any country Communist although he could do so if he wanted. That was a Russian affair!

Mick saw Stalin this evening – he was friendly and not discouraging over formation of united government. Mick fairly confident now wishes to start for London tomorrow and then return as quickly as possible.

October 19
Off to airfield at 9.30 a.m.

October 20
Arrive Cairo 7.30 a.m. Breakfast at Embassy. Sunshine. Rather weary.

Out to Mena at 5 to Moyne's villa, where P.M. is staying. Long conference about Syria. The old question of getting rid of Spears which P.M. can't bring himself to do. Moyne wanted both us and French to agree to clear out of Syria. But this clearly impossible. I impressed on A.E. that French position in Syria must be considered in relation to our own in Egypt, Iraq and Palestine. If we weaken the French in Syria, we weaken our own positions. Syrians incapable of governing themselves without some foreign supervision. French only people who can do it. We discovered that British army is using Syria as a training ground and building semi-permanent barracks there. This annoyed even P.M. who said it was gross waste of money to build in other people's country, apart from feeding French suspicion of our intentions. All G.H.Q. here – Paget[1] and Clayton and Moyne – very anti-French. P.M. let out about Arabs and Jews – "The Arabs have done nothing for us except to revolt against us in Iraq." He said

1. General Paget had become C-in-C Middle East 1944–46.

he didn't want to upset them in Syria because of the pill – Zionism – which he knew they would have to swallow in Palestine.

October 21

Off to Mena at 9 and on the airfield at 10.30. Take off at 11 for Naples. Land about 6 p.m. (4 p.m. local time). I drove to Naples with Harold Macmillan and Kit Steel[1] who had come out to meet us. P.M. and party staying at Wilson's villa and me at Macmillan's next-door one at Posillipo.

October 22

Airborne at 10.15.

November 4

I have neglected my diary. I've just had a few days off and before that I was clearing up the affairs of our trip.

Poles have subsided into hopeless discussion. Mick who talked of 48 hours only being necessary to get his Government's agreement, has failed and begun prevaricating himself by saying he must wait until he hears from President Roosevelt. He has also advanced a demand for Stettin which P.M. foolishly has conceded. No British Government could ever guarantee Stettin for Poland.

Meanwhile Russian activities in Roumania and Persia[2] are scarcely reassuring to us or to the Poles.

Recognition at last given to Provisional Government of France[3] giving us minimum credit for what should have been a major gesture. We couldn't have been more stupid – thanks to P.M. and President. De G. has now invited P.M. to visit Paris for armistice celebrations on Nov. 11th – just in time because the P.M. was determined to go anyway, even unasked, and would have been quite capable of driving up and down the Champs Elysées without even calling on de G.

November 11

No progress last week with the Poles after A.E. got back. They are

1. Later Sir Christopher Steel, later British Ambassador in Bonn.
2. They were demanding oil concessions from Persia.
3. Roosevelt had again bowled a fast one by asking the U.S. representative in Paris to recognise without telling the British Government, or his own State Department. This was later said to have been a mistake; but it is interesting that this confusing action took place whilst the Prime Minister and Foreign Secretary were flying about the Middle East.

still holding out for the moon, i.e. a U.S. guarantee as well as Lublin. The longer Mick delays here, the clearer it is to Stalin how weak and powerless he is in the hands of the emigrés. Meanwhile the Lublin Committee must be strengthening their hold and I hope they are, because I believe the future belongs with them. A.E. has rather lost interest. He lost hold by stopping off in Greece and Italy instead of coming straight back to London and pursuing it here with the Polish Government.

Meanwhile Roosevelt re-elected by thumping votes, proving wrong all the Gallup polls who were hedging on a fine-run thing. I think it is best so – all in all – though there is much which is reprehensible in that power-intoxicated old man, as in our own P.M.

P.M. and A.E. went off to Paris on Friday. We all tremble for the result. P.M. being still violently anti-de G. (and anti-French in consequence) and A.E. *boudeur* at having to play second fiddle. De G., on other hand, is believed to be in a nasty and clamorous mood, anxious for the Paris meeting to be a counterpart to the Moscow meeting, marking France's "come-back". Both P.M. and A.E. are determined that it shall be a visit of ceremony only and not a diplomatic discussion. The one bright spot is that agreement has been reached by Russia, ourselves and America to France joining the E.A.C. as a permanent member. This is immense and I doubt it would have happened so quickly had not Russia bounced us by agreeing at once and telling the French so first. We then had to follow.

Not only this but the P.M. has banned any discussion of the Western Group plan for closer association with the Dutch, Belgians and French. Spaak came over last week specially to talk of all this, having been encouraged by A.E. to do so, and when he came, we could only look down our noses and say H.M.G. had had no time to study it at all and what were Spaak's views? I'm afraid a good deal of this must be put down to A.E.'s failure to prepare the ground with the P.M. and in turn to his old trouble of trying to do too much – H. of C. etc. He never has time to read our papers now and so his handling has become very superficial. A mixture of "intuition" (ominous word!) and past experience. Neither he nor the P.M. have yet given serious thought even to the future of Germany. Bad enough in the P.M., but worse in the Foreign Secretary.

Against this it must be said, I think, that A.E. is tired of the constant struggle with the P.M. who becomes more headstrong every day. As the purely military problems simplify themselves, the old boy's tireless energy leads to ever closer attention to foreign affairs.

The prospect of the old septuagenarian girding himself for a party election next spring must be pretty disheartening for him.

November 14
P.M.'s visit to Paris an outstanding success and all our forebodings dispelled. He and A.E. had an overwhelming reception as we knew they would and its warmth melted the old man as well as de G. None of the thorny subjects were mentioned in the political conversations which the P.M. attended, above all not Syria. A.E. had further talks with Bidault whom he liked.

November 15
Off to Paris for the weekend and tried to go yesterday but weather impossible. Through these empty streets to the Embassy and then on to Adrian Holman's flat, Avenue d'Iena, for a very late lunch. A wonderful flat which had belonged to Mumm, the German champagne King.

After lunch I walked through empty streets again – a few horse cabs about – old fiacres painted yellow with broken down horses as in Sickert's fresco – and bicycles with trailers attached for hire. People in the streets tired-looking – hectic, not well dressed and wearing fantastic high hats – turbans, pyramids, mitres, and solid wooden high heeled shoes.

Talked with Duff sitting in the Ambassador's study. Duff told me how successful the visit had been. He also told me that the night before, stirred up by the Beaver, A.E. and the P.M. had rung him up to suggest the whole thing be put off because it wasn't safe for the P.M. Duff had replied that it would be just the same next week or whenever he came, and he took full responsibility for advising them to come.

November 26
Mikolajczyk resigned on Friday having found ¾ of his Cabinet against him over Moscow proposals. This in spite of the arrival of Harriman with a message from Roosevelt offering to make a further appeal to Stalin for Lvov! However, we all felt this clears the air. We were getting into an impossible position with the Poles continually pressing for further *précisions* and commitments from H.M.G. as a price for accepting the Moscow plan. They had got as far as asking us to guarantee Stettin and the British worm was just about to turn. We had in fact proposed to A.E. that it would be folly to guarantee any

line which British public opinion would not approve, that far-reaching claims up the Oder would never be approved by either British or U.S. opinion, thus bringing the whole settlement into disrepute, and that, late as it was, it would be wise to attempt to reach agreement with Stalin on a new Curzon Line for Western Poland, having some relation to practical reality, i.e. not going beyond Oppeln on the Oder. Stalin would of course have suspected our motives as softness for Germany, and the Poles would have screamed. However, the Polish Government by refusing have got us out of all that.

New P.G. not yet formed.

December 6
A new P.G. was formed by Archicevski, a Socialist leader, who had been until recently in Poland. This Government has no Peasants in it and is a façade for anti-Russian and reactionary forces. We are being "correct but cold".

Trouble with communists and Resistance leaders in Belgium and in Greece. In both British troops obliged to intervene. Greece particularly bad, Elam-Elas[1] trying to seize power. Trouble also in Italy where the Communists are also sabotaging the Government. I suppose these upsets are inevitable after 4 years of war and German occupation, but they are disturbing. France alone, so far, thanks to General de G., is standing up to it.

December 7
Bevin at lunch with A.E. today gave an exposition, a damaging one, of U.S. planning and strategy. He said the Americans had planned that the war would be over by Xmas and that all supplies and shipping thereafter should go the Far East. This had had calamitous consequences. Labour in U.S. had laid off war work in large numbers, and all ships newly built were being ear-marked for Pacific. But the U.S. strategy of the war had defeated their purpose. Our plan was that Alexander should go on pushing in Italy and that Montgomery should go on pushing in France – but the U.S. had insisted first on the South of France expedition which had hamstrung Alexander and made a disastrous diversion of our supplies. Then, after the collapse of German resistance in France and Belgium, the U.S. had insisted on attacking in five places between Holland and Switzerland instead of

1. The Communists. This revolt had started when the Papandreou Government had proposed that the guerrilla bands should be dissolved. British troops under General Scobie had been in Athens since October 14.

concentrating all on one, i.e. in the North. (A.E. confirmed this and said it was Monty's view.) In consequence we are now bogged down for the winter. The liberated countries of Europe are clamouring for food and raw materials, and the necessary shipping is earmarked for the Far East.

I always thought it was an unwise decision to put Eisenhower in command of the battle in place of Montgomery and I foresee a demand before long for a change in the high command. Poor E. who has never been in any war before, is not the man for this – admirable though he is as a manager of lines of communications. He is a conciliator, not a general.

A.E., in very good heart in spite of all our troubles, said P.M. very up and down. Yesterday he'd said he wanted "to fight it out" in Greece, today he wished to clear out of Greece altogether.

December 15
Stalin has told us he doesn't think Mick is now any use. Agents of Polish Govt. are attacking Soviet people. He thinks we should concentrate now on making something of Lublin Committee.

There is to be a debate on Poland on Friday so H.M.G. must make up their minds. There is no real alternative to gradual switch over, I think. We should reduce our dealings with P.G. here to a minimum necessary for maintenance of Polish troops in West, and begin discreet contact with Lublin. But Lublin Committee are pretty small fry and scarcely more representative than P.G. here. I hope we can defer matters till Warsaw is freed and some real consultation with Polish people in Poland is possible.

There is much to be said for Russian claims to play leading part in East (Poland, Czechoslovakia, Hungary, Bulgaria and Roumania) as we claim in West (Greece, Belgium, France, Italy etc.). We can't have our cake and eat it as H.M.G. always expect. We have no evidence that Joe has stirred up Communist troubles in our areas.

De Gaulle in Moscow, we hear today, has concluded a Franco–Soviet Pact. Stalin asked us in advance what our views would be. We replied we saw no objection and much advantage provided conditions harmonised with Anglo–Soviet Pact, and suggested there might be advantage in trying to make a Tripartite Agreement. Stalin agreed and told the French so. This sent de G. through the roof, he saw our cloven hoof in this and at once concluded we wished to diminish France in some way. The reverse was the case. We at once telegraphed to Moscow to reassure Bidault (who had never consulted us in advance as Stalin had done) and explained that our anxiety was to secure harmony between all 3 and if bipartite agreements were preferred, we had no objection.

As part of the U.S. planning for the F.E. war mentioned above, the President has proposed to switch all shipping over to Pacific as from January 1st apart from military supplies and bare disorder and disease standard of supplies for civilians. This would upset careful plans just made for gradual increase of supplies of food and raw material and spell confusion and chaos to all the liberated countries of Europe whose Governments anyway are having difficulty in maintaining themselves and can only do so if a fairly normal life can be quickly restored. This is another fight for Europe we have to wage with the U.S.

December 17

Polish debate went well. P.M. came out flat for Curzon Line and so did A.E. showing how we had always favoured that line in past and had warned Poles against going further East. But Right Wing opinion here, propaganded by the Poles, is very hostile.

Spears has been sacked at last. The P.M. was finally persuaded to recall him after the Paris visit. Our stupidity remedied after great and unnecessary harm done to Anglo–French relations and to the war effort.

December 21

A.E. summoned me to join him at a conference with P.M. at 10.30 p.m. last night about Polish communications. We met in the bowels of the earth in the Defence Map room. P.M. in his boiler suit rather sozzled, A.E. in his bottle green smoking coat, Portal, Archie Sinclair and Selborne.[1] P.M. bellicose and repetitive, repeating snatches from the long speeches to the Poles we heard in Moscow, very anti-Polish Govt. in London, but equally anti-Lublin Committee. It was decided to check the former's communications still more, to reduce their funds, to send liaison officers into German Poland to see what is going on, to send supplies also as far as possible, but not to send any corresponding mission to Lublin.

P.M. fired a burst at Metrop. of Athens[2] whom he accused of being a Quisling. He said we had got two fussy-wuzzies there – meaning

1. Lord Selborne, Minister of Economic Warfare 1942–1945.
2. Damaskinos. Leeper had suggested on December 10 that he should be appointed Regent. This the King refused to do.

Macmillan and Leeper. (I'm afraid he has got Greece very wrong; about Poland he is much sounder.)

Rundstedt's offensive is a shock to everyone.[1] We were taken by surprise.

December 24
Greek business at a standstill mainly because of P.M. who now wants to go out to Greece himself. As if he hadn't enough to do with attending to the battle. He is set against pressing the King any more to agree to the Metrop. of Athens becoming Regent, although both Alex. Macmillan and Leeper, as well as A.E., urge it. The King remains wooden and obstinate.

Battle news not very reassuring yet.

I heard this afternoon that P.M. and A.E. are off to Athens tonight. P.M. insisted on going and A.E. insisted on going too.

December 29
P.M. and A.E. home this afternoon. As a result the K. of Greece is to be told we insist on his appointing the Archbishop sole Regent with powers to form a new Government. This is the solution which the Embassy and the F.O. have been urging for weeks but which P.M. and King G. flatly refused to accept. Now however the P.M. has seen the Archbp., he has fallen for him. But the fighting still goes on.

1. The German attack through the Ardennes.

1945

January 13

Greek armistice signed at last. Not peace yet. But it looks that the Elam/Elas clique are near the end of their tether and that their followers will abandon them as soon as they dare. At least that is our hope because we cannot undertake operations extending over the rest of Greece. The Archbishop[1] is playing up well and Plastiras[2] seems to be the right man too – a guarantee against the Royalists and a guarantee against disorders.

I'm now responsible for Italy, having shed Poland and Czecho and Hungary in the recent F.O. reorganisation. I'm glad and find it amusing to bring up to date my old knowledge of Italy. And not so out of date either! The problem is to infuse any political life into the Italians. Then there is need to emphasise *unity* of Italy, the fact that Northern Italy must look to Rome Government and not be tempted to set up a new Government in rivalry. There are good partisans fighting in the North. They have more trouble with the New Fascists than with the Germans – a civil war there already. We must do all we can to knit N. and S. together – liaison and exchanges of personnel etc. to enhance position of Rome Govt. and to help with supplies of food, and raw material.

Military situation in West rather better. Our troubles there were due to SHAEF and local commanders being taken by surprise. This was pretty bad as it was the weak spot in the line and the classic point of German offensive in France. But this was due in turn to a faulty system of strategy. The old fault of spreading out the troops equally and evenly like butter on a piece of bread and making little attacks everywhere, which is exactly what Eisenhower did in Tunis till Alexander was brought in. Montgomery always opposed this at SHAEF, I believe, and it is an irony that he had to be brought in to take charge of the Northern half of the bulge when the break occurred.

Big Three are to meet at Yalta at the end of the month. Alec

1. The ELAS had asked for terms soon after the appointment of the Archbishop as Regent.
2. General Plastiras became Prime Minister.

Cadogan is going this time. It will be the usual scramble leading to the usual half-digested decisions.

January 18
The familiar struggle over the French has begun again. This time about their attendance at the Big Three meeting at the end of the month. We and Stalin favour it. The President is against. Are we going to acquiesce in the President's veto again?

January 20
Troubles with King Peter reaching bursting point. He refuses to sign the Tito–Subasic[1] Agreement, encouraged by his womenfolk. Now he has refused to see Ralph Stevenson[2] who was to tell him today on behalf of the P.M. that unless he agrees, we shall carry out the agreement without him.

January 24
A.E. and I dined with Massigli alone on Monday. A.E. put it point blank to Massigli "Do you want a treaty[3] with us or not?" M. said "Certainly" A.E. "We cannot go on our knees to you!" M. said the people in Paris were at present scratching their heads as to whether they should first try and reach agreement with us over joint policy to Germany or not. A.E. said he thought better not. Now was the time when neither the Russians nor the Americans could object. M. said he entirely agreed and this was what they had urged in Paris. A.E. also said he thought if the French tried to bring in the Levant etc. it would also be a mistake. M. again agreed.

We then discussed the next meeting of 3. Would the French be asked? A.E. said he couldn't say but he could say that we had favoured France being asked when the idea first came up. M. knew all about the U.S. attitude.

P.M. very anti-de G. again. I fear little hope of his agreeing to press the Pres. to let the F. come. But they have now asked to be asked and a reply must go.

February 3
Russian advance has carried the attack to within 50 miles of Berlin.

1. Ivan Subasic, Yugoslav Prime Minister 1944–1945.
2. Ambassador to Yugoslavia 1943–1946.
3. An Anglo-French Treaty had first been proposed by the French after the conclusion of the Franco-Soviet Pact.

374

We have now weighed in with a heavy air attack on Berlin. Unfortunately the W. front is static. But it must be pretty bad in Germany now. It looks as if it might end by a Nazi withdrawal southwards on to Bavaria.

P.M. flatly refused to press Pres. to invite de G. to the talks. We shall pay bitterly for these snubs to France later on. It is the old tragedy of Anglo–French relations after the last war renewing itself. Nobody else now wants to cold-shoulder F. – only those two power-besotted old men.

February 14

Crimean Conference over. General result not bad. An agreement has been reached over Poland. There is to be a new Polish Government, neither London nor Lublin, which all will recognise. Largely face-saving, as I suspect the new Polish Gt. will be much more Lublin than London.

Our people were impressed by strong opposition not only of President but of Stalin to allow French in on anything. We battled hard and won over giving the French a zone in Germany and a seat on Control Commission. But we lost over their being partners in Reparation Commission or in Committee of A.E., Gusev and Winant to consider Dismemberment.[1]

It is lamentable that Russia should be holding out over Reparations after all lessons of Versailles – but this Commission may help to bury it. To discuss Dismemberment without France is of course folly but I guess A.E. intends to bring them in it somehow. Our people have lightheartedly agreed in principle to "Dismemberment" without any profound thought on the subject or indeed Cabinet authority. Both Pres. and Stalin very strong on this. I hope however in the end dismemberment will be fined down to Rhenania, Austria, E. Prussia, Silesia, leaving the remainder a unit which we can hold down and control.

I hear Roosevelt was looking much older and scraggier – very different from the chubby smiling torso I saw in Washington 18 months ago. In the photographs he has a Wilson look.

February 25

Came down to Binderton yesterday to stay for the visit of Bidault, French Foreign Minister, who arrives this afternoon with Chauvel[2]

1. Of Germany.
2. Jean Chauvel, later French Ambassador in London 1955–1962.

and Duff. A.E. had invited him from Cairo on his way back from
Crimea to tell him of the Conference. Fortunately de G. allowed him
to accept. There has been something of a row over de G.'s refusal to
meet Pres. R. at Algiers at very short notice as latter was on way back
to U.S.A. – most people think de G. wrong over this.

February 28
Our Frenchmen duly arrived and we met them at Tangmere. Hardly
had we had tea than we settled down to business. Bidault v. highly
strung, kept returning again and again to the omission of France from
Yalta and the future meetings of Foreign Secretaries. A.E. could only
point to what was being done for France – a zone in Germany, a seat
in Berlin, invitation to San Francisco etc. but said he could not
possibly say the Big 3 should never meet again without France. It was
a case of the military weight of France at the present time and the
overwhelming responsibility of Big 3 for conduct of war. Bidault kept
jumping up and making impassioned little speeches, Massigli and
Chauvel both looking slightly embarassed. We had dinner for eight
and afterwards went on again till midnight. France claimed that she
must never be left out anywhere again or, as B. said, she would lead
the malcontents and "go the way of Italy after the last war". France
claimed an exclusive zone of occupation of Rhineland as far as Cologne,
the Ruhr and the rest being under international control. As for the
Anglo–French Treaty, France wanted it but wished first to have
agreement with us about Levant and Germany. A.E. pointed out that
the Russian treaties had not been held up for general agreement on
other things; it was concerned only with German aggression. Finally,
it came out that France had refused to accept to be an inviting party to
San Francisco because she hadn't been a party to the Dumbarton Oaks
and Yalta discussions. A.E. was aghast and pointed to the deplorable
impression which this would create in Washington. Could not France
accept but explain to U.S., S.R. and G.B. that she must be free to
propose amendments? Here Massigli intervened and made suggestions
for a change in text of invitation itself which would meet French. It
was agreed to go into this with Winant and Cadogan next morning.
Very tired.

Next morning we came up to London and Bidault and A.E.,
Massigli and Duff lunched with P.M. and stayed till 4.30. All over
much the same ground, I gather. In the evening we had a Government
dinner for Bidault attended by P.M. who couldn't have been more
friendly and mellow and made one of his famous speeches in French.

But the talks left us nowhere.

I'm afraid the Anglo–F. Treaty is down the drain for ever. How Daladier or Mandel or Poincaré would have jumped at it! I wasn't greatly impressed by Bidault, honest and sincere, but a light-weight, I thought, very jumpy understandably enough in an ex-resistance leader in Paris – but how much better poor Vienot would have been.

March 31
I have not written in my diary for days. I have just had a week in Paris and feel less tired. But goodness, how tired we all are!

The German war is rapidly ending. We are across the Rhine and racing across Germany almost unresisted. It looks as if we might reach Berlin even before the Russians.

Diplomatically it is not all so good. Relations with the Russians are deteriorating. Not a single one of the decisions of the much heralded Crimean Conference which has not been sabotaged by them. The Polish business drags on; the negotiations in Moscow to set up a new Polish Govt. are being steadily blocked by Molotov who is refusing to accept our nominees, even Mikolajczyk, to the conference. The Russians are behaving disgracefully in Roumania, setting up the worst, even collaborationist elements, and pillaging the oil wells. And now Molotov refuses to go to San Francisco. How on earth are we going to agree over Germany? They are even preventing our officers from visiting the released British P. of W. in Poland.

April 5
Steady and almost unresisted progress into Germany from West. But on East the Russians are still on the Oder. Are the Germans deliberately fighting harder in the E.? We know that Stalin suspects it.

Great doubts as to whether San Francisco should take place at this point. Cranborne[1] has developed personal doubts about the honesty of the proposals[2] themselves in view of Russian attitude and has written to P.M. to say he cannot honestly defend them in H. of L. P.V.E.E. told me about this and said Bobbety had authorised him to do so. I said I personally thought San F. should be postponed because it was too dangerous for A.E., Bobbety and Attlee to be away from London just when Germany cracking – it would leave the field free to the P.M., the Beaver and Lord Cherwell. But I did hope Bobbety wouldn't resign on it, which would be frightful.

1. At this time Secretary of State for Dominions.
2. The setting up of UNO.

And now at this moment the French have come forward with a proposal to conclude a treaty with us at once. If only they had thought like this before, in January or even in March, but now, on the eve of San Francisco, even I do rather doubt its timeliness and fear for the reactions of P.M.

April 8
Bidault, pressed by Massigli and Chauvel, has suddenly come forward with a jump and wants to conclude a Treaty or Alliance with us at once – in a week, in advance of San Francisco, and Chauvel proposes to come over here on Tues. armed with drafts. A.E. is all in favour and would welcome an Anglo–French Treaty now, because of Russia. P.M. is anti, and furious with Duff whom he suspects, wrongly, of having initiated the whole thing. We don't yet know where we are.

I would like Chauvel to come and discuss. But I am doubtful whether any quick agreement is possible because I think the French still cling to their old idea of clearing up Syria and Rhineland first – and that won't be simple – and also they have different ideas from us about automatic operation of Treaties.

April 11
Consent finally wrung out of reluctant P.M. to Chauvel coming to talk only, without commitment. What an absurd fuss.

April 13
Roosevelt dead. A tremendous shock to everyone. One thinks inevitably of Lincoln and the consequences of his death on the morrow of victory. How on earth will Truman be? Quite unknown abroad. Who will guide U.S. policy in this critical year?

A.E. goes off tonight to the funeral. San Francisco is still on.

April 18
As a gesture to Truman, Stalin has sent Molotov to San Francisco – so the three Foreign Secretaries will meet after all.

Chauvel has never come. We think because A.E. had to go off sooner than expected because of Roosevelt. I hope now that Bidault may tackle A.E. at San Francisco.

April 19
P.M. still pursuing savage vendetta against France. Nothing is right that the poor people do now! What folly this is. The old man will leave

us without a friend in the world. Instead of building the French up, we take every opportunity to denigrate them.

April 25
Himmler yesterday sent word through a Swede to Stockholm that Hitler was ill and nearly dead in Berlin and that he, Himmler, was now ready to order the armies on the West to surrender, but not those on the East. He was ready to meet Eisenhower for the purpose.

We are informing the Russians and telling them that we are replying that there can only be unconditional surrender simultaneously on all fronts.

Meanwhile the Russians have encircled Berlin and are fighting in the town.

In Washington complete deadlock in Polish talks between Molotov, A.E. and Stettinius.[1] We stated our position on the B.B.C. tonight. A show-down!

April 26
Pétain has arrived in Switzerland to give himself up to the French. The Swiss only allowed him in on this condition. The Germans allowed him to leave of course in order to embarrass the French.

For the same reason we expect Leopold of Belgium to turn up. From the German point of view neither of these hostages are worth shooting – quite the contrary they are delayed action bombs to be left among the Allies.

I'm only afraid the P.M. may rush to their rescue! He is now very definitely on the side of fallen royalty. Hapsburgs, Hohenzollens or Glucksburgs.

April 28
No reply from Himmler yet. Berlin nearly entirely occupied by the Russians. Junction of U.S. and Russian forces announced today near Dresden. Germany cut in two. Hitler still said to be in Berlin and half-dead. Goering sacked and reported fled or dead. Musso reported captured alive by the Italian partisans in the North of Italy. Nothing certain about any of them. It can't last much longer.

P.M. proposes that when resistance ceases the armies should stand still on their existing lines while 4 Power Control Commission is set up in Berlin to regulate the orderly withdrawal to the 4 allotted zones.

1. Edward R. Stettinius, U.S. Secretary of State 1944–1945.

He wishes before withdrawal to secure from Russians agreement to pooling of all German resources – i.e. food from Russian zone of Germany to be available for British and U.S. zones in West – hard bargaining is the only thing the Russians understand.

At San Francisco[1] Molotov behaving pretty badly. Cooperation with Russia in peace is going to be very difficult, if possible at all.

The French are demanding Cologne for their zone of occupation. Massigli came yesterday to say he had been told "to insist". This will cause fresh ill-will on both sides for they won't get it and it really is an unnecessary demand. Poor Massigli evidently quite agreed.

April 29
Soviet Government have announced setting up of a Provisional Government for Austria under Renner, an old Social Democrat of 75. This is a fast one. They told us only a day ago that they were contemplating this. We telegraphed at once to say wait till we, the U.S.A. and the French (who are all equally responsible) can think it over. Only 1/10th of Austria is yet free. It is quite unnecessary to set up a Government yet – apart from a town council for Vienna. In any case it is intended that representatives of H.M.G., U.S. and France should arrive any day now to discuss zones and provisional machinery. A very fast one. We are proposing to protest.

Musso alleged shot by Partisans in Milan. A general break-up of the front is taking place. First trouble will be at Trieste which Tito is claiming and which we intend to occupy for our communications to Austria. We are hoping for a *modus vivendi* by which Alex takes what he wants without reference to frontiers or their future. Behind Tito is of course Stalin – and here is another place for a clash.

April 30
P.M. is havering about appointing Montgomery as British C. in C. in Germany. He also wants to appoint Desmond Morton as deputy! Although possibly Alex would be better than Monty, I feel it would be an injustice.

German surrender on Italian front fixed for May 2. One war ended!

Meanwhile the Russians tell us they don't wish our missions to go to Vienna till all is clear at E.A.C. This together with the setting up of new Austrian Government seems to show an unpleasant determina-

1. The San Francisco Conference opened on April 25. Molotov immediately objected to Stettinius taking the Chair.

tion to fix things in Austria before we arrive. But Patton[1] and Patch[2] are now getting into Austria from Bavaria, and the German surrender on Italian front takes with it Vorarlberg, Tyrol and part of Carinthia. Then we have this impending row over Trieste with Tito.

May 2
Hitler dead today. Doenitz takes on.

We understand however surrender on Italian front still stands and will occur at midday today.

May 3
Surrender on Italian front took place last night. Over a million men.

May 4
Germans still trying to surrender to us and not to Russians. Monty told one lot that they couldn't surrender "backwards" i.e. to us, but only to the Russians whom they were facing.

We seem to be in Trieste after all – only a few Yugoslav partisans already there first.

May 5
Germans have surrendered in Holland and Denmark to Monty – another million men.

Today we believe Keitel will surrender Norway – only Czechoslovakia remains. Doenitz and Himmler said to be joining up there to resist the Russians.

Tito very angry about Trieste but we are there all right. We are also overrunning Southern Austria from Bavaria.

May 5 and 6
Days of expectation. Doenitz believed to be about to agree to sign universal capitulation on all fronts to us and Russians – instead of partial surrender of Norway etc.

We are only partly in Trieste, i.e. in the harbour, but the Partisans are in the upper town. Acrimonious messages between Tito and Alex.

Conversations over Poland at San F. suspended because of disclosure that the 15 non-Lublin Poles in Warsaw have been arrested by

1. Major-General George Patton, Commander of the U.S. 7th Army 1943–44, and Commander of the 3rd Army 1944.
2. General A. M. Patch, Commander of Ground Forces Guadalcanal 1943, was now commanding the U.S. 7th Army.

the Russians on charges of conspiracy. We are moving towards a
show-down with Russia. Meanwhile we are overrunning as much of
Germany and Austria as possible to increase our bargaining weight.

May 7
Total surrender of all of remaining German garrisons signed last
night at SHAEF HQ. Russian General signing also, effective from
midnight tonight.

A good deal of confusion. Eisenhower now off to Berlin tomorrow
to meet Zukov and obtain signature by Keitel of ratification of
surrender. This may delay announcement of V.E. day.

May 8
V.E. day at last though Russians finally wanted to hold everything for
9th because Germans still fighting Russians in Czechoslovakia.

May 9
Fighting in Czechoslovakia still going on. One bad thing. Eisenhower
refused to go on from Pilsen into Prague where the Germans were
fighting the Patriots though urged to do so by P.M. because of the
Russians. Another 12 hours at least might have been gained and we
would have had another pledge for Russian good behaviour.

June 10
I've left off my diary for a month since the day of peace. Since then
we've had a row with Tito over Trieste, now almost patched up; a
grave row with de Gaulle over Syria, really grave and far-reaching;
a sort of stale mate with Soviet Russia over Poland and Germany.

Tito jumped his claims to Venezia Giulia by shortheading Alexander's troops there. By standing firm and getting Truman to stand firm,
we have got a compromise by which Tito holds on to Istria but leaves
Trieste and communications northward to Alex. all without prejudice
to the peace-settlement. The Italians have little right to recover Istria
but Trieste is a different thing. It should be neither wholly Italian nor
wholly Yugoslav.

In Western Italy, encouraged by Tito's bad but successful example,
de Gaulle has ordered his troops who had advanced over the passes as
part of the general plan to lever out the Germans, to stay put, refuse to
allow Alex's Amgot officers and to resist by force if necessary any
attempt to turn them out. Truman has asked him to withdraw and in
face of the "unbelievable threat" to resist American troops, he has cut

off all American supplies to the French army – not unnaturally. De Gaulle by this action has of course also antagonised the new Italy which it was his opportunity to conciliate – stupidity.

But, gravest of all in Syria, wobble here and intrigue there has brought about the most disturbing situation. The Syrians have been allowed successfully to play us off against the French. Under threat of disturbances our soldiers have stepped in and taken charge. (We should of course long ago have withdrawn all our troops and handed over responsibility to the French.) We have asked de G. to a conference with ourselves and the U.S.A. He has countered with a plan for a conference to include Russia and China as well as to discuss the whole Middle East. Of course de G. doesn't want Russia nor do we, but we don't want to discuss the whole Middle East and he naturally does. Foolish as de G. has been, we have been inexcusably foolish too. We have publicly humiliated the French in Arab eyes. We have temporarily taken over Syria. We have set our American critics off again about our imperialist aims. Syria is incapable of governing herself and we have made it almost impossible for the French to do so. Who is to do so then if it is not us? Yet if we oust the French in this way, as they always said we were aiming to do, we raise the most appalling issue which will lie across our relations for a generation. And all this is muddled thinking. The P.M., H.M.G. and the British people have no wish to take over Syria. Local pro-Arab officials in subordinate positions are of course working for it. Spears certainly did so in spite of F.O. instructions while he remained there as the protégé of the P.M. carrying out the opposite of the P.M.'s policy. The stupid military mind fell of course for this nonsense, supposing that we should always have troops to waste in this way. Yet this policy is suicidal to British local interests which are identical with those of the French. We are both occupying Arab territory and the Arabs hate us both as Christians and Europeans. We should have emphasised French responsibility for the Levant by taking all our troops out. We are now in a false position.

Nonetheless, I'm afraid de G. has shown himself impossible. We can never have normal relations with such a man. But I'm not sure the same isn't beginning to be true of Winston and Stalin. The war lords are temperamentally incapable of conducting peace. Thank goodness, Roosevelt is gone and we have Mr. Truman, the plain American citizen, honest, forthright, we all want Trumans now. But Winston, pushed by Beaverbrook, has now launched out on a jingo election which is terrifying in its inappropriateness. He will have the

THE WAR DIARIES OF OLIVER HARVEY

whole country at war with itself soon. A.E. is ill with an ulcer and is
out of it for a month at least. But his health must now be taken as a
seriously limiting factor due to constant overwork, not least to
doubling the F.O. with H. of C.

There is to be a Big 3 Meeting in July in Germany while the
election is going on. Meanwhile we have at last issued the Declaration
on German surrender and Monty has been appointed our C. in C.
The four C. in C.s have met and signed but the Control machine has
not been set up because we are trying to avoid retreating out of the
Russian zone until we can get overall agreement with the Russians
about supplies for Germany. A stalemate therefore – except that the
Americans will not agree to delay much longer.

July 17
De G. has climbed down over Val d'Aosta and is going to evacuate
without a word. That is due to Truman. He has also agreed to accept
the proposed French zone of occupation in Germany which is good
too. But he is behaving in a childish way in Paris – refusing to allow
French officers to receive British decorations at a ceremony prepared
at the British Embassy, refusing to have Tedder at the dinner given
to Eisenhower. Syria is as bad as ever. We and Americans have
refused 5 Power Conference (Russia, China, U.S.A., Gt. B. and
France). De G. refuses so far a 3 Power Conference.

As to Germany Truman insists on not delaying evacuation of the
Soviet Zone any longer and we have fallen into line. We hope to set up
the Commission in Berlin shortly.

July 28[1]
I had just gone home last night when Bob Dixon rang up to say would
I come back to F.O. at 9 as Mr. Bevin (who had been appointed F.S.)
wanted to be given an idea of the Potsdam Conference[2] before starting
off the next morning.

We all met at 9 in the empty and gloomy office. Mr. B. very genial
and friendly. I congratulated him. He said "commiserate rather". He
had only known at 4.45 that he was to be F.S. – up till then he had
thought he was to be Chancellor of the Exchequer which he would
have rather liked. "However, I didn't mind taking this". The election
itself had been the surprise of his life. He was so sure the Tories were
in that he had taken a little cottage in Cornwall for the holidays.

1. The election result had been declared on the evening of 26 July.
2. The Potsdam Conference had opened on July 17.

384

We went over the doings of the Conference. I asked him whether he and Mr. Attlee proposed to carry it on. He said he hadn't had a talk with A. yet but believed the idea was that the latter would return on Sunday but that he himself should stay on. He was ready to do so and to stay as long as the Soviets and U.S. wished. He thought it wouldn't be at all desirable that we should propose an adjournment. He would leave that to the others.

Earlier in the day, A.E. had had a farewell tea-party in the Ambassador's waiting room at the Office. He called me to his room later to say goodbye. Poor man, he had heard while at Potsdam of the discovery of the aeroplane in the jungle with the bodies of his son and the crew. But otherwise he seemed well and not much concerned at the Government's defeat. He was worried about Winston, and wished he could get him away and out of the House. He would like now to be Leader of Opposition himself and mould the Party as he wants it. But he fears Winston will stay on and get everything wrong. I begged him to give himself a rest, saying that for him personally it couldn't have been better. He could never have stood another Government as No. 2 to Winston and as Leader of the House plus the F.O. Now he could make a complete recovery. He was worried about the Garter which Winston had offered to recommend him for. He was reluctant to accept it. He thought it would rather diminish him in the public eye.

August 7

The atomic bomb was used yesterday for the first time on the Japs. I must say I feel shocked and ashamed. Nobody knows what the effects of it, indirect or direct, will be on the area. I don't think posterity will think it was a very creditable action.

I've seen no more of Mr. Bevin, but those who were at Potsdam were extremely pleased with his performance there. He says he wants to improve Anglo–French relations, thank goodness!

I'm afraid Winston and A.E. had latterly become quite exhausted. They could no longer look at the problems properly or read the papers about them. It had become mere improvisation. Bevin, we hope, will really devote his mind to foreign policy, *read the papers*, and not divide up his time with other duties.

Index

Beaverbrook, Lord, 31, 32, 34, 37, 38, 44, 47, 48, 49, 51; in Moscow, 52; broadcast, 53, 54–55, 56–59, 60–63, 68, 81, 87–88, 91, 93–96, 98, 100, 104–106, 108–109; to America, 111, 113–114, 117, 119, 120, 122–124, 131, 133–134, 136, 143, 146, 147, 150, 161, 164, 167–168; asked to US, 244, 245–246, 255; and US Embassy, 257–258, 266, 298–299, to be Lord Privy Seal, 301, 365, 377, 383
Benes, Dr, 251, 313
Bergeret, 205
Berio, Signor, 284
Berling, 341
Bermuda, Conference at, 246
Berut, 363
Béthouart, 196, 198, 200, 235
Bevan, A., 147, 198
Beveridge, Plan, 228, 235, 267
Bevin, Ernest, 30, 31, 43, 47, 48, 58, 86, 91, 94, 98–99, 114, 122, 133, 137, 143, 146, 150, 152, 162, 176, 188, 246, 261, 271, 293; on U.S. planning, 367; Foreign Sec., 384, 385
Bidault, Georges, 357, 368, 375–377
Biddle, H., 201
Billotte, General, 211
Binderton, 153, 236, 249, 351, 375
Blanche, Maison, 306
Bloom, Sol, 233
Blum, Leon, 138
Boisson, 205, 264, 266, 267, 269
Bonomi, Ivanoe, 283, 345
Bor-Komarowski, General, 358
Bowhill, Air-Marshal Sir F., 242
Bracken, Brendan, 18, 21, 94–95, 100, 102–104, 124, 137, 162, 248–249, 298, 301
Bradley, General O., 354
Brand, 228
Brauchitsch, General von, 79
Brazzaville, 268

Briand, 138
Brooke, Field-Marshal Sir A., 50, 64, 145, 263
Bruce, 88, 110
Bullard, Sir Reader, 32, 36, 42
Burma Road, 60
Butler, Harold, 119, 230
Butler, R. A., 18, 96, 110, 152, 165, 176, 299, 337, 338

Caccia, Harold, 89, 111
Cadogan, Sir Alexander, 16, 69–71, 75–76, 78, 81, 103, 128, 131, 146, 158, 185, 188, 189, 202, 215, 252, 283, 298, 301, 315, 374, 376
Caen, 352
Cambon, Roger, 47, 107, 259
Campbell, Sir Ronald, 266, 267, 282, 285, 286
Campbell, Sir R. I., 19, 228, 231, 302
Camrose, Viscount, 299–300
Canaries, the, 36
Carton de Wiart, General, 287
Casablanca, 154–155, 172, 178, 179, 180, 181, 218, 222, 315
Casey, R. G., 88, 111, 116, 139, 147, 169, 263, 306, 319
Castellano, General, 285, 289
Catroux, General, 169, 196, 197, 198, 200, 203, 214, 215, 216, 225, 227, 244, 252, 259, 261
Cazalet, Victor, 19, 118, 271
Chamberlain, Austen, 61
Chamberlain, Neville, 18, 48, 49, 61, 135, 187, 237, 275
Channon, Sir H., 18
Charbonniere, 215
Charles, Sir Noel, 301, 305
Chauvel, Jean, 375–376, 377
Cherwell, Lord, 206, 377
Chetniks, 319
Chiang-Kai-Shek, General, 60, 74, 89, 90, 92, 93, 150, 319, 321

tov, 125–130, 131, 132, 133;
dines with P.M., 137, 140; on
P.M., 141, 142; to visit U.S., 144;
talks to Cripps, 144; visit to U.S.,
postponed, 145, 146; his position,
151–152; on Torch, 153–156, 157;
with U.S. Generals, 159; Government changes, 160–168, 162; and
de Gaulle, 163–164, 166; talks to
Beaverbrook, 167–168; post-war,
168; sees Maisky, 169–170; on
visit to U.S., 174; on post war,
175; 176, 177, 179, 182, 183, 186,
187; and India, 187; tel. to Halifax, 188, 189; to lead H. of C.,
191, 192; Jewish policy, 194;
secret session on Darlan, 195, 197,
198; on leadership of H. of C.,
201–202; sees de Gaulle, 205,
209; message from President, 214,
215, 216, 219, 220, 224, 226; to
U.S., 228–240; speech at Annapolis, 237–238; to Ottawa, 240;
addresses Canadian parliament,
241; sees de Gaulle, 244; and
P.M., 244; suggested as Viceroy,
245–251; Polish-Russian problems, 251; Viceroy question, 252–
254; and 255–258; sees Baldwin,
256; health 258; and de Gaulle,
259–262, to Algiers, 262, 263,
264; Viceroy question, 264–266;
French affairs, 266–272; with
P.M., 273–274; talks with
Winant, 276, 277, 282, 285, 286,
287; and P.M. and President, 288,
289, 290, 293; in H. of C., 297,
298; Government changes, 299–
301; Moscow plan, 301; and
P.M., 304; to Moscow, 305;
Algiers, 306; Cairo, 306–308;
Moscow, 310–319; Overlord
problem, 313; Turkish talks, 319,
321; to Tehran, 322–323; and
Poles, 330–331; and French

Committee, 335; on P.M., 337,
339; French problems, 335–347;
trip to France, 351–354; to
Quebec, 357; to Moscow, 358;
sees Molotov, 359; and Poles,
360–363, 365, 368, 369; to Athens,
370; and Massigli, 374–376, 377;
ill, 384; farewell party at F.O.,
385
Eden, Beatrice, 224, 248, 253
Eisenhower, General Dwight, 154,
158, 170, 173, 176, 180, 182, 185,
186, 187–188, 189, 190, 194–6,
198, 199–200, 202, 204, 205, 206,
210; becomes C. in C., 218 219,
222, 223, 226, 244, 252, 259, 261,
268, 269, 270, 271, 281, 282, 288,
289, 291, 292, 297, 301, 303, 305,
306, 312, 314, 329; directive on
France, 336, 338–340, 341, 342;
and military currency, 343, 352–
355, 368, 373, 379, 382
Elam-Elas, 367, 373
Emrys-Evans, Paul, 54, 67, 377
Esteva, Admiral, 185, 186, 245
European Advisory Council, 357

Farinacci, Roberto, 286
Farouk, King, 307, 309
Ferrard, Admiral, 342
Finland, 62, 64, 66
Flandin, Perre-Etienne, 51, 117,
190, 223, 224
Foreign Press Association, 24
Franco, General, 21, 28, 179, 263
Frankfurter, Felix, 28, 136, 233
Fraser, Peter, 35

Gamelin, General, 262
Gandhi, Mahatma, 90, 113, 148,
149, 150, 221, 222, 228, 230
Gascoigne, J., 283
Gaulle, Charles de, 45, 46, 47, 55;
broadcast, 107, 108, 110, 114, 121,
125, 133, 137, 138, 140, 144, 153,

391

Murphy, Robert D., 158, 169, 172, 182, 189, 199, 201–202, 203, 206, 214–215, 216, 218, 259, 268, 290
Muselier, Admiral, 45, 46, 107
Mussolini, Benito, 18, 201, 217, 263, 271; resignation of, 279, 281, 285; rescue of, 294; forms Salo Government, 296, 301, 379–380

Nahas, Pasha, 307
Namier, L. B., 19
Nash, Walter, 229
Naylor, General, 352
Negrin, Juan, 21, 193
Nehru, Pandit, 90, 113, 114, 115, 116
Nogues, General, 179, 182, 185, 187, 191, 196, 205, 214, 263
Norton, Sir Clifford, 23
Nuri-es-Said, 319
Nye, General Sir Archibald, 69, 75, 110, 263

Observer, the, 331
Oder, 330, 333, 367, 377
O'Malley, Sir Owen, 330, 331
Oppeln, 361, 367
Oran, 178–180
Orlando, Signor, 283, 345
Osborne, Sir d'Arcy, 285, 293
Ottawa agreement, 90, 91
Overlord, 294, 312, 315, 317, 323, 324, 329, 335, 340

Paget, General Sir Bernard, 60, 64, 359, 363
Palermo, 279–280
Palewski, Gaston, 164, 169, 262
Papandreou, 359, 367
Papen, Von, 217
Paris (Comte de), 138
Passy, 46
Patch, General A. M., 381
Patton, General G., 381

Paulus, General von, 219
Peake, Sir Charles, 31, 39, 86, 121, 137, 141, 160, 211, 212, 225, 227, 246, 257, 352, 354
Peasant Party, Polish, 331
Perkins, Miss Frances, 163
Pertinax (Andre Geraud), 232
Petain, Marshal, 118, 158, 172, 178, 179, 181, 183, 184, 191, 196, 200, 230, 267, 280, 294, 379
Peter, King of Yugoslavia, 273, 278, 306, 320, 374
Peyrouton, 211, 212, 214, 217, 263
Philby, St John, 58
Philippe, Andre, 262
Pilsudski, Marshal, 277
Pineau, Christian, 114
Pius XII, Pope, 201, 202, 223, 271, 289
Plastiras, General, 373
Pleven, Rene, 164, 169, 171, 211, 215, 218
Poincare, 138, 377
Polish-Soviet Pact, 26
Ponsonby, Sir Charles, 17
Portal, Air-Marshal Sir Charles, 263
P.Q. 17 Convoy, 139, 140
Pound, Admiral Sir Dudley, 116, 118, 263
Prisoners of war, British in Poland, 377
Pritt, D. N., 147, 163
Prussia, East, 45, 55, 74, 322, 323, 330, 333, 375
Pucheu, Pierre, 189, 190
Puma, 21

Quebec, Conference (Quadrant), 276, 277, 281, 283, 285, 286, 287, 312, 314
Queen Elizabeth (The Queen Mother), 275
Quisling, Vidkun, 117, 184, 193, 267, 286, 369

399